A HISTORY of the CHURCH

A HISTORY of the CHURCH

From Pentecost to Present

JAMES NORTH

COLLEGE PRESS
PUBLISHING COMPANY
Joplin, Missouri

Library of Congress Catalog Number: 82-074538
International Standard Book Number: 0-89900-371-0

Table of Contents

Maps

Appendices

INTRODUCTION

"Of making many books there is no end." So wrote Solomon in Ecclesiastes 12:12. Every author who presents another book to the public feels the need to justify the appearance of his product. This author presents his work with the hope that it will be useful to the students who read it — formal students in the classroom sense, as well as others who may want to study the history of the church. This book is intended to be a one-volume textbook for a one-semester survey of church history. Formal students will have the material supplemented by lectures and other assignments; church study groups may want to use the text as the basis for an examination of the history of the church, and the questions and projects at the end of the chapters are especially designed to stimulate their thinking about past developments; still other individuals may simply want to read the work as an introduction to the topic.

History consists of the events of the past and an interpretation of those events. All too often the facts of the past are meaningless without an adequate interpretation which demonstrates their significance. Every historian wants to be objective, but every interpretation carries with it subjective conclusions. As a result, every book on history must be watched for the bias of the historian. It will be obvious in its early chapters that this book is written from a non-Roman Catholic perspective. Perceptive readers may notice other biases as well.

Interpretation of the facts is essential to understand history, in spite of the inherent danger of not recognizing the historian's bias. A small corrective is to pay close attention to primary source documents. Every serious history student should read source documents rather than depend entirely upon secondary surveys such as this text. For this reason, the endnotes in this work provide constant direction toward original documents which have been printed in several collections. For classroom use it would be ideal if students purchased one of the source collections frequently quoted and digested the original documents themselves as well as the secondary interpretation of them. Petry-Manschrek is probably the best set for this purpose.

Frequent references in the footnotes will include the following:

ANF   *The Ante-Nicene Fathers*, edited by Alexander Roberts and James Donaldson (Grand Rapids: Wm. B. Eerdmans Publishing Company, 1978-1979), 10 Volumes.

Barry   *Readings in Church History*, edited by Colman J. Barry (Westminster, Maryland: The Newman Press, 1960-1965), 3 Volumes.

Bettenson   *Documents of Christian Classics*, edited by Henry Bettenson (New York: Oxford University Press, 1947).

LCC   *Library of Christian Classics*, edited by John Bailie, John T. McNeill, and Henry P. Van Dusen (Philadelphia: The Westminster Press, 1953-1960), 26 Volumes.

Manschreck   *A History of Christianity: Readings in the History of the Church*, Volume 2, *The Church from the Reformation to the Present*, edited by Clyde L. Manschrek (Grand Rapids: Baker Book House, 1981).

NPNF   *Nicene and Post-Nicene Fathers*. First Series edited by Philip Schaff, 14 Volumes; Second Series edited by Philip Schaff and Henry Wace, 14 Volumes (Grand Rapids: Wm. B. Eerdmans Publishing Company, 1978-1979).

Petry   *A History of Christianity: Readings in the History of the Church*, Volume 1, *The Early and Medieval Church*, edited by Ray C. Petry (Grand Rapids: Baker Book House, 1981).

Schaff   *Creeds of Christendom*, by Philip Schaff (Grand Rapids: Baker Book House, 1977), 3 Volumes.

While the author's name alone appears on the title page, this book bears the impress of dozens of people: teachers, colleagues, students, and friends. There is not enough space to mention the names of all who have had a major share in shaping this book. However, special attention is merited by three colleagues who read the text in its entirety and made numerous helpful suggestion: Michael W. Hines of Intermountain Bible College,

James B. Hunter of Ozark Christian College, and William J. Richardson of Emmanuel School of Religion. Others who read portions of the manuscript and made many useful suggestions were: Roger Chambers of Central Florida Bible College, Lynn Hieronymus of Lincoln Christian College, F. Sherwood Smith of Cincinnati Bible College, and Henry E. Webb of Milligan College.

A special thanks must go to the secretaries who did the typing: Mary Cannon, Barbara Smith, and Kathy Smith. Only those who have typed a manuscript through its several revisions can appreciate the labor involved in a text of this sort.

Chapter One
THE APOSTOLIC CHURCH

Christians believe that Jesus Christ was (and is) the Son of God, the only begotten Son of God, the long-promised Messiah sent to the Jews. Christians of every generation have found the life and ministry of Jesus to be the focus of their identity as Christians. In addition they accept as authoritative the New Testament writings because they contain (1) the concrete details of the life and ministry of Christ, and (2) the letters which reflect the theological and moral teachings of the apostolic period. Further, Christians inherited from the Jews their body of writings known as the Old Testament. Early Christians acknowledged both of these collections as authoritative for doctrinal and ethical teaching. Jesus and the sacred writings — these two sources became the matrix out of which Christian thinking developed.

Although most of Jesus' teaching was about Himself and the attitudes of religious service and worship which His followers were to cultivate, part of His teaching also included the idea that His followers would be related to each other in a corporate identity — the Church. In a noted passage in Matthew, Jesus said that if a dispute between brothers could not be settled by any other means, it should be taken before the church (Matt. 18:17). In Peter's well-known confession, he claimed that Jesus was the Christ, the Son of the living God; Jesus commended him for this statement, adding that upon this truth about Himself He would establish the Church.

Obviously Jesus had many followers during His ministry, but they were not organized into any type of group. Those who turned aside and "walked no more with him" (John 6:66) simply dropped out of the number of His followers. During the night of Christ's trial even Peter denied he was a follower (Mark 14:66-72). Obviously there was no master list of those who were Christ's followers; instead the number of them was very fluid, ever changing, even through the events of the crucifixion.

But the events of that first Resurrection Sunday galvanized the followers into a core of committed believers. The apostles were no longer a loose assembly of men, ready to go back to their fishing nets (John 21:3); now they became fully dedicated to the task of finishing the evangelistic work begun by their Lord. Jesus had told them to tarry in Jerusalem until they were clothed with power from on high (Luke 24:49), and then they were to preach the gospel to every creature (Mark 16:15), baptizing them, and continuing to teach them the words of Christ (Matt. 28:19-20).

Waiting for that kind of enabling power, the apostles were still in Jerusalem on Pentecost. The Holy Spirit came upon them and created quite a disturbance when the apostles began to speak a variety of languages. This drew a large crowd, for Jerusalem was crowded with Jews from all corners of the Roman Empire who had come to the city for the great Pentecost feast. On this occasion Peter got their attention and preached about Jesus, pointing out His special favor with God to the extent that God even raised Him from the dead — a death that the Jews themselves had inflicted on Him. This Jesus whom they crucified, God made Lord and Christ. When the assembled people asked what they were to do to make up for their actions, Peter commanded them to "repent and be baptized" for the remission of their sins, and God would give them the gift of the Holy Spirit. Three thousand responded to that invitation. Most church historians date the beginning of the church from this classic event. Jesus was proclaimed as the Christ; man's sinful condition was pointed out, and the invitation was given to be saved. Many responded and can now be accurately labeled as Christians — believers in Christ. Soon thousands of others joined their number. The men of the movement soon numbered five thousand (Acts 4:4), then "multitudes both of men and women" were added (Acts 5:14), and even a large number of priests became obedient to the new faith (Acts 6:7).

From these simple beginnings the church continued to multiply throughout the first century. At first the believers were limited to the city of Jerusalem. When the Jewish religious authorities began a persecution of the new faith, Stephen preached boldly in the synagogue and became the first martyr (Acts 7). (The word "martyr" comes from the Greek *martys* meaning "a witness"; a martyr is a person who "witnesses" of his faith to the point of dying for it.) Immediately after the death of Stephen the persecution caused the believers to scatter throughout Judea and Samaria (Acts 8:1) — the first known expansion outside Jerusalem. Philip preached to the Samaritans, as well as to the treasurer of Ethiopia who had been worshiping in Jerusalem and was now returning home.[1] Saul pursued the new believers to Damascus in Syria (Acts 9:2), a Gentile soldier in Caesarea named Cornelius soon believed (Acts 10), and other believers spread to Phoenicia, Cyprus, and the city of Antioch where they were soon called Christians (Acts 1:19,26).

With the eastern coast of the Mediterranean Sea now dotted with centers of Christian believers, the remainder of the story of the Acts of the Apostles deals almost exclusively with missionary travels of Paul. A first journey went through Cyprus and into central Asia Minor. A second trip cut northwest through Asia Minor to Troas, then through Macedonia, down into Greece, and back. A third journey began with a three year stay at Ephesus (from which the entire province was then evangelized), and included another swing through Macedonia and Greece. When Paul later arrived in Rome, Christians were already there and came out to meet him (Acts 28:14,15).

And so it went. From a provincial capital in Judea, the new faith of Christianity soon traveled to the major

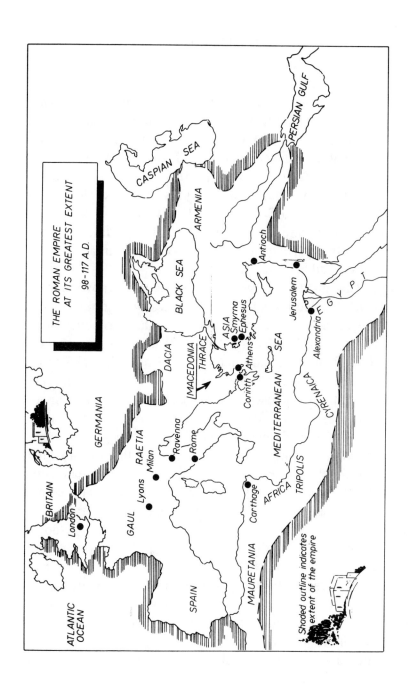

THE ROMAN EMPIRE
AT ITS GREATEST EXTENT
98-117 A.D.

CASPIAN SEA

PERSIAN GULF

ARMENIA

BLACK SEA

DACIA

THRACE

MACEDONIA

ASIA
Smyrna
Ephesus

Athens

Corinth

Antioch

Jerusalem

Alexandria

EGYPT

CYRENAICA

MEDITERRANEAN SEA

GERMANIA

RAETIA

Ravenna

Milan

Rome

Lyons

GAUL

BRITAIN

London

ATLANTIC
OCEAN

SPAIN

MAURETANIA

Carthage

AFRICA

TRIPOLIS

Shaded outline indicates
extent of the empire

cities of the Empire — Antioch, Ephesus, Athens, Corinth, Rome, and probably also Alexandria. The Book of Acts gives a great deal of information about the travels and ministry of Paul, some about Peter and John (particularly in the first half of the book). What happened to the rest of the apostles? There is little solid information. There are traditions that link Thomas to India, James to Spain, and others to various corners of the Empire and beyond, but most of these traditions are untrustworthy legend, and none of them can actually be considered historically sound.

This means that we have no accurate knowledge of what the remainder of the apostles were doing in the several decades after Pentecost. It is hard to believe that all of them remained in Jerusalem until the end of their days. Paul's offhand reference in I Corinthians 9:5 about having the right "to lead about a wife"as did Peter and the rest of the apostles seems to suggest strongly that not only were the apostles married, but they were traveling. But we have no details. Adolf Harnack, a significant historian at the turn of the century, stated that much of the evangelization that took place throughout the regions of the Roman Empire was done by "informal missionaries," just plain Christians who shared their faith and gave their witness wherever they went.[2] Even widows were credited with making converts. Numerous others who died for their beliefs held to their faith so securely and impressively that pagans were won to Christianity through their witness — they were *martyrs* in the purest sense of the word. Tertullian, the influential church leader whom we will meet again soon, was converted in such a way. He was talking about his own conversion when he exclaimed, "The blood of martyrs is the seed of the church."

Except for a few references in the Gospel accounts, Jesus did not place much emphasis upon the organized church as such. The writers of the New Testament letters, however, constantly reflect the background of the church as it then existed. These statements and reflections, plus some overt comments in the book of Acts, give us additional information as to how the church was organized and functioned in the apostolic era. To begin an examination of the church through the centuries after Pentecost, it will be important to first understand its first century composition.

In the apostolic writings, the church is referred to by many terms, but one of the most common and meaningful is that of being "the body of Christ." Paul in particular develops this idea, comparing the church to a human body with its various parts, many for specialized purposes, but each devoted to the good of the entire body (I Cor. 12:12-30). Paul's particular point here is that the Christians in Corinth ought to work in harmony with one another, each person utilizing his special abilities for the common good. Paul argued strongly against any division in the body of Christ — whether it be arguments over which person had the most significant spiritual function, or even over which evangelist was the most praiseworthy (I Cor. 3:3-9).

Not only is it obvious that Paul argued strongly for the corporate unity of the body of believers in any one place, but there are also numerous reflections in the apostolic writings of a unity that transcended geographical separation. When the Christians in Palestine suffered famine, Paul collected an offering for them from the Christians in Macedonia and Achaia (I Cor. 16:1-3; II Cor. 8-9). Christians in Antioch also responded to the needs of their brothers in Judea (Acts 11:27-30). The picture emerges of all Christians considering themselves part of the same corporate entity, the body of Christ. This spiritual relationship was a strong bond, tying them to each other as well as marking them off from the rest of the world. Thus there was a definite distinction between those who were members of the church and those who were not.

A crucial factor in determining the success of the first century church was the resolution of the Judaistic controversy represented in Acts 15. Peter had baptized Cornelius and his household in Acts 10, but he was soon criticized for his innovation. When Paul returned from his first missionary journey brethren from Jerusalem caused great agitation in Antioch with their claim that only those circumcised according to the law of Moses could be saved. This led to the Jerusalem council which decided that Gentile Christians did not need to undergo circumcision as long as they were sensitive to Jewish consciences on such things as idolatry, immorality, and the eating of blood. This allowed preachers a great deal of freedom and flexibility in adapting the Christian message to the Gentile world. Thus freed from Jewish restrictions, Christianity spread quickly in the Mediterranean world. This did not mean a separation between Jewish and Gentile Christians, but it did mean the basis of their fellowship was in Christ, not in Judaism. Gentile Christianity soon predominated over the original Jewish elements.

Another important factor for the apostolic church was its organization and officers. Various types of leaders are referred to in the New Testament: apostles, prophets, pastors, teachers, bishops, elders, deacons, evangelists. There is some dispute whether all of these are mutually separate officers, or whether perhaps two terms may refer to the same office. There is also concern over whether these are to be seen as "offices," that is positions of power and authority, or whether they are simply functions and positions of service. Perhaps even suggesting that there is a distinction between an "office" and its "function" is unrealistic. Undoubtedly these offices are service functions. But the individuals who filled these positions also exercised authority through their service. It is good to keep in mind that modern offices in the church are service positions. It is also necessary to keep in mind that the persons in the early church who performed these services achieved power as a result. Because struggles over church organization will occupy our attention through much of this book, it is good to review these positions in the apostolic church. A convenient way of analyzing these officers is to break them up into two categories: general and local.[3]

The general officers seem to be the apostles, prophets, teachers, and evangelists. The apostles are of course the original twelve, plus Matthias (Acts 1:26). Paul is also an apostle — which he vigorously defends in Galatians 1,2.[4] Apparently the apostles had the power to convey special gifts of the Holy Spirit, and this was a unique aspect of their ministry (Acts 8:14-17). The apostles, because of their first-hand acquaintance with Jesus and the special knowledge they had of His teachings, constituted a special group of leaders to whom difficult issues could be referred — as in the question of circumcising Gentiles before allowing them to become Christians, the issue of the famous Jerusalem council recorded in Acts 15. As is true with most of the general officers, the office of apostle was not to be a long-lasting office. There is no record whatsoever of a second-generation apostle. After the death of these men, there are no further references to apostles in the church. Their credentials made their teachings so authoritative that throughout the rest of the history of the church Christians always measured the doctrine, practices, and life of the church by the teachings of the apostles. Having received their authority directly from Christ, they formulated the teaching for the first generation of believers; that standard became normative for all later Christians.

The prophets were apparently special spokesmen (and spokeswomen![5]) for God. The word "prophet" in its Old Testament context means not only a person who can foretell the future, but a person who delivers a message on behalf of another. Prophets — whether in a thundering sense of doom, as we often use the word, or in a milder form of communication. Agabus predicted two events — a famine and the imprisonment of Paul (Acts 11:27; 21:10,11). Paul's writings often refer to people having the gift of prophecy. But this gift also died off in the first generation. As a special gift, it did not carry over beyond the first century church. In that modern preachers are speakers for God, they are prophets in a general sense; but in the special sense of having a unique gift from the Holy Spirit, this office ceased soon after the lapse of the office of apostle.

The office of teacher appears to be a bit more complicated. There has been a great deal of dispute with reference to Ephesians 4:11 as to whether Paul is referring to the office of "pastor-teacher" or whether he is referring to two different offices, "pastors" and "teachers." It probably does not make a great deal of difference. If it is a combined office, then these teachers were also doing some pastoring. If it refers to two different offices, as seems most likely, then the pastoral office can more properly be identified with the office of elder which we shall notice shortly.

We must remember that these three offices — apostle, prophet, and teacher — were general offices. That is, their authority was not limited to a certain location; it was general throughout the church. The apostles had their apostolic authority no matter where they were — in Jerusalem, in Antioch, in Samaria, in Galatia, or elsewhere. The same was true with the office of prophet. The prophet Agabus came from Jerusalem to Antioch and gave his prophecy about the coming famine. These were special offices, and the men who received these gifts were universally respected by Christians.

The same is true of the office of teacher. This was a general office, and the teachers were itinerant teachers. There are few clear New Testament references to these men, but when they are mentioned in Ephesians 4:11 and I Corinthians 12:28-29 they are mentioned in series with the other general offices, the apostles and prophets. Because these men were itinerant, it was a problem for the early Christian communities to know who were the true teachers and who were false. Apostolic writings constantly warn: "Beware of false teachers." II and III

John may reflect this dilemma. II John warns against false teachers (II John 7-11); III John refers to the opposite problem — good teachers who are not received by a local leader because he wants the preeminence (III John 5-10). A church manual of the second century, dated about the year 125, also refers to false teachers, although it combines the words apostles, prophets, and teachers in its references. But it indicates the standards often used to unmask a false teacher. A teacher may stay only one day, or two in case of necessity; if he stays three days, he is a false prophet[6] — he is obviously freeloading off the generosity of Christians. When he leaves he is to ask only for enough food to get to the next town; if he asks for money he is a false prophet.[7] Anyone who teaches the truth but fails to practice it is a false teacher.[8] By these means, the early Christian communities were to identify the false and the true teachers.

A fourth general office seems to be that of the evangelist. This word is not used often in the New Testament. Philip is called an evangelist — he preached in Samaria and to the Ethiopian treasurer along the road to Gaza (Acts 8:5-39). Philip is the only named evangelist in Scripture, although Timothy is told to do the work of an evangelist (II Tim. 4:5). The word "evangelist" simply means one who announces good news, and apparently the word was applied to those traveling preachers of the first century who proclaimed Christ from place to place.

These offices, then, are the general officers of the first century church. Apostles and prophets will die out in the first century itself, the teachers will linger on into the second century. Evangelists are heard of only rarely after the New Testament writings, although there are certainly many people doing the work of an evangelist, whether they are called that specifically or not. But all of these offices have general implications — none are tied down to a particular place or congregation. The situation is different with the local officers.

The occasion in Acts chapter six is usually taken to be the beginning of the office of deacon, although the word is not used there. The Grecian Jews were complaining because their widows were being overlooked in the daily food distribution within the Christian community. The apostles, mediating the situation, suggested that seven men be selected to oversee the distribution. All seven of those chosen bore Greek names, including Philip, the later evangelist. The word "deacon" is simply the Greek word for "servant," and that is what these men were — servants of the Christian community with responsibility for the physical needs of the members. Later references in I Timothy 3 list the qualifications expected of these men for the churches after mid-century had passed. But although the qualifications are given, the responsibilities and the job description are not. The normal assumption is that the deacons were charged with responsibility for the physical needs of the Christians, although no details are recorded, as to exactly which needs were involved, or how pervasive and extensive their responsibilities were. But there is no doubt that these were local officers. Whereas the general officers had authority and respect from the entire church universal, deacons and elders held offices of only local authority.

Although the office of deacon may have been instituted first, it was the office of elder that came to have the greatest weight in the local congregation. There were "elders" in the Jewish synagogues in the pre-Christian period, and Christian elders may simply have been an adaptation of this same office by the Christian assemblies. The first New Testament reference to specifically Christian elders is Acts 11:30, where Barnabas and Saul brought the Antioch offering to the Christians in Jerusalem and gave it to the elders there. On the return leg of Paul's first missionary journey, he and Barnabas appointed elders in each of the churches in Asia Minor they had established on the earlier part of the trip. When the dispute came up about the uncircumcised Gentile Christians, it was the "apostles and elders" in Jerusalem that were approached with resolving the question (Acts 15:2,4,6,22,23; 16:4). When Paul, at the end of his third missionary journey, wanted to speak to the leadership of the church at Ephesus, he called the elders to Miletus to meet with him (Acts 20:17).

It is also noteworthy that when these elders arrived to talk with Paul, Paul addressed them as "bishops" (cf. Acts 20:17 and 20:28). Paul lists the qualifications for elders in I Timothy 3 and Titus 1, and in the midst of the Titus passage he shifts to the term "bishop," the term used exclusively in the Timothy passage. It is obvious that for Paul the two terms apply to the same group of men. In I Peter 5:1-4, Peter talks to the elders who in vs. 2 are called "bishops." It is true that this word does not appear in some of the early manuscripts — but the fact that it appears in even *some* of the early texts indicates that the early church was still using the two terms as referring to the same group of men.[9] In this same passage, Peter uses the word "pastors," also used in Ephesians 4:11.

Thus the elders have the spiritual oversight of the congregation. The elders (or bishops, if you please) are to guard the flock, feed it, nurture it, and do the work of a shepherd. The word "elder" simply meant an older man, a respected figure among the community; the word "bishop" literally meant an "overseer" or "superintendent"; the word "pastor" meant a shepherd. Thus it can be said that "elder" denotes the man's attainment and respect, while "bishop" and "pastor" denote his function — spiritual oversight and shepherding. Of all these words, the term "bishop" became the predominant one. It is the term that continues to have a direct history all the way down to the present. The Greek word for "elder" is the word *presbyteros*. In English this word comes out as "presbyter," and this form of the word is used by many historians. Unfortunately, the word "presbyter" soon undergoes some changes in meaning, which we will notice in a forthcoming chapter. It will be important to pay close attention to them when they occur, and contrast the new meaning to its New Testament original meaning.

One thing more remains to be said about the office of elder: in the New Testament it is always plural. Although the terms "elder" and "bishop" are used interchangeably in the pages of the New Testament, there is never a reference to a single elder or bishop over any one church. The word is always plural — "elders," "bishops." When Paul and Barnabas appoint elders in the church of Asia Minor, the word is plural (Acts 14:23). When Paul instructs Titus to appoint elders in every town in Crete, the word is plural (Titus 1:5). When Paul writes to the Christian congregation at Philippi, he addresses his letter there along with "the bishops and deacons" — both words used in the plural (Phil. 1:1). As we will see in Chapter Three, there will soon be a move to a single bishop in a congregation. It is essential to note that the New Testament knows nothing of this arrangement. This is a major change that will have overwhelming significance for the later development of the church — but it is a change from the apostolic pattern.

Under these officers — some general, others local — the church finished out the first century. In these first decades, however, the church was more than merely an organization with certain officers — it was a fellowship, a new way of life. It had certain traits that marked it as peculiar in the first century and which continued to characterize its life down through the centuries. Probably its two most peculiar practices were baptism and the Lord's Supper. Jesus talked about baptism, apostolic teaching included it, and Paul's writing in particular emphasized its place in the life of the Christian. Concluding the "Pentecost" sermon, Peter invited his hearers to be baptized for the remission of their sins, and both Greek and Latin church fathers emphasized this as the cardinal purpose of baptism. Although there is some modern controversy about the form of baptism, there is overwhelming evidence, and an impressive consensus, that the early Christian baptism was by immersion, and only for those old enough to make a profession of faith. Paul's writings emphasized baptism as a death to the old life and rebirth in the resurrected Christ (Rom. 6:1-4), and Peter talked about baptism being more than merely getting wet — it was the answer of a good conscience to God (I Peter 3:21).

On the last night that Jesus was alive on earth He celebrated the Jewish Passover feast with His disciples, and in the process He instructed them to continue to remember His sacrificial death through the consumption of bread and wine which were to represent His body and blood. This act of communion with the risen Christ marked the apostolic worship services, held in honor of His resurrection on the first day of every week. Although preaching normally accompanied such worship services, it was the act of communally participating in the observance of the Lord's Supper that was the most significant element in early Christian worship.

Often in conjunction with the Lord's Supper, and slightly preceding it, was the *agape*-feast, or the love feast. This was a fellowship dinner for the entire congregation, reminiscent of the passover meal which Jesus had shared with the disciples prior to His instituting the Lord's Supper. Yet this agape-feast soon developed problems, because some of the congregation used it as an opportunity to display their abundant provisions: they failed to observe the "fellowship" aspect of the meal and share their provisions with those who did not have as much. As Paul relates in I Corinthians, these people were profaning the feast — if they were that hungry, he says, they ought to eat first at home, and not disrupt the spirit of the common meal (I Cor. 11:20-22; 33-34). It is doubtful that the love feast survived the first century as such — perhaps because of the very problems that came up at Corinth.

In addition to such observances, the early Christians worshiped through singing hymns, many surely borrowed from the Jewish Book of Psalms. There is good evidence to indicate that most early congregations met in houses, though undoubtedly a few in Palestine also met in synagogues. In fact, the Jewish Christians continued many of the practices of Judaism, and for a while there was a major dispute about whether Gentile Christians could be accepted without first becoming Jews. Yet by the time of the Jewish War which began in 66, the Jewish Christians made a virtual break between themselves and official Judaism. Most of them fled Jerusalem, and thus they escaped the destruction which the city experienced under the Roman armies in 70.

As we have already mentioned, a further mark of the early church was its sharing together — in earthly possessions as well as in things of the spirit. This general amity, generosity, and good will received special notice from the pagan world. Jesus had prophesied that the world would know they were His disciples if they had love for one another (John 13:34,35), and the history of the early centuries indicates that the Christians practiced it and that the world did note it.

To a great extent it was this spirit of brotherliness and burden-bearing which aided the evangelistic outreach of the church to the world. Many people in the ancient world — commoners as well as the intellectuals — were looking for answers to the meaning of life, and they saw that the early Christians lived above many of the problems of the world. These Christians seemed to enjoy a supernatural serenity which was the envy of much of the pagan world, and in turn that demonstrated serenity attracted people to the church.

This early church survived and grew. Originally simple in its organization and basic in its teachings about

Jesus and the salvation offered through Him, that church continues down to the present. In the process it experienced great pressure in the form of persecution, constant challenges in the form of false teachings, and continuing adaptation to the changing times of its environment. Such makes up the history of the church, and we will notice each of these elements as they come up, sometimes in sequence, sometimes simultaneously.

Bibliography for Chapter One

Bultmann, Rudolph. *Primitive Christianity in its Contemporary Setting.* Cleveland: The World Publishing Company (Meridian Books), 1956.

A thorough analysis of the cultural and religious context of first-century Christianity, though reflecting a liberal theological orientation.

Harnack, Adolf. *The Constitution and Law of the Church in the First Two Centuries.* New York: Williams & Norgate, 1910.

This has become a classic treatment of the organization of the early church, although it reflects some of Harnack's liberal presuppositions.

_____. *The Mission and Expansion of Christianity in the First Three Centuries.* New York: Harper & Brothers (Harper Torchbooks), 1961.

An assessment of the early expansion of the church, emphasizing the role of unknown Christians who spread the faith as they traveled from place to place.

Hort, Fenton John Anthony, *Judaistic Christianity.* Grand Rapids: Baker Book House, 1980 [reprint of 1894].

An investigation into the earliest years of Christianity in the context of Judaism, as reflected in the pages of the New Testament.

Martin, Ralph P. *Worship in the Early Church.* Grand Rapids: William B. Eerdmans Publishing Company, 1974.

A study of worship practices as reflected in the New Testament Church.

Tenney, Merrill C. *New Testament Survey.* Grand Rapids: William B. Eerdmans Publishing Company, 1961.

There are a number of New Testament introductions available, but this is one of the best. Tenney deals with the background, context, and content of the New Testament books.

Questions and Projects for Chapter One

1. Study the New Testament references that deal with officers of the church. Prepare a paper on the nature, function, and responsibility of these officers based on the New Testament information.
2. Study the New Testament references that deal with worship. Correlate this information and prepare a paper on what factors are essential to worship for the church.
3. Some people refer to baptism and the Lord's Supper as "sacraments"; others call them "ordinances." Look up both words in a good dictionary, and then study the New Testament references to each. Which word do you think Paul would use? Why?

4. Study the context of first century history and describe the factors that enabled the church to grow so quickly, both in numbers and geographical extent.

5. Do you think it was proper for the offices of apostle, prophet, and teacher to die out? Are there any valid counterparts to these offices today?

Notes for Chapter One

1. There is no evidence to suggest an Ethiopian Church resulted from this man's return to his homeland. There is no mention of Christianity in Ethiopia until the arrival of foreign Christians in the mid-fourth century. See J. Herbert Kane, *A Concise History of the Christian World Mission: A Panoramic View of Missions From Pentecost to the Present.* (Grand Rapids: Baker Book House, 1978), p. 12; and also Stephen Neill, *A History of Christian Missions* (Vol. 6 of "The Pelican History of the Church"; Baltimore: Penguin Books, 1964), pp. 52-53.

2. Adolf Harnack, *The Mission and Expansion of Christianity in the First Three Centuries* (New York, Harper & Brothers, 1961), pp. 366-368.

3. The division of officers into general and local and the enumeration of what officers belong in the two categories is suggested by Adolf Harnack in his *The Constitution and Law of the Church in the First Two Centuries* (New York: Williams & Norgate, 1910), pp. 23ff., 53ff., and 121ff.

4. I am using the word "apostle" here in its strict sense — *the* apostles. But the word itself simply means "one sent forth," and it can mean much the same as our word "missionary." Such New Testament usages include Barnabas (Acts 14:14), Andronicus and Junias (Romans 16:7), Titus (II Corinthians 8:23), and Epaphroditus (Philippians 2:25). But in talking about the apostolic office, I am restricting the term to its strict application.

5. Philip the evangelist had four daughters who exercised the gift of prophecy (Acts 21:9).

6. *The Teaching of the Twelve Apostles*, 11:5. This work, commonly referred to as the *Didache* (from the Greek word for "teaching"), can be found in various sources, including LCC, I, pp. 171-179; also in ANF, VII, pp. 377-382.

7. *Ibid.*, 11:6

8. *Ibid.*, 11:10.

9. The texts used as the basis for the King James translation of 1611 contained the root word for "bishop," but better texts used as the basis for more modern translations omit the word.

Chapter Two
THE CHURCH
UNDER PERSECUTION

"Blessed are ye when men shall revile you and persecute you" (Matt. 5:11).

Jesus, knowing what kind of death He would have to face, also knew what His followers would have to face. Persecution came in various forms: social ostracism, hatred and misunderstanding, physical abuse and torture, and death. Stephen was martyred for his faith; he was soon joined by thousands of others.

The early Christians received considerable harassment from the Jewish authorities, and King Herod even killed the Apostle James (Acts 12:1,2). By contrast, the official policy of the Roman government was to tolerate the various religions then current in the Empire. Whenever Rome annexed a new area to the Empire, policy dictated that local customs be left intact as long as they posed no political threat to the Empire; this policy of toleration extended to the local religions also. Such religions were then known as *religio licita* — a licensed religion, or a legal religion. When the Romans occupied Judea in the first century B.C., they tolerated Judaism as the national religion of the Jews.[1] As long as the Romans considered Christianity a branch of Judaism (as they initially did), it enjoyed the benefits of Judaism's status as a *religio licita*. Thus officially the Romans tolerated Christianity as a variation within Judaism.

The Jews, of course, objected to this association. They argued that Christianity was a new religion, not a part of Judaism at all. Technically they were right, but in the meantime Christianity grew under the protection of Judaism. Shortly after mid-century, however, things began to change. The Jews were successfully making the point that Christianity was not a Jewish sect. At the same time Christianity grew in Rome itself and attracted attention because it seemed to be a religion of lower class people and slaves. Slaves numbered about one-third of the entire population of the Empire, and scores of thousands of them resided in Rome. Organizing them, even in the name of a religion, seemed to pose a threat to social and political stability, and this made many of the rulers uneasy. It also earned Christianity the disgust of the upper classes who looked down upon anything associated with the lower classes.

There were also popular misunderstandings about Christianity. Most people knew very little about the new faith, but there were some vague rumors about its being involved in immorality. The Romans also picked up the information that the Christians owed allegiance to a new king called Jesus; certainly this seemed a serious threat to the state.

Moreover, some Christians were heard to talk about the destruction of the world by fire, and among the wooden tenements of Rome, arson would be a serious affair.

Then there was Nero, the Emperor (54-68). Historians consider him to be tinged with insanity, particularly toward the latter part of his life. In the summer of 64 fire broke out in Rome, devastating two-thirds of the city. Many people blamed Nero for the fire, noticing that the very area where the fire started was an area he wanted cleared so he could build new imperial palaces. Other people remembered that the Christians had talked about a destruction by fire, and they thought the Christians must be responsible. Nero also found it convenient to blame the Christians, and thus began the first official persecution of the Christians. Thousands of the believers were arrested and thrown into prison. Some were used to provide entertainment for the Roman populace either as combatants in gladiatorial contests or as prey for ravenous lions. According to some reports, others were dipped in tar, tied to posts, and used as living torches to provide illumination for Nero's nocturnal parties.[2] This last charge, however, comes from Nero's enemies, and there is reason to believe it may not be quite true. What is true is that numerous Christians were killed during this persecution, which lasted the remaining four years of the emperor's life (64-68).

Exactly how many Christians were killed during this time is unknown, but it probably ran into the thousands. Apparently, however, the persecution was fairly well limited to Rome and its immediate vicinity. There is no record of official persecution extending farther into the Empire at this time. The only exception may be the Apostle Paul. From the suggestions made in II Timothy, Paul appears to have been on the run through western Asia Minor, leaving Troas so quickly that he forgot his cloak and books (II Tim. 4:13). Paul is obviously in prison at the time of this writing (II Tim. 2:9), his case has already come up once, with no one standing by him (II Tim. 4:16), and he is ready to finish his course and depart this life (II Tim. 4:6-8). The implication seems to be that Paul was arrested in Asia Minor, taken to Rome for trial as a Christian, and was now about to die. Reliable tradition places his death in the year 67. Since he was a Roman citizen, he was allowed the dignity of being beheaded, rather than being subjected to some more onerous form of death. The death of Peter also occurred at this time. There is evidence that he was in the city at the time of the persecution, and he was crucified about A.D. 68. According to Origen, he was crucified, but Peter requested that he be placed on the cross upside down, since he did not feel worthy to be killed in the same manner as his Lord.[3]

Nero died in 68, and with him the persecution ceased. For a couple of decades the church enjoyed another period of relative peace. But a second persecution began in A.D. 91 under Emperor Domitian (81-96). Domitian was an autocrat and a tyrant. He is the first emperor to demand to be called *dominus et deus* ("Lord and God"). When he was finally assassinated in 96, the Senate rejoiced and removed his name from the public monuments. Again, most of the persecution occurred around Rome, but it also extended elsewhere. It was at this time that the Apostle John was exiled to Patmos where he received his vision and wrote the Book of Revelation, with its basic thrust of encouraging Christians to persevere through this persecution.

In the year 95 Domitian condemned his cousin Flavius Clemens to death on the official charge of "atheism." This was a favorite charge against the Christians. How could Christians be accused of atheism? Christians believed only in the Lord God Jehovah; they did not believe in all the other gods of the Graeco-Roman pantheon. Monotheism was something most of the Roman population could not understand. Anyone who disbelieved in all these gods could only be an atheist! Therefore the accusation of being an "atheist" was a general indication that a person was really a Christian. This accusation against Flavius Clemens indicates that Christianity had penetrated even to the immediate members of the Emperor's family — in this instance, his own cousin.[4] Obviously Christianity was making inroads into pagan strongholds. In the year 96 Domitian sent Clemens' wife, Flavia Domitilla, into exile on the island of Pontia. But that same year Domitian was killed, and the persecution ceased.

But not completely. There remained a general attitude of official hostility to the Christians. They were still a *religio illicita*. Under Domitian's successor, Nerva (Emperor 96-98), John returned from Patmos, and under the next emperor, Trajan (Emperor 98-117), John finally died, certainly the longest-lived of all the apostles, outliving his brother James by almost sixty years.

In spite of John's release, and the obvious softening of the policy under Nerva, Christians were still experiencing persecution. It was not so much a policy personally initiated by the emperor, but a general policy of persecution and harassment throughout the Empire. This policy is aptly depicted in a famous exchange of letters between Emperor Trajan and the Governor of Bithynia, Pliny the Younger, member of a noble and famous Roman family.

Written in 112, Pliny's letter to Trajan requested information on how to deal with Christians. He stated that he first asked these people if they were in fact Christians; if they admitted it he asked them twice more. If they still admitted it, he sentenced them to death. As a result, anonymous information against a large number of alleged Christians came to his attention. All who denied any Christian identification, he released, since they repeated an invocation to the gods phrased by the governor, and they did reverence to the emperor's image with incense and wine. Others admitted they had been Christians earlier, but they were no longer; these also worshiped the emperor's image and the statues of the gods, and cursed Christ. The governor's question to the emperor was then, what more should he do, or do differently.

Trajan's reply commended Pliny for his actions. Trajan also stated that no concrete policies could be laid down for universal application. Under no circumstances, however, were Christians to be sought or ferreted out; if informed against and the charge was proved, they were to be punished. But if they denied the charge and proved it by worshiping the pagan gods, the charge was to be dropped, even if they had been Christians in the past. Anonymous information was also to be discarded.[5] This exchange of documents demonstrated that Christians were being executed for their faith, but it was not a thorough attempt to exterminate the church. Christians were executed only if they were informed on by a reliable source, and if they refused to change. Otherwise, Christians were not to be sought out. This half-way measure produced a number of executions, but it also allowed for the survival of large numbers of Christians.

Apparently the same basic policy continued under Hadrian (Emperor, 117-138). In Justin's First Apology he quoted a document from this emperor addressed to another local governor, Minucius Fundanus, proconsul of Asia. Hadrian instructed him to proceed against Christians if accusers came forward and charged them with particular crimes. But if anyone slandered them without proof — that is, just called them Christians for the negative connotations involved — the charges were to be dismissed, and the accuser himself was to be punished.[6]

Through most of the second century the same general policy continued. Christians were punished on the basis of reliable information against them. Anonymous or slanderous accusations, however, would not hold up in court. There was no attempt officially to annihilate Christians. But they were seen as stubborn and peculiar. It is in this context of trying to explain their beliefs and attitudes that a number of Christian writers did their work. Styled "Apologists," they wrote formal "apologies." This is using the Greek word *apologia* in its technical sense of defense, a formal response to an accusation, explaining why a person believed or acted in a certain way. The Christians were not making apologies in the sense of saying "I'm sorry," and asking for forgiveness — far from it. They were simply making a legal defense and explanation of their faith and their actions. Their purpose was two-fold: on the one hand they were trying to answer the false rumors that were current about them, gross misunderstandings and untruths; on the other hand they were trying to gain a hearing for Christianity and explain its fundamental doctrines. In general, these apologists were not theologians, but logical thinkers, some of them trained in philosophy and law.

Although dates are sometimes arbitrary, the period of the

Apologists is usually put at 120-220. Some of the early ones mentioned by the later historian Eusebius include Quadratus and Aristides, both of whom wrote under Hadrian. The first really important Apologist is Justin (100-165). Justin was born in Shechem in Samaria of pagan parents; his father was in the Roman civil service at the time. Although most of the details of his biography are not known, he was something of a professional student for a while, then he became a philosopher. The latter portion of his life he spent in Rome. He wrote his First Apology in 155, addressed to Emperor Antoninus Pius (138-160) himself. He wrote his Second Apology a few years later, and ultimately he himself came before the judges. Ordered to sacrifice to the gods, he refused, and he was executed in 165. He is often called Justin Martyr, although the latter word is not a name, but a description of faith unto death.

Justin's First Apology[7] was an attempt to prove on rational grounds that the empire had nothing to fear from Christians. He pointed out that Christianity was superior to paganism, partially because Christians had a higher morality than pagans. In this explanation, Justin demonstrated the falsity of some of the rumors making the rounds against the Christians — such charges as Christians' having sexual orgies and practicing cannibalism in their secret meetings. Christians usually met at night in fields, caves, or other out-of-the-way places, and this led the Romans to suspect the nature of their meetings. Romans knew the Christians practiced love toward one another, and this along with their nocturnal meetings in isolated places led the Romans to believe the meetings consisted of wholesale sexual promiscuity and incest. When the Romans heard that Christians at these meetings also ate someone's flesh and drank his blood (actually a reference to the Lord's Supper), they concluded that Christians devoured in such feasts the children born to such illicit relations. These charges Justin refuted. In the process he also explained what really happened at a Christian worship service, and thus he provides us with our best glimpse of the nature of second century worship. He talks about baptism as the initiation into the fellowship, the reading of Scripture and sermon by the "president" (apparently simply a presiding officer), the prayers, the kiss of peace, and the celebration of the Lord's Supper. He also points out that deacons then dispatch the elements of the Supper to those who are unable to be present.[8]

Justin also makes the argument, based on Old Testament prophecy, that Christ was prefigured before He came to earth. This particular item is a standard argument of Christian apologetics all the way down to the present — just as it had been a staple item even in the preaching of the apostles. A bit more suspicious is Justin's later argument that Plato and other Greek philosophers borrowed many of their ideals from Moses and the Old Testament writings, and that paganism itself was only a poor imitation of Christianity. Justin developed this argument to explain away many of the similarities between paganism and Christianity while at the same time he was arguing that Christianity was a unique religion. He even argued that the demons tried to compromise baptism by having some pagan religions copy such a ceremony of washing. Some later Christian apologists picked up this argument. although pagans never found it convincing; modern scholars find it an embarrassing example of begging the question.

Another significant apology of the period is that of Athenagoras,[9] dated about 176 or 177, addressed to Emperor

Marcus Aurelius (160-180). He also offers a lengthy response to the charges of sexual irregularity. Not only does he again deny these charges, but he also points out that these charges, heinous as they are, are actually things believed of the pagan gods — some of them ate their own children, committed incest with mothers or sisters, and certainly carried on numerous adulterous affairs with other deities and even mortals. Athenagoras refers to the proverb "The harlot reproves the chaste" — the pagans are embarrassed by the holy lives of the Christians and want to slander them to bring them down to the pagan level. Athenagoras is also anxious to deny the charge of atheism. He wants to gain a hearing for monotheism, and he argues at length that Christians are indeed theists — although they believe in only one god, not many.

Thus Christianity continued through mid-century. The general policy of persecution continued, although persecutions were brought on more by local conditions than by official decision. Where there was much local hatred against Christians, there usually was persecution. Quite often antagonistic Jews instigated it. In the time of Antoninus Pius such a persecution broke out in Alexandria. He tried to prevent it, but the Jews were so numerous and the Christians so few that he decided that it was politically undesirable to interfere and suffer the wrath of the Jewish population. A similar instance occurred in the city of Smyrna in Asia Minor in 155 which resulted in the death of many Christians, including Polycarp, a disciple of the Apostle John.

In spite of the sporadic persecution under both Antoninus Pius and Marcus Aurelius, Christians thought well of both men. Both emperors were men of good character —

devout in their paganism, noble in their value systems, committed to the peace of the Empire, and capable rulers. Marcus Aurelius was himself a practicing Stoic philosopher. Very few men had his ability to lead a difficult military campaign against the Pannonian barbarians (on what is now the border between Austria and Hungary), and then spend his evenings in his tent writing philosophical meditations in Greek by candlelight.

This very campaign indicates another major transition that occurred under Aurelius. For about two hundred years the Roman Empire had enjoyed a period of relative peace on its borders, a time called *Pax Romana*, the Roman Peace. Then, about the year 170, war broke out almost simultaneously on the eastern border with Persia, and on the Danubian frontier with the Germanic tribes. What could have caused this sudden threat to the Empire? In the minds of many people it was obvious — the old Roman gods were displeased because so many atheists were at large within the Empire. Who were these atheists? The Christians. The Emperor himself came to the conclusion that the gods must be propitiated by an observance of the traditional worship of the old Roman deities by all citizens — including the Christians. Thus Aurelius developed a new official policy of persecution, one much more stringent than any before. The Jews, being a *religio licita*, were exempt, so the full fury of the persecution fell upon the church.

Persecutions were not limited to Rome. They occurred as well in Asia Minor, Palestine, and Egypt, but one of the most famous was that which took place in southern Gaul (southern France), particularly in the towns of Lyons and Vienne. Here the persecution broke out in its full severity about the year 177. Pothinus, the ninety year old bishop of

Lyons, was arrested, beaten, and scheduled for execution in the amphitheatre, but he died in jail. The death of Pothinus led to the appointment of Irenaeus (130-200) as the new Bishop of Lyons, and from that position he became one of the most significant churchmen of the late second century.

One of the most famous (and fantastic!) executions in Lyons concerned the slave girl Blandina. Numerous soldiers tormented this thirteen year old girl, trying to get her to deny her faith. When these threats did not succeed, she was tortured, thrown to wild beasts (which apparently refused to touch her), placed in a red-hot metal chair, and finally wrapped up in a net and gored repeatedly by a wild bull.

Marcus Aurelius could not understand the stubbornness of the Christians. He saw himself as only trying to safeguard the Roman state, and the Christians were hindering his plans. Their continued resistance could only be seen as rebellion, as well as hard-headed obstinacy. There seemed to be no reason whatsoever why these Christians should be so stubborn. Obviously, then, they must be some kind of subversives, committed to the destruction of the Roman Empire. Such could not be allowed to live, and the Emperor was in favor of eliminating all Christians he could discover.

Many earlier historians paint the persecuting emperors as depraved beasts, maliciously and sadistically enjoying the tortures experienced by the Christians. These historians saw all persecuting emperors as bad emperors. Actually, the opposite seems to be the case. With the exception of Nero and Domitian (both of whom probably were rather depraved), the emperors doing the most persecuting were the better emperors. They were the ones concerned about the stability of the Empire. Actually, bad emperors were not really concerned about the condition of the Empire — a situation we will see, particularly in the third century. They were content to allow the Empire to fall apart. As a result they were not interested in doing anything constructive, and since they wasted no time thinking about the Christians, they allowed the church free reign. Thus we must see persecution, not as an indicator of the depravity of an emperor, but as a measurement of his sincere desire to do what he thought was best for the Empire.

This is also aptly illustrated in the son of Marcus Aurelius, Commodus (Emperor, 181-192). He was hardly the man his father was. Not a philosopher, he fancied himself an athlete. He regularly appeared in the public arena as a hunter of wild animals and conqueror of gladiators, although both classes of opponents were carefully selected to present no significant danger to the willful emperor. He was more interested in a life of sensual pleasure than the stability of the Empire, so the persecution begun by his father lightened, although it never lapsed completely.

Another interesting item pertaining to this emperor and the status of the church at the time was that his favorite mistress, named Marcia, was a Christian — that is, at least she was a member of the Christian community at Rome. At the time many of the Christians were condemned to life-long slavery in state-owned mines in Sardinia (the equivalent to a Russian's being sent to the mines in Siberia). Through her unique relationship with the emperor, Marcia was able to intervene on behalf of many of these condemned Christians, get them released from their captivity, and returned to Rome. Some of those released later attained high office in the Roman church, including at least one Bishop, Calixtus I (217-222). The relationship between

Marcia and Commodus points out two things: (1) Commodus, a far less capable emperor than his father, was not as consistent in pursuing the church as his father had been; and (2) the mere fact that the emperor's mistress could be identified as a member of the Roman Christian community also says something about the depth of commitment that some Christians were able to get by with in the late second century and still be considered Christian. It is difficult to imagine this having happened in the apostolic age. The second century had brought changes to the church — both in the life-style of its members, and in the structure of the organized church itself. To that internal structure we must now turn.

Bibliography for Chapter Two

Eusebius Pamphilus, *Ecclesiastical History*. Grand Rapids: Baker Book House, 1962 (reprint from 1885).

> This is the most important single source for the history of the church down to the early fourth century, written by a respected historian who died in 340.

Roberts, Alexander, and James Donaldson (eds.). *The Ante-Nicene Fathers*. Grand Rapids: Baker Book House, 1979 (reprint of 1886).

> This series, of ten volumes, contains most of the writings of the early church fathers prior to 325, including such men as Tertullian, Cyprian, Origen, Justin, and Irenaeus.

Richardson, Cyril R. (ed.). *Early Christian Fathers*; Vol. I of *The Library of Christian Classics*. Philadelphia: The Westminster Press, 1953.

The twenty-six volumes of the *Library of Christian Classics* are also an important series of source writings. Volume One includes some of the writings of Ignatius, Justin, and Irenaeus.

Questions and Projects for Chapter Two

1. Examine a modern book on Christian evidences or apologetics (examples: Francis Schaeffer, *The God Who Is There*; Arlie J. Hoover, *The Case for Christian Theism*; or Josh McDowell, *Evidence That Demands a Verdict*) and see how its presentation compares to the approach of the early Apologists. Do you think the Apologists would change their style if they were writing in the twentieth century?
2. The twentieth century saw persecution of Christians in Nazi Germany, Soviet Russia, Red China, and elsewhere. How do these compare to the Roman persecutions suffered by the early church?
3. What do you think of the idea that it was the better of the Roman emperors who led in the persecutions? How would this compare to twentieth century persecutions?

Notes for Chapter Two

1. See the treatment in Simeon L. Guterman, *Religious Toleration and Persecution in Ancient Rome* (London: Aiglon Press, Ltd., 1951), pp. 11-12, and 103-122.

2. This information, as well as the statement that Christians were dressed in wild animals' skins and attacked by dogs, is in Tacitus, *The Annals of Imperial Rome*, translated and with an introduction by Michael Grant (Harmondsworth, England: Penguin Books, 1971), p. 365.

3. This statement about the manner of Peter's execution is attributed to Origen by Eusebius, in his *Ecclesiastical History*, Book II, Chapter 1.

4. Some scholars believe that Christianity had penetrated the Emperor's family as early as Paul's Roman imprisonment, for he writes in Philippians 4:22 about those in "Caesar's household." But I believe this means household servants or soldiers, not members of the Emperor's family. Flavius Clemens is the first concrete evidence of a Christian in the imperial family.

5. The correspondence between Pliny and Trajan can be found in Bettenson, pp. 5-7.

6. This letter can be found in ANF, I, p. 186; as well as LCC, I, p. 288.

7. The entire Apology is found in ANF, I, pp. 163-187; and LCC, I, pp. 242-289.

8. Justin's description of the worship service is in ANF, I, pp. 185-186; and LCC, I, pp. 285-287.

9. Athenagoras' work can be found in ANF, II, pp. 129-148; and LCC, I, pp. 300-340.

Chapter Three
DEVELOPING STRUCTURE
IN THE CHURCH

The church of the second century experienced significant changes. These changes were brought on by two factors: the pressure of persecution from the state (an exterior threat), and the pressure of heresy (an interior threat). The church's answer to this dual problem was three-pronged: changes in the office of bishop, development of a creed, and the creation of a canon of sacred writings.

As we have seen, the apostolic church was composed of various officers, some general, some local. The general officers soon faded out of existence, while the local ones endured, giving the church much of its structure down to the present. While these local offices endured, however, the function changed considerably. The most important of these changes concerns the office of bishop. This brings us to the story of Ignatius of Antioch.

Ignatius is not just one of a number of bishops or elders in the church in Antioch — he is *the* Bishop of Antioch, in the sense in which the word "bishop" is normally used today. Since he was the leader of the Christian community there, the Roman government arrested him shortly after the turn of the century and marched him overland to Rome to stand trial and execution. His execution took place either in 107 or 115. Ten soldiers formed his escort (he referred to them as his "leopards"), and they accompanied him through Asia Minor, Greece, and Italy. As he passed through Asia Minor he made contact with many of the other Christian leaders located in Smyrna, Ephesus, Philadelphia and Troas. Later he wrote letters to many of them, and these letters, the only work from his pen that has survived, give an indication of his thinking. These seven letters (including one sent to Rome in which he pleaded with the Roman Christians *not* to interfere with his execution) reflect his view of the office of bishop, a view that is markedly different from the New Testament writings.

In his writings, he always makes a distinction between the "bishop" and the "presbyters" or elders — the word "bishop" always used in the singular, the word "presbyters" always used in the plural. Whereas in the New Testament the terms "bishop" and "presbyter" are used interchangeably, for Ignatius this was no longer true. He always pictured a single bishop over a church, assisted by a group of presbyters who were directly under him. The unity of the church was personified in the singleness of the bishop. He suggested that the bishop took the

place of Christ as an authority figure, while the presbyters were like the apostles.[1] This development is
known as the monarchical episcopate, or the mon-epis-
copate — a single bishop ruling as monarch.

In his letter to Smyrna, Ignatius stated that nobody
must do anything that had to do with the church without
the bishop's approval. The only valid Lord's Supper was
that which was celebrated by the bishop or someone he
appoints.[2] Without the bishop's permission, no baptism
or love feasts were permitted. In his letter to Polycarp he
even suggested that marriages ought to wait for the bishop's approval.[3]

Part of Ignatius' concern was definitely a concern for
unity. Dangerous teaching could be avoided and schismatic tendencies in the church could be eliminated if
everyone remained loyal to the leadership and direction
of the bishop. But in the process, he made the office of
bishop something more than it had been under the apostles.

It is difficult to explain how this change could have
come about. According to early tradition, Ignatius
became Bishop of Antioch about the year 69 — still
within the apostolic period. If he had been a member of
the Christian community in Antioch for some time previously — as would be expected: Paul said the bishop
should not be a novice — then he would have known the
Apostle Paul personally. Ignatius obviously overlapped
the apostolic period. How could he depart from the apostolic precedent? One of the interesting things about his
writings is that he seems to assume everybody shares his
views. He does not seem to be aware that his views are
different from those of the New Testament. This would

indicate that the change is not recent, that it must be placed well within the first century.

Another factor is that although Ignatius seems to assume that all churches are like his own, the historical record indicates that they are not. The church at Rome was still using the terms "bishop" and "presbyter" interchangeably until the year 140.[4] Soon thereafter, the monarchical episcopate developed in Rome. It became common throughout the Christian churches so that by the year 200 it was universal throughout Christendom. The process occurred everywhere, but at different times. But Ignatius was not aware that the pattern at Antioch was different from others. Another interesting factor in Ignatius is a significant omission: he says nothing about "apostolic succession," even when it would have been very useful to his argument about Christian unity to do so. This suggests that he is unaware of the idea, which in turn indicates that the idea that bishops succeed directly to the authority and position of the apostles is a later concept. In fact, this idea received its first clear treatment by Irenaeus, several decades later.

As mentioned earlier, Irenaeus became the Bishop of Lyons in 178 after the death of Pothinus the previous year. Irenaeus grew up in Asia Minor and, while still a young lad, he received Christian instruction from Polycarp, Bishop of Smyrna. Polycarp, in turn, had received instruction from the Apostle John. This makes Irenaeus a second-hand disciple of John — an important link back into the apostolic period. As Bishop of the important city of Lyons, Irenaeus also became concerned about the purity of Christian doctrine. His attention was directed particularly to Gnosticism, a false teaching that existed as early as Paul's letter to the Colossians. Gnosticism was a philosophical perversion of Christianity which had numerous variations among its different sects. A common element, however, was its intellectual emphasis, trying to make Christianity compatible with reason and philosophy. Gnostics made a major distinction between things of the flesh and things of the spirit. They believed an inferior god had created the physical world; therefore, all things of earth, including human bodies, were by nature evil. Most Gnostic groups denied the real humanity of Christ; from their viewpoint, Christ could not be both divine and incarnate. Christ came to save men through *gnosis* (the Greek word for "knowledge"). For the Gnostics, this saving knowledge came through special teachings that only they knew, but which had been handed down from the apostles. Thus many Gnostics claimed to have the true apostolic faith while the majority of the church had lost the truth.

Irenaeus responded to this heresy by arguing that the best way to be sure of the apostolic teaching was to look at those churches established by the apostles and which, therefore, had a clear succession of bishops down to the present. In these churches, he claimed, the apostolic teaching was continued in its purity. As a case in point, Irenaeus pointed to the church in Rome. Although the Roman church was technically started before the arrival of either Peter or Paul, both these apostles worked there in its early years, so the church was considered the equivalent of having what was called an apostolic foundation. And the teaching at Rome, Irenaeus triumphantly concluded, refuted the teaching of the Gnostics.

In a troublesome passage, Irenaeus went on to say, "It

is a matter of necessity that every Church should agree with this Church [the Church in Rome] on account of its preeminent authority, that is, the faithful everywhere, inasmuch as the apostolic tradition has been preserved continuously by those who exist everywhere.[5] The statement is not even grammatically correct, which adds to its difficult interpretation. Many have used this statement to prove the primacy of Roman authority — that Irenaeus states every church must be in harmony with Rome. Others assert that Irenaeus' point seems to be that the church in Rome is made up of individuals from all of Christendom; since it is a microcosm of the church throughout the entire Empire, it can only represent the basic common teachings of the church universal; any peculiar teachings of a church in some region of the Empire will be countered by its absence in others, so that what is taught at Rome can be assured to be taught everywhere — and Gnosticism is definitely not taught at Rome; therefore it is a false teaching. Irenaeus is important, therefore, not only because he continues the evolution of episcopal authority, but also because his statement — whatever he might have meant by it — will be used by others in later generations and centuries as proof of Roman primacy in the second century.

Another reaction to heretical teaching was the use of creeds. A creed is simply a statement of faith (Latin *credo*, I believe). Simple statements of faith include Peter's "Good Confession" of Matthew 16:16 and may also be reflected in such biblical statements as "Jesus is Lord" (I Cor. 12:3) or "He is Lord of all" (Acts 10:36). In the early church additional simple statements of faith came about, many of them framed on the tri-partite divi-

sion of Matthew 28:19, "Father, Son and Holy Spirit."
The major such statement in the West was the Early
Roman Baptismal Creed, developed sometime around
the year 150. It stated:

> I believe in God the Father Almighty;
> And in Christ Jesus, His only Son, our Lord;
> And in the Holy Spirit, the holy church, the resurrection of the
>   body.[6]

This was an interrogative creed, phrased in three parts,
and answered "I do" by the person being baptized after
each phrase. Thus "trine immersion" developed. The
person baptizing asked, "Do you believe in God..."
upon which the person answered "I do" and was baptized. The second and third phrases repeated the procedure, resulting in three immersions.

But by the end of the century church leaders felt it
necessary to expand the creed to weed out the Gnostics.
The Old Roman Creed, formulated about the year 200,
was one the Gnostics would not use or repeat because of
its statements about Christ, which was the whole point.
The creed served as a convenient doctrinal summary to
check the theological orthodoxy of people. The first
point was unchanged, but the crucial statement about
Christ was expanded to state:

> And in Christ Jesus His only Son our Lord:
> Who was born of the Holy Spirit and the Virgin Mary,
> Who under Pontius Pilate was crucified and buried,
> The third day He rose again from the dead,
> He ascended into heaven,
> And sitteth on the right hand of the Father,
> Whence He shall come to judge the quick and the dead.

Because Gnostics denied the Incarnation of Christ, they

would not repeat such statements as "born," "crucified and buried," "rose again from the dead." Thus the creed served its purpose. The Apostles' Creed was a later development, formulated in Spain about 650, although it is clearly based on the original tri-partite division. The legend developed that the apostles stated it immediately after the Ascension, but this is a later idea.

One of the reasons creeds were needed was that there was as yet no officially selected New Testament. No one could argue "The Gnostics are wrong because the New Testament plainly teaches...." All the various books we have in our New Testament were in circulation, but they had not yet been definitively collected as such. The Gnostics claimed to have special teaching represented in books of their own, and thus there was a conflict of written authorities in the second century church. An early conflict of this sort is represented in the story of Marcion.

Marcion (?-c.160) was from Pontus, but he had been excommunicated from the church there for gross immorality. He shortly arrived in Rome, about the year 140, as a wealthy young merchant. He was soon a recognized figure in the Roman church until his Gnostic views came to light, which led the Roman church to excommunicate him in 144. To substantiate his claim to represent pure apostolic teaching, Marcion drew up a list of canonical New Testament books that were genuine Scripture. "Canon" is a Greek word meaning literally a "reed," but one that was used as a measure, as a yardstick. "Canon" came to mean a body of writings that could be used to measure the accuracy of other teachings. Marcion's list was good — as far as it went. He included the Gospel of Luke (but he omitted the first two chapters which dealt with the human birth of Jesus; since Gnostics denied the Incarnation, this was a troublesome passage), and ten of Paul's letters — excluding the three Pastorals and Hebrews. This list was fine, except it suggested that they were the *only* accepted Christian Scriptures. To defend the authority of other writings as well, the Roman church had to come up with its own list to counter the list of Marcion.

This development led to the creation of numerous lists, as Christians in various places began the serious task of coming to a consensus as to which books were to be considered scriptural. The Muratorian Fragment is an example of such an early list, dated about 170. It lists all the books in our New Testament except Hebrews, James and the two letters of Peter, although it includes the Revelation of Peter.[7] This latter book is typical of dozens of various writings which were not authentically apostolic, but were often used by early churches. Other such books are I Clement, the Shepherd of Hermas, the Didache, and numerous revelations and books of acts.

Origen (184-254), an important church leader in Alexandria, compiled lists from various Christian centers around the Mediterranean, and he was the first person to begin a systematic and comparative check to arrive at a consensus in this listing. One of his lists was the *homologoumena*, those books accepted by all churches. The list included the four Gospels, Acts, Paul's thirteen, I John, I Peter, and Revelation. That is, all churches around the Mediterranean basin accepted these twenty-one books as scripture. His other list was the *antilegomena* — books that were accepted by some churches, but not by all. This list included Hebrews, II Peter, II and III John, James, Jude, Barnabas, the Shepherd of Hermas, the Didache, and the Gospel of the Hebrews. It is obvious that by the time of Origen the churches were well on their way to achieving a consensus on what writings were to be considered scripture — but there were still some discrepancies with regard to a final list. The Council of Nicaea did not discuss the canon, but a council at Carthage in 397 did, and it came up with a list of 27 books — the very same as are in our New Testament today. The significance of this list is that it is not just the list of one person, but the decision of an entire assembly, an assembly which included the great Augustine in its number.

It may also be important to point out that this is not a case of the church "making" the canon. Later scholars, particularly Roman Catholics, will make the argument that since the church formed the canon, the church is superior to the New Testament in its right to interpret those books as it sees fit. Actually this is not the case. It is not a matter of the church's *forming* the canon. The various books were written well within the apostolic period without any approval by the church as such. Virtually all churches recognized these books as authoritative. Thus, rather than "making the canon," the church, after a long period of research and consideration, simply came to a unanimous consensus as to which books were to be counted as authentic and of scriptural import. This places the New Testament over the church, recognizing that New Testament as apostolic in authority, while the church then must constantly refer itself to the pattern of apostolic Christianity.

The major tests used by the church to decide which books were canonical were two: was it written by an apostle, and does it coincide with the remainder of genuine apostolic teaching? Hebrews and Revelation were accepted into the canon on the strength of the belief that they were apostolic in authorship — by Paul and John respectively. Mark and Luke were not written by apostles, but Mark was strongly connected with the preaching of Peter, and Luke was written after his research in Palestine, and blessed by his association with Paul. James and Jude were not apostles, but they were half-brothers of Christ, and this gave their books authority, particularly for Jewish Christians. So it was through this process that the authoritative books for the church — the New Testament — were gathered and considered canonical.

Two other items remain to be treated in a consideration of structural developments in this era, and both of them pertain to the changes in the office of bishop. One of them has to do with the term "presbyter." As we noticed earlier, originally this term was interchangeable with the term "bishop," but it had been separated by Ignatius and made into a lower office. The universal development of the monarchical episcopate meant that each church had a ruling bishop and a group of presbyters under him. The bishops often delegated the presbyters to preach, preside at the Lord's Supper, and do pastoral work among the people. Usually the presbyters also lived with the bishop, probably in quarters near the church building. These men became known as the bishop's family, a phrase that remained current through the medieval period.

As the third century moved along, another development occurred. The church was growing and expanding, particularly in the cities and surrounding urban areas. It reached the point where many churches had to go to multiple services to accommodate the crowds of people. The presbyters played an active part in these extra services. Then things reached the point where suburban churches began to develop, so that people in the outlying areas were not traveling to the inner city church on Sundays anymore. Presbyters, who assisted the bishop in the first service at the city church, took portions of the Lord's Supper elements (blessed directly from the hands of the bishop, a concept that Ignatius would have approved of) to these outlying churches. Here a full worship service was held, under the delegated authority from the downtown bishop. The presbyter then returned to the bishop's house.

But with additional process of time, more and more of the presbyter's time was spent in that outlying church — in pastoral work particularly. It was more and more awkward and inconvenient for him to come back daily to the bishop's residence. Thus he soon stayed with that suburban or outlying church. He was what a later age will call a parish priest. Our English word "priest" is in fact derived from the word "presbyter." Although there is a different Greek word for "priest" (*hierus*), quite often scholars today will translate the word "presbyter" as "priest." His function was not that of a pagan priest, but it is that which is commonly associated with priests in modern denominations. So the second and third centuries not only saw a growing distinction between "bishop" and "presbyter," which in the New Testament were interchangeable terms, but they also saw the bishop-presbyter relationship becoming that between a modern bishop over a diocese and his subordinate parish priests.

Meanwhile the church was growing throughout the Empire. The first half of the third century saw a relaxation in the persecution. There was a significant persecution in the year 202 under Septimius Severus, but most emperors in the next half century ignored the church. This made it less dangerous for people to become Christians, with the result that many people did so with less than full commitment to Christ. When persecution flared up again, some of these people were unwilling to maintain their Christianity to the point of death.

Most of the emperors in the first half of the third century were greedy, incompetent men. Decius (Emperor, 249-251) was an exception. He was as concerned about the empire as Marcus Aurelius had been, and he came to the same conclusion. The Empire was in a bad way, and the old state gods must be appeased. Therefore, all citizens in the Empire must publicly worship the state gods. Those who refused were to be killed. Even pagans of long standing repute were forced to throw incense into the altars of the deities of Rome. Those who sacrificed received a certificate (*libellus*) saying they had. Many Christians knuckled under to the demand of the state and secured their *libellus*. This included several bishops in North Africa; in fact two bishops in Spain led their congregations in a wholesale worship at the altars of Rome. Their feeling was much like those of first century Christians who ate meat sacrificed to idols — since Christians did not believe in the existence of these gods, their action could not be considered worship, only as obedience to the state. Other Christian leaders, particularly bishops, fled into exile and hiding. Still others did not sacrifice, but obtained *libelli* on the black market which simply *stated* that they had sacrificed.

The persecution began in the year 250 and ended the next year when Decius died fighting the Goths on the northern frontier. His persecution was the first attempt to totally abolish Christianity, but his early death made it ineffective. However, its efforts were to rock the church for some time to come. For now the church was faced with the question of what to do with all the people who had offered sacrifice and thus lapsed in their faith (the *lapsi*).

This situation was complicated by the great number of martyrs who had died for their faith, and the even larger number of people who had confessed their faith through torture and punishment, but survived the ordeal. These people were called *confessors*. (The theologian Origen was one such person; tortured in 251, he finally died of his injuries in 254.) Christianity had always respected its martyrs, and local custom did the same to the confessors. In North Africa, confessors were considered so exalted that they could handle serious cases of church discipline, forgive people of their sins, and allow them back into the church. Officially these were prerogatives of the bishop alone.

With the persecution over, what was to be done with the thousands of *lapsi* who now wanted back into the church? Basically there were three schools of thought. The hard-liners saw the action of such people as unquestioned apostasy — they had denied their Christ, and this was a serious offense. The only way to remove the sin of apostasy was to die as a martyr to the faith. On the other hand were those who wished to be lenient, and most of the *confessors* were in this category. They had experienced the horror of torture, and they probably realized how thin the line was between holding out and giving in. They felt that the *lapsi* were the people who needed shepherding the most, and that they needed to get back into the church to receive the proper spiritual growth. Therefore, return to the church ought to be made as easy as possible to allow these people to come back and be strengthened. Then there was a third option between the two — the moderates. Their view was that the *lapsi* ought to be welcomed back, but apostasy was no light thing; therefore, they ought to prove their commitment through a period of probation of two or three years first. These were the three options: make it hard, make it easy, make it realistic.

Into the midst of this conflict came Cyprian, Bishop of Carthage (248-258). Cyprian thought the *confessors* were making things too easy; he was a moderate. But the hard-liners formed a significant block of opposition to him. Into this dispute in Carthage came the overflow of a Roman problem. The Bishop of Rome had been killed in the persecution, and in 251 two men stood for election. Cornelius was a moderate, Novatian was a hard-liner. Cornelius was properly elected, but the hard-liners refused to accept him; they elected Novatian instead. Both men then wrote to Cyprian asking for his endorsement. Cyprian investigated, determined that Cornelius had been properly elected and gave his support there. But Novatian refused to yield; he formed a schism in the Roman church, gathered support elsewhere, including the hard-line Carthaginians, and even appointed a "proper" bishop for the church in Carthage. Thus there was a wide-spread split, called the Novatian schism.

The Novatianists were also evangelistic, and they won a number of people to their churches, baptizing them as Christians. But after a while the steam went out of the Novatian schism, and many of that group returned to the church under Cyprian, including some new converts who had been baptized by the Novatians. Now another question was raised. Was baptism in a heretic or schismatic church valid? Cyprian concluded it was not. Against him, however, was the new Bishop of Rome, Stephen (254-257) who contended that as long as the proper motive was present and the proper words were used, the baptism was indeed valid. Actually Stephen's position became the general position of the church — even down to today. This means that the validity of the church's ministry does not depend upon the personal morality or orthodoxy of the preacher or priest, as long as the sacraments/ordinances are done with the proper motive on the part of the recipient and the proper formula. Cyprian outlived Stephen (by one year), so he appeared to win, but in the next century the other side became victorious.

The dispute involved here is important for additional considerations. Although Cyprian lost the central issue, he developed a line of thinking that became orthodox thinking even for the Roman church. In arguing against the validity of heretic baptism, Cyprian began asking questions about the structure of the church. He picked up Ignatius' ideas that Christians must be in obedience to their bishop and that outside the bishops there are no valid sacraments, and he carried these a step further. He now enunciated the slogan *extra ecclesiam nulla salus* — outside the church there is no salvation. All Christians will probably accept this. But Cyprian identified the church as those who are in proper obedience to their bishop. Ultimately Roman Catholicism will advance the idea that there is no salvation outside the church, and the church properly defined is those under the submission to the Pope. Therefore, outside the Pope there is no salvation.

It is both interesting and instructive to compare Cyprian's position to that of Rome in these two disputes. In the controversy over the *lapsi* he and Cornelius agreed against the African rigorists. Cyprian was a great believer in the unity of the church, and in his book *On the Unity of the Church*, he based this on the unity of the episcopal body in communion with the Bishop of Rome. He also upheld the primacy of Peter and thus the primacy of Peter's successor, the Bishop of Rome. Soon afterwards, however, he had his run-in with Stephen over the question of rebaptism. He then put out a second edition of his book in which he modified his statements about Peter's primacy and emphasized the theory of local episcopacy. He saw the bishop as the principle of unity in the church (in agreement with Ignatius), with each bishop sovereign in his province. Thus he stressed to Stephen that Carthage was an episcopal see as much as Rome was, and that Stephen had no authority in Carthage.[8] This position comes to be known as "the collegiality of bishops" — the authority of the church resides in the bishops collectively, and not in any of them in particular. The bishop of Rome was already coming to be known as *primus inter pares* — first

65

among equals. This means that all bishops are equal in authority, but that Rome stands first in their number.

In Cyprian's disputes we notice a pattern we will return to again. That is, whenever a bishop finds that Rome agrees with him, he emphasizes the primacy of Rome. He tells his opponents that Rome must be right, so they had better shape up and fall in line with the teaching of Rome, as he has done. But whenever a bishop in a local dispute discovers that Rome agrees with his opposition, he will emphasize that all bishops are equal and that Rome has no authority in his local diocese. Thus the claim that later Roman Catholics will make that Roman primacy is accepted in the early church is misleading; it is accepted only by those who have political advantage they want to make out of it. It is not accepted by those in disagreement with Rome. They will uphold the earlier tradition that each bishop is independent and authoritative in local matters. *Primus inter pares*? It simply depends upon which side of the dispute the local bishop and the Bishop of Rome are on. If they are on the same side, Rome is *primus*; if they differ, Rome is *pares*.

In all of these developments, from Ignatius to Cyprian and beyond, the structure of the church was changing. The administrative machinery was growing, the church was enlarging, and the office of bishop became even more authoritative.

Bibliography for Chapter Three

Gregory, Caspar R. *Canon and Text of the New Testament.* New York: Charles Scribner's Sons, 1907.

Although this is an old work, it is still an excellent study of both canonical development and the New Testament text.

Harnack, Adolf, *The Constitution and Law of the Church in the First Two Centuries.* New York: Williams & Norgate, 1910.

Already quoted in Chapter One.

Lietzman, Hans. *The Founding of the Church Universal;* Vol. II of *A History of the Early Church.* Cleveland: The World Publishing Company (Meridian Books), 1961.

Lietzman's liberalism colors his presentation of the New Testament period, but this is still a valuable comprehensive treatment of the early church.

Westcott, Brooke F. *A General Survey of the History of the Canon of the New Testament.* London: Macmillan, 1896-97.

This is a classic treatment of the development of the New Testament canon, quite comprehensive.

Questions and Projects for Chapter Three

1. Construct a hypothetical situation where you can illustrate some of the pressures on a local church that would lead it to move toward a monarchical episcopate. Try to be imaginative but still plausible.
2. What is your personal opinion about the use of a creed

in a local church? Would it change your position any if such a statement were considered simply a personal statement rather than an authoritative position of the church?

3. Write a paper in which you try to argue convincingly that the church produced the New Testament, and therefore has authority over it. Write another paper to refute this position.

4. Do you think Novatian was right in demanding that standards of church membership should not be lowered for those of weak faith or courage? What would Jesus say? What would Paul say? Give supporting scriptural references for these last two answers.

5. What do you think of the early church's decision that the sacraments are valid as long as the proper words are used and the proper motive is present? How would this apply to modern practices of baptism, including persons who want to transfer membership from a Baptist church?

Notes for Chapter Three

1. Ignatius, *Trallians* 2:1-2. The letters of Ignatius can be found in LCC, I, pp. 74-120; and also in ANF, I, pp. 45-96.

2. Ignatius, *Smyrnaeans* 8:1.

3. Ignatius, *Polycarp* 5:2.

4. I Clement, Chapter 44 uses the terms interchangeably; this work was written about the year 97. The reference can be found in LCC, I, 64, or ANF, I, 17. Hans Lietzman states that a "college of presbyters" was still at the head of the church in Rome in the year 140. See his comment in *A History of the Early Church*, Volume II: *The Founding of the Church Universal* (Cleveland: The World Publishing Company, Meridian Books, 1961), p. 60. For his coverage of the development of the monarchical episcopate, see *Ibid.*, pp. 58-68.

5. Irenaeus, *Against Heresies*, III, 3,2. This work can be found in ANF,

I; the reference is on pp. 415-416.

6.   A useful discussion of these early creeds is in B.A. Gerrish (ed.), *The Faith of Christendom: A Sourcebook of Creeds and Confessions* (Cleveland: The World Publishing Company [Meridian Books], 1963). Both the Early Roman Baptismal Creed and the Old Roman Creed are given on p. 55. Further information can be found in Schaff, II.

7.   For a copy of the Muratorian canon, see ANF, V, pp. 603-604.

8.   On this change in Cyprian, for both the text and commentary, see LCC, V, pp. 122, 126 and 142.

Chapter Four
THE TRIUMPH OF
THE EARLY CHURCH

The persecution under Emperor Decius was the most rigorous the church had faced up to that time, but it lasted only a year. The church then enjoyed peace for several years, but persecution flared up again under Valerian (Emperor, 253-260). This persecution represents a new development, because it was not initiated by the Emperor himself, but by his Finance Minister, Macrianus. Macrianus was a member of one of the Egyptian mystery religions, and he was jealous of the growing success of the Christians. Previous persecutions had been in the name of the state, to preserve the ancient ways and honor the old gods. This persecution originated in a jealous hatred of Christianity by a person not loyal to the old gods either. In addition, Christianity by this time was beginning to accumulate property, including significant buildings for worship. Many Christians were wealthy. Macrianus, in charge of the fiscal stability of the Empire, was keenly sensitive to the fact that the imperial treasury was just about empty. So he combined his zeal for his own religion and his hatred of the Christians with the financial needs of the Empire. The persecution allowed him to confiscate the estates of the church and individual Christians, as well as advance his own religion at the expense of Christianity.

The first edict of this persecution came in 257 with a prohibition of worship — the first time Rome forbade Christian worship. The decree further prohibited Christians from gathering in their cemeteries, and it forced them to sacrifice to the Roman gods. A second edict in 258 ordered the execution of members of the clergy who had not sacrificed and the confiscation of property belonging to Christians of the upper class. This persecution was even worse than that under Decius. This was a major attempt to wipe out the Christian clergy. Cyprian himself died in this struggle, in 258. But in the year 260 Valerian was killed in battle against the Persians on the eastern frontier, and the persecution ceased. For approximately the next four decades, the church again experienced another period of peace. As a result, the faith spread, more church buildings were erected, and the Christians by the end of the century came to number about ten percent of the entire population of the Empire.

This was the situation when Diocletian came to the throne (Emperor, 284-305). Diocletian has sometimes been called the savior of the Empire, because the Empire was, in fact, experiencing extremely difficult times.

Most of the emperors of the third century were greedy and incompetent. Many of them were army generals who used their military power to seize the throne. As a rule, they were more interested in power than in actually working for the stability of the Empire. Most of these died violent deaths, either at the frontiers battling attacking tribes, or by assassination due to political intrigues at home. Army generals were constantly vying with each other for the imperial throne. The result was almost constant civil war, which led to wholesale killings, financial corruption, and economic chaos. Many people thought the Empire was about to come completely apart.

But Diocletian seized control in 284 and restored peace and order to the situation. He reformed both the army and the civil government, and his accomplishments are credited with having saved the Roman Empire for another two centuries. One of the conclusions that Diocletian came to was that the Empire represented too much responsibility to be administered effectively by one man. So he raised an army colleague named Maximian to be a co-ruler with him; Diocletian exercised control over the eastern half of the Empire, Maximian over the west. Soon each man had a junior assistant: Constantius in the West, Galerius in the East. Thus, there were four rulers, an arrangement known as the Tetrarchy.

Because of Diocletian's administrative reforms, peace and stability did return to the Empire. The Church also shared in this time of peace and prosperity. But, as we saw earlier in the time preceding Decius, when it was easy to become a Christian, many people became Christians without total commitment to Christ. The majority

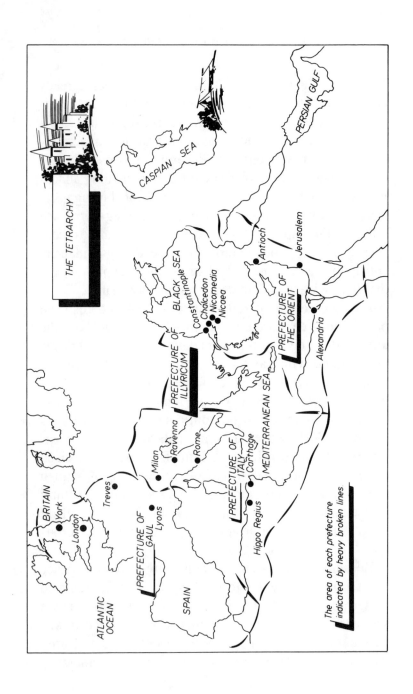

THE TETRARCHY

CASPIAN SEA

PERSIAN GULF

BLACK SEA

Antioch
Jerusalem

Constantinople
Chalcedon
Nicomedia
Nicaea

PREFECTURE OF ILLYRICUM

PREFECTURE OF THE ORIENT

Alexandria

Ravenna
Rome

MEDITERRANEAN SEA

Milan

PREFECTURE OF ITALY
Carthage

BRITAIN
York
London

Treves

PREFECTURE OF GAUL
Lyons

Hippo Regius

ATLANTIC OCEAN

SPAIN

The area of each prefecture indicated by heavy broken lines

of the church, however, was genuine in its commitment to its Lord.

Persecution began again in 303. Galerius, the junior ruler in the east and also the son-in-law of Diocletian, apparently was the person who convinced Diocletian to begin another persecution against the church. Early in the year 303 Diocletian yielded to his entreaties and dismissed Christians from all posts in the army and in the government. But Galerius was not satisfied with such partial measures. From February of 303 to about January of 304, the Roman government promulgated four edicts against the Christians. The first one was directed mainly at Christian worship: sacred books and vessels were to be confiscated and church buildings destroyed. The second edict ordered the arrest of all clergy; the third edict compelled them to sacrifice to the gods. The fourth and final edict made such worship mandatory to all inhabitants of the Empire. Failure to sacrifice would mean deportation to state mines, torture, or death. The Christians always referred to this persecution as "the Great Persecution," and there is no doubt it was the most severe the church ever faced. Uncounted thousands of Christians were cruelly tortured and killed, throughout the Empire.

The persecution was not equally severe everywhere, however. Galerius and Diocletian led the fury, with Maximian not too far behind. But Constantius, who ruled over Gaul and Britain, had as his first wife, Helena, a Christian woman. Constantius enforced only the first edict, and even that one not thoroughly. He confiscated copies of the Scriptures and destroyed church buildings, but he refrained from harming the Christians.

The persecution was most severe in the east, where Diocletian and Galerius ruled. But it was in the east that Christians were most numerous. It has been estimated that at the time Christians constituted 10-15% of the population in the eastern half of the Empire, but only 5-10% in the west, for an overall 10%. The population of the eastern half was significantly higher than that of the western half, so that in terms of actual numbers, there were far more Christians in the east than in the west.

The persecution continued, but after 305 things became even more complicated. Diocletian retired that year, and forced his colleague Maximian to retire also. That meant that Galerius and Constantius became the new co-rulers of the Empire, though Diocletian had chosen new junior rulers for each of them. Diocletian worked this out so that the whole arrangement would be a self-perpetuating process. Augustii retired, Caesars moved up to become Augustii, and new Caesars were appointed. Thus stable government prevailed, with no fear of incompetent sons or a military takeover. Unfortunately, this whole system disintegrated in 306 when Constantius died in York, Britain, while at the head of his troops. With him at the time was his son Constantine. The troops reverted to the common practice of the third century, proclaiming Constantine the new emperor in his father's place — the very kind of military takeover Diocletian's system was designed to prevent. This opened up the way for other men to put their bid in for the imperial throne, and soon there were seven claimants to the Emperor's position in the west, and several more in the east. Galerius managed to keep a firm hand on most things in the east, and under him the persecution continued.

The continuing executions, however, soon sickened even the pagan population. Most Christians maintained their faith even in the face of such pressure, and it appeared that further persecution would cause nothing but continued social disruption. Then in 311 Galerius became mortally ill. On his death bed, he finally issued an edict cancelling the persecution, giving Christians their freedom to worship and rebuild their churches as long as they did not offend public order. In the process Galerius took the occasion to voice his resentment at the Christians for their stubbornness and madness for not returning to the ancient gods of Rome. He issued his edict on April 30, 311 — six days before he died. In the east he was succeeded by Maximin, and for six months this new emperor continued the policy of religious toleration. But by fall he had reinstated the persecution. By the spring of 312, however, even Maximin gave in — partially because of new developments in the west. In spite of the brief persecution under Maximin, and another brief period which we shall note a little further on, the edict of toleration granted by Galerius in April of 311 is usually considered the virtual end of official persecution of Christians in the Roman Empire. They had been through a lot in the last two and a half centuries, but their numbers had grown considerably since the days of their apostolic beginnings.

Meanwhile, in the west, Constantine, after his elevation to the office of Emperor by his father's troops, had been busy consolidating his own position in England and Gaul. The various claimants in the west began to wipe each other out until by the spring of 312 only two remained — Constantine and Maxentius, the son of

Maximian (please try to distinguish between Maximian, Maxentius, and Maximin). Constantine held England and Gaul, Maxentius held Italy. In the summer of 312 Constantine invaded northern Italy, fighting hard battles, but constantly winning his way south. By autumn his advance guard was nearing Rome, and it was at this time that he had his famous vision.

He claimed that in full daylight he saw a Christian symbol in the sky: the monogram of two Greek letters, "Chi" and "Rho" which are the first two letters in the name "Christ." This popular monogram looked somewhat like a cross, and above the Chi-rho Constantine saw the words, "In this sign, conquer." Constantine was not yet a Christian, but he took this vision as a sign from the Christian God that he would be victorious in the coming battle if he fought under the Christian symbol. As a result he had the monogram painted on the shields of his soldiers (scholars disagree whether this included only several dozen soldiers of his bodyguard, or several thousands of his infantry) and made into his personal standard, his *labarum*, as he prepared to fight Maxentius.

Maxentius was strongly entrenched in the city of Rome and it would have been difficult to defeat him. But Maxentius was also confident of success, and he sallied forth to give battle to Constantine in the open field. A few miles outside of Rome the two armies clashed, and Constantine, the far better military strategist, soon outmaneuvered his enemy and won the battle. Maxentius escaped from the disaster on the battlefield and fled back to Rome, but some of Constantine's cavalry met him at the Milvian Bridge crossing the Tiber into the city, killing Maxentius in this little skirmish. Thus on October 28, 312, Constantine emerged the unopposed victor of the entire west.

One of the ongoing arguments among historians through the centuries has been whether Constantine can be considered a genuine Christian. Was he "converted," or was his "Christianity" only a political façade for his selfish ambitions? A leading nineteenth century historian, Jacob Burckhardt, saw him as only a political opportunist who used Christianity for his own interests. In the twentieth century, most historians have gone the other way, seeing Constantine as genuinely of the Christian position and doing his best to implement it. Christians numbered only 10% of the Roman population, and by showing favor to them, Constantine risked the support of the other 90% of the inhabitants of the Empire. Burckhardt argued that the populace was sick of further persecution and was ready to grant toleration to the Christians; but granting toleration is a very small thing compared to the huge favors that Constantine now began to shower upon the church. This can hardly be considered going with the popular tide.

The day after the Battle of Milvian Bridge (the name given to the entire battle, not just the skirmish at the bridge itself) Constantine entered Rome in triumph. There were the usual games, appearances before the Senate, distributions to the people, but no sacrifice. Constantine never again offered a sacrifice, and he suppressed those offered him as part of the imperial cult. In letters sent to North Africa in the next several months, Constantine ordered church lands returned to their owners, public relief distributed through the hands of the

Bishop of Carthage, and clergy exempted from various public services. One of his first acts in Rome was to present the Lateran Palace (inherited through his wife Fausta) to the Bishop of Rome along with the adjacent grounds of the recently razed barracks of the Praetorian Guard. Constantine had dissolved the Praetorians, and this cleared land was used to erect a magnificent church building to become the bishop's seat — St. John's Lateran. For the next thousand years the Lateran Palace was the residence of the Bishops of Rome.

Christian symbols began to appear on imperial coinage as early as 314. The Unconquered Sun (Sol Invictus) began to disappear from the coins by 321, and by 323 all pagan symbols were removed from the coins. Church cases tried by a bishop's court were recognized as legally binding, and churches were also given the right to inherit property. Constantine had his children educated as Christians, and he even began to proscribe certain pagan rituals. Much controversy has also centered on the relationship of Constantine, Christianity, and the cult of the sun, Sol Invictus. Emperor Aurelian (Emperor, 270-275) had made the sun cult one of the official religions of the Empire, and the birthdate of the Unconquered Sun was made a public holiday — December 25. Constantine had Sunday declared an official holiday in 321. By the end of his reign (Constantine had nothing to do with it, it was a custom developed by the people) December 25 was turned into the celebration of Christmas. Many have argued that this is a base syncretism: Christianity advantageously adding elements from other religions. But it is just as viable to contend that Christians are merely taking older symbols and turning them to their own account, without necessarily accepting all the old symbol stands for.

It is true that Constantine delayed his baptism until the end of his life. Although not normal at this period, such "death-bed baptisms" were not rare. Rather than an indication that the person is not serious about Christianity, it actually indicates just the opposite. The church's basic teaching was that baptism washes away sins. Therefore sins committed after baptism presented a problem; it was commonly believed that nothing was as powerful in washing away sins as baptism. Thus if a person could delay baptism until the last possible moment, and then died immediately after baptism, he would enter eternal life without any sins charged against him. The theology may be poor, and the concept of God's forgiveness woefully inadequate, but the whole idea certainly underscores a person's seriousness about Christianity. Constantine delayed his own baptism until a few weeks before his death on May 22, 337.

There seems little doubt that he was serious in his commitment to Christianity. Just a few months after his victory over Maxentius he met in Milan with a colleague, Licinius, who was about to engage Maximin in a death struggle for control of the eastern half of the Empire. At Milan, in February of 313, Licinius married Constantia, Constantine's sister, and Constantine and Licinius both agreed to what has been called the "Edict of Milan." Not an edict as such, it was a decision between the two men on how Christians were to be treated. This decision called for religious freedom for all, but it specifically stipulated the Christians. The wording was sometimes vague; at one point it referred to "the

Supreme Godhead," at another place it was "whatever divinity is enthroned in heaven." But some of this vagueness may have been due to the insistence of Licinius, who was a convinced worshiper of Sol Invictus. Certainly from the Battle of Milvian Bridge on, Constantine referred to himself as a Christian.

Licinius was soon victorious in his battle in the east, defeating the armies under Maximin on April 30, 313. Maximin himself escaped, but he died later that summer. Unfortunately, Licinius and Constantine soon disagreed over various policies of their joint-rule. For ten years or so petty harassments crept in to create friction. Licinius apparently even resented the policy of tolerating Christians, who were more numerous in his sector of the Empire than in Constantine's. So Licinius developed a policy of harassment. On the excuse that church buildings were not properly ventilated, Licinius ordered that worship services take place out of doors. In order to guard public morals, the sexes must worship separately, nor could a priest instruct female catechumens. Christians visiting those in prison impeded civil justice, so it was ordered stopped. He forbade bishops from meeting in synod. Some overzealous local officials did execute Christians, apparently with Licinius' knowledge and approval.

After a number of minor political disagreements between Constantine and Licinius, the final clash came over a dispute concerning defense of the northern borders and resistance to German tribes. Some Germans broke into northern Greece, and Constantine moved east to stop them. Licinius accused Constantine of invading his territory and trying to stab him in the back, so the war was on. In battles in July and September 324, Constantine defeated his brother-in-law. At first he spared his life, but when Licinius conspired with the Goths, Constantine had him executed. Thus by 324 Constantine became the sole emperor for the entire Empire. He was supreme, and there was no doubt that he favored the Christians.

Although Constantine's conversion should be seen as genuine, there is also no doubt that he hoped to use Christianity as a means of binding up the wounds that had developed during the years of civil war. Previous emperors had tried to keep the Empire united by maintaining service to the old gods. Constantine tried to use the church to unite the Empire. He was deeply disappointed, then, when he discovered that the church itself was divided.

In his first year of rule, Constantine granted large gifts of money to churches for building programs, as well as tax exemptions to the Christian clergy. But word came back from North Africa that there was considerable rivalry over who was the true church there. The dispute went back several years, to the pressures of the recent persecution. When Diocletian's first edict was being enforced, some bishops handed over copies of the New Testament writings. Since these writings were considered of equal authority to Christ Himself, some Christians considered this the equivalent to betraying Christ, and thus they called these men *traditores* — traitors.

When the Bishop of Carthage died in 311, the local clergy elected chief deacon, Caecilian, to succeed him. Consecration of a new bishop must take place at the hands of three other bishops, but in Caecilian's consecration, one of the bishops involved was under accusation of being a *traditore*. The result was that a number of people refused to acknowledge him as the legitimate Bishop of Carthage. They elected their own man, Majorinus; he died shortly and was replaced by Donatus, who gave his name to the movement as well as the idea it emphasizes. The Donatists were continuing much the same battle that Cyprian had fought some decades earlier: they believed that a taint in the theological orthodoxy or personal morality of a priest/bishop invalidated any sacramental ministry received from his hands.[1]

When the imperial commissioners came to North Africa to dispense Constantine's gifts, the Donatists protested, claiming that Caecilian and his followers were not the true church. This confused Constantine, who called a council of church leaders in Rome to settle the issue. This council, held in 313, went against the Donatists, but they appealed from its decision on the grounds that too many Italian bishops were involved, Italians who were influenced by their neighbors down in Carthage. So Constantine arranged another meeting, in Arles, southern Gaul, in 314. Here again the Donatists lost. Thus both Cyprian's fight against the Novationists, and Caecilian's struggle with the Donatists came to the same conclusion: the validity of the sacraments does not depend upon the theological orthodoxy or the personal morality of the person officiating. This idea remained standard for the rest of the history of the church, including down to the present day.

The Donatists, however, refused to accept the decision. They remained a strong splinter group in North Africa until the next century, and some of them persisted until the Muslims overran the area in the late seventh century. Another interesting factor in this episode is the increasing use of the name "catholic." The word means "general," or "universal," and originally meant those who belong to the one church. Caecilian and his followers used the term, suggesting that what they believed was practiced by the rest of the church in the Roman world, while the Donatists were a small sect located only in North Africa. After this adoption, the term came to represent "orthodox" doctrine, particularly that represented by the Bishop of Rome. Its ultimate use will come with the phrase, "Roman Catholic," but that is still some centuries in the future.

The conversion of Constantine to Christianity did more than make Christianity the favored religion. It now became the socially accepted religion. Men soon learned that if they wanted to advance in the army or the governmental bureaucracy, it paid to become a Christian. The result was a flood of conversions to the church. Granted, many of these conversions were for the wrong reasons, and this created some troubles later, which we will come back to in Chapter Six. Nevertheless, the church in the fourth century experienced a period of tremendous growth. The number of Christians in the early fourth century has been estimated at about 10% of the population of the Empire. By the end of the century the number is estimated at about 90% of the population. The population of the empire at this time is estimated to be between 50 million and 75 million people. Even if we take the smaller figure, that means the number of Christians jumped from 5 million to 45 million in less than a century. Keeping up with this kind of church growth put a severe strain on the church, in terms of facilities and personnel. That is one reason why Constantine was granting so many favors to the church. It became obvious that the church, to stay up with rampant growth, would have to streamline its own organization.

At that time the Empire was divided into provinces. Each province had its own capital, and in the capital were the governor, the bureaucracy, and the provincial troops. Usually the provincial capital was also the largest city of the province, commonly called the "mother city," the "metropolis." At the time, Christianity had penetrated all provinces of the Empire, and it was represented in virtually all the cities. Therefore every city of any size had a local church, under its monarchical bishop. Gradually, however, the bishop in the provincial capital began to exercise control over the bishops in the province. We ought not to interpret this as a subversive power grab, but the normal shifting of power into fewer and fewer hands. Most people in the province were accustomed to looking to the metropolis for guidance in political affairs, and it seemed natural for the spiritual leader there to exercise spiritual leadership over the entire province. This is, in effect, one bishop ruling other bishops — an archbishop. The origins of this development are reflected in the Greek terminology, for in Orthodox lands, the word "metropolitan" is still used rather than "archbishop." And the "metropolitan" is simply the bishop of the provincial capital (the "metropolis"), called in western Europe "the archbishop." The creation of archbishop is another crucially important stage in the evolution of the church's organization.

There is another factor. Parallel with the creation of

archbishoprics was the growth of what came to be called the "patriarchates" — areas ruled over by a "patriarch." By the fourth century, there were a few bishops that came to have immense power and prestige. This prestige stemmed from a number of sources: the outstanding personalities of the bishops in a particular city, the size and strength of the Christian community in that city, the theological or spiritual leadership exercised by earlier bishops of that city, and the mystique attached to a church with an apostolic foundation.

In the fourth century, five cities stood out in this rivalry for prestige and leadership. Four of these cities were in the east: Jerusalem, Alexandria, Antioch and Constantinople. Jerusalem was accorded the honor of being the "Mother church of all Christendom," because that was where the church started, but this position was more one of honor than any acknowledgment of real leadership. In practical terms, the other three were more important. Both Alexandria and Antioch were important centers of Christianity as early as the first century, and in the intervening centuries both had maintained positions of leadership over their respective areas. The Bishop of Alexandria controlled the church in Egypt, Libya, and adjacent parts. The Bishop of Antioch controlled Syria and its neighbors. The city of Constantinople was founded by Constantine in 330, but as the new capital of the empire, which Constantine made it, the city immediately became important. Thus the Bishop of Constantinople soon exercised leadership over much of Greece and Asia Minor. Each of the four men who occupied these positions was called the "patriarch" of his respective city.

In the west there was only one city that rose to the top

in this fashion — the city of Rome. Carthage was its only rival, but Carthage had no apostolic foundation. Christianity did not get to Carthage until late in the second century. Rome claimed an undisputed apostolic foundation — the only such city in all the west. Moreover, Peter and Paul, the two most illustrious apostles, were involved in the early years of the Roman church. For this reason, the bishops of Rome often claimed authority and jurisdiction over the entire west. As we have already seen in the disputes with Cyprian, other bishops in the west did not always accept these claims. But Rome was certainly consistent in making its claims and working energetically to enforce them. This struggle is part of the background for later troubles in the early church. Not only was Rome contending against others, but in the east the three main patriarchates were battling for supremacy. This will become immensely important for understanding the theological difficulties of the fourth and fifth centuries.

Bibliography for Chapter Four

Burckhardt, Jacob. *The Age of Constantine the Great.* New York: Random House Vintage Books, 1967.

A thorough biography of Constantine and his era by a renowned scholar who doubts the Emperor's conversion, considering him only a political opportunist.

Dorries, Hermann, *Constantine the Great.* Trans. Roland H. Bainton. New York: Harper & Row, 1972.

A recent work done by a historian sympathetic to Constantine's conversion and his Christian identification. A helpful counterbalance to Burckhardt.

MacMullen, Ramsay. *Constantine.* New York: Harper & Row, 1971.

Another recent work on Constantine, also sympathetic to identifying him as a Christian.

Ricciotti, Giuseppe. *The Age of Martyrs: Christianity from Diocletian to Constantine.* Trans. Anthony Bull. Milwaukee: The Bruce Publishing Company, 1959.

Reflects a Roman Catholic position, but a thorough investigation into the Great Persecution and its effect upon the Church.

Questions and Projects for Chapter Four

1. Do you think Constantine's statement in the Edict of Milan about "whatever divinity is enthroned in heaven" compromises any assessment of him as a Christian? Write a paper either defending or attacking Constantine in this regard.
2. What parallels do you see between the Donatist schism and that of the Novatians of the previous century? Do you agree with the final decision of the church regarding the validity of the sacraments?
3. There is little doubt that Constantine tended to "secularize" the church. Write a paper describing the details of this, and also what Constantine could have done to avoid it. How does that apply to modern Christians who may happen to be political leaders?
4. Contrast this "Great Persecution" to the earlier ones. In what ways was it worse?
5. Prepare for a debate and be able to defend either of

these two positions: (1) The development of archbishops was a great benefit to the church because it gave better structure to the organization, thus allowing better efficiency and better supervision of local bishops and churches. (2) By creating authoritative officers in a structured organization, the development of archbishops was harmful to the church, causing it to become political, secular, and power-oriented.

Notes for Chapter Four

1. Another element in the Donatist dispute, and certainly an important one, was that the Donatists were mostly rural Berbers, while the Caecilian party were mostly urban Carthaginians. These latter were descendants from Roman colonists; thus the dispute was intensified by social and ethnic differences as well as a theological contention.

Chapter Five
THEOLOGICAL DIFFICULTIES
IN THE EARLY CHURCH

The original apostolic message about Jesus Christ was a relatively simple one. But that simple message also contained great ideas that have challenged profound thinkers ever since the apostolic days. Theologians who have wrestled with some of those ideas have often come to conclusions that have been unacceptable to other Christians. Such theological differences occurred in the lifetime of the apostles themselves, and they have proliferated in the centuries since. Thus the early church directed a great deal of attention to the controversies that developed out of historical differences.

We have already mentioned the Gnostics. With its denial of an Incarnate Christ, Gnosticism was already a threat within the apostolic period. Scholars are convinced that the second chapter of Paul's letter to the Colossians was aimed at a Gnostic-type heresy. Much of the flavor of I John also reflects Gnostic errors — John's emphasis that "we have seen and touched Him" (I John 1:1), as well as his emphasis that the spirit of the antichrist is in those who deny that Christ came in flesh (I John 4:3). In spite of such apostolic denunciations, Gnostic teachings continued in the early church, attacked by such writers as Irenaeus and others.

Another struggle in the early church was with Montanism. Montanus, a newly baptized convert in Phrygia in Asia Minor, began in 156 to speak in tongues and prophesy; two prophetesses, Priscilla and Maximilla, soon joined him. On the one hand, Montanism was an enthusiastic, prophetic, rigorist brand of Christianity seeking to preserve the expectation of the Second Coming. Some historians have seen it as a reaction to growing centralization in the spreading monarchical episcopate. On the other hand, different scholars have seen it as an attempt to return to the original simplicity and independence of the believers in the apostolic church. The Montanists, however, did not see themselves as a "return" to anything, but as a "new" spiritual outpouring.[1] This movement lasted only a half century or so, because most church leaders uniformly attacked it as a definite threat to the stability and order of the churches. Further, they feared that it encouraged enthusiastic excesses which could compromise moral integrity. Tertullian, the great church leader in North Africa in the third century, became a convert to Montanism, not because of its emotional excesses, but because he saw in it a moral and spiritual rigorism which the contemporary church lacked.

The date of Easter is not itself a theological matter, but it became the occasion for a great deal of theological infighting for the early church. Many Christians, particularly those in Asia Minor in the second century, continued to celebrate Easter by the Jewish calendar. They observed Easter on the 14th day of the Jewish month of Nisan, which tied it always to the celebration of the Passover. Other Christians believed Easter ought to coincide with a Sunday, so they celebrated Easter on the Sunday following 14 Nisan. Those Christians who remained tied to the date of 14 Nisan were often called Quartodecimanians (literally, "the Fourteenthers").

Trouble broke out in the year 120 when some Quartodecimanian Christians were in Rome. They fasted during Passover, then feasted; the Romans continued their fast until Sunday. Thus some Christians were fasting while others were feasting, and this created hurt feelings, snide remarks, and fears about theological purity. Bishop Polycarp of Smyrna came to Rome to discuss the situation with Bishop Anicetus, but they could come to no agreement other than mutual toleration.

The situation became acute toward the end of the century, when Victor of Rome (Bishop 189-199) excommunicated the churches of Asia Minor over this issue. This episode is important, not only because of the Easter dispute itself, but because it highlights the growing claims of the Bishop of Rome. Polycrates, Bishop of Ephesus, protested that Victor had no right or authority to excommunicate the churches of Asia Minor, for they were convinced they were within the apostolic traditions. Irenaeus of Lyons, a westerner who was a native of Asia

Minor, practiced the western form, but he also protested that Victor had no authority over Asia Minor churches. Victor withdrew his excommunication, although ultimately the Roman date for Easter won out. Various "cycles" were developed to determine the Easter date: there was a 19-year cycle, an 84-year cycle, and an 111-year cycle, plus others. The Council of Nicaea also investigated the problem, and it determined the formula which we still use today — that is, Easter is the first Sunday following the first full moon following the vernal equinox (March 21). In spite of this decision, however, the differences in determining the Easter date created more problems in the future.

A problem which became acute in the West in the early third century was Monarchianism. The issue concerned the relationships between the Eternal Father and His Son, Jesus Christ. Some early thinkers simply stated that Father and Son were two different figures. The Monarchians, however, felt this created two gods, and they were committed to monotheism. One group of Monarchians was known as Adoptionist or Dynamic Monarchians. They believed that Jesus was a man who was simply "adopted" as the Son of God (misinterpreting the words of Peter in Acts 2:36, "God has *made* Jesus to be both Lord and Christ"). The word "Dynamic" comes from the Greek word *dunamis* which means "power"; the "power" of God came upon Jesus. Thus, this view of Monarchianism preserves the singleness of God by keeping Jesus human — a human used in the divine plan, but definitely not a god.

A second group of the Monarchians was called Modalistic, for they believed that God the Father and

God the Son are one; the only difference is in the "mode" of their appearance. This position was also called Sabellianism, from its early teacher, Sabellius; it was called Patripassionism because it taught that in the crucifixion of Jesus (the Passion) the Father himself was on the cross.

This idea, in turn, created a fear in the minds of many people that Modalism denied the separate existence of Christ, and this was unacceptable. Tertullian (160-220) was one of the outstanding writers who came out in opposition to Modalistic Monarchianism. He insisted that the Father is God, the Son is God, and the Holy Spirit is God; yet there are not three gods, but one. His formula was to understand this as one substance (one Being) in three persons. In so doing, he safeguarded the uniqueness of each of the three figures of the Godhead; at the same time he defended the basic position of monotheism.

The problem of the relationships within the Godhead, and the corollary question of the nature of Christ, continued to plague the church for the next two centuries. In fact, these Christological Controversies, as they are called, were undoubtedly the major theological issues of this period.

The first of these significant controversies was Arianism, a complex phenomenon. It centers on the teaching of Arius (250-336) a presbyter in Alexandria, but there are other elements as well. An important one was the growing rivalry between the patriarchates of Antioch and Alexandria, which we mentioned in the last chapter. Another factor was that different schools of biblical interpretation were already developing in the eastern church. Biblical studies in Antioch emphasized a literal interpretation of Scripture, placing the writings in their historical context. This tended to emphasize Christ as a human person walking in history. The dominant method of interpretation in Alexandria, however, was allegorical, developed a century previously by Pantaenus, Clement, and Origen. They tended to "spiritualize" the text, because they could explain away any unwanted literal reference[2] by claiming it was an allegorical allusion. Arius brought the controversy to a head. He was a native Libyan, but he went to school in Antioch, where he absorbed the historical method. He then came back and served a local church in a suburb of Alexandria.

In the year 318 Bishop Alexander of Alexandria (313-328) had used the word *homoousios* ("same substance") to describe the relationship between Son and Father. Arius considered this dangerously close to Sabellianism. To counter this he argued that the Father alone is true God, and Jesus, while divine, is a subordinated deity. His proof texts were Proverbs 8:22 ("The Lord formed me," which makes the Son a *created* being) and John 14:28 ("My Father is greater than I"). Arius concluded that since the Son is created, He was created at a certain point in time, and before that, there was no Son. This was expressed in the Arian slogan "there was when He was not."

Alexander and the majority of the church in Alexandria found this intolerable. Alexander convened a council of over a hundred bishops from Egypt and Libya. The council anathematised the errors of Arius and excommunicated him and several of his followers. This would have been bad enough if it had been confined to Egypt, but since Arius was a product of the Antiochian school, other Antiochian graduates rushed to his defense. Within a couple of years this theological dispute became a major controversy throughout the eastern church. Constantine had been disappointed that Donatism threatened the unity of the church in the West, but he hoped after the defeat of Licinius in 324 that Christianity could still become the means of uniting the divided Empire. He was now even more disappointed to discover that the Eastern church was even more divided. Constantine decided a council of bishops would be the best way to handle the situation. He issued a call for all bishops of the Empire to gather at Nicaea in the summer of 325. This became the first of a long series of "Ecumenical Councils."

It was not really ecumenical, because of its approximate 300 bishops, only three or four were from the West. It was certainly the most illustrious assemblage of church leaders since the famous Jerusalem Council of Acts 15. There was also no doubt that the issue was momentous, both for the theology and for the organization of the church. Constantine paid all the transportation expenses, as well as the food and lodging expenses for the duration of the council. He wanted this council to be a success. The Emperor was anti-Arian, so many felt the decision of the council was foreordained.

The council spent a month debating the Arian issue. It was obvious that the full Arian position did not stand a chance for majority acceptance, but many bishops might have voted for a compromise position. Several were suggested, but the Alexandrian leaders inserted the word *homoousios* into the new creed being formulated, as well as such phrases as "Very God of Very God" and "begotten, not made." They concluded by adding anathemas against the slogans used by the Arians, such as "there was when he was not," and others.[3]

All bishops present signed the document but two; Arius and these two bishops were banished. The Council of Nicaea also dealt with other matters, including the formula for computing Easter. At the conclusion of the council, Constantine entertained the bishops at a splendid banquet — so splendid that Eusebius, the famous church historian, said the whole thing seemed a dream. To those who had survived the persecutions of the previous decades, it was probably just that. So far had the church come in the last few years.

With the Council over in two months, the Bishops returned home. It soon became apparent, however, that most bishops had signed the Nicene Creed out of respect for the emperor's wishes, and not because they actually accepted the Nicene position. Although Arianism was condemned, Arians lived on, many of them in high positions in the church. Known as Semi-Arians, they formed a political action group that worked to discredit the three major speakers who had led the attack on Arius. Within a decade, they had succeeded in getting these men exiled, including Athanasius (296-373), the very orthodox leader of the Nicene party who was now the Bishop of Alexandria.

The religious strife continued. When Constantine died in 337, he divided the Empire up between his three sons. The son who inherited the East, Constantius, was an Arian. During the twenty four years of his rule (337-361) the theological turmoil continued, although increas-

ingly there was a growing shift toward the Nicene position. The extremists of the Arian parties were losing support, and the spokesmen for the orthodox position were
making that viewpoint more and more acceptable in the
East.

By the end of his life, Constantius had gained control
over the territories in the West which had been willed to
his two brothers, so that once again the Empire was
reunited. When he died in 361, the imperial throne
passed into the hands of Julian, his nephew and the last
of Constantine's family. Julian had grown up a Christian,
but as a young man he had converted back to paganism.
He is often referred to as Julian the Apostate. He spent
the two years of his reign (361-363) trying to reinstitute
paganism. He tried to copy the church's lines of organization and rebuild paganism on a system of bishops,
archbishops, etc. In all this, however, he was totally
unrealistic. As a viable system of religion, paganism was
dead, but Julian was unwilling to accept that. He was an
anachronism in the fourth century, and when he died
fighting on the Persian frontier in 363, it was indeed the
death knell for paganism.

Two other Emperors followed Julian in short order.
Emperor Valentinian (364-375) was Nicene, but he gave
control over the eastern half of the Empire to his brother,
Valens, who was Arian. When Valens was killed fighting
the Goths in 378, he was succeeded the following year
by Theodosius, a Spanish general who was Nicene.
Theodosius was concerned about the continuing theological unrest in the East, so he called another Ecumenical
Council to meet at Constantinople in 381.

This council dealt with four major issues. The first

concerned the Nicene Creed, which the council promptly reaffirmed. This virtually marks the end of Arianism in the East. A second topic treated was Macedonianism. This position, named for Macedonius, Bishop of Constantinople from 352 to 362, says about the Holy Spirit what the Arians said about the Son — he is a subordinate deity, and a creature. The Macedonians were sometimes called *Pneumatomachoi* — fighters against the Holy Spirit. The Nicene Creed now received the added phrase that the Holy Spirit proceeds from the Father, which made the Spirit more than subordinate, yet the creed remained ambiguous on this point. The East apparently believed this meant the Spirit proceeded from the Father "through the Son," while the West believed the Spirit proceeded from the Father "and the Son." The Eastern position is slightly subordinationist, while the Western makes Father and Son fully equal. This Western phrase, "and the Son," later created the famous *filioque* controversy. At Constantinople, thirty-six Macedonian bishops left the Council when their position was condemned.

A third issue at the Council was Apollinarianism. Apollinarius (310-390) was decidedly anti-Arian, and he wanted to emphasize that Jesus was full deity. In fact, he went the other direction, undercutting the teaching that Jesus was fully human. He believed the Son was not subject to change, and therefore Christ must have been without a human spirit or human soul. The more orthodox party reacted by arguing that if this position was true, then the Incarnation was incomplete. They pointed out that what the Son had not assumed, He could not redeem, and therefore the crucifixion accomplished nothing. So the Council also condemned Apollinarianism.

A fourth matter brought up at Constantinople had nothing to do with these Christological disputes, but it reflected the continuing struggle for leadership among the churches. One of the decrees of the Council stated that the Bishop of Constantinople was to have primacy of honor after the Bishop of Rome, since Constantinople was the New Rome. This decree has several implications: one is that Constantinople was now accorded the position of leadership in the East, thus beating out the other patriarchates of Alexandria and Antioch; another is the political overtones. Constantinople was the new capital built by Constantine in 330. Since that date it had functioned as the capital of the combined Empire, not Rome. Rome was still the city of the founding of the Empire, and Rome was still accorded primacy of honor. Constantinople was acknowledged the second city in the Empire. Therefore, while the Bishop of *Rome* was to be given first honor in the church, the Bishop of *Constantinople* was given second honor. The implication is that this was not because of anything inherent in his position as bishop, but only an acknowledgment that the political prestige of the city had carried over to the spiritual leader of the city. Later defenders of papal primacy used this decision at Constantinople as proof that Rome was accorded primacy in the early church; detractors from that theory point out that the primacy is only political in nature, and Rome had first honor only because it was the first capital. Therefore, this primacy had nothing to do with the primacy of Peter's successor as such; it is only in recognition of the secular politics of the fourth century.

In spite of the decisions at this Council, unrest continued. There were theological loose ends not tied down by the conciliar decisions, and there was still serious rivalry among the three eastern patriarchates for spiritual supremacy. Actually the two issues were intertwined. Each city tried to win leadership and power in the church by defending its favorite theological positions. It was inevitable that the theological conflict would continue and worsen.

While these disputes were going on in the East, other issues were capturing the attention of the West. They are represented in the life and career of Augustine (354-430). Born in North Africa of a pagan father and a Christian mother, the brilliant young Augustine spent his youth seeking for wisdom and understanding in philosophy. He chased after the doctrine of Manicheanism, then the philosophy of Neo-Platonism. He was thirty years old when he wound up in Milan and heard the preaching of its great bishop, Ambrose. Finally converted, Augustine returned to his native North Africa and soon became its leading churchman, even though he was located in an unlikely place — Hippo Regius, about 130 miles west of Carthage. As a bishop he inherited the problem of the Donatists, and the part he played in a major African council in 411 led to the collapse of most of the Donatist resistance.

Another major issue in the early fifth century was the teaching of a British monk named Pelagius (?-419). Pelagius had lived in Rome for some ten to twenty years. He found there a moral atmosphere that was both lax and scandalous. He was convinced that not enough was being said about man's responsibility to lead a proper moral life. He discovered the culprit in the teaching of original sin. This doctrine teaches that sin is inherited from Adam, that man's nature is so corrupt that it cannot obey God's commands. Pelagius wanted to discourage moral lassitude, but in the process he emphasized a self-originating morality, suggesting that man can live without sin just as Jesus did.

Augustine countered this teaching by emphasizing the hereditary nature of original sin, total human depravity, and predestination. Infant baptism had become increasingly common in the previous century and a half, and Augustine correctly saw infant baptism as a vote of ratification for the idea of original sin. Infant baptism makes sense only if infants have inherited sin. Augustine's influence on theology was immense, not only for the fifth century, but also beyond. His stature became such that he has more influence on the theology of the church than any other writer outside the apostles. The ideas of original sin, human depravity, predestination, infant baptism, and the need for man to wait upon God's grace operating upon him — all these immeasurably influenced the church through succeeding centuries.

Meanwhile the East reached a new stage in the Christological conflict when Cyril was Bishop of Alexandria (412-444) and Nestorius became Bishop of Constantinople (428-431). Nestorius was from Antioch, where he had learned the historical method of biblical interpretation and its idea that the humanity of Jesus must be safeguarded. Thus he wound up emphasizing the humanity of Christ more than His divinity. The thing that sparked his concern was the use of the phrase *Theotokos* (literally God-bearer," or "Mother of God") applied to Mary.

Nestorius wanted to apply only the phrase *Christotokos* ("Christ-bearer") to her. He went on to deny that the word "God" could be applied to a two or three month old infant.

Nestorius' basic teaching was that there were two separate persons in the Incarnate Christ — one human, the other divine. These two remained unaltered and distinct in their union within Jesus of Nazareth. He believed the Alexandrian theology improperly emphasized the divinity of Christ, as reflected in the word *Theotokos*. Although much of the controversy focused on the use of this term, the deeper problem was Nestorius' conviction about two persons in the historic Christ.

As a result the eastern Emperor Theodosius II (408-450) called another Ecumenical Council, the third, this one to meet in Ephesus in 431. The Alexandrian bishops attended in strength, but Nestorius refused to come. Cyril of Alexandria read a statement on the union of the two natures of Christ which the council approved. The bishops of the Antioch area had not yet arrived, so when the council passed a sentence deposing Nestorius, all 198 bishops present signed it. Four days later the 43 bishops from around Antioch came, but it was too late to reverse the decision. The Emperor deposed Nestorius and sent him into exile.

Because Nestorius was the Bishop of Constantinople, and also a disciple of the school at Antioch, Cyril felt that the decision at Ephesus had allowed Alexandria to upstage the other two cities. Exulting in his victory, he began to get rather wild in his statements. His statement at the council on the two natures of Christ had offended some of his radical followers, so he added that although he could in the abstract distinguish two natures united in Christ, yet in the Incarnate Lord there is only one nature after the union. Eutyches, a monastic official in Constantinople, picked up this word *monophysis* ("one nature") and made it more popular. The idea was called Eutychianism as well as the more common term Monophysitism. Monophysitism was, of course, very similar to Apollonarianism, except instead of "one soul" it was "one nature." But the very same objections were made by the orthodox party — what Christ had not assumed He could not redeem. Men by definition have a human nature, and if Christ does not, then there is no way He can be the example for mankind.

To help smooth out the renewed controversy, Emperor Theodosius called another council for Ephesus, for 449. Cyril had died a few years previously, to be succeeded by Dioscorus (444-454), his nephew. Dioscorus was even more extreme than Cyril. He brought a number of monks with him who turned the streets of Ephesus into mob scenes. The Bishop of Constantinople, Flavian, was beaten by the Egyptian delegation and died of his injuries within three days. Bishop Leo I of Rome (440-461) had sent a letter expressing his view of the theological issues, but it was not even read to the council. The council simply rubber-stamped the Monophysite position. Leo later called this meeting not a council but a *latrocinium,* a "robber synod."

Emperor Theodosius was killed by a fall from his horse the next year, and this allowed Marcian to come to the throne (450-457). Theodosius had been friendly to the Alexandrian camp, but Marcian was firmly on the orthodox side. The result was another council, held in

Chalcedon, in 451. There was talk of holding the council in Nicaea, but Marcian wanted it closer, so he could keep tabs on it. He wanted no repetition of the disorders of Ephesus. Chalcedon was just across the Bosporus from Constantinople. More than five hundred bishops took part, making it the largest council of the early church. In its early proceedings, the council condemned Dioscorus and some of his leading supporters for heresy and deposed them.

The Council of Chalcedon clearly condemned Monophysitism. Part of the problem through all four of these councils was that they were good at condemning heresy, but weak in actually explaining the correct doctrines concerning the nature of Christ. Controversy often creates polarization and extremes, and that had been occurring here. The nature of Christ is a doctrine that has two poles — His humanity and His deity. The problem was to keep these natures in tension, without one overcoming the other. Arianism had overemphasized the subordinate nature of Christ, thus diminishing His deity. Apollinarianism reacted to that by minimizing His humanity; Nestorianism responded by further undermining His deity, and Monophysitism reacted by again reducing His humanity. It was easy to condemn the errors; but what was the real nature of Christ?

The letter from Leo[4] had been ignored at the council in Ephesus in 449, but it was now read in full session at Chalcedon. Leo condemned both Nestorianism and Monophysitism. In very simple terms, he said three things: 1) Jesus is 100% God; 2) Jesus is 100% Man; 3) there is no problem between these two positions. Very God; very man; union.[5]

These first four Ecumenical Councils were extremely important for the theology of the early church. Christological controversy would reappear, but the foundational positions had been worked out. It was now agreed that the nature of Christ was an undefined blend of deity and humanity. The Chalcedonian creed formulated the recent consensus on the nature of the Trinity and the nature of Christ. These decisions became and remain theological orthodoxy.

But just as Arianism lived on after its condemnation by the Council of Nicaea, Monophysitism persisted after the Council of Chalcedon. Monophysitism had gained such a hold in certain parts of the eastern church that it continued to survive for centuries to come. Three distinct geographical areas of the East became overwhelmingly Monophysite: Egypt, Syria, and Armenia, the northeastern part of Asia Minor. Within a century Monophysitism was so strong here that these regions resisted control by the more orthodox, Greek-speaking portions of the Empire. When the Muslims came out of Arabia on their wave of conquest in the seventh century, the Monophysites preferred a Muslim ruler to a Greek Orthodox one.

Leo's Letter highlights the significance of Chalcedon. Rather than solving the abstract theological issues represented in the unique blend that is the nature of Christ, Leo as much as said, "That's the way it is," and accepted it. The East had been trying to explain the Incarnation in philosophical language for some centuries. Leo did not even try. This reflects one of the growing differences between the eastern and western parts of the Roman Empire. The East was much more speculative, based on

Greek philosophy. The West was much more practical, reflecting the Roman specialty in engineering and military success. It perhaps was no coincidence that while the East was battling Monophysitism, which has to do with the abstract nature of Christ, the West was battling Pelagianism, the nature of man, with implications for how man is expected to live his daily life. Such differences grew even more pronounced in the succeeding centuries. Ultimately it led to the first major split in Christendom.

Bibliography for Chapter Five

Hefele, Charles Joseph. *A History of the Councils of the Church.* Edinburgh, Scotland: T.&T. Clark, 1872-1896.

A five-volume work by a Roman Catholic scholar on the first seven councils, down to 787; more extensive than any other treatment available in English.

Jedin, Hubert. *Ecumenical Councils of the Catholic Church: An Historical Survey.* Trans. Ernest Graf. New York: Herder & Herder, 1960.

A simple, one-volume overview of the councils of the Church, from Nicaea to I Vatican.

Kelly, J.N.D. *Early Christian Doctrines.* New York: Harper & Row, Publishers, 1960.

An overview of doctrine and doctrinal development in the first few centuries, including the Christological controversies. An important source and assessment.

Sellers, Robert Victor. *The Council of Chalcedon: An Historical and Doctrinal Survey.* London: S.P.C.K., 1961.

An outstanding investigation of this significant council, comprehensive and detailed.

Stevenson, J. (ed.). *Creeds, Councils, and Controversies: Documents Illustrative of the History of the Church, A.D. 337-461.* London, S.P.C.K., 1966.
Provides the source documents for understanding the doctrinal controversies of this period. Quite helpful.

Questions and Projects for Chapter Five

1. Do you agree that Easter should be tied in to lunar cycles, or should it be a particular Sunday every year (as Thanksgiving is always the fourth Thursday of November)? Should we call it "Easter" (named after a Teutonic goddess of spring) or "Resurrection Sunday"?
2. Do you think the Christological controversies were important matters, or were they simply theological speculations that were not of significant value?
3. Study the doctrine of Christ taught by the Jehovah's Witnesses, and compare it to that of Arianism.
4. If Mary is the mother of Jesus, and if the Godhead consists of God the Father, God the Son, and God the Holy Spirit, then why shouldn't Mary be acknowledged as "Mother of God"?
5. Write a paper analyzing to what extent the first four centuries reflected major amounts of political pressure and manipulation.
6. Some historians have stated that it seems the theological problems of the early church in the East are speculative (the concept of the Trinity and the nature of Christ), while those in the West are more practical

(the nature and organization of the church, and the nature of man). Do some additional research and analyze the validity of this position.

7. Prepare a chart of the Christological controversies, paralleling similarities where possible and noting differences.

Notes for Chapter Five

1. For a brief treatment of Montanism as a return or an innovation, see J.W.C. Wand, *A History of the Early Church to A.D. 500* (London: Methuen & Co.., Ltd., 1965), p. 60.

2. "Unwanted" in the sense that a literal interpretation of numerous passages would prove offensive to sophisticated Greek culture.

3. The Nicene Creed and its anathemas can be found in Schaff, I, p. 29.

4. Older history books usually refer to this document as "the Tome of Leo." This word suggests something heavy and pretentious. Actually the letter is only a few pages long. But students need to be aware of the older designation.

5. Leo's Letter can be found in Barry, I, pp. 97-102. The Chalcedonian Creed is in Schaff, II, pp. 62-63.

Chapter Six
THE RISE OF MONASTICISM

Christian monasticism as a movement within the church began in the late third century, though there are precedents that go back to the very beginnings of Christianity. The New Testament itself reflects some antecedents and impetus for monasticism. A number of elements combine to furnish the momentum for the monastic life. Some of the most important are:

(1) Scriptural passages taken in an ultra-literal sense are direct origins of monasticism. Later monasticism emphasized the Christian life as opposition to the things of the world. Scripture teaches us not to love the world. The story of the rich young ruler warns of the danger of earthly possessions. Other passages teach the crucifying of self. Thus, much of the desire for monasticism was a

desire to be faithful to scriptural teaching that Christians should avoid entanglement with the world.

(2) There is also the influence of Greek philosophy. Greek philosophy often taught that the desires of the flesh were there to be overcome. Stoicism taught that life was to be experienced without emotional highs and lows. Gnosticism, which had been intellectually defeated in the second century by Christianity, returned in the third and later centuries to influence the church through asceticism — giving up the desires of the flesh. Historian Herbert Workman refers to the development of monasticism as another chapter in the "history of renunciation." Gnosticism taught that the flesh was evil, the creation of an inferior deity. Monasticism embraced the concept that all fleshly desires are evil. The early monastic vows of poverty (renunciation of the world) and celibacy (renunciation of sex and fleshly desires) represent a Gnostic view of life. These two ideas combined to form the basis of monasticism. To them can be added three desires: achieve spiritual victory over physical existence, live a hermit's life, and spend long periods of time in prayer and fasting. These five elements together fairly well summarize the activities of early monasticism.

(3) Another element appears about the time of Constantine. There had always been a number of people in the church who felt the need to prove their faith (if not to others, at least to themselves) by going to the ultimate of dying for it. As long as the church was being persecuted, such people could always experience martyrdom. However, after Christianity achieved favored status in the Empire, the persecutions ceased and the road to martyr-

dom was closed. With no more opportunity to die for the faith (called "red martyrdom" because of the shedding of blood), more people began to seek the path of asceticism ("white martyrdom"). Ascetics are those people who practice strict self-denial as a religious discipline. Only through asceticism could these people show their ultimate devotion to Christianity.

(4) A final element of monasticism emerged under and after Constantine. With hordes of people now coming into the church, many of them for the wrong reasons, the quality of spiritual life in the churches began to decline. Many new converts were social parvenus with no real dedication to the Christian life. Many of the rigorists and purists were disillusioned by the caliber of membership in the churches. These people desired to separate from the worldly church and withdraw to commune with God in isolation. These people became the first real monks.

As mentioned, there were early instances of the monastic impulse. Even in the lifetime of Ignatius some people dedicated themselves to lives of virginity or celibacy while living at home. But the real start of monasticism began with Anthony (251-356; that's right — 105 years).[1] Born in central Egypt into a wealthy family, he walked into a church service one day when he was 20 years old just as the reader was beginning the passage about the rich young ruler. When he heard the words of Jesus, "Sell all you have and give it to the poor," Anthony was convinced Jesus meant that for him. So he sold everything and became a hermit monk. He spent fifteen years living with a venerable old man as an "apprentice" monk. In 285 he went off into the desert to live completely alone. He became an anchorite (Greek *anachoreo*, "to withdraw"), the first stage of classical monasticism. Our word "monk" comes from the Greek *monachos*, which means "single," or "alone."

In his solitude, Anthony often engaged in what he thought were jousts with the Devil. Merchants and others passing by on the edge of the desert often heard the shrieks and cries of this physical combat. Anthony soon attracted a considerable amount of attention, which meant a number of followers. These began to crowd around him, wanting to emulate his lifestyle and devotion, but actually interfering in his solitude. So in 305 he came to the edge of the Egyptian desert to organize his followers into a community of hermits, called a *laura* (from the Greek word for street, or lane). These *lauras* were a collection of individual huts on a common street, directed by a single abbot (from a Semitic word for "father"). In essence these men were alone, but they were alone together. They had no common life, each remaining to himself in his hut. Because they were still alone, they were monks.

Others soon came to realize that not everyone was able to adapt to that kind of life. Pachomius (290-346) became a hermit monk about 317, but in 320 he began the first real monastery, located in Upper Egypt along the Nile River. The emphasis here was upon the common life of the group (Greek *koinos bios*, "common life"), and therefore this stage of monasticism is called coenobitic. Not only did he organize men into a monastery, but he also wrote rules for orderly living in the community. This was the famous "Rule of Pachomius" (there will be numerous other rules later). In

Latin "rule" is "regula," so these monks are usually referred to as "regular clergy." In most respects, however, they were still considered laity, for they were not ordained to the normal clergy as bishops, priests or deacons. The monks took specific vows when they joined the community. These included the normal vows of poverty and celibacy, but Pachomius added the vow of obedience — particularly obedience to the abbot. Pachomius also made manual labor a part of the working day for the monks. This enabled the community to become self-sustaining. When he died, there were eleven monasteries under his direction, including two for women.

Monasticism at this stage was highly individualistic. As a result, many hermits went overboard in their attempt to repress the desires of the flesh. Extravagant eccentricities began to appear, all in the name of spirituality. Some monks lived on a meal a week. Others trained themselves to sleep standing up in the middle of a room. Others stood chin-deep in a stream of water all night. Some made cages for themselves too small for sitting, standing, or lying down. One man lived this way for sixty years. He became so bent that when he was walking through a field a farmer shot him, mistaking him for a wolf. One man gave up a position in the Court of Egypt with its fine clothes and perfume; he became a hermit along the Nile making woven baskets of reeds. He changed the soaking water of the reeds only once a year so its foul odor would be a penance for the years he breathed the sweet perfume of the court.[2]

Probably the classic example of extremism is Simeon Stylites (390-459). At age 23 he started out as an anchorite in a cave, where he lived for forty days with his right leg chained to a large stone. A piece of leather protected his leg from the ankle clasp, and when the chain was removed after the forty days, his admirers found under the leather 20 fat bugs which Simeon had refused to disturb. He considered them part of his penance. One summer he had himself buried in a trench up to his chin every day, and he was dug out every night.

The thing that made Simeon most famous was that at age 33 he built himself a pillar about six feet high upon which he lived for the rest of his life. Gradually he had it raised until it was a small square platform 60 feet in the air. As a holy man suspended between heaven and earth, he attracted a large number of followers and fans, including kings and emperors who came to be blessed by him and to ask his advice. He took no baths, and his followers cherished the worms that fell off his body. He was constantly cutting himself to open new wounds and reopen old ones, letting the bugs feed on them. Once when a bug fell off, he replaced it on the open wound, saying, "Eat what God has given you." One of his religious exercises was to touch his forehead to his feet; one admirer counted this act 1244 times in succession before he lost count.

Probably the most important person in the development of eastern monasticism was Basil (330-379), Bishop of Caesarea. He established a monastery in Pontus in 358, and the Rule that he wrote became the foundation for all later eastern monasticism, even in Russia. Basil was concerned about the proliferation of extreme eccentricity among the hermit monks. He wanted to transform the institution from a life of bizarre competi-

THE RISE OF MONASTICISM

tion in outlandish asceticism to a devotion to the common life of the monastery.

Basil designed his Rule to do four things. (1) Suppress the anchorites, bringing them into monasteries. (2) Remove the monasteries from the deserts to the cities. (3) Restrict the austerites and self-inflicted suffering. One means of doing this was to limit the time spent in contemplative devotion. Previously the monk's entire day might be given to spiritual contemplation. Basil reduced the times of prayer to seven a day (based on Psalm 119:164), plus one in the middle of the night. These became known as "the monastic hours." (4) Encourage learning.

By these measures, Basil directed much of the energy of monasticism into more productive channels. He limited the number of monks in a community to manageable proportions (30 to 40 monks), tried to keep the monasteries under the direction of the bishops in the area, made the monasteries self-supporting with manual labor, and involved the monasteries in social relief work.This included working in hospitals and schools, as well as aiding farmers during harvest time. Basil was not the originator of eastern monasticism, but his influence was such that he is considered its founder.

Keeping the "monastic hours," sometimes called the "canonical hours," was characteristic of monasticism both east and west. These consisted in seven chapel services for the monastic community. These periods, and their approximate time of the day, were as follows:

Lauds	Daybreak
Prime	6 a.m.
Tierce	9 a.m.

Sext	12 noon
None	3 p.m.
Vespers	sundown
Compline	darkness
Matins	Night Office, 2 a.m.

Matins was set in the middle of the night for two reasons: first, to interrupt a good night's sleep and thus prevent the monks from enjoying this satisfaction of the flesh; and second, to conform to Psalm 119:62, "At midnight I will rise to give thee thanks." This service often lasted an hour — and falling asleep was cause for severe punishment.

The seven offices of the day were of varied length. Some might last an hour or more, others only a few minutes. Those monasteries emphasizing manual labor might have shorter services than the contemplative orders. The offices of Prime through None were at set times, the others corresponded to the passage of the sun. Because winter and summer have a radically different time for daybreak and sundown, these offices varied considerably from January to June. In the dead of winter Prime was often postponed until the break of day; it would then immediately follow Lauds, whatever time it happened to be. Depending upon the geography and climate, Vespers and Compline might also be held back-to-back. Yet the result was that the times of prayer and contemplation for the monks were put on a regular schedule.

Meanwhile, monasticism developed differently in the West. When Athanasius was exiled to Rome in 339, he brought two hermit monks with him, the first to appear in the West. The idea soon spread, particularly in the city of Rome itself, encouraged by the example and teaching of Jerome (342-420). About the year 374 Jerome went to the East, lived as a hermit in the desert for a while, and learned Hebrew. From 382 to 385 he was back in Rome, where he served as the secretary to Damasus, Bishop of Rome (366-384). By 386 Jerome was back in Palestine, where he settled in a monastery in Bethlehem for the rest of his life. He promoted monasticism during his brief return to Rome. In Palestine, his greatest accomplishment was the translation of the Bible into Latin, which Damasus had commissioned him to do. This translation achieved great popularity in the western church. Known as the Vulgate, it became the standard text of Scripture for Latin-speaking Christianity.

A few decades after monasticism first appeared in Rome, it took hold in southern Gaul, brought by individuals who had traveled in the East. The first monastery in Gaul was established by Martin of Tours (335-397). For a while monasticism in the West went through an episcopal stage, with bishops setting up monasteries under their own direction for their own clergy. Martin did this, as did Augustine a few years later. John Cassian (360-435) was from the East, but he came west and established two influential monasteries near Marseilles.

What Basil was to the East, Benedict of Nursia (480-550) was to the West. He is certainly not the first monk in the West, but he was the significant organizer of western monasticism. Disgusted with the worldliness of Rome, he retired to a cave about the year 500. He developed a reputation for holiness, attracted followers, and organized them into small monasteries. In 525, local jealousies drove him south to Monte Cassino. He established a new monastery that became the headquarters for all later Benedictine monasticism.

His Rule became the basis for most later monasticism in western Christendom. It is a very practical handbook of advice on how to run the monastery. The Rule encourages humility, poverty, and obedience, although it says nothing about celibacy — which simply means that celibacy by this time is assumed. In addition, the Rule of Benedict emphasizes the Book of Psalms, which is to be chanted through every week in the course of the daily monastic hours. Specific Psalms are sometimes mentioned for each of the daily services. Benedictine monasticism expanded throughout Europe, absorbing other monasteries in the process. With the exception of Celtic monasticism, it was the only form of western monasticism from the seventh to the later eleventh centuries.

Another important figure in early western monasticism was Cassiodorus (485-580). He was a Roman civil servant who retired from the government under the Ostrogoths in 540 to establish a monastery on his family farm in southern Italy. He was fond of books, and he had his monks make copies of old Latin texts. This became a major preoccupation of the monks — there as well as in other monasteries. By the exposure to books monks not only became experts at copying, but also became educated. Benedict emphasized reading in his Rule, and the policies of Benedict and Cassiodorus combined to make monasteries the most important libraries and educational institutions of Europe until the creation of universities in the 13th century.

Christianity among the Celtic tribes is a separate study, but since it had much to do with the flowering of monasticism, it is treated here. The Celts were tribes that moved into central Europe about 500 B.C. and then into much of western Europe, including most of the British Isles. Celtic Christianity can be identified in southern Gaul by at least the late first or early second century. Information is sketchy, but apparently Christianity reached Britain by the late second century. At least when Constantine called the Council of Arles to deal with the Donatist trouble in 314, three bishops from Britain were present — indicating a sizable growth of Christianity in the country by that time. Christianity was probably a minority religion in Britain at the time of Constantine — not so much overshadowed by Roman paganism as by the latent heathenism of the Celtic tribes.

Ninian (360-432) was the first significant missionary to the Scots. In 394, he established a monastery in Whithorn in southwestern Scotland. It became the base for evangelization of the area, although he apparently had limited success. Patrick (389-461) was a native Briton from northwestern England, kidnapped by pirates and sold as a slave in Ireland, where he worked for a number of years. He later escaped, and in 432 he returned to Ireland to do missionary work.

There is much controversy and confusion about the place and work of Patrick in Ireland. There is no doubt that he was there, and that he became the most famous Christian figure in their history. He was not the first Christian there, nor even the first missionary. Most of his work was in the northern part of the island, and he later became the Bishop of Armagh. It is important to note that Patrick worked in a land that had never become part of the Roman Empire; the foundation of Roman culture that Christianity built upon everywhere else was not present here. This had a significant effect on the development of Christianity in Ireland, the form that became Celtic Christianity.

The Irish were not a unified people. Socially, they were still in a clan/tribe stage of development. There were no large cities. The Roman Empire was a highly urbanized, organized society. Christianity growing in a culture totally different from Roman society took on organizational forms totally different from the rest of western Christendom.

Apparently Patrick and other early missionaries initially planted the diocesan form of Christianity they knew from Britain and the Continent. But this failed to take hold in Ireland because Ireland lacked the towns which served as centers of commerce and influence. As a result, episcopal, diocesan Christianity soon disappeared, replaced by a series of monasteries. The abbots of the monasteries were, in fact, soon exercising the powers of bishops over the land, appointing priests to do work in outlying areas, sometimes even appointing bishops. Even in the fifth century the bishopric of Armagh was reorganized on monastic lines.

Monasticism in Ireland was similar in some ways to eastern monasticism. Perhaps Patrick and others visited monasteries in southern Gaul that were directly influenced by the East. Whatever the connection, there were in Ireland many of the same excesses; men stood with their arms extended in the form of a cross all night; they recited the entire Psalter while standing in water up to their necks; anyone who did not say "Amen" after the grace at meals received six lashes. Desire for solitude led monks to build individual cells on tiny islands off the coast and live like the hermits in the Egyptian desert. As Celtic monasticism later flowed into northern Britain, it developed a unique institution — the "double monastery." Here, under the same roof, were monks and nuns, although there was a stout wall separating the quarters of the two. But it was a single institution, and always under the direction of an abbess, never an abbot.

Celtic Christianity was also influenced by a changing political situation. In the early fifth century, the Roman Empire, as we will see in the next chapter, was increasingly unable to defend its northern borders along the Rhine and Danube rivers against the pressing Germanic tribes. The Roman outpost in Britain became a luxury the Empire could no longer afford. Soldiers were being continually taken out of Britain to hold the line in northern Italy. By 406 all soldiers were gone from Britain. In 409 Emperor Honorius told the Britons to defend themselves; the rest of the Empire could not help them.

This left the Britons virtually defenseless. By mid-century the Germanic tribes of the Angles, Saxons, and Jutes began to invade from the Continent — from modern Denmark and northwestern Germany. By this time the Britons were mostly Christian, but the invading Anglo-Saxons were entirely heathen. The barbarian Germans had no pity for the civilized Celts. Most of the native Celts were wiped out. Those who survived were pushed west into Cornwall, Devonshire, Wales, and northwestern Britain. A number of Britons went across the English Channel into the old Roman province of Armorica, which was soon renamed Brittany. In the process British Christianity in eastern and central Britain was wiped out by the invaders. The Britons were not faultless in this. They had no desire to convert the invading heathen. The Anglo-Saxons had killed Celtic men, women, children, burned their homes, and taken their land. Celtics did not want to see the Anglo-Saxons converted — they would then have to spend all of eternity with them! They were content that the Anglo-Saxons go to Hell. But the result was that except for some pockets in the western part of Britain, Christianity was eliminated from the island. The work of converting this country would have to be repeated.

By the end of the fifth century what Celtic Christianity survived, in western Britain and in Ireland, was effectively cut off from the rest of Christendom on the Continent. Celtic Christianity went its own way, developing its own traditions. An example is the books called *penitentials*. Previously penance was public and applied to the "big" sins in life. These were to be openly confessed before the assembled church. But the Irish changed penance to a private rite in which every sin was confessed to a priest, who assigned a proper work of penance to make up for it. The *penitential* was a list of appropriate penances for the priest to consult, so that a scale of penances was established, varying with the gravity of the sin, the degree of will involved, and whether the sinner was a monk/clergyman or a layman. In addition, a sinner could substitute a long mild penance for a shorter, more severe one.

Another difference was in the observation of Easter. As we have seen, Easter computations had already been worked out, and agreement was achieved at Nicaea. But the western churches soon fell away from the Nicene formula. In the year 455 Rome, after much discussion

124

and study, went to a 19-year cycle for computing Easter. Unaware of this because of their isolation, the Celtic churches continued on their 84-year cycle. This had serious repercussions in the seventh century, as we will see in the next chapter.

Another characteristic of the Irish-Celtic Christians in this period was a great fondness for education and literature. A remarkable flowering of culture took place in early Celtic Christianity, both literary and artistic. In a couple of centuries, when much of Europe was experiencing what some historians have called the "Dark Ages," Ireland and northern Britain were the shining lights of culture and learning. This cultural refinement is reflected in the colorful and exquisite drawings and paintings that were put into such productions as the Lindisfarne Gospels and the Book of Kells. Both of these works came from northern Britain, but they reflect Celtic Christianity at its best.

Columban (521-597) was an Irish monk who also loved books. In fact he became so jealous over the possession of a book that a tribal war erupted which resulted in the killing of 3000 people. Sobered by this loss, Columban decided to convert a soul for each person killed, so in 563 he began a monastery at Iona off the coast of Scotland. From this base Celtic Christianity penetrated all of northern Britain.

Another Irish monk, Columbanus (550-615), went to Gaul in 590 where he set up several monasteries. He was outspoken in condemning the immorality of the Christian rulers of the Franks and Burgundians, so in 610 he was forced out of the area. He moved on through Switzerland and northern Italy, planting monasteries after the Celtic fashion. The differences between Celtic monasticism and Roman monasticism created a good deal of friction, and the Celtic practices were soon discarded. But he brought with him copies of the Irish *penitentials*. The Romans, being of practical bent of mind, saw the advantage of such a list for the use of the priest in assigning penance, and the *penitentials* came into common use by the Roman Christians. Though the monastic framework of their Christian expression was ultimately replaced by the normative Roman style, the use of *penitentials* is one of the lasting contributions Celtic Christians made to the development of the church.

Bibliography for Chapter Six

Athanasius, "Life of Anthony," in *A Select Library of Nicene and Post-Nicene Fathers of the Christian Church*, Second Series, Vol. IV, *St. Athanasius: Select Works and Letters*. Grand Rapids: Wm. B. Eerdmans Publishing Company, 1978 (reprint of 1891).
    This is the classic source for the biography of Anthony.
Duckett, Eleanor Shipley. *The Gateway to the Middle Ages: Monasticism*. Ann Arbor, Michigan: The University of Michigan Press (Ann Arbor Paperbacks), 1963.
    A brief but valuable overview of western monasticism.
Gregory the Great. *The Dialogues, Book Two: Saint Benedict*. trans. by Myra L. Uhlfelder. Indianapolis: The Bobbs-Merrill Company, Inc. (The Library of Liberal Arts), 1967.

From Gregory's writings, the classic biography of Benedict.

Workman, Herbert B. *The Evolution of the Monastic Ideal From the Earliest Times Down to the Coming of the Friars: A Second Chapter in the History of Christian Renunciation.* Boston: Beacon Press, 1962.
An excellent overview of both eastern and western monasticism down to the twelfth century.

Questions and Projects for Chapter Six

1. Locate a monastery (or convent) in your area. Arrange for an interview and tour.
2. Monasticism has often been accused of being selfish — that is, the focus is on saving self rather than ministering to others. Do some research to determine whether this is a valid criticism either for past history or for modern monasticism.
3. Are there any modern counterparts to the extreme asceticism and bodily punishment of the early eccentric monks?
4. Write a paper in which you compare and/or contrast the thrust and development of the three main branches of early monasticism: eastern, western, and Celtic.
5. How would you assess the contributions of monasticism to the life of the church in this early period?

Notes for Chapter Six

1. The original source document for the biography of Anthony can be found in Athanasius' "Life of Anthony." In NPNF, Second Series, IV, pp. 188-221.

2. For these and similar examples of eccentric conduct, see Herbert B. Workman, *The Evolution of the Monastic Ideal From the Earliest Times Down to the Coming of the Friars: A Second Chapter in the History of Christian Renunciation* (Boston: Beacon Press, 1962), pp. 41-53.

Chapter Seven
THE SHIFT TO A
GERMANIZED EUROPE

The Germanic tribes along the northern border of the Empire — the Rhine and Danube Rivers — began to cause trouble for the Empire as early as the time of Marcus Aurelius. He fought the Marcomanni Wars beginning in 170, and sporadically after that the various Germanic tribes continued to harass the frontiers. Constantine began the process of recruiting Germans to serve as soldiers in the army, and for the next century and a half the percentage of Germanic soldiers in the Roman army rose higher and higher until ultimately Roman officers had to give military commands in German dialect in order to be understood.

Other than minor border troubles, the Goths were the first to cause serious trouble for the Empire. In the fourth century the Goths located in Eastern Europe, northwest of the Black Sea, on both sides of the Dniester River. Those west of the river came to be known as Visigoths, and those east of the river were Ostrogoths. They were virtually separate tribes. The Visigoths, closer to the borders of the Empire, became a problem about a century earlier than their eastern cousins.

Thanks to the work of Ulfilas (311-383), the Goths were already Christians when they came into the Empire. Ulfilas was apparently of civilized ancestry, but he was born among the Goths. About the year 340 he was in Constantinople on some kind of official embassy on behalf of the Goths. While there he was converted to Christianity — Arian Christianity. In 341 he was consecrated a bishop at a council in Antioch and sent back to the Goths. He was a successful missionary, and although he had a difficult time, eventually Arian Christianity became the dominant religion among the Goths — not only the Visigoths, but also the Ostrogoths. Filtering through them, it influenced numerous other tribes as well. As a result, many of these Germanic tribes entered the Roman Empire not as barbarian heathen, but as Arian Christians. Some of them were adamantly Arian, and this created a good deal of difficulty in those portions of Europe where these tribes settled. Early in the process of evangelizing the Goths, Ulfilas reduced their language to writing and provided them with an alphabet. He then translated the Bible into their language. He left out the Old Testament books of Kings, for he felt the Goths were sufficiently warlike without the encouragement of reading these biblical tales of battle and bloodshed.

About the middle of the fourth century the Huns, an Asiatic tribe moving into eastern Europe, were pushing various tribes before them and each tribe began to push against its neighbors. The Visigoths were pushed into the Roman Empire in modern Romania. They requested permission to come into the Empire as *foederati* (confederates, allies) rather than as citizens, and Emperor Valens gave permission for them to enter in 372. Many of their men served in the army, guarding the Danube frontier. Unfortunately, the government did not always deal honestly with them, and minor bureaucrats often discriminated against them. Friction increased until the Visigoths finally revolted in 376. When Valens came with the flower of the Eastern army to put them down, the Romans were defeated and Valens killed. Theodosius became the new emperor in the East, and after putting down the revolt he treated the tribespeople fairly and restored peace in the area.

But when Theodosius died in 395, things changed. In 391 Theodosius united the entire Empire under his personal rule. At his death only four years later, he willed the Empire to his two sons, thus again dividing it. This was hardly the first time the Empire had been divided. It had been divided by Diocletian, Constantine, and Valentinian within the previous century. But each time a later ruler reunited it. After the division in 395, however, the Roman Empire was never united again. There was a brief attempt at that under Justinian which we will notice shortly, but the attempt never reached its goal. After 395, the western part of the Empire and the eastern part went their separate ways. Much of what happened in the next millennium was a direct result of this separation.

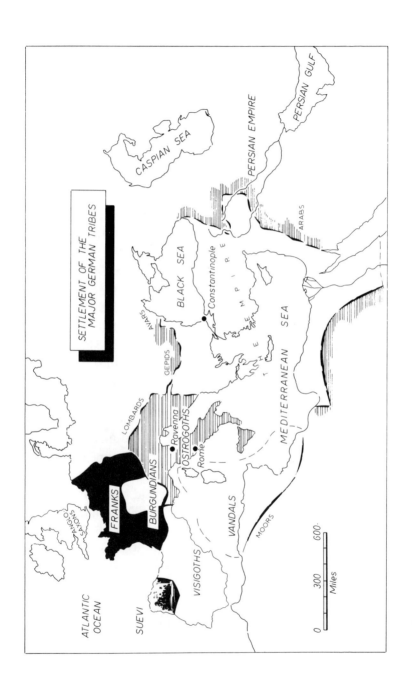

SETTLEMENT OF THE
MAJOR GERMAN TRIBES

CASPIAN SEA

PERSIAN EMPIRE

PERSIAN GULF

BLACK SEA

Constantinople

ARABS

AVARS

GEPIDS

THE EMPIRE

MEDITERRANEAN SEA

LOMBARDS

Ravenna

OSTROGOTHS

Rome

ANGLO SAXONS

FRANKS

BURGUNDIANS

ATLANTIC OCEAN

SUEVI

VISIGOTHS

VANDALS

MOORS

0   300   600
Miles

The sons of Theodosius (Honorius in the West, Arcadius in the East) were not the capable rulers that he was. Arcadius allowed additional mistreatment of the Visigoths, with the predictable result that in 398, under their chieftain Alaric, they went on the rampage again. They ravaged parts of Greece, turned west to follow the coast of the Adriatic through modern Yugoslavia, and were about to enter northern Italy. This, of course, put them in the jurisdiction of the western part of the Empire. In the effort to stop the Visigoths from breaking into Italy, western leaders rushed troops to the area — stripping soldiers from the Rhine and from Britain. Ultimately, however, the effort was fruitless. In 409 the Visigoths were in central Italy and attacked Rome; the next year they came back and sacked the city. From there they went into southern Italy where Alaric died in 411. Under their new leader, Athaulf, the Visigoths turned north, left Italy, and moved into southern Gaul. Eventually they moved into Spain and finally settled down. Because they were Arian Christians rather than orthodox Catholic Christians, there was a great deal of friction between them and the local religious leaders. Reconciliation to the Catholic position would take another century and a half; at the Third Council of Toledo in 589 King Recared renounced Arianism.

Significantly enough, it was this same Council that formalized the *filioque* tradition developing in the West. As we mentioned in an earlier chapter, the eastern theologians understood the Holy Spirit to proceed from the Father "through the Son," while the western theologians seemed to understand the Spirit as proceeding from the Father "and the Son" — *filioque*. Actually the eastern position is somewhat subordinationist, while the western idea places the Son on more of an equality with the Father. It is significant that this idea is first formalized at the very time and place that a group of Christians is abandoning Arianism — for Arianism itself is a subordinationist concept. It is theologically congruent for the Visigoths to give up Arianism and insist on the *filioque* at the same time. Their step forward in doing so was a spur to other western theologians to follow suit, so that within a few centuries the West identified the *filioque* with true Christianity.[1]

The sacking of Rome by the Visigoths was a severe blow to the prestige of the city and the Empire. Their attack on the city in 409 was the first time a foreign army had been at the gates of Rome since Hannibal — 625 years earlier. Rome had not been sacked in 790 years. This was a traumatic shock from which the ancient world never recovered. Many people were of course asking "Why?" and they concluded that it was because the gods were angry that so many people had become Christians. Those who still held on to paganism proclaimed that if Rome had remained faithful to the old gods, this kind of thing could never have happened.

This crisis caused Augustine to write what was probably his most famous book, the *City of God*.[2] He spent fifteen years on it, beginning in 412, finishing it only three years before his own death. In this work, Augustine claimed that Rome's greatness was due not to its gods, but to God's purpose for it. It is an earthly city, and therefore subject to decay. He argued that Rome's fall was not an argument against Christianity, but a final proof for it — all else falls, but Christianity lives on.

Even such an "eternal city" as Rome can fall into the hands of invaders, but the City of God will never be conquered. He concluded by stating that the Roman Empire is the City of Earth, while the orthodox Catholic Church is the City of God. This important work provided the significant Christian rationale for the current troubles the Roman Empire was experiencing, and it also gave the people optimism that God was still in control, working out His will, and directing men's affairs.

Somewhat earlier, when the Romans were drawing troops away from the Rhine to defend northern Italy, another major invasion of the Empire occurred. The troops left along the Rhine were too few to defend that stretch of the border. In 406 the entire tribe of the Vandals broke into Gaul, plundering as far as the Pyrenees. They entered Spain in 411 and quickly conquered the entire peninsula — at about the time that Alaric of the Visigoths was dying in southern Italy. When the Visigoths moved toward Spain, they found the Vandals already in possession of it, so they settled down temporarily in southern Gaul. Under their leader Gaiseric (428-477) the Vandals crossed the Straits of Gibraltar in 429 and began their conquest of North Africa. This allowed the Visigoths to move into Spain, while the Vandals took over the entire coast from opposite Gibraltar all the way to Carthage. In fact, while Augustine lay dying in Hippo Regius in 430, the Vandals were laying siege to the gates. Carthage fell in 439, and once this magnificent seaport was in their hands, they became masters of the western end of the Mediterranean. They attacked the Balaeric Islands, Sardinia, Corsica, Sicily, the coast of southern Italy, and in 455 sacked Rome, plundering it more savagely than the Visigoths had done 45 years previously.

The Vandals were also Arians. The Visigoths were not very militant about their Arianism, but the Vandals were. (This is indicative of their general behavior, which is why we have the word "vandal" in our vocabulary today.) They considered themselves the true Christians, the true "Catholics" and that the people both in Constantinople and Rome were wrong. The orthodox people when persecuted had a tendency to appeal to Rome for help, and this convinced the Vandals that such people were untrustworthy traitors. They closed down many Catholic churches, exiled bishops, and prevented the appointment of new ones. When Carthage fell in 439, its bishop was driven out, and the position was empty for twenty-four years. Many of the Donatists who were still in existence aided the Vandals in their attack on the Catholics. The depredations upon Christian institutions in this area were so severe that the church never fully recovered. It was still very weak when the Muslims came through two centuries later.

The Burgundians were another tribe that filtered down into southern Gaul after the Visigoths had moved on, having crossed the Rhine about 413. Apparently much of Richard Wagner's work, *The Ring*, reflects Burgundian legends and traditions. Shortly before midcentury they settled in the area of western Switzerland. Later they dominated the area down to the Visigoths and had two centers of strength located at Geneva and Lyons. They were also Arian, but under King Gundobad (480-516) several princesses converted to the Catholic position. His son and successor, Sigismund (516-523) converted to Roman orthodoxy, the first of the Germanic chieftains to do so. This was significant for the future, as we will notice shortly.

Meanwhile, Italy was coming apart at the seams. Most of the western emperors during the fifth century were ineffective, and the commanding general of the army was in charge more often than not. At the beginning of the century this was Stilicho, a Vandal. However, he fell afoul of the emperor's jealousy and was assassinated in 408. At the mid-century point the leading general was Aetius. When the Huns finally broke into central Europe, it was Aetius who assembled the Huns at Orleans and Troyes. In these battles orders to the "Roman" troops were given in German dialect. It is ironic that what defense the Roman Empire had left was being manned by Germans. Emperor Valentinian III assassinated Aetius in 454 and was himself assassinated by some of the latter's soldiers the next year. By 456 Ricimer, a German of Suevi and Gothic ancestry, was the virtual ruler of Italy until his death in 472, even though there was a succession of emperors upon the throne. But none of these were effective.

German mercenaries, a few Roman patricians, and appointees from the eastern emperor briefly vied for power in Italy. When Odovacar, the leader of the mercenaries gathered from various minor tribes, took charge in 476, the current "emperor," Romulus Augustulus simply abdicated. Odovacar sent the imperial insignia back to Emperor Zeno (474-491) in the East, informing him that one emperor was enough for the Roman world, and that he would administer Italy as the agent of the Emperor in Constantinople. This, of course, is the classic date for the fall of Rome — 476. Actually little changed. Roman administration had been collapsing in the West for some decades, and by 476 all parts of the West were ruled by Germanic *foederati*, Germans in independent kingdoms: Vandal North Africa, Visigothic Spain, Anglo-Saxon England. Odovacar became simply the King of Italy, although he considered himself a *foederatus*, an extension of the imperial power in the East. Thus was Rome entirely suffocated under Germanic invasions.

A tribe with immense impact upon the future was the Franks. By about 350 some of these people were beginning to move into what is modern Netherlands, where they settled permanently. The Franks fought as loyal allies of Rome against the Huns in 451, and their King Childeric (458-481) remained a faithful *foederatus* throughout his life and reign, often fighting the Saxons and Alans. His son Clovis (King, 481-511) came to the throne when he was only fifteen years old, but he is the most significant in the early line of the Frankish rulers. His conquests greatly increased the size of the Frankish dominion, reaching out to the east, the south, and the southeast.

About 492 or 493 Clovis married Chlotilde, a niece of King Gundobad of the Burgundians. Chlotilde was a Catholic Christian. The Franks were one of the few major tribes that had come into the Empire directly from heathenism. They were not Arians, nor any other kind of Christians. But Clovis had already shown a favorable disposition toward Christianity. Chlotilde now began to urge her husband to accept the new faith. Remigius, the Bishop of Rheims, added his words of argument and persuasion. In various teaching sessions, Remigius explained the principles of Christianity to the young but powerful king. When he heard the story of Jesus' crucifixion, he gripped his sword and remarked that if he and his Franks had been there, it would have been a different story! In the year 495 Clovis faced a particularly important battle with the neighboring Alemanni. He vowed that if the Christian God gave him the victory, he would accept Christian baptism. He won, and he fulfilled his vow by being baptized in 496. Shortly thereafter, the Franks as a whole converted to Catholic Christianity.

This was important because it made the Franks the only major Germanic tribe within the old bounds of the Empire that was of the same religious persuasion as the orthodox Christians in the West. The church leaders located in Rome always had a deep interest in these Franks. In the meantime, the native population in the areas overrun by the Germanic hordes, suffering under the Arian rule of these barbarians, often looked to the Franks for deliverance. As the Franks reached out to the south, the east, and the southeast, they made contact with Visigoths, Burgundians, and Ostrogoths, all Arian tribes. Not only were portions of these territories gobbled up by Frankish conquest, but the Franks often came as holy deliverers freeing Romanized Christians from the hands of these alien Arians. All this helped make the Frankish name both feared and respected in western Europe.

Meanwhile, the Ostrogoths were also beginning to move. Located east of the Dniester River, they had fallen under the control of the Huns when the Huns moved into eastern Europe. After the death of Atilla, however, the Hunnish Empire fell apart. The Ostrogoths soon threw off the Hunnish yoke and achieved a new sense of unity and power. So strong were they becoming, that Emperor Zeno in Constantinople began to see them as a threat. To eliminate any problem the Ostrogoths might cause on the Danube border, Zeno decided to kill two birds with one stone. He resolved to get rid of the Ostrogoth problem by sending them west, encouraging them to attack Odovacar, who was getting somewhat independent of Zeno's nominal control.

So it was that in 488 the Ostrogoths under their king Theodoric moved west, following much the same path as their cousins a century earlier, the Visigoths. With about 20,000 warriors, Theodoric soon became master of the Italian peninsula, although he was unable to drive Odovacar out of his fortified capital at Ravenna. Finally in 493, Theodoric proposed a truce feast. In the midst of the celebrations, however, he drove a dagger into the ribs of Odovacar, and thus the King of the Ostrogoths became King of Italy.

The Ostrogoths were, of course, Arian, but in spite of this religious difference, Theodoric ruled Italy with tolerance. He respected the church and there was no persecution. He used a number of Roman civil servants in his administration, including the philosopher Boethius, and also Cassiodorus, whom we noticed in Chapter Six. In theory he still recognized the primacy of the Eastern Emperor; in fact he was an independent ruler. All coins struck at Rome, Ravenna and Milan carried the Emperor's name; only the reverse side bore the name of Theodoric. Theodoric was an enlightened ruler, retaining many aspects of Roman government and administration. He was a powerful ruler, indicated by the fact that most

Germanic kingdom-states were tied to him by marriage alliances. Theodoric gave his sister to wed the King of Vandals, his daughters were married to the kings of the Visigoths and Burgundians, and he himself married the sister of Clovis, King of the Franks.

In spite of Theodoric's enlightened ways, toward the end of his life he became increasingly concerned about the ambitions of the new Emperor in the East, Justinian (527-565). Justinian indeed did have designs on the West, and Theodoric read him correctly. Theodoric also knew that his Catholic subjects from the Italian population resented their Arian masters. Fearful of designs against his throne, Theodoric began to harass the Catholics in various ways. In 523 he had his high administrator, Boethius, thrown into prison for suspected treason. There Boethius wrote *The Consolation of Philosophy.* He was tortured and executed the following year. John, Bishop of Rome (523-526), was sent to Constantinople to soften Justinian's anti-Arian edicts, but the results were disappointing. When John returned, Theodoric had him thrown into prison, where the old man died of ill treatment in 526. Theodoric himself died the same year. Things in Italy were headed for a crisis, finally resolved by Justinian in 535.

In the East, meanwhile, the Monophysite controversy lingered as a major problem, even after its condemnation at Chalcedon. The Monophysites had such strength in some localities that the emperors recognized it as a threat to the stability and integrity of the Empire. Unity was necessary if the Empire was to survive the attacks of the Germans and Slavs to the north, as well as the renewed Persian attacks on the East. Consequently,

Emperor Zeno tried to mediate the problem by reconciliation and compromise through imperial declaration. In 482 he issued a decree called the *Henoticon* (Decree of Union)[3] which was an attempt to settle the differences between the orthodox and the Monophysites by going back to the statements of Nicaea and the Council of Constantinople, ignoring the decisions of both Ephesus and Chalcedon. Any statement about the definitive nature of Christ was avoided. Both sides found such a procedure unacceptable, so little was accomplished through this maneuver.

Justinian came to the throne in 527, and he is one of the most significant eastern emperors. He revised the legal code, reformed the army and bureaucracy, and reformed the financial policies of the Empire. It was also about this time that the name of the Empire began to change. We remember that the old Roman Empire had been divided in half several times, most notably by the sons of Theodosius in 395. Each half went its own way, with the western line of emperors ending in 476. The eastern half of the Empire continued, sometimes called the Eastern Roman Empire, sometimes just Roman Empire. For some time these people called themselves Romans, but with the capital in Constantinople, people soon acknowledged that they were Greeks. About the time of Justinian, the Empire came to be called the Byzantine Empire, after Byzantium, the original name for the city that had become Constantinople. Historians find it convenient to refer to "the Byzantine Empire," and its people as Greeks, or "Byzantines," even though many of these people for centuries still referred to themselves as "Romans."

Justinian was significant for a number of things, but one of the most notable was his plan to recapture the West and restore the glory and the grandeur of the Old Roman Empire. He moved first on North Africa. He launched an amphibious invasion in 533 against the Vandal stronghold. The Vandals had never developed a strong government, so resistance collapsed quickly, and after six months North Africa was in Byzantine hands.

In 535 Justinian launched a two-pronged attack against the Ostrogoths in Italy. A naval force from North Africa attacked Sicily, while a land force marched along the coast of the Adriatic to attack Italy from the north. Sicily fell in one year, and the Byzantines moved into southern Italy. But the Ostrogoths were far better organized than the Vandals had been. Justinian's invasion turned into a bitter contest that lasted eighteen years. The city of Rome changed hands seven times. Byzantines and Goths chased one another up and down the peninsula, and in the process wiped out villages and fences, destroyed orchards and vineyards, and ruined grain fields. Italy was devastated by this war far more than it had been by all the Germanic invasions combined. In addition the severe financial and manpower drain all but exhausted the Byzantine Empire. Justinian finally regained Italy, and he added a little bit of Spain along the Mediterranean coast, but that was all. He did not reestablish the glory and power of the Roman Empire. But he did put Italy into the control of Byzantine forces, where some of it remained for centuries.

Meanwhile, Justinian still faced the Monophysite problem. The fact that his beautiful wife, Theodora, was a Monophysite increased his burden. In an attempt to

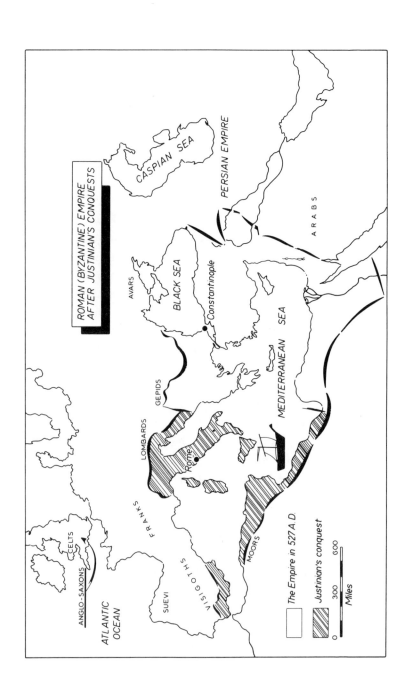

ROMAN (BYZANTINE) EMPIRE
AFTER JUSTINIAN'S CONQUESTS

CASPIAN SEA

PERSIAN EMPIRE

ARABS

AVARS

BLACK SEA

Constantinople

GEPIDS

MEDITERRANEAN SEA

LOMBARDS

Rome

FRANKS

CELTS

ANGLO-SAXONS

ATLANTIC OCEAN

SUEVI

VISIGOTHS

MOORS

The Empire in 527 A.D.

Justinian's conquest

0   300   600
Miles

win Monophysite confidence and show that he was not intractable in his orthodox position, Justinian about mid-century decided to have the church condemn the writings of three theologians approved at Chalcedon: Theodore of Mopsuestia (350-428), Theodoret of Cyrrhus (393-458), and Ibas of Edessa (Bishop of Edessa 435-457). To give the condemnation more authority, Justinian commanded the bishop of Rome, Vigilius (537-555), to come to Constantinople and affirm the denunciation. Since the condemnation was motivated purely by political reasons, Vigilius was reluctant to attack three men approved by an ecumenical council, but imperial troops ushered him to Constantinople anyway.

The western church as a whole protested this procedure, and finally Vigilius claimed that only another general council could undo the words of Chalcedon. Justinian obliged by calling the Second Council of Constantinople, the Fifth Ecumenical Council, in 553, which duly condemned the three men. Justinian's handling of this issue indicates that in spite of Rome's claim to primacy, he saw the Roman bishop as subservient to himself. Rome still claimed to be the supreme tribunal concerning all questions of Christian faith. But obviously Justinian never accepted the idea that the Bishop of Rome had jurisdiction over the eastern churches.

Actually Justinian's hard bargaining accomplished nothing. The condemnation of the Three Chapters (so called because of a document that recounted the suspicious doctrine of the three men, devoting a chapter to each) did not reconcile the Monophysites to the Eastern Orthodox churches. They continued to go their own way.

145

By the time of Justinian's death in 565, the Christians in Egypt, Syria, and Armenia had cut themselves off from the Patriarch of Constantinople, who by now was the ruler of the Eastern Orthodox churches. This division produced tragic political repercussions (to be discussed in the next chapter), which was exactly what the emperors had been afraid of for the previous century.

Meanwhile in the West, the last Germanic tribe made its entrance. The Lombards (also Arians) were being pushed by other tribes into the Empire, and in 568, just three years after the death of Justinian, they entered northern Italy. Within three years they conquered the valley of the Po (which to this day is called Lombardy), and by the next year had carved out a duchy in Spoleto (north of Rome, on the main communications link between Rome and the Byzantine governor in Ravenna) and another in Benevento (southeast of Rome, threatening Naples). The Byzantine authorities, strapped for money and manpower, did nothing. They simply held on to their fortified capital at Ravenna, while most of northern and central Italy fell into Lombard hands.

The Lombard advance was stalled in 573 when their king was assassinated, but about twenty years of relief brought no great improvement to the Byzantine position. When the Lombard invasion was resumed in the early 590's, the Byzantines were still virtually powerless to stop them. When Lombards advanced on Rome, she was thrown on her own resources. This brought Gregory I, Bishop of Rome (590-604), into the spotlight. Gregory came from an old, wealthy patrician family. Born in 540, he was a witness to the devastation Italy experienced during the Byzantine campaign against the Ostrogoths.

As a young man he began to hold office in the Roman municipal government, and he became city prefect (a position equivalent to our title of "mayor") in 573, the year the Lombards threatened siege, until the assassination of their king. Gregory was experienced in the use of bureaucratic power, and he was a skilled administrator. But in 575 he became a simple monk, going so far as to turn his family estate in Rome into a monastery. In 590 he became the Bishop of Rome, and he dramatically increased the power and prestige of that office.

Over the years numerous people had made large bequests of land to the Roman Church, and the Bishop of Rome was responsible for the administration of these properties. These lands were scattered throughout Italy, Sicily, Sardinia, southern Gaul, and Illyricum. They included farms, vineyards, orchards, mines, timber tracts and other businesses. Gregory's experience in city government was now useful as he oversaw the operations of this far-flung corporation. Profits were used to finance the operations of the church, gifts to the poor, and defense needs.

Some of these lands were in danger from the Lombard depredations. Gregory had a pastor's heart, and he was concerned about the lives and fortunes of the thousands of Italians that occupied farms and villages in the way of the advancing Lombards. When the Lombards increased their aggression in the early 590's, and since the Byzantine authorities were either unwilling or unable to do anything about it, Gregory filled the power vacuum that existed in central Italy and took charge.

It is important to note, however, that this was not an aggressive attempt to seize the reins of power. Gregory considered himself a loyal citizen of the Byzantine government. If the Byzantines had met the political, military, and social needs of the people of the peninsula, Gregory would have been content. But experience had taught him that such help would not be forthcoming. So Gregory, unwilling to see the situation deteriorate further, took over civil operations in central Italy.

When the Lombard invasions disrupted communications between Ravenna (the Byzantine provincial capital) and the rest of the peninsula, many of the managers of the church's estates assumed the duties of the absent imperial officials. Gregory provided the grain subsidies which the peasants received from the imperial government, often paying for the grain out of church funds. The land-tax was collected by officials of the church estates, not officials of the Empire. For a time the imperial garrison stationed in Rome depended upon Gregory for its maintenance and supplies.

Gregory initiated negotiation with the Lombards. He appointed a military governor to Nepi, thirty miles north of Rome. In 592 he arranged a peace with the Duke of Spoleto. When the Exarch (the Byzantine governor) in Ravenna disregarded this, the enraged Lombards made an assault on Rome itself. Gregory interrupted his series of sermons on Ezekiel to organize the defenses of the city. To save Rome he paid the Lombards five hundred pounds of gold as ransom. In 595 Gregory arranged a peace with the Lombard King. Emperor Maurice in Constantinople protested, but the peace stood and formed the foundation for peaceful relations in Italy for another century. Bishop Gregory now had more political influence on the Lombards than the Exarch did.

As the Patriarch of Rome, Gregory was energetic and efficient, welding the ecclesiastical organization of Italy into a tight, compact structure. He wrote to archbishops in Spain, northern Africa, and along the Adriatic coast, offering advice, being a friend in need, and constantly advancing the claim of Rome to supremacy. It was partially through his influence that a child of the King of the Lombards received orthodox baptism in 602, thus weaning the Lombards away from Arianism. Gregory firmly believed that the Bishop of Rome was more than just the Patriarch of the West; he was the primate of all the churches and responsible for the government of the universal church. He believed that all bishops and patriarchs must answer to Rome if guilty of heresy or disobedience to the canons of the church. He particularly liked to announce that the church at Constantinople was subject to Rome.

A famous incident in 588 underscored the struggle for primacy between Rome and Constantinople. When the Patriarch of Constantinople, John the Faster (582-595), assumed the title of Ecumenical Patriarch, Pelagius II, Bishop of Rome, loudly protested, as did Gregory when he ascended the bishop's throne in 590. Rome complained that the title suggested that Constantinople was the sole source of episcopal power and the most important bishopric in the entire Church — both of which Rome claimed for herself. Gregory sent a stiff rebuke to both Patriarch John[4] and Emperor Maurice. Both ignored him, and Maurice was offended at Rome's presumption and arrogance. Later Patriarchs of Constantinople used the title for a while yet, and then Roman Bishops picked it up too. It appears that Gregory did not expect his protest over John's title to result in change — but it was necessary to protest for the record or else it might appear that Gregory tacitly recognized the title.

Thus tension developed between East and West, but in the West Gregory was firmly mending his fences with the other western rulers. He was delighted when the news reached Rome that the Visigoth King Recared of Spain had converted from Arianism to Catholicism in 589 — though it apparently took a couple of years for the news to arrive. In summary, the Burgundians, Lombards, and Visigoths had all converted from Arianism; the Franks had converted directly from heathenism to Catholicism; and the Vandals and the Ostrogoths had been conquered by the Byzantines, meaning their land was back in orthodox hands. Arianism was gone for good, and all Christian areas in the west were in doctrinal harmony with Rome. The only exception were the Celts in the British Isles, but these were almost unknown to the Romans anyway.

Thus a number of developments converged in Gregory: he managed the civil affairs of central Italy, virtually all Christian areas in the west acknowledged him as the unrivaled patriarch, the Roman Church became very wealthy, and all western religious leaders looked to Rome for advice and direction. As a result, Gregory emerged as the first Bishop of Rome to display fully the power and authority that is connoted by the word "Pope." The word is a bit confusing, since it comes from the Latin word for "fathei." In the second century every bishop was called a "pope," though the word did not mean what it does now.[5] It is always difficult for Protestants to answer the question, "Who was the first Pope?"

because one must first talk definitions. Roman Catholics, of course, believe that Peter was the first Pope, but as we have already pointed out, there is no evidence that Peter was ever the Bishop of Rome, and the evidence indicates that the early church did not unilaterally accept the primacy of the Roman bishop. Some have suggested that Leo I merits the title of "Pope" because of his influence at the Council of Chalcedon and his success at keeping Attila the Hun out of Italy. But all things considered, it seems that Gregory (called "the Great" for understandable reasons) is the first person to function with the respect and authority of a modern pope. With this definition, then, we can date the beginning of the papacy at about 600.

Another development that helped underscore Gregory's growing European authority was his successful missionary expedition to England, launched in 596. As we noted earlier, Britain was once Christian, but fell to the heathen Anglo-Saxons and Christianity was wiped out, except for Celtic holdouts in the western part of Britain and in Ireland. The remaining Christian Celts had no desire to convert the invading Germans; for a century and a half the land remained heathen. Even before he became Bishop of Rome, Gregory had learned of these people, and he desired to see them converted. Once he became Bishop, and the immediate danger of the Lombard situation was over, Gregory sent a missionary team under Augustine (destined to become famous as Augustine of Canterbury, ?-604).

The mission landed in England in the spring of 597. England was divided into seven small kingdoms at the time, and Ethelbert (560-616) was King of Kent, where

151

Augustine landed. His queen was a Frankish princess, already a Catholic Christian. She had been unable to convince her husband of the superiority of Christianity, but when Augustine arrived, Ethelbert converted within a few months. Southeastern England was rapidly evangelized. Canterbury was the capital city, and Augustine located here. Canterbury is the oldest surviving Christian bishopric in England, and the Archbishop of Canterbury remains the leader of today's English church. Other bishoprics were established in Rochester and London.

It was about the turn of the century when Augustine learned that there were other Christians (Celts) in the western parts of the islands. In 602 or 603 Augustine went to meet them. He traveled in the knowledge that he was the direct emissary of the Bishop of Rome, the Patriarch of the West. He had word from Gregory that these western Christians were to be under his authority. The Celts had been cut off from Rome for a century and a half; they had no idea that the Bishop of Rome was in charge of all of Christianity. They had their differences from Roman Christianity, including the dating of Easter, the tonsure,[6] and distinctive monastic institutions. At the meeting the Celtic Christians did not appreciate Augustine's presumption of authority. They thought him a vain and prideful man. As a result, the Celtics rejected his authority, and Augustine took them to be evil-minded rebels against the rightful power of Rome. Here began a struggle for power between the two forms of Christianity that would last for six decades.

In 625 Ethelbert's daughter married the King of Northumbria, one of the kingdoms in the northern part of England. She tried unsuccessfully to plant Roman

Christianity there. By 633, however, the Northumbrian Oswald became king (633-641). He was a Celtic Christian, having been baptized at Iona a few years earlier while in exile from Northumbria. After his victory, he invited Celtic monks to come and evangelize the kingdom, which they did. Soon the other heathen kingdoms in the center of the island were converted, some to Roman, others to Celtic Christianity.

The traditional customs of both Romans and Celtics often hindered fellowship. The actual differences in practice between the two were very minor, but they focused on the authority of the Bishop of Rome — a big issue indeed. Things came to a crisis in 663 when Oswy, King of Northumbria (641-670) and brother of Oswald, realized that on the same Sunday his Roman Catholic wife would be celebrating Palm Sunday, he would be celebrating Easter. How could he feast while his wife was fasting? To resolve this dilemma once for all, he called a national synod at the double monastery of Whitby in 664. Learned arguments were presented from both Celtic and Roman advocates. What seemed to settle it for Oswy was the Roman argument that their practices came from Peter, who held the keys to the kingdom of heaven. Oswy did not want to oppose the doorkeeper of heaven, lest he arrive there and not be admitted.

Although the Celtics had made a remarkable comeback in the conversion of many of the English, the most powerful of the kings in England now favored the Roman form of Christianity. This had a tremendous impact upon the future of European Christianity. The English church from now on would be doggedly loyal to the Bishop of Rome, and it was English missionaries that had the greatest influence on the fate of Christian Europe in the next two centuries.

Thus the situation of European Christianity changed dramatically since the year 400. At that time the Roman Empire was still alive and well, with virtually all Germanic tribes outside the borders of the Empire. Now the Germans have come in, and most parts of the Empire have become Germanic kingdom-states. Because of political complications, the prestige and leadership of the Bishop of Rome have increased to the point of being almost unrecognizable. In these two centuries the patriarch of the West became the pope, and he picked up much of the power and prestige of the now defunct Roman Empire. For the next nine centuries Rome held undisputed sway over western Christendom.

Bibliography for Chapter Seven

Baker, John W. *Justinian and the Later Roman Empire.* Madison, WI: The University of Wisconsin Press, 1966.

A good treatment of Justinian and his place in the sixth century.

Barraclough, Geoffrey. *The Medieval Papacy.* New York: W.W. Norton Company, 1979.

The early portion of this book details the growing political power of the Bishop of Rome.

Bede. *A History of the English Church and People.* Trans. by Leo Sherley-Price. Baltimore: Penguin Books, 1955.

This is a priceless treasure of English church history, written in the early eighth century.

Boethius. *The Consolation of Philosophy.* trans. by V.E. Watts. Harmondsworth, England: Penguin Books, 1969.

A modern reprinting of Boethius' classical statement.

Deanesley, Margaret. *Augustine of Canterbury.* London: Nelson, 1964.

A good biography of this strategic missionary.

Dudden, F. Homes. *Gregory the Great: His Place in History and Thought.* New York: Russell & Russell, 1967.

A reprint of a 1905 work, still the best biography of Gregory.

Gregory of Tours. *The History of the Franks.* trans. by Lewis Thorpe. Harmondsworth, England: Penguin Books, 1974.

Gregory lived among the Franks in the sixth century; this is a first-class history by an eye-witness and contemporary.

Neill, Stephen. *A History of Christian Missions.* Vol. Six of *The Pelican History of the Church.* Baltimore: Penguin Books, 1964.

An encyclopedia of missions information, including works among the Germanic tribes.

Pirenne, Henri. *A History of Europe: From the Invasions to the XVI Century.* trans. by Bernard Miall. New York: University Books, 1955.

Early chapters provide a good overview of the Germanic migrations.

Procopius. *Secret History.* Harmondsworth, England: Penguin Books, 1982.

An inside look at Justinian and his court by a somewhat biased contemporary.

Questions and Projects for Chapter Seven

1. Do you agree that the year 476 is as good a date as any for dating the "fall of Rome"? Why or why not?
2. Contrast the various ways in which different portions of Europe are brought to a uniform Catholic position from the fifth to the seventh centuries.
3. Can you think of any way the eastern emperors could have resolved the Monophysite problem? Would it have been better if they had ignored the situation completely?
4. Prepare a paper in which you chronicle and analyze the gradual development of the power of the bishop of Rome. Could you defend the proposition that the year 600 is the beginning of the Roman Catholic papacy?
5. Summarize the achievements of Gregory I. Can you point to any earlier Bishop of Rome who accomplished more?

Notes for Chapter Seven

1. For this idea, see Paul Hutchison and Winfred E. Garrison, *20 Centuries of Christianity: A Concise History* (New York: Harcourt, Brace and Company, 1959), pp. 84-85. Also see Schaff, I, p. 26.

2. Augustine's classic work can be found in NPNF, First Series, II, pp. 1-511.

3. A copy of Zeno's *Henoticon* can be located in Bettenson, pp. 125-128.

4. Gregory's letter to Patriarch John can be found in NPNF, Second Series, XII, pp. 166-169.

5. Geoffrey Barraclough, *The Medieval Papacy* (New York: W.W. Norton & Company, 1979), p. 9.

6. The "tonsure" refers to the shaving of the head done by clergy. Roman clergy shaved the crown and the sides, leaving only a circular fringe around the top. The Celts drew a line over the top of the head from ear to ear and shaved the back half. In itself the difference is insignificant, but it gave the Romans the opportunity to make snide remarks about their Celtic opponents.

Chapter Eight
THE RISE OF ISLAM

In the early part of the seventh century, the Byzantine Empire was again under great pressure. The Persians on the eastern frontier resumed the offensive. In 606 they took over Armenia and Mesopotamia, Syria-Palestine in 607, and in 608 moved through Cappadocia as far as Chalcedon — just across the Bosporus from Constantinople itself. Emperor Heraclius (610-641) came to the throne inheriting a desperate situation. In the early days of his reign the Persians besieged Jerusalem for 20 days, and the city was delivered over by the Jews. There was a frightful three-day massacre of the Christian inhabitants. The Zoroastrian Persians zealously desecrated the Christian shrines, and carried off the "True Cross." As if affairs on the eastern border were not enough, Slavic tribes in the north came roaring down the Danube, in 617 coming down to the walls of Constantinople itself. In 619 the Persians invaded Egypt, aided by the disaffected Monophysites, as other Monophysites in Syria-Palestine had aided the Persians a decade earlier. This was the very thing the emperors had feared for over a century and a half: that the religious dissidents would be so disturbed over religious issues that they might betray the Empire. This simply emphasized the need to settle the religious controversy over the nature of Christ.

In the year 622 Heraclius counterattacked. He recovered most of Asia Minor, and in 623 he swept through Armenia. In Armenia he treated the holy city of the Zoroastrians the same way the Persians had treated Jerusalem. Driving deep into Mesopotamia, he achieved a great victory over the Persian king at Nineveh in 627. The Persians sued for peace, returned all land taken in the previous fifty years, and also returned the "True Cross." This relic Heraclius returned to Jerusalem, restoring it to its shrine. By 629 peace was restored, but it was still a disorganized Empire devastated by much of the Persian conquest. Both Persians and Byzantines were exhausted.

Meanwhile, the religious problem refused to go away. Heraclius was sorely bothered by the obvious dissatisfaction of the Monophysites who would welcome the invading Persians as liberators rather than continue to live under the Byzantine government. As a result, he worked closely with the Patriarch of Constantinople, Sergius I (610-638) to work out a compromise formula. Sergius drew up a statement which acknowledged the

Two Natures in Christ, but it defined them as being manifested in a single operative or active Force. Cyrus, the new Patriarch of Alexandria appointed in 630, became a strong proponent of this policy. But Sophronius, Patriarch of Jerusalem after 634, led the orthodox opposition. In this controversy, Sergius appealed to Honorius I of Rome (625-638). Honorius accepted the new compromise movement, but he replaced the term "one energy" with "one will," which in Greek gave the new name to the position, Monothelitism. In 638, when Emperor Heraclius put all this in an official document named the *Ekthesis* (Greek, "statement of faith"), he used the phrase "one will" coined by Honorius.

The orthodox, of course, raised the same objection against the "one will" as they had earlier made against Monophysitism and Apollonarianism, that is, if Jesus had no human will, He could not be an example for men, and He could not redeem man's fallen will. In the same year that *Ekthesis* was issued, Honorius died, and all later Roman Popes refused to sanction the doctrine he had endorsed. The doctrine of Monothelitism never did any good anyway, for even in the East the Orthodox saw it as a compromise which undermined the two natures of Christ taught at Chalcedon. Heraclius' successor, his grandson Constans II (641-668), tried to forestall further discussion and bitterness by forbidding all further discussion of this issue in his decree *Typos* in 648.

But Martin I, Bishop of Rome (649-655), refused to keep quiet. He not only called a synod in 649 to endorse the idea that Christ had two wills and two energies, but he also condemned and excommunicated the Patriarch of Constantinople and a number of other leading Eastern clergymen for supporting Monothelitism. This made Constans furious. Thanks to the stabilizing work of Gregory, central Italy was still nominally under Byzantine control, so in 653 Constans had Martin arrested and brought to Constantinople. Here he was humiliated, tortured, tried for treason, and exiled to the Crimea where he died in 655. This episode is instructive in seeing how the East really did assess the claims of Rome to primacy. Sergius was willing to use Rome's argument when Rome was saying what Sergius wanted to hear. But later actors in this scene stoutly denied that Rome had authority in the East. This again illustrates that the claim of Rome to universal supremacy does not parallel the actual attitudes of the time.

The story of Honorius becomes significant in later attempts to prove the infallibility of the Roman papacy. We will return to this point when we come to the nineteenth century. Meanwhile, the decree of *Typos* was doomed to failure as much as *Ekthesis* had been. Constans' son, Constantine IV (668-685), recognized this, particularly since the Arab invasions removed Monophysite lands from the Empire's control. As a result, Constantine called the Sixth Ecumenical Council, which met in Constantinople (the Third Council of Constantinople) in 681. This Council condemned Monothelitism and reaffirmed the strict doctrine of Chalcedon. In addition, the Council anathematized Honorius I. Pope Leo II (682-683) refused to approve this anathema, but he condemned Honorius for neglecting to denounce the Monothelite heresy when he should have done so. For a time all popes similarly denounced Honorius when they came to the throne.

By 681, however, things had changed so much in the eastern Mediterranean that any concern for the disciples of Monothelitism was unnecessary. The Muslim movements out of the Arabian peninsula were completely redrawing the map of history.

Mohammed (570-632) was born just five years after the death of Justinian, but they belonged to entirely different worlds. Mohammed was born in Mecca, in the Arabian peninsula. He became a small-time merchant and accountant, soon working for a wealthy widow named Khadija, fifteen years his senior. In 595 Mohammed married her. She bore him two sons (both of whom died in infancy) and some daughters, of whom only one survived, Fatima. They had a happy marriage until her death in 619.

There were many Christians in Arabia, including some in Mecca, though most of them apparently were Nestorians. Since his father died in Medina, about two hundred miles northwest of Mecca, Mohammed often visited there. The city had a large colony of Jews. In the year 610 he had his first alleged vision, in which Allah, the tribal god of his family, appeared to him announcing him as Allah's messenger. From then on he had numerous visions, many of which he dictated and had written down — on paper, parchment, leather, palm leaves, or bone. Not until after his death were these fragments collected and compiled as the Koran.

Meanwhile, in Mecca Mohammed announced himself as Allah's prophet, particularly down at the Kaaba, a square building which housed numerous idols, including a Black Stone seven inches in diameter (now thought to be a meteorite) which was a symbol of Allah. Many of the Meccan merchants flourished from the profitable pilgrim trade of the various idols, and they disapproved of Mohammed's monotheistic preaching. They saw him as a threat to their financial stability and future. There were occasions of violence between the two sides, but Mohammed slowly added members to his following.

In 620 he preached to some Medina merchants on pilgrimage at the Kaaba; in 622 seventy-three citizens of Medina invited him to their city. About two hundred of his followers accompanied him on this move, called the *Hegira* (flight). Later the Islamic calendar was dated from this event. There were some problems in Medina, but ultimately he converted most of the local citizenry, and it became his headquarters. The responsibility for the welfare of his followers fell upon him as the leader of this religious band. He usually supplied their needs through raids on the camel caravans that passed nearby. Such camel raids were hardly new. The various Arabian tribespeople had been raiding and feuding with each other as far back as their oral history went.

These raids, however, led to war with Mecca, and the fortunes of war shifted back and forth for a while. In 628 he pledged a ten-year truce with Mecca; in return his followers were allowed to return to the Kaaba. When he decided that he was getting a respectable following back in Mecca, he marched on the city in 630 and conquered it. He destroyed all the idols except the Black Stone.

The Holy Book of Islam is the Koran, which means "reading," or "a discourse." The modern composition of the Koran has the longest chapters (called "suras") first, down to the shortest. Most scholars believe this is almost exactly the reverse order of their composition. The earlier revelations were shorter, more poetical and spiritual. The suras written in Medina are longer, more prosaic, and more practical. They all take the form of a discourse from Allah or the angel Gabriel to the Prophet Mohammed.

As a religion, Islam consists of some relatively simple guidelines, though ethical content is included. The word *Islam* means "submission," and a member of this religion is called a Muslim (or Moslem), which means "one who has submitted." Muslims are offended to be called Mohammedans, just as Jews would be offended to be called "Mosesites." They acknowledge Mohammed as a prophet, but their worship is directed solely toward Allah.

A major thrust of Islam is to emphasize the unity of god. The central creed is the statement, "There is no God but Allah, and Mohammed is his prophet." Many scholars point out how much borrowing there is from Jewish traditions and the Scriptures. It may even be possible that *Allah* is an adaptation of a common Semitic root that is also the basis for *Elohim*, one of the major Old Testament names for God. One-fourth of the Koran can be traced to the Talmud, the authoritative body of Jewish tradition. It is obvious that Mohammed got many of his ideas from the Judaeo-Christian literature that was a part of the religious context in the Arabia of his day. The basic ideas of Islam — monotheism, prophecy, faith, repentance, the last Judgment, heaven, and hell — seem Jewish in origin, while other ideas, details of angels, resurrection, and heaven seem more Talmudic than derived directly from the Old Testament. Where Koran narratives vary from the standard Old Testament story, as in the tale of Joseph (Koran, chapter [or "sura"] 12), the variations accord with Talmudic legends. There are also borrowings of worship ritual, ceremonial purification, and details on diet and hygiene.

Mohammed accepted the Hebrew and Christian Scriptures as divinely revealed (Koran, 3:48). He stated there have been one hundred four revelations from God, but only four of them were recorded: the Pentateuch to Moses, the Psalms to David, the Gospel to Jesus, and the Koran to Mohammed. But the first three suffered corruption and could no longer be trusted. There were seven inspired prophets: Adam, Noah, Abraham, Moses, Enoch, and Jesus, but the last, the greatest, and the final one was Mohammed. He had a Docetic view of the crucifixion — Jesus was not really crucified, the disciples only thought He was (4:157).

In addition to these borrowings from Judaism and Christianity, Mohammed also borrowed from Zoroastrianism. In his travels as a merchant, Mohammed had occasion to meet representatives from all three of these major religions, for they were easily found in the trading cities along the north shore of the Red Sea.

The heart of Islam is the "Five Pillars." First is the basic creed, "There is no God but Allah, and Mohammed is his prophet." The other four are: (1) prayer toward Mecca five times a day; (2) the giving of alms; (3) fasting for the twenty-nine days of the month of Ramadan, but only during the daylight hours: at night food, drink, and sex were permitted; (4) taking a pilgrimage to Mecca "as often as he can," which soon came to be interpreted as meaning once in a lifetime.

In addition to these basic guidelines were numerous

166

injunctions. Alcoholic drink was prohibited, and other dietary restrictions were added. A man could have only four wives, though as many concubines as he could afford. Polygamy was nothing unusual to the East, and it seemed to go along with a limited life span and high infant mortality, plus the loss of many men through constant inter-tribal fighting (which Islam did not significantly reduce). Mohammed himself was monogamous until Khadija died. Then he added wives until he had ten, plus two concubines (actually, slave girls). A special revelation gave Mohammed permission to have more than four wives and even allowed him to have the pretty wife of an adopted son. Mohammed's picture of heaven was extremely sensual and explicit. Those who got to heaven would recline on couches, drink from rivers of milk, honey, and wine (wine is forbidden to them in this life), and with regard to the latter, there will be no after effects! Each man will have chaste, "high-bosomed" "bashful virgins" for his own (4:56, 37:48, 78:33). The Muslim view of life both on earth and in heaven is decidedly male chauvinistic. One Muslim teaching that did change value systems on earth, however, was the prohibition of infanticide (17:31), which was common — particularly for infant girls, who were buried at birth if the father desired.

This was Islam. It must be added that Arabia had been all but ignored by all the classical civilizations of the ancient world. The Bedouin nomads were poor, undisciplined, jealous, and strife-ridden.

Islam was able to weld them into a force and unite them in religion. Raised in privation, these hardy warriors fought zealously, believing that death in battle gave them instant admission to Paradise and its sensual allures. As a result, the direction of world events changed drastically.

Mohammed died in 632, two years after his triumphant return to Mecca. A successor was appointed (the Caliph, literally, "the successor"), and by the year 633, fervent missionaries scattered over the Arabian peninsula and succeeded in subduing the entire area to Islam. Arab tribes in Syria harassed the Byzantine Empire. In 633, Arab warriors raided into Persia, only to be hastily recalled into Syria when Heraclius directed his Greek army against the advancing Arabs there. The Byzantines, who had defeated the Persians a few years earlier, had not entirely recouped their strength, but they did not take the Arab threat too seriously. After all, the Arabs had never been a threat to the rest of the Near East.

Nevertheless, the Byzantines massed their forces for one decisive blow. According to contemporary sources, 40,000 Arabs met a Byzantine army of 240,000; modern historians scale this down to 25,000 Arabs and 50,000 Byzantines. But the result was the same: total disaster for the Greeks. The fast Arabian horses and their skillful riders were far superior to the plodding cavalry and infantry of the Greeks. The Byzantines had risked everything on one encounter; disaster meant there were no reserves to meet the continued Arab advances. Damascus fell to the desert warriors in 635, Antioch in 636, Jerusalem in 638, and by 640 all Syria was in Muslim hands.

When the Caliph Omar visited Jerusalem after his victorious warriors had conquered it, he treated Patriarch

Sophronius with kindness and courtesy, allowing the Christians to keep their shrines. The temple area, however, became Muslim holy ground. In one of Mohammed's earliest visions, he was taken to Jerusalem and the Wailing Wall. From there a winged horse took him to heaven and back. Thus Jerusalem became the third holy city for Islam, after Mecca and Medina. This made Jerusalem a holy city for three religions — Judaism, Christianity, and Islam. Because of Mohammed's vision, Omar chose the temple site for the location of the mosque that bears his name today. For centuries Jews and Muslims have bitterly wrangled over possession of the temple site. Christians fought for sole possession of this site during the crusades, but they have no such obsession today.

The onslaught of the Arab forces, once they were released from the Arabian peninsula, was rapid and bewildering to the people of the seventh century. Within the years 630 to 640, Islam passed from the religion of a handful of Mohammed's followers to the conquering force of some major cities that had existed for thousands of years. And that was only the beginning. By 641 the Arabs launched out in two directions at once and were successful in conquering both Egypt and Persia. It was in Persia that the later capital of the Caliphate was relocated in 750 at Baghdad. Meanwhile, the disaffected Monophysites and Monothelites in Alexandria again indicated their reluctance to continue as part of the Byzantine Empire. It was the Monophysite Patriarch of Alexandria that opened the gates of that city to the Muslim armies, after a twenty-three month siege. Monophysite Christians received the Muslim conquerors with open arms, guided them through the city, and helped them take the ancient city of Memphis.

Once they conquered Syria and Egypt, the Muslim leaders realized they would be unable to hold their coastline without a fleet. The doughty warriors of the desert adapted to the seas and soon seized Cyprus and Rhodes, and defeated the Byzantine navy in two battles (652, 655). To protect their western frontier, the Arabs marched from Egypt into Libya. By 670 they were only eighty miles south of Carthage. Here, however, the Greeks finally sent reinforcements, and with the aid of the local Berbers, they held off the Muslims until 698, when Carthage finally fell. Muslim control soon extended all the way to the Atlantic. Who could have foreseen this a mere seventy years earlier?

Muslim Moors crossed into Spain in 711, under their general Tariq, who led a force of 7,000 Berbers and 300 Arabs. The rock at whose foot his forces landed was called Gebel al-Tariq, "the Rock of Tariq" — later shortened to Gibraltar. In 712 there came a combined force of 18,000 Arabs and Moors. The victors gave the Visigothic Christians religious freedom and did not increase their taxes beyond what the Visigothic kingdom collected. The Muslims went on to cross the Pyrenees and entered Gaul. It began to look as though the Muslim wave would advance over all of Christendom, engulfing Christianity completely. Finally in 732, between the cities of Poitiers and Tours, Charles Martel (the name Martel meant "hammer," given him because of his battering blows at the Muslims), the de facto ruler of the Christian Franks, met the Muslims and stopped them. The seven day battle left the Muslims defeated and retreating. Yet in the next few years they captured Arles and Avignon, and threatened Lyons. Not until 759 were they expelled from southern Gaul, and they returned the next century.

Much has been made of the famous battle of Tours. Historians have stated that this battle alone stood between the death of Christian Europe and the survival of Christendom — that if the battle had gone the other way, we would all today be adherents of Islam. That may be a bit too sensational, but there can be no doubt that this was a significant contest. As we will see in the next chapter, the elimination of the Franks from the ranks of the Christians would have altered the shape of the next few centuries, and indeed all of subsequent history. But the Muslims were stopped and soon pushed back into the Iberian peninsula. Most of Europe remained free of their threat, but Spain blossomed as a home of Muslim culture, regained by Christians only in the fifteenth century.

Thus the century following the death of Mohammed dramatically altered the balance of power in the Mediterranean, as well as the history of the West. Islam captured Arabia, Persia, Syria, Palestine, Egypt, Libya, North Africa, and Spain. The Mediterranean became a Muslim lake, with Christianity limited to Europe and Asia Minor. Christianity was thrown back upon itself. So it would remain for centuries.

It is easy to answer the question, "What happened?" It is more difficult to answer, "Why?" How could so many areas, Christian for centuries, convert so quickly to Islam and remain so to the present? The answers are not easy to find, but several factors present themselves.

For one thing, in many of these areas, Christianity had not changed the underlying ethnic rivalries. We have already mentioned Monophysitism in Syria and Egypt. That Monophysitism was also a veneer for latent ethnic opposition to Greek domination. The same was true of the Berbers of North Africa. These areas welcomed the Muslims as deliverers. Resentment against Greek and Roman rule took advantage of the political transition.

A second factor rested in the Muslim decorum toward those of other faiths. Generally, it is not true that Islam spread at the point of the sword. Very few people were told, "Convert or die!" The Muslims were content to allow Christians, Jews, Zoroastrians, or others to continue in their faith, but they were excluded from first-class citizenship. Non-Muslims paid higher taxes and were excluded from certain occupations. They could always be blamed for military reverses or economic difficulties and persecuted accordingly. As a result, many such people converted to Islam. As we have seen, much of the pagan world converted to Christianity when it was socially profitable to do so. The same thing happened with Islam three centuries later.

The combination of these two factors led to widespread conversion to Islam. Most areas that embraced Islam remain Muslim today. Spain is the major exception, but even there the struggle was long and bitter. Most of Spain remained Muslim for centuries and, once begun, the Christian conquest of the peninsula took three centuries. Even then it had to employ such devices as the Spanish Inquisition to ferret out superficial converts to Christianity. Military prowess established the Muslim empire; fanatical devotion to Islam maintained it.

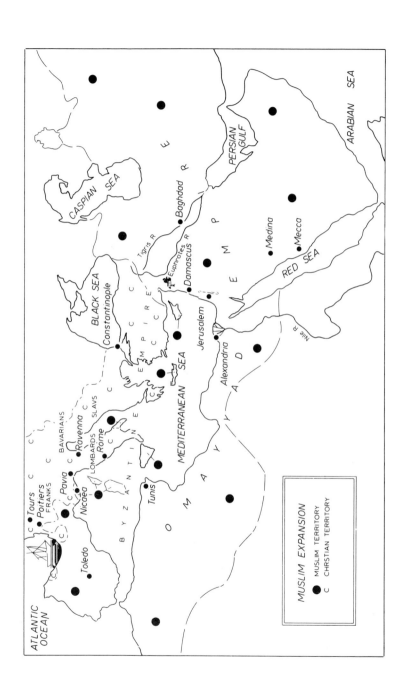

MUSLIM EXPANSION
● MUSLIM TERRITORY
C CHRISTIAN TERRITORY

ATLANTIC
OCEAN

ARABIAN SEA

CASPIAN SEA

BLACK SEA

PERSIAN GULF

RED SEA

MEDITERRANEAN SEA

Tigris R
Euphrates R
Baghdad
Damascus
Jerusalem
Alexandria
Nile R
Medina
Mecca

Constantinople
Tours
Poitiers
FRANKS
Pavia
BAVARIANS
Ravenna
Rome
LOMBARDS
SLAVS
Nicaea
Tunis
Toledo

EMPIRE
BYZANTINE
OMAYYAD
EMP

Bibliography for Chapter Eight

Andrae, Tor. *Mohammed, The Man and his Faith*. New York: Barnes and Noble, 1957.
This is a standard text, covering the main features of Mohammed's life.

The Koran. Trans. by N.J. Dawood. Harmondsworth, England: Penguin Books, 1974.
The Koran, the sacred scriptures of Islam, is of course available in various editions.

Pirenne, Henri. *Mohammed and Charlemagne*. Trans. by Bernard Miall. New York: Barnes & Noble Books, 1956.
Pirenne's major thesis is that it was the Muslim capture of the Mediterranean rather than the German invasions of civilized Europe that broke Europe's continuation of Roman civilization and led into the Middle Ages.

Questions and Projects for Chapter Eight

1. Do some research and write a paper noting the similarities between the Koran and either the Old or New Testament.
2. If you can find a Muslim in your area, ask him to describe the similarities and contrasts between Islam and Christianity.
3. Locate on a map the territory conquered by Islam in the first century after the death of Mohammed. Has any other empire or religious movement in history

done as much so quickly?

4. How do you account for the rapid spread of Islam into areas that were previously Christian?
5. Locate the areas of the world that are dominated by Islam today. Has there been any significant change in its doctrines since its establishment?

Chapter Nine
THE FRANKS AND
THE HOLY ROMAN EMPIRE

From time to time we have had occasion to notice the Kingdom of the Franks, and we have also added that in time to come this group would achieve great significance. The line of kings among the Franks was known as the Merovingian dynasty, so named from Meroveg (448-458), the grandfather of Clovis. By the mid-seventh century, however, this dynasty had become a line of "do-nothing" kings. Whenever there is a power vacuum, someone (or ones) will move in to fill the vacuum. With incompetent kings, various families of the Frankish upper nobility began to take over functions of the power of the king. The kings were willing for this to happen because it gave them more leisure time to enjoy hunting, drinking, and chasing concubines around the palace.

One family in particular began to gather up most of the power that the kings were losing. This family, the Carolingians, attained firm hold on the position of Mayor of the Palace, the rough equivalent of a prime minister today. Pepin of Heristal defeated a coalition of other nobles in 687 to secure this position, and he was the virtual ruler of the Franks until his death in 714. There were still kings through this period, but the Mayor of the Palace was the important figure. Upon Pepin's death his son Charles Martel (714-741) succeeded him. That is why we were careful to mention in the last chapter that Martel was the "de facto ruler" of the Franks at the time of the Battle of Tours in 732. He was not the king, but he was the ruler.

The Franks had been Christians ever since the time of Clovis, and they were desirous of extending the faith. They controlled Frisia (in what is now Netherlands) though the Frisians still had their own king. Pepin of Heristal supported the English missionary Willibrord (658-739) in Frisia, where he labored for fifty years with a great deal of success.

Another English missionary, Boniface (680-754) served as an apprentice missionary under Willibrord from 719 to 722, and then he launched out into the area of Germany, at the time totally heathen. The Roman papacy also recognized him as a special missionary on its behalf to this region. Boniface's success was a major factor in the spread of Roman Christianity into central Europe. Boniface evangelized Thuringia and Hesse and reorganized the church which had already been planted in Bavaria. After the death of Charles Martel, with whom Boniface never got along well, he was invited into the homeland of the Franks and was the instrument that revitalized the Frankish church in the next decade. Part of the significance of Boniface is his English origin. After the Synod of Whitby in 664, the English remained devoted to Roman Christianity, and it was missionaries from England that evangelized much of central Europe. As a result, these areas were infused with that special English commitment to the Roman Church. This was true of the areas later to be called Germany, as well as France. In no small part was this due to Boniface. Without a doubt he was the most important missionary of the early medieval period.

Relations between Charles Martel and the papacy were satisfactory, but none too cordial. On the one hand, he had saved Europe from Muslim invasion by his victory at Tours in 732, but on the other hand he was despoiling church lands. These properties he gave to the nobility so they could have the income to give themselves to long years of military training and service. This was a major stage in the development of medieval knighthood and feudalism. The church was none too happy about these confiscations, but there was little it could do. Martel gave basic protection to Boniface east of the Rhine, but the two had little contact.

Another problem between the papacy and Martel had to do with the Lombards. We left the Lombards in a peace signed with Gregory I. Over a century later, under their new king Liutprant (712-744), the Lombards again aspired to unite all Italy under their rule. Liutprant absorbed the Lombard duchies of Spoleto and Benevento, and indicated he wanted Rome as well. Pope Gregory III (731-741) was unwilling for the papacy to become just a Lombard bishopric, so he called upon the Byzantines for help. They did nothing. In 739 Gregory called upon Charles Martel for aid in battling the Lombards. Although Charles was willing to fight for the church, he was unwilling to battle Liutprant. In 732 Liutprant had brought a contingent of Lombards and had fought at the side of Charles at Tours against the Muslims. Charles was not willing to attack his erstwhile ally. He politely refused Gregory's request, and this further strained relations between the Franks and the papacy.

Theoretically the popes properly asked for help from the Byzantines because the Byzantines were the nominal overlords of central Italy. In effect, however, as we have repeatedly seen, the Byzantines were unable to respond. In addition, the East was going through the iconoclastic controversy at the time (a situation we will cover in detail in Chapter Eleven), and the papacy was opposed to the basic iconoclastic impulse. So the Pope was trying to chart his own course in the confused stream of Italian politics in the mid-eighth century. In effect there were three powers contending in Italy: the Lombards, the Byzantines, and the papacy. The latter two often teamed up against the Lombards, but it was an uneasy alliance. Increasingly the popes felt uncomfortable with the Byzantine connection.

Both Charles and Gregory III died the same year, 741. Charles was succeeded by his two sons, Carloman and Pepin the Short (741-768). Both sons worked closely with Boniface in reforming the Frankish church, which brought delight to the new pope, Zacharias (741-752). When Carloman went into a monastery in 747, Pepin became sole ruler. In 749, Pepin decided he was no longer happy to be second in command to a do-nothing king. He wished to be king in his own right, but the Germanic tribes had always believed that the blood of royalty was somehow better than that of others; furthermore, if Pepin simply overthrew the current king (Childeric III, King of the Franks, 741-51), then the other families of the nobility had a precedent to do the same to him. So Pepin needed some authority other than his own to legitimize any take-over. He wrote to the Pope, asking who should wear the crown, the man with the title but no power, or the man with the real power. Zacharias knew exactly what Pepin was asking, and he gave the proper reply. This got back to Pepin in 750. He spent the next several months communicating this to the nobility, and at the annual March assembly in 751, the Frankish nobles elected Pepin their king. He immediately sent Childeric off into a monastery where he died about four years later. Boniface was in Frankland (as it was called) at the time, and he participated in Pepin's coronation ceremony. Boniface consecrated the new king with oil, a practice borrowed from the Old Testament.

Meanwhile the Lombards in Italy had become more aggressive, particularly after King Aistulf (749-756) came to the throne. In 751, the same year that Pepin became King of the Franks, Aistulf conquered Ravenna, thus finally eliminating the Byzantines as a power in northern and central Italy. In the next few years he made menacing moves toward Rome. He claimed that since Rome had legally been under the Byzantines, it now belonged to him. The new pope, Stephen III (752-757) urgently sent for aid to the Byzantine Emperor Constantine V, but all this emperor did was to send Aistulf a letter. Stephen sent an equally urgent message to the Franks.

In 753 Stephen went north to the Lombard capital at Pavia to negotiate with Aistulf, but he accomplished nothing. According to some sources, he was physically abused and placed under house arrest for a couple of days. When Stephen left Pavia, he did not return to Rome, as all expected. Instead he turned to the northwest, crossed through the Alps, and in January of 754 met Pepin in southern Gaul. Pepin held the reins of the pope's horse and knelt before him, assuming the role of the pope's servant. To indicate papal approval of the changes in Frankland, Stephen recrowned Pepin as king. In return for giving God's blessing on Pepin's new position as King of the Franks, Stephen now asked for help against the Lombards.

Charles Martel had been unwilling to march against his one-time ally Liutprant; but now both Charles and Liutprant were gone. Pepin and Aistulf had no such bond, and the recent recipient of the pope's favor agreed to lend a helping hand. Some scholars think that Stephen had with him a copy of the document known as the Donation of Constantine. This document came out of an old legend that Constantine had once become ill with leprosy and was cured by Pope Sylvester (314-335). As partial recompense, Constantine decided to vacate Rome and move his capital to the East, since it was not right for an earthly emperor to rule where the head of all Christians had been established by the Emperor of Heaven. Thus Constantine gave the Pope the Lateran Palace (this much is true) and "all provinces, palaces, and districts of the City of Rome and Italy and of the regions of the West," as a permanent possession of the Roman Church.[1] The legend goes back to the fifth century, and it was a convenient addition to the papal claims on central Italy, particularly against the Lombards. From this time on the popes combined their claim to spiritual oversight over all Christians with this further claim to physical ownership of Rome and its environs.

In 755 Pepin led his armies south through the Alpine passes and immediately brought Aistulf to terms. But when the Franks left, Aistulf resumed his old ways and marched on Rome. At this point Stephen sent three letters to Pepin: one from himself calling upon the king for help, another from the people of Rome to the people of Frankland, and a third from St. Peter promising aid in the hereafter if the Franks would help Rome in this time of crisis. The Franks came roaring back in 756, devastating Lombardy and deposing Aistulf. Lombardy itself was made a Frankish fief, and all of central Italy was given to the papacy in the "Donation of Pepin."[2]

The Byzantine emperor Constantine V thanked Pepin for reconquering his lands and requested them back. But Pepin said he was under no obligation to the Byzantines; what he had done he had done for Peter. Byzantine authority was now completely ended in northern and central Italy, though they still held much of the south. This land given by Pepin to the papacy continued to be a church possession for eleven centuries. Called by various names (the Papal States, the States of the Church, the Patrimony of St. Peter, etc.) these lands made the pope a political/temporal ruler, just like any king. The implications of this development influenced papal activities well into the twentieth century.

Pepin died in 768, succeeded by his two sons, Carloman and Charles. Carloman's death by natural causes in 771 left the entire Frankish dominion in the hands of Charles, soon to be called Charles the Great (or more familiarly, Charlemagne). He became the most important single ruler in Europe in the entire medieval period. His influence upon political, religious, educational, and social developments was immense. He ruled more of Europe than any other single ruler between the Caesars and Napoleon.

One of his first problems was with the Lombards. Under their new king Desiderius, the Lombards again made plans for both independence from the Franks and conquest of Rome. Desiderius prepared a ruse to enter Rome as a pilgrim and then take over the city, including the custody of the papacy. Pope Adrian I (772-795) rebuked him, prepared for siege, and threatened Desiderius with anathema if he entered Roman territory. This was apparently the first time such spiritual penalty was placed on a temporal ruler; previously it was used only for schismatics and heretics. Responding to papal pleas, Charles came down to Italy in 772, besieged several of the Lombard strongholds, including Pavia, and then went down to Rome to meet with Pope Adrian. When the Lombard cities finally gave in, Charles this time removed their king and had himself crowned King of Lombardy, in 774. This completed the annexation of Lombardy to the Frankish empire. Charles also ratified the Donation of Pepin, leaving the papacy in control of the territory stretching across the peninsula from Ravenna to Rome.

Charles was constantly engaged in military activities

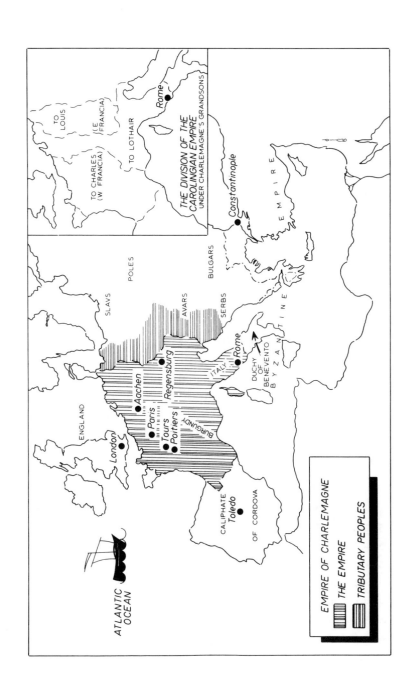

ATLANTIC OCEAN

ENGLAND

London

SLAVS

POLES

Aachen

Paris

Tours
Poitiers

Regensburg

AVARS

SERBS

BULGARS

BURGUNDY

ITALY

Rome

DUCHY OF BENEVENTO

B Y Z A N T I N E

CALIPHATE Toledo

OF CORDOVA

THE DIVISION OF THE
CAROLINGIAN EMPIRE
UNDER CHARLEMAGNE'S GRANDSONS

TO LOUIS

(E FRANCIA)

TO CHARLES
(W FRANCIA)

TO LOTHAIR

Rome

E M P I R E

Constantinople

EMPIRE OF CHARLEMAGNE

THE EMPIRE

TRIBUTARY PEOPLES

in expanding and policing the borders. Lombardy was added, as were additional areas to the east and south. In 778 Charles led his first invasion into Muslim Spain. It accomplished little, and in the departure from Spain his rear guard under his cousin Roland was caught in ambush at Roncesvalles, which gave occasion to the popular medieval "Song of Roland." Later expeditions into Spain did consolidate a slice of northern Spain into the Spanish March (or Mark), a designation given to a military area on the borders. A similar designation for an area to the east, the Ost Mark, ultimately became the name for Austria. Charles gave a great deal of attention to the conquest and evangelization of Saxony. Many preachers were sent there, and in 772 he made his first military foray into the territory. The Saxons resisted bitterly, however. They saw Christianity as the religion of the Franks, and they feared that evangelization would result in their political absorption (which was virtually correct). It required almost fifteen years of bitter gain and loss before Saxony could be considered more than temporarily Christian. It was in this period that Charlemagne punished the Saxons for their repeated resistance by beheading 4500 Saxon warriors in one day.

The incident for which Charlemagne is most famous occurred in 800. Adrian died in 795, replaced on the papal throne by Leo III (795-816). The news of this caused a shock in Frankland, for there were suspicions that Leo was corrupt, perhaps engaged in simony. Even though it was a proper papal election, there were many enemies of Leo in Rome, among both nobility and people. On April 25, 799, as Leo was proceeding on horseback to a church, he was ambushed, beaten to the ground, and left half-dead. Rumor also had it briefly that his eyes had been put out and his tongue torn out. The conspirators soon returned, gathered up the helpless pope and kept him prisoner in a monastery. His chamberlain brought a rope at night, and Leo escaped the city. When Charles heard of the events, he demanded that Leo appear before him in Saxony. Leo came that summer, and the two had long discussions. Leo returned to Rome in the fall, with a contingent of Frankish bodyguards. A commission of Frankish envoys, both bishops and counts, heard the charges against Leo, but they declared the pope not guilty, and the accusers were sent to Charles.

In March of 800 Charles left his capital in Aachen and began a tour of his realm, arriving in Rome in November. He convoked a full-scale synod of Roman clergy to hear the charges against Leo. The conspirators were there, brought back from Frankland, and the trial lasted a full three weeks. In the end, so much incriminating evidence had been presented against Leo that it was impossible to give a full acquittal. Instead the Frankish court resorted to an old legal stratagem where the accused swore to his innocence. Leo did this on December 23, and the trial was over.

Two days later, Charles took in the Christmas mass at St. Peter's which was crowded with worshipers. He was in the front of the church, kneeling, and there just happened to be a magnificent golden crown on the altar. At a certain point in the service, Leo took the crown and placed it on the head of Charles. At that point the worshipers, obviously coached in advance, shouted: "Long life and victory to Charles Augustus, crowned by God, the great and peaceful emperor of the Romans." Three times they roared this chant, and then Leo knelt and kissed the hem of Charles' cloak, a Byzantine custom. Charles' son Charles was also crowned and anointed as King of Old Frankland. This is the beginning of the "Holy Roman Empire," although the word "Holy" was not added officially until the time of Frederick Barbarossa in 1155.

The whole ceremony has remained somewhat of a puzzle to historians, for it appears that Charles was very upset by the coronation. He said that if he had known what the pope was going to do, he would not have gone to the church that day. Yet it is difficult to believe that Leo would have taken such a drastic step without Charles' knowledge; Leo owed too much to Charles to offend him. And there are indications that Charles wanted to be an emperor. Two factors may explain Charles' dissatisfaction. One is the title, Emperor of the *Romans*. The Franks did not want to lose their monarch to the Romans. In fact, from this point on Charles always referred to himself as "King of the Franks and Lombards," and he never again wore Roman dress.

Secondly, Charles was probably unhappy with the way Leo had managed the coronation: "crowned by God," with the pope as the mediating agent. Leo had arranged the ceremony in such a way as to suggest that the crown came through the papacy. The papacy later pointed out how in the Donation of Constantine the Emperor even gave his diadem to Sylvester, suggesting that the Pope could dispense with it as he saw fit. Young Charles soon died, and the Emperor's son Louis was the only son to survive him. Before Charlemagne died, he had Louis crowned, in 813, but he saw to it that Louis crowned himself (much as Napoleon would do a millennium later), suggesting that he did not need the Pope to confer the title or crown. This very point became a troublesome one for the next several centuries. Does the Pope make the Emperor, or is the Emperor independent of the Pope? By and large the church convinced later generations that it takes papal coronation to create an Emperor. Herein was a significant area for troublemaking in succeeding centuries.

In spite of the various interpretations and controversies surrounding the coronation, there is no doubt that Charlemagne was a significant figure in the cementing of relationships between the Franks and the papacy — what some have called the Franco-Papal Alliance. Charles was devout in the things of the church. He supported the monastic reform movement of Benedict of Aniane, used political authority to suppress heresy in the state, and used state powers to collect the tithes of the people. He insisted upon proper discipline of the clergy, and he approved most of the episcopal elections held in the kingdom. He also regularized the distinctive dress of the clergy and saw to it that Roman liturgy was used throughout his territory: in the newly conquered areas as well as in Frankland.

Charlemagne put a new emphasis on education, within the church as well as without. The best centers of learning were to be found in Italy and in the British Isles. Charlemagne brought Peter of Pisa and Paul the Deacon to Frankland as teachers. He brought cantors from the Roman school to instruct the Frankish clergy in the Gregorian chant. From England he imported Alcuin of York (735-804). From 781 to 796 Alcuin was at Charles' court; the last eight years of his life he taught in St. Martin's monastery at Tours. Alcuin led his students into an intense study of Augustine and Gregory the Great. Charles, his family, and his courtiers sat under Alcuin's instruction. Charles insisted that each bishop have a cathedral school to train the clergy of his diocese. Few such schools were formed, but Charles' order indicated his concern that education be widespread. Such was the revival of learning under his court that historians refer to it as the Carolingian Renaissance. Charles was a significant boost to the fortunes of the church. To a great extent, he created the atmosphere of life in the Middle Ages.

Charlemagne was a giant that strode across the Europe of his generation. When his tomb was opened in the 19th century, his skeleton measured 6 feet, 3-3/4 inches, although in the eighth and ninth centuries a five-foot adult man was not unusual. He had blond hair, flashing blue eyes, a powerful nose, a mustache with a clean chin. It was his personality and the power of his presence that kept his vast empire together. The territory he had inherited from his father he had increased dramatically, but there was not enough time for so disparate and scattered an empire to be welded into a united kingdom. The people did not have the bureaucratic machinery to maintain it as a unit after his death. He bequeathed to his heirs something which they could not manage. They were not cut from the same piece of cloth.

Emperor Louis I (814-840) was tall and handsome, as was his father, but he was the youngest of several sons. The eldest had been groomed for the throne, the youngest was raised by priests, but he was the only son that survived Charlemagne. He had neither the administrative experience nor the temperament to rule as his father had. In 816 the new pope Stephen V (816-817) journeyed to Rheims and re-enacted the coronation of the Emperor, making sure everyone understood the Pope's involvement in the process. When the Pope first arrived in Rheims, Louis prostrated himself before the pontiff three times. Nicknamed Louis the Pious, this emperor allowed the Pope to perpetuate the idea that the emperor's crown was at the disposal of the papacy. Charlemagne would not have been happy.

Nor would Charlemagne have been pleased with the further disposition of the Empire. It had always been the custom of the Franks, even back in the days of the Merovingian dynasty, to divide the kingdom up among the sons of the ruler. Under the Merovingians this had led to a constant cycle of civil wars among the sons, until one of them conquered the others. Unfortunately, the new king divided the kingdom among *his* sons and the wars began anew. It was only by chance that the Carolingians had no problems with this for a century and a half. Louis had no brother in 814, and the three previous rulers had outlasted rival brothers. But Louis himself had three sons, and in 817 he divided the kingdom among them. The problem became worse when his wife died and Louis remarried, and in 823 had a fourth son. Louis insisted that the kingdom was to be redivided four ways instead of the earlier three, but the three older brothers protested. In 825 this began a bloody eight-year civil war which only ended in 833 when Louis was forced to surrender to his sons, who had been joined by most of the nobility, the clergy, and even Pope Gregory IV (827-844).

The Frankish bishops were very disturbed by this papal intervention. They did not want any precedent of papal interference in Frankish affairs. But the popes claimed that anything that happened to the crown that was at the pope's disposal also affected the papacy. The popes liked to quote Matthew 16:19, where Jesus gave the keys of the kingdom to Peter. The bishops, however, liked to quote Matthew 18:18, where the same power of binding and loosing was given to the collected apostles. The pope claimed sole monopoly of the power of the keys: the bishops claimed that it was given to the collected apostolate, and therefore to the collected episcopate. This problem remained basically unresolved throughout the entire medieval period. The papal concept led to a strong monarchical development within the church; the episcopal concept led to a decentralization of territorial units in the dioceses and to a conciliar concept of authority. To some extent, the battle is still unresolved. Even in the Second Vatican Council of the 1960's, modern bishops were arguing for a share in the authoritative power of the church.

Part of the dispute over the division was settled in 838 when one of the three older brothers died, allowing again a three-way split. Emperor Louis died in 840. The eldest son, Lothair, received the imperial title and tried to make his brothers his vassals. His full brother Ludwig (Louis the German) and half brother Charles (Charles the Bald) refused, combined their military forces, and fought for three years until the Treaty of Verdun was signed in 843. An extremely important document, it had to be read to the various troops in two languages — the equivalents of early French and early German. This showed how disparate the Empire had become, and how inevitable was the division into France and Germany. According to the document, the Empire was to be divided three ways: Charles received the lands west of the Rhone (West Frankland); Ludwig received the lands east of the Rhine (East Frankland); and Lothair received the land in between, running from the Netherlands down into northern Italy. He also received the title of emperor. His lands north of the Alps took the name *Lothari regnum*, which became Lotharingia, and ultimately Lorraine.

When Lothair died in 855, his three sons divided up his middle portion. Louis II received Italy and the imperial title; Charles received the middle section, and Lothair II the northern part. When Charles died without children in 863 his brothers divided up his middle portion. When Lothair died in 869 his northern half went up for grabs between his two uncles, Charles the Bald and Ludwig the German. Generally East Frankland was able to control this land most of the time, but to a great extent this section of territory, running from the Netherlands down into Switzerland, was a battleground between France and Germany well into the twentieth century.

Thus the powerful empire of Charlemagne was divided. Perhaps it was inevitable. Only a person of Charlemagne's strength of character could have ruled it effectively. By commingling the appointive power of the papacy into his Frankish lands, Charlemagne bequeathed to his successors a church-state problem that caused immense grief in future centuries.

Bibliography for Chapter Nine

Duckett, Eleanor Shipley. *Anglo-Saxon Saints and Scholars*. New York: The Macmillan Company, 1947.
  A scholarly though very readable account, containing a good treatment of the missionary Boniface.
Einhard and Notker the Stammerer. *Two Lives of Charlemagne*. Trans. by Lewis Thorpe. Harmondsworth, England: Penguin Books, 1969.
  Both Einhard and Notker were court officials of Charlemagne; their biographies are important source documents for this period.
Fichtenau, Heinrich. *The Carolingian Empire: The Age of Charlemagne*. Trans. by Peter Munz. New York: Harper and Row, Publishers, 1964.
  This brief treatment is an excellent introduction into the court life and history of the Empire under Charlemagne.
Ullmann, Walter. *A Short History of the Papacy in the Middle Ages*. London: Methuen & Co., Ltd., 1972.
  Ullmann is a renowned medieval historian, and he here presents the historical development of the papacy rather than a series of individual popes.
Winston, Richard. *Charlemagne: From the Hammer to the Cross*. New York: Random House (Vintage Books), 1954.
  A modern assessment of the life of Charlemagne, very thorough and comprehensive.

Questions and Projects for Chapter Nine

1. Write a paper comparing and contrasting Constantine and Charlemagne as Christian emperors. Who was the more important? Who was the more Christian?
2. Write an assessment of what you think are the virtues and vices represented in the church-state entanglements of the Holy Roman Empire.
3. Analyze the role the papacy played in the political developments among the Franks from 749 to 843.
4. Do some research on the topic, and then prepare a paper on the coronation of Charlemagne in 800. What motives do you think emperor and pope respectively might have had as they went into the ceremony?
5. Write a paper on the Papal States. In the long run, were they more of a benefit or a curse to the popes for the next hundred years?

Notes for Chapter Nine

1. For the Donation of Constantine, see Barry, I, pp. 235-240. A shorter version can be found in Bettenson, pp. 137-142.
2. The Donation of Pepin can be located in Petry, pp. 206-207.

Chapter Ten
THE MEDIEVAL PAPACY

Some of the struggles that marked the interests of the
church in the early ninth century dealt with issues of
long-range consequence. The struggle for supremacy
between pope and emperor was more than symbolic — it
was a matter of life and death. The struggle within the
episcopacy for independency was also a harbinger of
things to come — bishops fought archbishops, archbishops fought the popes, and both fought lay interference
from nobles and kings. In the midst of this situation,
some clerics at Le Mans (about 130 miles southwest of
Paris) came up with a good idea. They produced a series
of documents to come to the aid of the embattled bishops.

They wished to strengthen the power of the episcopacy against the Carolingian nobility, and they provided

the paperwork to give bishops independence from lay interference. At this stage the bishops decided to look to the pope for protection, feeling papal claims were less of a threat than lay interference. Using some records of the early bishops of Rome, plus a generous amount of historical imagination, they produced a series of documents: some were genuine, some had a genuine core but added new material, and some were complete fabrications. The whole was put out under the name of Isidore, whom contemporaries thought must be the noted Spanish bishop, Isidore of Seville (560-636). This collection of papal decrees became known as the Isidorian Decretals; centuries later, when the nature of the forgery was proven, they were known as the Pseudo-Isidorian Decretals. Probably the most important feature of these decrees was the antiquity which they ascribed to some later pretensions of the papacy. Trying to protect the bishops from interfering archbishops and counts, the documents provided the arguments and historical evidence for the papacy to receive the sum of power and authority among the Frankish bishops. Knowledge of this collection soon spread from France to Rome, where it was quickly used by Nicholas I (858-867), and even more extensively by later popes, particularly in the eleventh century. It was centuries before any one even suspected that the documents were not genuine. By that time they had become the foundation for many additional papal decrees. These were years of relative weakness for the papacy, and thus local bishops were willing to appeal to papal protection. At the time there was no concern about the interfering power of a strengthened papacy. Certainly there was no awareness of the long-range implications and applications of the collection in the next several centuries.

When Nicholas I came to the papal throne in 858, he took on the characteristics of a strong pope and he was soon discipling other important clerics. John, the Archbishop of Ravenna, a personal friend of Emperor Louis II, was accused of graft, theft, and inefficient administration. Nicholas summoned him to Rome for an investigation, and when John refused to come, Nicholas deposed him, in spite of John's friendship with the Emperor. Lothair II of upper Lotharingia wanted to divorce his wife and marry another; he was supported in this by the two archbishops of Cologne and Trier. Nicholas commanded Ludwig the German and Charles the Bald to resort to arms to rescue their wayward nephew, and in a synod of 863 he deposed the two archbishops. The next year Nicholas ran into difficulty with Hincmar of Rheims, the strongest cleric in West Frankland. Archbishop Hincmar had excommunicated one of his bishops for disobedience; this bishop appealed to Nicholas, who reversed Hincmar's decision, quoting from the Isidorian Decretals which gave the pope this authority. Nicholas also had problems with the Eastern Orthodox, but this incident we will save for the next chapter.

Nicholas emerged as the strongest pope of the ninth century, but his immediate successors could not follow his example. In fact, they were enslaved by it. The medieval papacy alternated between times of papal strength and papal weakness. In the times of strength the popes contended with kings and emperors and often won. In the times of weakness, they needed an outside force to protect them from power-hungry Italian nobles who wanted to control the papacy for themselves. Stephen III needed help from King Pepin against Aistulf; Leo III needed help from Charlemagne against his enemies in Rome. The popes soon grew leery of imperial domination, but times of papal weakness were even worse. Disaster came to the papacy when there was no strong outside protector. Nicholas bequeathed to succeeding popes a powerful position. But later popes lacked both the forceful personality of Nicholas and strong emperors who could protect them in the style of Pepin and Charlemagne.

When Emperor Louis II died in 875, Pope John VIII (872-882) crowned Charles the Bald of West Frankland as Emperor, but Charles died in 877. The choice of emperor then went to the three sons of Ludwig the German, and various groups began to put tremendous pressure on the pope to choose their particular candidate. Finally John chose Charles the Fat, even though Duke Lambert of Spoleto had entered Rome in 878 and tried to starve John into appointing a different brother. The papacy was rapidly coming under the influence of families of the local Italian nobility. When the papacy became little more than the plaything of petty Italian politics, each family trying to increase its power base, calamity overtook the papacy.

This was already happening with John. Not only was he subject to great pressure because of the appointment of an Emperor, but he also had to hold off members of his own family who wanted him to use the office to enrich the family coffers. When he refused, they poisoned him. When the poison did not work fast enough, they burst into the papal bedchamber and crushed his skull with a hammer.

Three other popes followed in rapid succession, but they were of minor importance. Formosus (891-896) came to the papal throne having previously earned a reputation as a skilled diplomat for the church; he was an austere, ascetic man, and no one ever saw him eat meat or drink wine. Yet his friends consisted of thieves and assassins, and he was a constant schemer. Charles the Fat had been deposed as Holy Roman Emperor in 887, and although the German nobility elected Arnulf of Carinthia, a grandson of Ludwig the German, to the position, he had not been crowned by the pope. In this state of confusion, Formosus crowned Duke Lambert of Spoleto the Holy Roman Emperor in 894. Two years later, Arnulf came down to Italy, and Formosus reversed his action. He now crowned Arnulf as the Emperor. Formosus died in April of the same year, and the situation deteriorated rapidly.

The next pope was assassinated in less than a month. Then came Stephen VII (896-987). Agiltrude, Lambert's mother, was outraged at Formosus' double-dealing. In February of 897 she had his body exhumed, clothed in papal robes and put on trial for his crimes. Formosus was found guilty of treachery (he could not say much in his own defense). All his ordinations were declared invalid, his decrees null and void. His three fingers used to bestow the papal blessings were cut off, the papal robes were stripped from his body, and his corpse was dragged through the streets of Rome and cast into the Tiber. Throughout the trial Pope Stephen screamed his vengeance at the corpse.

But in August of 897 the party to which Formosus had belonged got the upper hand in local politics. Stephen was strangled and the next pope restored the name of Formosus to honor. That pope lasted only four months, followed by another who lived only 20 days. In 903 Leo V was elected pope, but after only two months in office his chaplain killed him and took over the office. This man, Christopher, is considered an antipope in official Roman Catholic lists, not a legitimate pope.

Sergius III (904-911) killed Christopher in early 904 and began the period often known as the Pornocracy. Theophylact was the powerful Count of Tusculum, and he was in political control of Rome at the time. Sergius took as mistress Theophylact's daughter, Marozia, a young girl of twelve or thirteen, who soon bore him a son. Sergius and Theophylact ruled Rome, and after the pope's death, the mother of the family, Theodora, appointed the next three popes. The third of these was John X (914-928).

In 927 Marozia took over the city. She killed John's brother, put out the eyes of the pope and threw him into prison; he died there the following year. Marozia appointed the next three popes, the last of which was John XI (931-935). He was in fact her illegitimate son by Sergius III. Still looking for ways to cement her control of Rome, Marozia in 932 killed her husband and married another nobleman of local power. In the same year, Alberic, Marozia's son from her first marriage, overthrew his mother and took control of Rome. He threw John XI in prison, but allowed later popes their freedom. Altogether, Alberic ruled Rome from 932 to 954. When he felt death coming on, he forced the

Roman Senate to agree that at the next vacancy, his son Octavian wold be made pope. When Pope Agapetus died in 955, Octavian succeeded to the throne and took the name of John XII — only the second time in history a pope changed his name, though it has become standard procedure ever since.

John XII has the distinction of being the most immoral pope of this period, certainly one of the most immoral popes in history. His sexual appetite seemed insatiable. According to contemporary reports, he turned the Vatican into a brothel and did not mind raping female pilgrims right in St. Peter's basilica. He and his friends often scooped the money out of church collection boxes to finance their evenings out on the town. He had many mistresses, and he rewarded some of them with grants of church land. If for no other reason, John was important because he proved the rule that in the eyes of the church authority rests in the office, not in the man. His moral pronouncements were an indictment of all that he did, yet they were flawless, as were his statements on matters of faith. Later contenders for the infallibility of the papacy were not worried about John because his official teachings were orthodox. His personal life was another matter, but that was beside the point.

At the very time that the papacy was reeling under these debaucheries, there were serious-minded Christians who were concerned about the spiritual state of things, and they intended to do something about them. In the year 910, Berno, a Burgundian monk, began a new monastery at Cluny in southern France. Duke William of Aquitane gave the initial land for the monastery, and William bequeathed to the monks the right to select their own abbot. The problem with many monasteries of the time was that a powerful lay lord in the neighborhood often selected the abbot, a man who would remain under his influence. Thus the spiritual integrity of many monasteries was undermined. This was exactly what the Cluniac reform movement wanted to eliminate — the interference of laymen in church affairs. Once things were under way at Cluny its reputation for holiness and integrity spread, and many other monasteries soon came under its influence and control. Whereas the Benedictine system allowed each monastery to have its own abbot, the reformers at Cluny allowed only one abbot — at Cluny. Other houses in the Cluniac system were run by priors, appointed directly from Cluny. That way local pressures could not interfere with the discipline of the local monastery. The whole Cluniac system expressed the church's desire to be free of the interference of powerful laymen.

Meanwhile, the title of Holy Roman Emperor had fallen into the hands of the rulers of East Frankland, or Germany. The Carolingian dynasty in the East died out in 911, and a Saxon dynasty came to power when the German nobles elected Henry Duke of Saxony as the new emperor (918-936). He was followed by his son, Otto I, also called "the Great" (936-973). Otto became emperor at a delicate time. Recent developments in Germany demonstrated that Otto would not be able to lean upon other families of the nobility for help in administering his kingdom; they would use any power he gave them to further their own family interests, not his. Unfortunately, the same was true of members of Otto's own family. They rebelled against Otto when they thought they had a chance to gain the throne. In looking for capable and trustworthy men to help with governing the kingdom, Otto finally decided to use members of the upper clergy, particularly the bishops and archbishops. Usually these men were at least moderately educated. In supervising their own diocese, they had gained administrative experience. And since the church insisted on celibacy for the clergy, there was no danger of untrustworthy sons inheriting the position and thus working against the emperor. But in order that the bishops might have the power to govern effectively, it was necessary for Otto to give them authority. In the Middle Ages, authority always came from control of the land. Thus Otto distributed vast amounts of royal land into the hands of the bishops. Certainly he would want to keep personal enemies out of positions that he had made powerful by grants of his own land.

As a result, more and more of the selections of bishops and even their installation fell into the hands of the emperor. This was not a situation of a free church being subverted into a state-controlled church; the choice rather was between a church controlled by local, unscrupulous counts and dukes, and a church controlled by the king for the good of the country as a whole. In general Otto made good episcopal appointments. He also participated in the installation service, called investiture, by "investing" the new bishop with control over his lands, and giving him the seals of authority of his office: the bishop's staff, the episcopal pallium to be worn around his neck, the bishop's ring, and often a scepter, to symbolize his authority over the king's land. The criticism that came later was not that the emperor was installing incompetents, but that a layman was both selecting the bishops and investing them with the symbols of their office. This is the very thing that concerned the Cluniac reform movement. But in the context of the tenth century, the Cluniac movement was not very significant yet, and Otto was making good appointments for the improvement of the church.

Otto showed further interest in church reform by his involvement in Italian politics and the papacy itself. After the death of Alberic in 954, petty Italian figures began to build positions of power for themselves, and they cast greedy eyes upon the papacy. Thus once again the papacy needed a strong outside protector. John XII had earlier resisted Otto's efforts to mediate in the Italian problems, but in 960 the pope requested Otto to come down. Otto came the next year, and early in 962 John crowned him Emperor.

Otto protected John from some of his enemies, but that did not mean Otto approved of John's lifestyle. Rather, he was appalled. Immediately after the coronation ceremony, the emperor took the young pope aside and gave him a lecture on his moral habits. John promised repentance, but he worked instead to undermine Otto's position in Italy. The local politics became complicated, but Otto could forget about John after May of 964. An outraged husband came home to find the pope in bed with his wife; he beat the pope so badly that he died of his injuries three days later. For the next several years, Emperor Otto supervised appointments to the papacy.

Otto III (982-1002), the grandson of Otto I, decided to take a firm hand in Rome in 996. The papal throne was vacant at the time, and Otto appointed his cousin Bruno as Pope Gregory V (996-999), the first German pope. When he was killed by poison, Otto put in the first French pope, his former tutor Sylvester II (999-1003). Otto himself was poisoned in 1002, and rumor had it that the same hand poisoned the pope the following year. The new emperor in Germany, Henry II (1002-1024), was not interested in the Italian situation, which meant that the local families of the nobility again fell to power plots among themselves, each trying to secure the papacy as a basis of strength. The Crescenti family controlled three papal appointments from 1003 to 1012, and then the Tusculum family controlled three more from 1012 to 1045. Moral and spiritual deterioration of the papacy set in again.

The first two popes the house of Tusculum put into office were brothers, Benedict VIII (1012-1024) and John XIX (1024-1032). John was only a layman when elected, and he had to be put through various consecrations before being made pope. On his death a nephew came to the papacy — Benedict IX (1032-45/48). Statements as to his age vary from twelve to eighteen, but certainly he was but a youth. As he became older, he followed the immoral lifestyle of John XII of the previous century. Technically Benedict is considered the pope until 1048, although three other legitimate popes appear from 1044 to 1047. This indicates the confusion and scandal in Rome. In 1044 the people drove Benedict from Rome and elected Sylvester III (1045). After three months, Benedict returned and took over again. Within three weeks, however, he decided to leave the office, but wanted to make as much money out of it as he could. He sold the papacy to his god-father who became Gregory VI (1045-1046).

Gregory's father was a converted Jew, and he therefore counts as the first Jewish Pope (unless we count Peter). Gregory surprised everybody by being a reforming pope. The money he paid for the papacy came from his own funds — fifteen hundred pounds of gold he had been saving to restore some of Rome's dilapidated churches. Yet his act of ransoming the papacy from immoral hands had involved him in the sin of simony — purchasing spiritual office with money, named from the sin of Simon the sorcerer in Acts 8. In addition, in less than a year and a half, Benedict wanted his throne back, as did Sylvester.

Such a situation demanded help, and Emperor Henry III (1039-1056) came down late in 1046 to oversee a synod to decide the issue. Sylvester's claims to the papacy were easily set aside, but Gregory's situation was more difficult. After all the discussion, however, the synod decided that in spite of his reasons for purchasing the papacy, the act of purchase had nullified any claim he might make to the papacy, and Gregory too was deposed. Benedict was canonically deposed also, and with all three popes out of the way, Henry had a German pope put into office, Clement II (1046-1047). Ten months later he was dead of suspicious causes, and some whispered it was done by poison. Benedict returned, but when Henry III also came back in 1048, Benedict departed again, this time for good. In official lists, Benedict is listed as pope three different times, surely a confusing situation for the legalist.

Henry installed another German, but he died of

malaria within twenty-three days. The next pope was also a German, Leo IX (1049-1054). Leo rescued the papacy from the unsavory reputation that had recently settled upon it. He had heard of the Cluniac reform movement, and his reign as pope emphasized the reforming demand to eliminate simony and immoral clergy from the church. He condemned a bishop for simony in Rome, and he traveled into France and Germany to implement the same message. He made a smashing impression, forcing both nobility and archbishops to yield to his demand for moral reform.

One of the difficulties Leo got involved in, however, was with the Normans in southern Italy. The Viking invaders had long since settled down in northern Europe, as well as in the area that came to be called after them in France, the duchy of Normandy. Early in the eleventh century some Normans began to arrive in southern Italy looking for new worlds to conquer, and they were soon successful in setting up a new kingdom for themselves. By mid-century the leader of this group was Robert Guiscard ("the Fox"). In the process of adding more and more land to their territory in southern Italy, they ran into papal estates. This led to a pitched battle between the Normans and papal forces led by Leo himself in 1053. The Normans won, although they protested their loyalty to the pope, requesting permission to become his vassals. Kept a prisoner for nine months, Leo finally agreed, but he died a month later in Rome. Leo was also involved in the great schism in 1054, to which we shall turn in our next chapter.

During the reign of the next couple of popes a monk named Hildebrand became more and more of a factor in

papal councils. Hildebrand had been a friend of
Gregory VI, and he encouraged Leo to accept the Norman offer of vassalage. Hildebrand was a major voice in
papal decisions and, in fact, influenced several papal
elections. Apparently it was his advice that formulated
the significant decree of Nicholas II in 1059 placing the
power to elect the Bishop of Rome in the hands of the
cardinals — a major step in the development of the college of cardinals as we know it today.[1] When the papal
office fell vacant in 1073, the people of Rome, who had
become very vocal in their admiration of Hildebrand,
demanded that he become pope. He protested his unwor-
thiness, but the people carried him to the cardinals, and
they elected him to the office. He took the name of Gregory VII (1073-1085).

Gregory wasted little time in focusing the attention of
the church on two matters still needing reform —
simony and clerical marriage. Decrees condemning the
practices were renewed, but the practices were so
widespread that it was difficult to stop them. So Gregory
decided to approach the issue from another direction. He
felt that as long as the upper clergy were appointed by
monarchs the moral level would remain low. Therefore,
he put first priority on the need to eliminate temporal
rulers from the business of appointing church officers.
The focus of his attack would be on the ceremony of
investiture. This policy put Gregory in direct opposition
to Henry IV (1056-1106) of Germany. Henry was
involved in a serious civil war with his upper nobility,
and he was using the bishops and archbishops as a major
element to restore royal control over Germany. To maintain control over their positions, he was carefully making

episcopal appointments.

Yet the qualifications for office that Henry was looking for were not the same as those of the church. Henry
needed bishops who were loyal to him; he did not care
whether they were devout churchmen. Gregory knew
that kings and emperors tended to appoint bishops on
political grounds rather than spiritual ones. However,
this not only eroded the church's control over religious
office, it also destroyed the possibility of proper spiritual
nurture for the people. Both kings and popes felt they
needed to control the office of bishop. They were on a
collision course.

In February, 1075, another Roman synod renewed the
usual decrees against simony, fornication, and lay
investiture. At the same time Gregory suspended for
simony five of Henry's bishops, and he deposed other
German bishops as well. Henry refused to yield, and he
continued to appoint bishops in his lands. By December
of that year Gregory threatened excommunication if the
Emperor persisted. Henry still refused, so in February of
1076 Gregory not only excommunicated him, he also
deposed him from the imperial throne and released all
subjects from allegiance to him. The following month he
released his noted document, *Dictatus Papae,* in which
he claimed that he had the power to depose emperors
and bishops, but that he was totally above the judgment
of everyone else. The document enunciates the highest
claim of papal power up to this point in history.[2]

This hit Henry at a bad time. His nobles took advantage of the excommunication and release from allegiance due him as a feudal lord. The nobility of Germany approved the excommunication and threatened to

replace him on the imperial throne if he did not receive absolution from the pope by the next February. Because of the combination of spiritual demands and political realities, Henry was caught. So he decided to go through all the motions of complying with the Pope's order. He journeyed down to northern Italy and appeared before the Pope in the garb of a penitent, begging forgiveness. Gregory was sure Henry was being deceitful, but as the chief pastor of Christendom he could not afford to turn down a penitent sinner. So he forgave Henry completely, lifted the excommunication, and restored his subjects to their oath of allegiance.

This was exactly what Henry wanted. He turned north and dealt harshly with the nobility who now had no legal excuse for their rebellion. As a result, Henry's position was stronger than it had been before. Most importantly, he still continued to appoint bishops. Gregory excommunicated him again, but because Henry was now fully in control of the political situation in Germany, the excommunication had no effect. Instead Henry marched south in 1082 and besieged the Pope. Gregory was rescued by his Norman allies under Guiscard in 1084, but he had so alienated Rome in the process that Guiscard had to take him to Naples where he died in 1085.

Henry continued to maintain his position against the church, and similar troubles arose across the English Channel. The Normans had invaded England under William the Conqueror in 1066, and they brought Continental customs to the island. One of these was the practice of royal investiture. William's sons, William II (1087-1100) and Henry I (1100-1135) abused various privileges in controlling the English church, and this angered religious authorities both in England and in Rome. After a lengthy series of confrontations, a compromise was finally worked out in the Concordat of London of 1107. According to its provisions, bishops were to be freely elected by church officials, but they must also swear allegiance to the king. At the actual investiture ceremony, the pope's representative presented the pallium, the ring, and the crozier, while the king's representative invested the bishop with his lands. This solved the problem, and it seemed to work very well.

Yet it took another fifteen years for the same issue to be resolved in Germany. In the end the Concordat of Worms of 1122 was very similar. The clergy elected their own bishops, but if the candidate was unacceptable to the emperor, the emperor could refuse to invest the bishop with the lands. This effectively eliminated the possibility of purposefully nominating the king's enemies to the episcopal positions. Yet the king could not impose his own man — he must be elected by the church. In the long run the Concordat worked in the favor of the church, since the Emperor would be under pressure to approve a worthy cleric. There were still occasional difficulties, but the basic principles of the reform movement nurtured by the Cluniacs and Gregory VII had triumphed.

With the continuing growth of Cluniac reform, Gregorian reform, and monastic reform which we shall notice in Chapter Thirteen, the end of the twelfth and beginning of the thirteenth centuries represent what one historian has called "the zenith of the medieval papacy."[3] This is represented in the pontificate of Innocent III (1198-

1216). In terms of actual power, Innocent may have been the most powerful pope in the entire history of the papacy.

Innocent had a lofty concept of his position as pope. He stated that as pope he was the vicar of the King of kings and Lord of lords and that Christ had left Peter not only the governance of the Church, but also of the whole world. He conceded that God had given kings divine commissions, but he also insisted that as the moon drew its light from the sun, so royal power derived its dignity and authority from the papal power.[4] He supported the Fourth and Fifth Crusades, and as we shall see in Chapter Twelve, he benefited from the Latin conquest of Constantinople. Closer to home, he asserted the right of the papacy to arbitrate all cases of disputed elections to the episcopacy, and he furthered the tendency to draw all appeals to Rome.

But it is probably in the political dealings that Innocent is most well known. He desired to reclaim total power over the Papal States since so much of it had been put in other hands during the disputes of the previous two centuries. To cement his hold on central Italy, he challenged the Hohenstaufen dynasty of Holy Roman Emperors. The Hohenstaufens had developed designs on Italy, particularly with the marriage of Henry VI (1190-1197) to the Norman heiress of the southern kingdom. The combination of imperial holdings in northern Italy and Norman holdings in southern Italy represented a Hohenstaufen stranglehold on central Italy and the Papal States. Innocent fought to dissolve this Hohenstaufen combination, and he was willing to intervene in German affairs to do so. When a dispute as to the succession occurred in 1197, Innocent played both parties off against each other and thus managed to maintain his own freedom of maneuver. Ultimately he recognized Frederick II (1212-1250) as the legitimate ruler, but only when it appeared he could control the young Emperor. When the King of France, the powerful Philip II (1180-1223), got into matrimonial problems, Innocent intervened. Philip wanted to put away his wife and install his mistress as the new queen, but Innocent protested. The protest normally might have been meaningless, but Philip was also facing a serious war with England. He could not afford possible excommunication and loss of support among his people. Because of the political realities, Philip accepted the Pope's commands. Whatever the rationale, this increased the Pope's influence and respect throughout Europe.

Perhaps Innocent's most famous conflict was with King John of England (1199-1216). The initial dispute had to do with the selection of a new Archbishop of Canterbury. Both the monks of Canterbury and the King had made selections, but Innocent annulled both and sent over his own candidate, Stephen Langton. John, however, refused to recognize him. Innocent excommunicated the King and placed the entire country under an interdict — an order forbidding any cleric to celebrate any of the sacraments. Innocent also encouraged Philip of France to invade England.

After five years of the struggle, John finally gave up in 1213, to the extent of *giving* England to the papacy and receiving it back as a fief. This vassal-lord situation between king and pope lasted for a hundred fifty years, until it was finally ignored late in the 14th century.

It may be necessary to point out that in every instance where Innocent forced rulers to yield to him, it was because there was always an internal political problem that the Pope could use to his advantage. Innocent did not get his way simply because of his recognized authority. It was only when he had a useful lever handy that he was successful: political rivalry in Germany, wartime pressures in France and England. This is further demonstrated in John's submission to the demands of his barons in 1215 in the Magna Carta. Innocent protested this act, because John had not consulted him in it (and after all, Innocent owned England; John was only his vassal!), and it was a threat to the Pope's theoretical sovereignty over England. But there was no way Innocent could turn the baronial rebellion to his own advantage. The English safely ignored his protests since the Pope lacked any political instrument to use against them. As a result, historians continue to raise the question whether medieval Europeans really accepted Innocent's authority at face value, or whether they accommodated themselves to his claims only when it was useful to do so.

The crowning glory of Innocent's pontificate was the Fourth Lateran Council, the twelfth ecumenical council, held in Rome in 1215. For the first time it made the teaching of transubstantiation dogma for the church. It also decreed that all good Catholics must receive communion at least once a year. This entailed the responsibility to go to confession, do penance, and receive absolution. This council is considered the most significant church council in the medieval period.

If the Lateran Council was Innocent's greatest

achievement, one of his more infamous acts was his crusade against the Albigensians. These people appeared
early in the eleventh century, centered on the town of
Albi in southern France. Their doctrine was a form of
dualism: physical matter was created by evil forces and
therefore Christians should avoid everything material.
This led them to become vegetarians, deny the Incarnation, disapprove of marriage and procreation, and refuse
to take the New Testament literally. Because the
Catholic Church did, the Albigensians hated the
Catholics. In spite of their heretical notions, the Albigensians won wide-spread support because of their pure
lives. A nobleman from southern France, Raymond of
Toulouse, supported their cause. But when some of Raymond's agents murdered a papal legate in 1208, the
Albigensians received the blame. The Church had condemned them several times in the twelfth century, but
Innocent in 1209 launched the crusade which led to their
virtual annihilation. Thousands of villagers were massacred: men, women, children, and elderly. The hunting
and killing lasted until 1228. Unfortunately, the killing
of so many innocents was not inconsistent with many of
the brutalities of the Middle Ages.

After a pontificate of eighteen and a half years, Innocent died in 1216, aged only fifty-six. He had put the
medieval papacy at the apex of its power. Considering
the previous four centuries, the papacy had had its ups
and downs. But in general it had been reformed and
strengthened, made into an organization of vast political
power as well as spiritual influence. Other men tried to
match Innocent's record for papal influence, but they
were unable to maintain his position. Given another

century, the papal situation was again in the lowest depths. But that will take us beyond the medieval period.

Bibliography for Chapter Ten

Barraclaugh, Geoffrey. *The Medieval Papacy*. ("Library of World Civilization," Geoffrey Barraclough, gen. ed.) New York: W.W. Norton & Co., 1979.

Done by a respected scholar, a brief but insightful analysis of the medieval papacy.

Chamberlin, E.R. *The Bad Popes*. New York: New American Library (Signet Books), 1979.

Not a very edifying subject, but Chamberlin gives some detailed history of some of the worst popes of the medieval period.

Hill, Bennett D. (ed.) *Church and State in the Middle Ages*. New York: John Wiley & Sons, Inc., 1970).

A combination of source documents plus commentary from various historians on this lively topic that is crucial to understanding the medieval period.

Painter, Sidney. *The Reign of King John*. Baltimore: The John's Hopkins Press, 1949.

A penetrating look into the complex reign of a major English king, particularly significant for his church-state entanglements.

Prinz, Joachim. *Popes from the Ghetto: A View of Medieval Christendom*. New York: Schocken Books, 1968.

A study of three popes with Jewish backgrounds, including Gregory VI and Gregory VII.

Tellenbach, Gerd. *Church, State and Christian Society at*

the Time of the Investiture Contest. Trans. by R.F. Bennett. Oxford: Basil Blackwell, 1966.

An extremely penetrating discussion of the problems represented by investiture.

Tierney, Brian. *The Crisis of Church & State, 1050-1300, With Selected Documents.* Englewood Cliffs, New Jersey: Prentice-Hall, Inc., 1964.

An excellent presentation of the church-state problem, with various documents to illustrate the positions taken.

Ullmann, Walter. *A Short History of the Papacy in the Middle Ages.* London: Methuen & Co., Ltd., 1972.

Annotated at the end of Chapter Nine.

Questions and Projects for Chapter Ten

1. Do some reading in medieval histories published by Roman Catholics to see how they treat such men as John XII and Benedict IX. Prepare a paper on your findings.
2. Compare and/or contrast Nicholas I, Gregory VII, and Innocent III. How does each contribute to the development of papal power?
3. Do you think the Concordats of London and Worms were effective means of resolving the investiture problems? What other solutions could you propose?
4. Was there any possibility of achieving total separation of church and state in the Middle Ages? Is it possible for today?
5. Prepare for a debate between Henry IV and Gregory VII. Which do you think has the best case? Why?

Notes for Chapter Ten

1. For a copy of this decree, see Barry, I, pp. 240-242.
2. This document can be found in Petry, pp. 236-237.
3. This is a chapter title in Walter Ullmann's *A Short History of the Papacy in the Middle Ages* (London: Methuen & Co., Ltd., 1972), pp. 201-226.
4. Examples of Innocent's views can be found in his letter *Sicut Universitatis Conditor* of November 3, 1198, printed in Barry, I, pp. 438-439; and in his 1213 agreement with King John of England, printed in Petry, pp. 319-321.

Chapter Eleven
THE EASTERN CHURCHES

During the centuries that the western papacy was achieving the height of its power and authority, the Christian churches in the East were battling the continuing aggression of Islam as well as suffering internal problems of their own. The loss of Mesopotamia, Syria, Palestine, Egypt, Libya, and North Africa could not help but be detrimental to the vitality of the Byzantine Empire. In 715 the Muslims even used Asia Minor as a staging area to march on Constantinople itself. In the resultant political chaos, the commander of the army garrison stationed in the capital rose to the throne in a successful coup, becoming Leo III (717-741). Leo was able to hurl back the Muslims and give the Empire another lease on life. He is also credited with saving western Christianity from direct Muslim attack and perhaps domination a decade and a half before the Moors met defeat at Tours.

Although Islam was a serious threat to the eastern churches, there were also beneficial aspects to the Muslim advance. The Monophysite areas had been explosive problems as far as the Empire was concerned. Their loss to Islam now meant that a major problem was eliminated from the Byzantine list of liabilities. What was left of the Empire was far more compact and homogeneous and, in fact, the Empire survived another seven centuries.

Another influence the Muslims might have had on the eastern churches at this time was to focus attention on the issue of icons (or ikons). These are paintings of Christ and the saints, displayed in churches or private homes.

Emperor Leo grew up in Isauria, an area in eastern Pisidia where Islam had made inroads, and the Muslims made numerous verbal attacks on "idol-worshiping" Christians, convinced that paintings were idols forbidden by the Second Commandment. Actually attacks on the use of these objects of religious devotion were not new. A Syrian bishop in the sixth century had denounced the veneration of representations of Christ, the Virgin, apostles, and other saints. Yet the icons became increasingly numerous. Christ and the saints, as well as scenes from the Bible, were made into pictures in mosaics, frescoes, and bronze or ivory carvings. For the simple minded, they were not only objects of reverence, but magic talismans. People prostrated before them, kissed them, burned candles before them, crowned them with flowers, sought miracles from them, adored them.

Church leaders and councils repeatedly warned that the images were not deities, only reminders; but the people usually did not make such distinctions.

Having grown up with this tension over icons, Leo, after first dealing with the Muslim's military threat, turned his attention to icons. In 726 he called a council of bishops and senators which demanded the complete removal of icons from the churches. It forbade representations of Christ and the Virgin, and ordered church murals covered with plaster. Many of the higher clergy supported the edict, but the bulk of the lower clergy and monks did not. Horrified and infuriated worshipers attacked soldiers trying to enforce the edict. When the Patriarch of Constantinople joined the revolt in 730 and sought to achieve greater independence of the church from the state, Leo deposed him. Pope Gregory II anathematized the iconoclasts (literally, "image breakers"), and this increased the tension between Rome and Constantinople.

The implications of the controversy go deeper than the icons themselves. To an extent the iconoclasts were puritans who resented the latent idolatry they saw in the use of the paintings. Because the iconoclastic emperors were from Isauria, the contest represented an Asiatic protest over the Greek sympathy for art. A further issue had to do with the theology of the Incarnation. Iconoclasts wanted no pictorial representation of deity. But those who wanted icons (they were called iconodules) protested that the iconoclasts denied the reality of the Incarnation. Icons of Christ were a reminder that Jesus came in human form; the iconodules identified the iconoclasts with the Monophysites.

Although Leo was the main force behind iconoclasm, he did not enforce the 726 edict harshly. At his death in 741, most of the churches retained their frescoes and mosaics unharmed. But his son, Constantine V (741-775), was much more strict. In 754 he called a council of more than 300 bishops, the Synod of Hieria, which condemned image worship as abominable and asserted that through such means Satan had reintroduced idolatry into the church. The synod recorded that the only proper representation of Christ was in the Eucharist. Severe persecution of iconodules followed. The Patriarch of Constantinople was tortured and beheaded in 767. Because monasticism was the backbone of the resistance, Constantine closed many monasteries and convents, confiscating their property, turned many of the buildings into secular uses, and sold others at court. Resistant monks were imprisoned and tortured, eyes or tongues were torn out, noses cut off. At Ephesus the imperial governor, with the approval of the Emperor, assembled the monks and nuns of the province and gave them the alternative to marry one another or be killed. The peak of the persecution was in the years 765-771.

Constantine's son Leo IV (775-780) reigned only briefly, followed by his ten year old son Constantine VI (780-797). Because of his youth, Constantine's mother Empress Irene served as regent until 790. Irene was an iconodule, as was true of most women. She ended the enforcement of the edicts, permitted the monks to return to their monasteries and pulpits, and called the Seventh Ecumenical Council which met at Nicaea in 787. At this council 350 bishops, including representatives from the Pope, restored the veneration — though not worship —

of sacred images as a legitimate expression of piety and faith.

Unfortunately, this did not end the controversy. Many iconoclasts in the East still held to their convictions, and the Emperors from 802 to 842 continued harassment, which turned to open persecution under Theophilus (829-842). Then another woman ruled as regent, Theodora (842-856). In 843 she allowed the reinstatement of icons, and the controversy was virtually over.

When the decisions of II Nicaea came west, the Franks had only a faulty Latin translation from the original Greek, and the distinction between "reverence" and "worship" was not fully made in the Latin. As a result Charlemagne denied the ecumenical character of the council, and in 794 he called his own council at Frankfurt, attended by western bishops and two legates of the Pope. They rejected the decrees of the Council of Nicaea on the ground that they were not ecumenical, although the council could not get Pope Adrian I to withdraw his recognition of them, or excommunicate the Byzantine Emperor. But the whole iconoclastic controversy did foster schism between East and West, particularly in the early years under Leo III and Constantine V, when the popes began to look to the Frankish kings for political protection from the Lombards rather than to the Byzantine Emperors. It was the eleventh century before northern Europe accepted the Second Council of Nicaea as the Seventh Ecumenical Council.

Another issue that had to do with increasing tension between East and West was the *filioque* clause. The original Nicene-Constantinopolitan creed of 381 referred to the Holy Spirit "who proceeds from the Father." By 589 a Spanish council at Toledo had inserted the phrase "and the son" (in Latin, *filioque*) after this clause in the Creed. By the end of the eighth century the western rulers turned it into a controversial issue, particularly Charlemagne, at his synod of Aachen in 809, which approved the *filioque* clause. The East condemned the West for blatantly *inserting* a clause into the creed without having it discussed and agreed upon by an ecumenical council, while the West blamed the East for *omitting* it.

If nothing else, these two issues showed how increasingly different the two halves of Christendom were becoming. The Seventh Ecumenical Council was the last council accepted by both East and West, although western Christians continued to recognize and hold such councils down to the present. Tensions between East and West continued to mount as each became defensive of his own position, and distrustful of the other's.

Just a decade or two after Theodora finally resolved the iconoclastic problem in the East, another issue came up, one that would strain east-west relationships to the breaking point. In 858 the Patriarch of Constantinople, Ignatius, was deposed because of some disagreements with the royal family. The newly elected Patriarch was Photius, but he was only a layman, who had to be rushed through all the various stages of consecration. Ignatius and his friends made a great outcry, and for several years there was discord in the East. In 861 a synod was called to resolve the situation. Two legates from Rome were also present, and they agreed with the synod's findings approving of the deposition of Ignatius.

But when the two legates returned to Rome, Pope Nicholas refused to accept their actions, stating they had acted without his authority. Claiming to be chief appeals judge in all of Christendom, he reserved the right to decide the issue for himself; in 863 he decided Ignatius ought to be reinstated, and he consequently deposed Photius. Both the Byzantine Emperor Michael III (856-867) and Photius refused to accept Nicholas' decision, much less his claim to authority. Photius was also alarmed at the spread of western influence in the Balkans, particularly the presence of Frankish[1] missionaries in Bulgaria and their insistence on using *filioque* in the creed. In 867 Photius wrote an encyclical letter to other eastern patriarchs denouncing the *filioque* and charging those who used it with heresy. He called a council at Constantinople later that year which excommunicated Pope Nicholas. This brought on the Photian Schism.

Both Nicholas and Emperor Michael died that same year. The new emperor, Basil (867-886), deposed Photius and put Ignatius back on the patriarchal throne. When Basil called a council in 869 to confirm the action, Pope Adrian II (867-872) sent three legates. This council of 869-870, the Fourth Council of Constantinople, is considered the Eighth Ecumenical Council by the west, although it was not accepted as such until the twelfth century. The East has never counted it as ecumenical. The Council reversed the decisions of Photius' council of 867; that is, it approved the reinstatement of Ignatius, condemned Photius as "a courtier and intruder," and it restored relationships with Rome.

The situation was further complicated by the death of Ignatius in 877, and the quite legitimate election of Photius as his replacement. Photius then called a council in 879-880 which reversed the condemnations of 869. The current Pope John VIII admonished Photius for his lack of humility but accepted his reinstatement. Early in the tenth century Photius was canonized as a saint by the Byzantine church. The Photian Schism represents the increasing tension between Rome and Constantinople. Some of it was caused by the particular issues, but much of it was political in nature. Each leader was maneuvering for prestige and authority over his rival. In general, the Pope was trying to claim authority over the East, but his claims were being consistently rejected.

Meanwhile the situation in Bulgaria continued the tension. King Boris converted to Christianity in 865, but he was not sure whether to align himself with the Romans or the Byzantines, even though it was missionaries from Photius who had baptized him, and many Greek missionaries came to spread the faith. But Boris wanted an independent church, and he was trying to see which side would give him the most. He asked for a separate patriarchate under Rome, but he could only get the promise of an archbishopric. Upset over the realization that Rome would continue to control the clerics in his country, Boris finally threw out the Latin mission and accepted a Byzantine archbishop. He allowed nominal Byzantine control while the Byzantines allowed the Bulgarians to use their Slavonic language in the services. This rivalry over Bulgaria was just one more irritant in the growing friction between Rome and Constantinople.

If Rome lost out in Bulgaria, it at least gained more in Moravia. Its king, Ratislav, secured missionaries from Constantinople in 863, two brothers, Cyril and Methodius. In spite of their Byzantine background, however, in

868 they journeyed to Rome and became loyal workers for the pope. Upon returning to Moravia, they brought that country into the column of Roman Christians. Thus although Bulgaria became Eastern Orthodox, Moravia (modern Czech Republic) became Roman Catholic. At the same time that the missions in Bulgaria and Moravia were taking place, changes were occurring in the great Slavic heartland that became Russia. In the ninth century market towns were just becoming established, the prelude for further political organization. Kiev became a major center, located on the Dnieper River and ruled by its Grand Duke. Vladimir (956-1015) became the Fifth Grand Duke of Kiev in 978, and in 988 he married Anne, the sister of the Byzantine Emperor Basil II (976-1025). Two years later Vladimir converted to Christianity, and he spent much of the rest of his life actively encouraging the evangelism and conversion of the native Russians. Eastern Orthodoxy soon dominated the entire country.

By the eleventh century the disputes between East and West had reached another crisis. Ever since the days of Justinian, the Byzantines had controlled southern Italy, even through all the disturbances of the Lombard troubles. But early in the eleventh century the Normans arrived and began to carve out a kingdom for themselves. The Byzantines resisted, but they were unable to mount enough of a military defense to hold off the warriors from the north. By mid-century the Byzantines still held on to Bari on the Adriatic coast, but there was even fear of losing this to a combined Norman-papal attack.

In addition to this problem over land possession, there were the personalities of the men involved. Michael

Cerularius was Patriarch of Constantinople (1043-1058). Although he had been destined for a political career, Cerularius became a monk on receiving the news of his brother's suicide in 1040. Within three years he became Patriarch. He was violently anti-Latin and deeply resented the papal claims to primacy. He felt the Patriarch was at least equal to the Pope, but he could get no recognition of this, certainly not in the West. Thus, when Norman forces claiming allegiance to Rome seized areas of southern Italy that had been directly under Byzantine jurisdiction since the seventh century, Cerularius was very upset.

In 1053 the Patriarch closed down various churches of the Latin Rite in Constantinople — churches used by westerners in town on business or on diplomatic missions. Latin monasteries were also closed down. In the process of closing down one church the soldiers trod upon the consecrated bread of the Eucharist, which according to the western understanding of transubstantiation meant the soldiers were actually tramping on the body of Christ. The situation was ripe for an explosion, but Cerularius added theological issues to the powder keg.

He began circulating some documents which accused the West of doctrinal error. It had probably been at the Patriarch's bidding that Leo of Ochrida, the Archbishop of Bulgaria, sent a letter to a bishop in southern Italy which was in reality an open letter to the West, actually addressed to the "bishops and priests of France," but intended for Pope Leo IX. In this document the Bulgarian cleric outlined four errors on the part of the western church: (1) The West used unleavened bread in the

Eucharist. The East considered this too similar to the Jewish Passover, and thus a continuation of Judaistic tendencies, and therefore in error. (2) The West encouraged fasting on Saturday. Since Saturday was of course the Jewish Sabbath, this too was considered a continuation of an inferior Jewish practice, and ought not to be done by modern Christians. (3) The West allowed the eating of the meat of strangled animals, in direct violation of the Jerusalem conference in Acts 15. It is ironic that the first two charges are made because the Roman Christians are too close to the Jewish practices, while the third charge is because the Romans do not adhere to an apostolic decision that was made to soften tender Jewish consciences. (4) The Western churches forbade the singing of the choral Alleluia during Lent. For the West the Lenten season was a time of mourning, not of rejoicing. The East considered that any custom that prohibited the expressing of joyous worship to God was an improper Christian requirement.

In addition to these four points brought up by the Bulgarian Leo, Cerularius also circulated another document, this one written by a monk in Constantinople. This condemned the West for (1) adding the *filioque* clause without proper authority from an ecumenical council and (2) prohibiting the marriage of priests. Eastern Orthodox churches allow the ordination of married priests (though no married priest can hope to become a bishop). Total celibacy seemed to the East to resemble Manichaean dualism, which the early church condemned. Actually, of course, none of these issues by themselves were particularly significant, although some of them, like the *filioque* clause, had been sources of friction for centuries.

Except for some theological implications of the *filioque* clause, there were no major theological issues involved; the differences were more cultural and traditional than significant. But it is obvious that Cerularius was spoiling for a fight. He apparently wanted to push the western religious leaders into rash behavior.

Early in the year 1054 Pope Leo IX sent delegates to Constantinople to try to resolve the sources of friction. When the three western delegates arrived, under the leadership of Cardinal Humbert, they were treated with insolence. During their stay, things got no better. Even though Leo died on April 19 of 1054, he may have already given approval to the procedures to be followed by the embassy or he may have given them blanket approval in advance. Whichever way it was, on July 16, 1054, the papal legates walked in on a mass in the prestigious church of St. Sophia in Constantinople and laid on the altar a sentence of anathema against Cerularius and all those who followed him. Four days later, on July 20, 1054, the patriarch excommunicated the Pope and his followers. This event is often referred to as the Great Schism, because it represents the final sundering of relationships between Eastern Orthodoxy and Roman Catholicism — the first major, long-lasting rupture in the universal Church.

As we have seen earlier in this chapter, as well as in earlier chapters, disagreement between East and West, disruption, and even mutual excommunications have occurred before. But previously, the division was always short, always reverting to the restoration of nominal fellowship and good will. From 1054 on the situation was reversed. There were short periods of officially restored relations, but the majority of the time the situation reverted to hostility, excommunication, and mutual recriminations. For all practical purposes, the split between East and West was now complete. The immediate issues, of course, were secondary. The schism came as a long development reaching back for centuries, mostly reflecting different cultural tendencies. Probably the most serious obstacle was the papal claim to primacy and authority, which the East never accepted. In spite of continuing modern negotiation between the Patriarch of Constantinople and the Pope in Rome, it is difficult to think the East ever will accept papal primacy. These pretensions to authority were more significant in the events of 1054 than the actual issues in dispute.

Bibliography for Chapter Eleven

Dvornik, Francis. *The Photian Schism: History and Legend.* Cambridge: University Press, 1948.
    A comprehensive assessment and study of the Photian situation.
Every, George. *The Byzantine Patriarchate, 451-1204.* London: Society for Promoting Christian Knowledge, 1947.
    An excellent survey of the period, stressing that perhaps too much has been made of the 1054 division.
Ware, Timothy. *The Orthodox Church.* Baltimore: Penguin Books, 1963.
    An excellent introduction to Orthodox thinking, the first half of the book is a survey of the history of the Eastern Church.

Questions and Projects for Chapter Eleven

1. Visit an Orthodox church and note the number of icons and the iconostasis. Ask the priest there to explain their use and function.
2. Interview a Roman Catholic priest and ask him about the use and placement of religious statues in the church. Ask him to clarify the distinction between veneration and worship of these statues. Do you think most people attending such churches observe such a distinction?
3. Do some research on modern attitudes of the Orthodox toward the Roman claim to primacy. Do you think there is a possibility of future union on this issue?
4. Write a paper detailing the contrast between Byzantine emperors' efforts on iconoclasm and western rulers' efforts on investiture. What does this say about church-state differences in East and West?
5. Why was it that women and monks tended to be iconodules during the iconoclastic controversy?
6. Write a paper in which you list and develop the factors that finally led to the Great Schism of 1054. Was this schism inevitable? If not, how could it have been avoided?

Notes for Chapter Eleven

1. The Byzantines designated all men from the West as "Franks."

Chapter Twelve
THE AGE OF THE CRUSADES

The Crusades were a major phenomenon of European history which captured the attention of Christians from the late 11th century through the next two hundred years. In the long run of history, the Crusades had little significance in the areas of the Holy Land where they were directed. Secondary results of the Crusades, however, were of immense significance in influencing later world history.

The causes of the Crusades were many. (1) The original unity of the Muslim movement had collapsed in the face of overwhelming geographical problems and personal ambition. An empire that stretched from the Atlantic to the Indus proved incapable of remaining under one ruler. Separate political caliphates in Baghdad,

Cairo, and Cordova (Spain) developed as leaders established power bases in these areas. All three areas remained Muslim, to be sure, but there was no concerted political or military unity among them. In addition, there were the divisions between Shi'ites and Sunnites which had occurred over early succession to the places of Mohammed. The Shi'ites contended that the caliphate was reserved for the family of Mohammed; the Sunnites observed no such restriction. It was only because of these political and religious divisions that the Crusades could have occurred. If Islam in the eleventh century still had the unity it had in the seventh century, it is difficult to believe that the Crusades could have had any success whatsoever.

(2) Pilgrimages had come to occupy an important place in the religious life of Christians. Apparently it was Helena, the mother of Constantine, who first made pilgrimage to the Holy Land. Ever since the fourth century, Christians had kept up a lively tourist trade with Palestine. But in the eleventh century, a new group of fanatic Muslims came into the Holy Land — the Seljuk Turks. Originally from Turkestan, north of Mesopotamia, the Seljuks had migrated into Muslim territory in the eighth and ninth centuries and accepted the new faith. In the early eleventh century the Seljuks began conquering neighboring Muslim areas, and in 1055 they captured Baghdad, where their leader was acclaimed the new sultan. More fanatical than the preceding Arabs, the Seljuks were so anti-Christian that they refused to allow the pilgrimage traffic, even if there were financial profits in it. They harassed, robbed, and even killed the Christian pilgrims. They kindled the ire of Christian nations in

Europe who demanded that Christians have access to the Holy Places.

(3) As a result of the Battle of Tours, the continuing presence of Muslims in Spain, and Islamic conquest in Sicily, Christians in various European countries had been inculcated to hate the Muslims. Denied access to the Holy Land, such Christians were ready to declare war against the Muslim "infidels."

(4) The Cluniac movement had fostered a deep religious devotion, which now manifested itself in the desire to visit the shrines in the places where Jesus walked the face of the earth.

(5) Finally there was the simple recognition on the part of the Byzantines that they were getting into desperate straits because of the surging Seljuk advance. Perhaps no one of these reasons would have been sufficient impetus by itself; taken collectively, however, they provided the thrust that led to the Crusades.

In the year 1071 the Seljuks met the Byzantine army and defeated it at the Battle of Manzikert, thus gaining control over central Asia Minor. In 1085 they took Antioch, and within a few years they had spread so deeply into Asia Minor that even Nicaea fell into their hands. The Byzantines sent an urgent request to the West for military assistance after Manzikert, but Gregory VII had so many problems of his own at the time that nothing resulted. After the fall of Nicaea, however, Byzantine Emperor Alexius I (1081-1118) sent another appeal, to Pope Urban II (1088-1099).

Urban was sympathetic to the plea of Alexius, even though the Great Schism had occurred only a few decades before. But Urban also had his problems. At the

time, he was not even able to hold Rome. The imperial-
ists under the sponsorship of Henry IV had elected an
antipope, and Urban was in exile. But Urban saw in the
request for military assistance a chance to win points for
himself, get a good thing started, and perhaps even gain
enough prestige to return to Rome. At a local council in
Piacenza in March of 1095 he supported the idea of
sending help to the East, but he asked for a more widely
attended assembly to meet in Clermont in southern
France that November.

Urban toured northern Italy and southern France in
the months before the council. Alexius wanted western
mercenaries to help the Byzantine armies win back central Asia Minor, but he also added the idea of reclaiming
Jerusalem. It was this latter idea that Urban emphasized
to get more support. On November 27, 1095, Urban
preached a holy crusade before the Council of Clermont.
He promised that all who went on this expedition would
receive a plenary remission of all sins. Citizens who
went were to be exempted of taxes, prisoners were to be
freed, and those under sentence of death could have it
commuted to service in Palestine. The church promised
protection to the lands and families of those who left on
Crusade, and the combination appeal of adventure, war,
travel, and absolution was enough to lead thousands to
volunteer. They were marked with a red cross — *cru-
sada*, thus crusade. The idea became so popular that
Urban rose to heights of new prestige. On the strength of
the popular support, Urban was able to re-enter Rome in
1097, driving out the antipope. Urban in this way
achieved his own personal goal.

With regard to the crusades, Urban had appointed the

month of August, 1096, as the time for departure, but the impatient peasants were not willing to wait. The armed knights would take months to get ready: amassing the military supplies, filling out recruitments, arranging for passage, readying their arms and equipment. But the peasants needed no such preparation. They simply left for the Holy Land. There were about five different aggregations of them, under the general control of nobody. One group decided that it was best to clean out the infidels at home before setting out for Palestine, so they went down the Rhine River Valley, massacred thousands of Jews, and disbanded. Another got into Hungary, but without any commissary or logistics preparations, they had neither food nor the money to procure it. They began looting along the way, and the local authorities slaughtered the whole lot of them.

Another group, numbering about 12,000, but only about eight knights, was led by two monks, Peter the Hermit and Walter the Penniless. Without an adequate organization or preparation, they also were forced to steal, pillage crops, and loot on their way across Europe, bound for Constantinople. Raping the land, they also raped women along the way. When they arrived in Constantinople in the summer of 1096, it was not exactly what Alexius had had in mind when he requested mercenaries from the West. These men were not trained soldiers, and they had no intention of enlisting in the Byzantine army. Alexius wanted them out of Constantinople before they caused riots there, so he quickly ferried them across the Bosporus. He advised them to wait for better reinforcements, but the peasants had come to march to the Holy Land, and march they did.

They advanced on Nicaea, only to have a strong detachment of Turkish archers come out and annihilate virtually the whole group. Only a handful returned to Constantinople.

Meanwhile the knights were also making their preparations. Philip I of France, William II of England, and Henry IV of Germany, the most significant kings of Europe, were all under excommunication at the time. This eliminated them from participation in the crusade, but many dukes and counts enlisted, most of them French (or Norman in Italy). Unfortunately, there was no one overall commander. Each main leader had his own body of troops who were loyal to him alone, and this prevented full cooperation at important points in the expedition. The various contingents proceeded to Constantinople, arriving in 1097. Some of them even considered the possibility of seizing the city itself.

Again, this uncoordinated body of troops was not what Alexius had in mind. These soldiers were no more interested in enlisting in the Byzantine army than the peasants had been the previous year. Alexius was fearful of the glint in the eye of many of these Franks, so he hurriedly ferried them across the Bosporus after the knights had taken a feudal oath to him. A few Byzantines went along as liaison. The appearance of this body of men before Nicaea was rather different from that of the peasants a year earlier. On pledge that their lives would be spared, the Muslim garrison surrendered on June 19, 1097, and the Byzantines immediately raised the Emperor's flag. This greatly surprised the Crusaders. They thought *they* had conquered the city, and that the Byzantines were now using religious devotion to hide their design for imperial conquest. As a result, there was bad feeling between the Byzantines and the Crusaders throughout the history of these ventures.

The Crusaders then marched on Antioch. Once they got into the vicinity of Tarsus, however, several of the leaders decided to carve out kingdoms for themselves, the first of which was Edessa. The crusading band was delayed while some contingents were adventuring. They finally got to Antioch and were victorious after a brutal, eight-month siege. Within a few days of their victory, however, a large Muslim army appeared, and besieged *them*. They were cut off from fresh food and water, and hopes were dim until someone discovered (or *claimed* to discover) the spear that had pierced Jesus' side, and three horsemen were planted in the hills to simulate angelic knights. The combination of the two ruses inspired the resistance that led to victory over the Muslim siege. Thus Antioch became another independent principality and joined the new Crusader states in the East.

Finally, on June 7, 1099, the Crusaders stood before Jerusalem. The two years' campaign had diminished their number from 30,000 to 12,000. Egyptian Fatimids had expelled the Turks the previous year, and the city was held by only 1,000 soldiers. They held out for forty days, when finally one contingent of Crusaders from Lorraine went over the walls on July 15. According to some sources, the blood ran ankle deep in the streets, all the defenders were killed plus the 70,000 Muslim inhabitants of the city, and the Jews were herded together in the synagogue and burned. Thus was Jerusalem restored to the hands of western Christians.

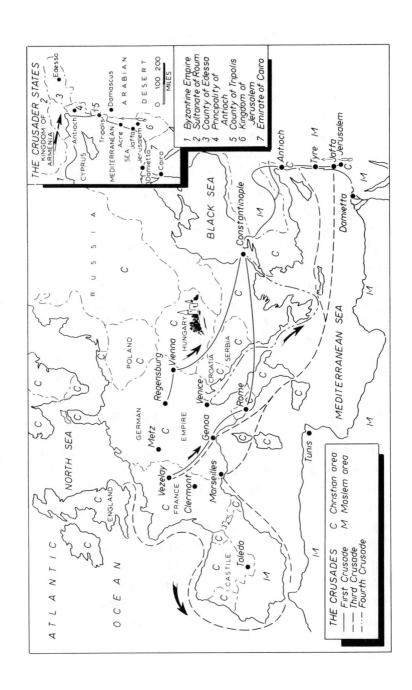

THE CRUSADER STATES

KINGDOM OF
ARMENIA

1 Byzantine Empire
2 Sultanate of Roum
3 County of Edessa
4 Principality of
   Antioch
5 County of Tripolis
6 Kingdom of
   Jerusalem
7 Emirate of Cairo

Edessa

Antioch
Tripolis   Damascus
         ARABIAN
Acre
Jaffa   DESERT
Jerusalem
CYPRUS
MEDITERRANEAN
SEA
Damietta
Cairo

0 100 200
MILES

ATLANTIC

OCEAN

NORTH SEA

ENGLAND

RUSSIA

POLAND

GERMAN
Metz   EMPIRE
Regensburg
Vezelay   Vienna
Clermont   HUNGARY
FRANCE   Venice
Genoa   CROATIA
Marseilles   SERBIA
Rome

BLACK SEA

Constantinople

MEDITERRANEAN SEA

Antioch
Tyre   M
Jaffa   Jerusalem
Damietta

Toledo
CASTILE

Tunis

THE CRUSADES   C Christian area
                M Moslem area
——— First Crusade
— — Third Crusade
·—·—· Fourth Crusade

Godfrey of Bouillon was chosen as the ruler of Jerusalem, but when he died the next year his brother Baldwin became the first King of Jerusalem (1100-1118). There were four independent states erected in Palestine — Jerusalem, Antioch, Edessa, and Tripolis — plus coastal cities under the control of Genoa, Pisa, and Venice, rewards for their naval support. Many of the Crusaders, their goal achieved, now left for home, leaving the Latin states in a precarious situation surrounded by aroused Muslims. Meanwhile, on the north the Byzantines watched for an opportunity to pick up more pieces from the Latins and reconstitute their Empire.

Muslims from Baghdad recaptured Edessa in 1144, and the news of this in Europe led to the Second Crusade. St. Bernard of Clairvaux took the responsibility of proclaiming this particular crusade, and he inspired Conrad III of Germany and Louis VII of France into action in 1147. In Asia Minor there were numerous skirmishes and Muslim ambushes (which the Crusaders were convinced included Byzantine plotters), and the two rulers got to Jerusalem in 1148 with only ten per cent of their initial army. They besieged Damascus, but could not take it. They were divided among themselves by jealousies and Muslim bribes among some of the lesser nobles. The crusade collapsed in disappointment, Louis staying behind an additional year to visit the holy places in Palestine.

Meanwhile, Saladin (1138-1193) united Egypt and Syria under one rule in 1175, in the forty-year period of truce which followed the collapse of the Second Crusade. But when in 1183 a minor noble beyond the Jordan tried to destroy Medina and intended to destroy Mecca,

Saladin was infuriated by the Frank's insolence. Previously he was content with minor raids, but now he threw himself into a vigorous war with the Latins — particularly when his sister was captured in a caravan in 1186. The next year he took up position near the Horns of Hattin, near Tiberias west of the Sea of Galilee. He controlled all the wells, and when the Latins marched over the plains, dusty and ravaged with thirst, he started a brush fire which drove smoke into their ranks. His warriors charged, cut down the footmen, and wiped out the cavalry. All members of the military orders were slain, and all Palestine except Jerusalem was in his hands. He marched to that city and demanded its peaceful surrender. When Jerusalem refused, he conquered it after a twelve-day siege. The number of captured Christians was about 60,000 but nearly all were released — rather in contrast to the Christian example some ninety years earlier.

The loss of Jerusalem in 1187 was another severe blow to Christian Europe. It responded with the Third Crusade, the Kings' Crusade. Frederick Barbarossa, Emperor (1152-1190), and a veteran of the Second Crusade, could not wait for the forces of Philip II of France (1180-1223) or Richard the Lion-Hearted of England (1189-1199). He set out immediately, sixty-seven years old. Marching through Asia Minor, his troops were subject to Muslim raids and death by starvation. Frederick himself drowned in the little river of Salef in Cilicia in 1190. Only a handful of his army ever reached Palestine.

In 1190 Philip and Richard set out, Richard demanding that Philip accompany him to prevent French attack on English possessions in his absence. After dallying in

Sicily and taking Cyprus from the Byzantines, Richard reached Acre, where the Christians had been besieging the city for nineteen months. Philip had preceded him there, but after the capture of the city, Philip, ill with fever, returned home, leaving Richard in charge. Richard maneuvered around Palestine for another year (1191-1192), but he was unable to get more than an additional coastal city or two, Saladin fighting him to a standstill. Finally, he signed a peace agreement with Saladin accepting the status quo, with each side able to enter peacefully the other's territory. By the terms of this truce, Christian pilgrims would be able to enter Jerusalem, which remained in Muslim hands. Yet Europe grieved over the failure to recapture the Holy City.

When Pope Innocent came to the papal throne in 1198, he strongly preached another crusade, but the monarchs of Europe were not interested. The kings of France and of England were bitterly fighting each other, and Germany was up for grabs between the Hohen-staufen dynasty and its enemies. Within a few years, however, a large number of knights had been recruited, but they suffered from a lack of cash which the kings could have supplied. Innocent and other preachers were the main force behind the crusade, and Innocent's idea was to send the force straight across the Mediterranean to Egypt, establish a base there which could provide food for the army, and then march up to Palestine.

Venetian merchants agreed to provide the ships for this, but the price for their transport and supply would be 85,000 marks plus half the spoils of conquest. At the same time, however, the Venetians also made a secret deal with Egypt to send the Crusaders elsewhere. In the summer of 1202 the crusading host gathered at Venice, but fell short of the required transportation money by 34,000 marks. The Venetians agreed to overlook the shortage if the Crusaders did them a favor. The Christian city of Zara down the Adriatic coast was cutting into their trade, and the Venetians wanted it destroyed. Innocent denounced the proposal, but the warriors went anyway and wiped out the Christian city in five days, dividing the spoils.

Meanwhile an invitation arrived from Constantinople. Alexius, the son of the deposed Emperor Isaac II (1185-1195), came to Venice in 1202 to request help to get the throne back. The Venetians and Crusaders agreed, on the condition that they be paid 200,000 marks, the Byzantines to equip an army of 10,000 men for service in Palestine, and the Orthodox Church to submit to the Pope. In spite of this last attraction, Innocent forbade the expedition, but it went anyway, 480 vessels strong.

The Latins arrived off Constantinople in the summer of 1203, and with little opposition they placed Alexius on the throne. But when the Greeks learned the price of the bargain, they were bitter and refused to honor Alexius' agreement. One incident soon led to another, and by the following spring the Latins declared war on the Byzantines, besieged Constantinople for a month, and captured it. What they then did to Constantinople was equivalent to what any group of barbarians had ever done to Rome. The soldiers appropriated the palaces of the nobility; they took from shops, churches, and private homes whatever took their fancy. Maidens, matrons, and nuns were raped. Gold, silver, and jewels accumulated over the previous thousand years were looted, and many sacred relics appeared in Europe over the next few centuries. Four bronze horses were shipped to St. Mark's Piazza in Venice, where they remain. Fires broke out in the city, destroying churches and libraries. A number of ancient manuscripts were irreplaceably lost. The Latins chose a new King of Constantinople, parceled out lands in feudal style, and set up a Latin Kingdom which lasted for fifty-seven years. Most historians agree that this blow to the fortunes of Constantinople was so severe that the Empire was never as strong again, and this led to the final fall before the Turks two centuries later. This was the infamous Fourth Crusade, and it never got close to the Holy Land.

Another tragedy shortly thereafter was the Children's Crusade. In the year 1212 a young boy in France named Stephen received the idea that the purity of children could succeed where the rapaciousness of their parents had failed. He preached a crusade in France, recruiting thousands of young children, the average age of which was twelve, to march to Jerusalem. They believed that their faith would open up the Mediterranean and they could walk on dry seabed to the Holy Land. Getting to Marseilles, they found that the sea did not open, but some merchants arranged transportation for them. Instead of taking them to Jerusalem, however, the merchants took them to Tunis where the children were sold into Muslim slavery. A similar group marched from Germany to Genoa, although more of them returned home than from the fateful French expedition. Historians estimate that about 100,000 children may have been involved, and about one-third of them never returned.

Most parents tried to forestall the departure of their children, and it may be that the later story of the Pied Piper of Hamelin had its origin in the departure of these children.

At the Fourth Lateran Council of 1215 another crusade was preached, and it got under way in 1217, with mostly German and Hungarian contingents under King Andrew of Hungary. This one was launched against Egypt, directed at Damietta, at the easternmost mouth of the Nile. They captured the city after a year's siege, from 1217 to 1218, but then spent another three years futilely trying to enlarge their base of operations. The Egyptian commanders were able to block any further move, and finally in 1221 the Crusaders abandoned Damietta. The Fifth Crusade had no permanent accomplishment, and it was the last time that the Church directly sponsored any more crusading activity against the Muslims.

The Sixth Crusade revolved around the Emperor Frederick II. In 1227 he had married Isabella, the fourteen-year-old daughter of the titled (but exiled) King of Jerusalem, and he claimed the Jerusalem throne. He sailed for Jerusalem, but became sick and returned. Pope Gregory IX (1227-1241) excommunicated him for this, but Frederick, undaunted, sailed again, in spite of the prohibiting excommunication. In Palestine Frederick signed an agreement with the Muslim rulers that placed the coast of Palestine, plus Bethlehem, Nazareth, and Jerusalem except for the temple area into Christian hands. Pope Gregory refused to ratify this treaty. In March of 1229 Frederick crowned himself King of Jerusalem. In 1244, however, a different group of Turks came into the area and captured Jerusalem again.

This same year King Louis IX of France (1226-1270) took up the cross and organized the Seventh Crusade. The Crusaders sailed for Egypt, reaching Damietta in June of 1249. They quickly captured the city, but when pressing upriver, they were surrounded by Muslims, defeated in one battle, and harassed along the line of retreat. Halfway back to Damietta, and fainting with dysentery, on April 6, 1250, Louis surrendered his army of 10,000 to the Egyptians. He ransomed himself for a large sum of money, spent four years visiting the holy places in Palestine, and returned to France in 1254. The Seventh Crusade accomplished nothing.

Shortly after his departure from Palestine, the Christian nobility and the Italian maritime cities with interest in Palestine began to fight among themselves, exhausting most of the Christian strength. Thus the new ruler in Egypt was able to move up the coast, taking Caesarea in 1265, and Antioch in 1268. Antioch had been in Christian hands since 1098, and its fall was an omen of doom. Captured Christians were either slaughtered or enslaved, and the city was so devastated that it never recovered.

The fall of Antioch made a great impression on Europe. Louis took up the cross again in 1267 at the age of 53. His sons followed his example, but most of the French nobility refused. Louis decided to attack Tunisia, convert its ruler, and march upon Egypt from the west. He hardly touched Tunisian soil when he died, with the word "Jerusalem" upon his lips. The rest of the army concluded a truce with the Sultan and returned home.

This eighth crusade was to include Prince Edward of England, but he arrived too late for the attack on

Tunisia. So he sailed on to Acre and in 1271 led an attack from there. But in 1272 his father died, leaving him King of England, and he soon departed Palestine. Acre was the strongest outpost of the Christian regime in the Holy Land, with 40 churches, more than 20,000 inhabitants and a double line of walls. But in 1291 it fell after a 43-day siege to a Muslim army with over 100 siege machines. The Christians from the surrounding countryside had swelled its numbers to 60,000. The Muslims slaughtered many of these, including the Dominicans who were cut down singing chants in their chapel. This was the virtual end of Christian presence in Palestine. After the fall of Acre, the other coastal cities also fell — Tyre, Sidon, and Beirut. The Muslims devastated the entire coast to dissuade the return of the Crusaders. The title of King of Jerusalem hung around for a while, claimed by secondary rulers of Europe, but the days of the Latin Kingdoms in Jerusalem had ended. The Crusades, with their goal of capturing the Holy Land, were over.

The results of the Crusades are somewhat difficult to decipher. The First Crusade and its victory gave added strength to the papacy; the later crusades and their failures reduced papal prestige. The fact of coming to grips with Muslims and realizing they were human was a weakening effect on the Christian faith. By the time the Crusades were over, some thinkers in Europe were asking tentative questions about the proposed universality of Christianity. Some of the upper classes lost their dogmatic devotion to Catholicism.

A second result of the Crusades was the creation of the Military Orders. These were basically armed knights who assumed monastic vows and devoted themselves to Christian militarism. The Templars were founded in Jerusalem in 1118, devoted to protect pilgrims on the roads to Jerusalem. The red cross of their mantles became the symbol of the modern Red Cross. The Hospitallers, or the Knights of the Hospital of St. John in Jerusalem, dated from a hospital which merchants from Amalfi had organized in Jerusalem in 1023. It was organized in the early twelfth century to protect pilgrims, and it became a military order. When the Holy Land was lost, Hospitallers resettled in Rhodes, and later in Malta. A third order was the Teutonic Knights, founded at the siege of Acre in 1190 by German knights who had accompanied Frederick Barbarossa. At the fall of Acre they removed to Prussia which they held for some time. Because of numerous bequests, the Templars became strong in various European countries, particularly France, where Philip IV (1285-1314) saw them as a threat to his own throne and finally had them dissolved in the early fourteenth century.

The Crusades also played a significant part in the development of the indulgence system. Indulgence was the remission of temporal punishment for sin: not guilt, which was forgiven by God, but the temporal punishment, which if not paid for in this life, would be satisfied in purgatory. Earlier visits to the tombs of the apostles in Rome had received some allowance of penance, but no complete remission was granted until Urban's pledge at Clermont. By 1198, in the aftermath of the failure of the Third Crusade, Pope Innocent was allowing the same plenary indulgence to any man who paid and equipped another man to go on crusade. Early in the next century the popes elevated their Italian campaigns against the Hohenstaufens to the status of crusades and also granted indulgences for them. Innocent's crusade against the Albigensians in southern France carried the same provisions. By the thirteenth century indulgences were being offered in a much wider variety of ways than was originally intended. Continually using this offering as a leverage for the welfare of the church led to its debasement. Eventually indulgences were granted for rather minor things such as contributing a few coins to the papal coffers. This development led directly to Martin Luther and the church door at Wittenberg.

A further result of the Crusades was to weaken the feudal structure of Europe. The spirit of military adventure in the Holy Land diverted the warlike activities of many nobles, thus allowing the kings to increase their power without constant rebellion. The knights who traveled on Crusade experienced a wider sphere of the world and lost their parochial narrowness. All of this helped to expand national consciousness in Europe and diminish the feudal infighting that marked the tenth and eleventh centuries. Feudalism was dying and nationalism was growing. Nationalistic struggles in the fourteenth century profited from this development.

One final result of the Crusades was its influence on the awareness of world geography and world trade. For centuries Muslim merchants had acted as middlemen in the silk and spice trade with the Far East. Europe's direct involvement in the Crusades brought more and more people in direct contact with this trade, and it whetted the appetites of the nobility and royalty of Europe. The maritime cities of Italy not only got involved in the coastal cities of Palestine for the profitable business of supplying the Latin warriors; they also wanted to tap the eastern trade. Many of their agreements with the crusaders included a monopoly for commercial privileges. Even after the loss of the crusader states, these Italian maritime cities — Venice, Genoa, Pisa, and others — continued to take over much of the silk and spice trade that previously had gone to Constantinople. Now there was more of a European market for such luxury goods, and lush profits were made. This became a major factor in the creation of the artistic flowering of the Renaissance. Artists can survive only where there are people with sufficient leisure time and wealth to enjoy the arts. The capital to allow such leisure and artistic indulgence could be made only in commerce. Thus it was the crusades that created the economic conditions for the flowering of the Renaissance, although this did not come until almost two centuries after the crusades ended.

The crusades in the short run accomplished little. The military states built up by the Crusaders evaporated within a century or two. Instead of strengthening the Byzantine Empire as Alexius I originally wanted, the Crusades (particularly the Fourth) distinctly weakened it, contributing to its fall in 1453. But if the military results of the crusades were inconsequential, the economic and cultural results were important. Europe became aware of a different culture, and many Europeans came to respect that culture. The economic results of the crusading activity drastically altered the life style of Europe.

Bibliography for Chapter Twelve

Gray, George Zabriskie. *The Children's Crusade: A History.* New York: William Morrow & Company, Inc., 1972.

A detailed treatment of this important but tragic phenomenon.

Mayer, Hans Eberhard. *The Crusades.* New York: Oxford University Press, 1972.

A one-volume treatment that does a thorough job.

Runciman, Steven. *A History of the Crusades.* 3 vols. Cambridge: Cambridge University Press, 1952-1954.

A thorough account by an accepted scholar, considered the finest work on the subject.

Villehardouin & De Joinville. *Memoirs of the Crusades.* Trans. by Frank T. Marzial. New York: E.P. Dutton & Co., Inc., 1958.

Eyewitness accounts by two French crusaders who took part, respectively, in the Fourth and Seventh Crusades.

Questions and Projects for Chapter Twelve

1. Do additional research on the Crusades and then construct a chart with the Crusades listed down the left-hand side of the page. Across the top of the page put: where took place, leaders, date, numbers involved, objectives, and accomplishments. Fill in the appropriate information in each column for each crusade.
2. Why was the First Crusade so much more successful than the others?

3. Prepare for a debate on the proposition: "The Crusades were beneficial to Christian Europe." Be able to argue for either side.
4. What do you think Jesus would have said to the whole idea of the Crusades? What about Paul? What about Constantine or Charlemagne?
5. The Crusades brought about greatly increased contact between Muslims and Christians. Do you think this was a good thing? Why or why not?

Chapter Thirteen
RENEWED MONASTIC VIGOR

Throughout the history of monasticism, a definite cycle takes place: desiring to lead lives of purity and holiness, men withdraw from the world; having withdrawn, often they attain a great reputation for holiness; this reputation attracts the attention of followers and the curious who throng to become disciples, while others desire to aid the endeavor by granting lands and other forms of wealth; suffused by large numbers of monks and much income-producing property, the monastery grows lax, and ultimately corrupt; after some time, a new leader emerges who sees the need for reform, and the entire cycle is repeated.

The story of monasticism is filled with numerous instances of this phenomenon. The major figures in western monasticism in the sixth and seventh centuries were all sincere leaders in the true spirit of monasticism. Benedict had arranged the Rule and charted the course for the future of the institution in the West. Cassiodorus, while remaining true to the monastic call, also added the element of book copying which ultimately included an emphasis on book learning. Augustine of Canterbury, while leading the missionary successes in England, established a monastery at Canterbury, which was the first Benedictine monastery outside of Italy. Benedictine monasticism was sweeping the field in the seventh century. When Boniface went to central Europe in the eighth century, he also planted the monastic form then dominant in England — Benedictine monasticism.

Boniface worked among the Franks from 741 to 751 and saved them from decline. He called synods and supervised the work of the church there, bringing reform not only to the bishops and parish priests, but also upgrading the quality of the monasteries in the country.

But even the work of Boniface was unable to stop the cycle. Within half a century after his death in 754, monasticism in Charlemagne's empire needed reform. The leader of the movement was Benedict of Aniane (750-821). He became a monk near Dijon in 773, and in 779 he founded a monastery on his own property in Languedoc. He revised the Benedictine Rule, and in his efforts he was aided by the active support of Charlemagne. Emperor Louis also gave strong support to his reforms, which led to their adoption at the national Synod of Aachen in 817. Louis made Benedict his advisor on monastic affairs.

In the ninth century, troubles hit the churches in

England. Danish Viking attacks plundered and destroyed numerous monasteries, and these depredations also wiped out many bishoprics. In the tenth century, as the Saxon kings began to push the Danes back north and to stabilize the frontier of the Danelaw (a region of eastern and northern England that was occupied by the Danes and administered under their laws), monastic revival also began to grow in the south and southeast. The key figure in this movement was Dunstan (909-988). Born in Wessex and nephew of a bishop, he was also related to the royal house. Dunstan attended the abbey school at Glastonbury, but he also spent time periodically at the royal court. Unpopular there because he was bookish and dull, his contacts were still sufficiently good to make him Abbot of Glastonbury in 943. Under the patronage of King Edmund I (940-946), Dunstan ruled this monastery for thirteen years, and gradually he was able to lead the clerics there from a semi-monastic, semi-secular form to the full Benedictine norm. Under him the monastery became famous for its learning. Political changes forced him out of the country in 956, and he made his way to Flanders where he made contact with a number of monasteries already influenced by the Cluniac reform movement.

Because of a political turn-around in England in 959, Dunstan returned and was made Bishop of London, then Archbishop of Canterbury in 960 until his death. From this position he had no continuing effect on monastic life, though he did play a commanding role in church-state affairs. His earlier reforms at Glastonbury paved the way for monastic reform in England. He was not aggressive or violent in these changes, but in a wise and patient way he showed what the monastic life could be. This ideal soon spread through England.

A contemporary worker of Dunstan's was Aethelwold. He was from Wessex as was Dunstan, and the two were ordained priest on the same day. He became one of Dunstan's monks at Glastonbury, but he was not satisfied with the moderate monasticism which Dunstan initiated. Through the king, he became the Abbot of Abingdon. From there Aethelwold sent monks to France to determine what the original Benedictine Rule was; their reports on their return led to the restoration of the original discipline at Abingdon. This monastery was soon famous as a center of monastic revival, and in 963 Aethelwold was made Bishop of Winchester. He expelled the secular canons[1] and installed monks in the cathedral. Not only did Aethelwold run both Winchester and Abingdon, but he also purchased ruined monasteries despoiled by the Danes at Peterborough and Ely and restored them.

A third individual working for the same goals was Oswald (?-992). He had come up through a lax monastery in Winchester, but he spent the years 954-960 studying monastic life in Europe. He became Bishop of Worcester in 960, bringing monks from the Continent to aid in the reform of monasteries in the diocese. In addition, Oswald founded several others, and refounded still others which had been despoiled by the Vikings. In 972 Oswald became Archbishop of York, using that position to further the cause of monastic reform.

With several men now working in the same cause, they felt some need for general direction for the movement. They influenced King Edgar (959-975) to call a national synod at Winchester in 970 in order to establish general rules for all monasteries. There were now about forty new or refounded houses, mostly in southern England. The new code which came out of this meeting was the *Regularis Concordia*, which became the general monastic code for all England. It is the original Benedictine Rule, as modified by Benedict of Ariane and the Cluny reformers. Yet the Cluny arrangement of having all houses under one abbot was not followed. As a result all English monasteries continued to be independent. One significant development out of this English monastic revival was the English tradition of having monastic chapters in the cathedrals, with a monk as bishop. In the decades prior to the Norman conquest, most bishops in England were monks.

We have already alluded to the Cluniac movement. Little more need be said, except merely to mention that this movement was spreading rapidly all over Europe. Its most significant characteristic was that all monastic houses in the Cluniac system were under the direction of the single mother house — one abbot with individual priors in the individual houses. More and more monasteries in Europe now came under the ownership of some famous abbey, partly to escape the corrupt influence of a lay proprietor and partly to insure strict observance of the monastic rules. Not always were these houses added under Cluny. It could just as well be a different monastery that had a good reputation. Some monasteries had hundreds of dependent priories. Cluny was begun in 910; by 942 there were 17 houses in the system; 37 in 994, 69 in 1048, over 300 by 1109. These were all full monasteries. In addition there were numerous smaller "cells" affiliated with the larger units. By 1100 there were about 200 of these cells.

Reform tends to breed reform. The Cluniac reform movement had been successful indeed. By the end of the eleventh century, it had largely achieved its twin goals of removing simony and clerical fornication from the church. The process of eliminating laymen from making church appointments was also gaining ground, to be finalized in the Concordats of London and Worms early in the twelfth century. The Cluniac Reform became the Gregorian Reform, and under papal auspices, it too achieved success by 1122. But the Cluniac reform movement bred reform concern in other places as well, with specific thrusts beyond the rather narrowly defined twin concerns of the original Cluniac focus. Some of this we have already seen in England.

Another aspect of this new reform was the development of a whole series of new monastic orders that developed from the late eleventh to the early thirteenth centuries. Before the year 1098 virtually all monastic establishments in Europe were of the Benedictine order. The only major exception was the Celtics. But the Viking raids on England, Scotland and Ireland had destroyed the Celtic monasteries. After the Viking attacks had subsided, all monasteries that were rebuilt were built along the lines of Benedictine, or Roman monasticism. However, by the eleventh century, many Benedictine monasteries had become lax, corrupt, and some of them quite immoral. Some of the reform came not only from within the Benedictine establishment, but also from new rival orders.

St. Bruno of Cologne (1032-1101) began a new order

in 1084. Having declined an archbishopric at Rheims, he found a desolate spot in the Alps in southeastern France near the town of Grand Chartreuse. Many reformers wanted out-of-the-way locations to prevent the acclaim that preceded fame, wealth, decline, and fall. In his chosen location Bruno established a new monastery and began a new order which took its name from that of the area. The Latin form of the name Chartreuse provided the name Carthusians. Not a part of the Benedictine Order, the Carthusian monks had a much more isolated life even within the monastery. Each monk lived in a separate cell, ate only bread and milk, and practiced almost perpetual silence — broken only by worship services in common three times a week. On Sundays and holy days the monks could talk and enjoy a common meal. The Carthusians became the most austere of the monastic orders. The order never became extremely popular, but Charter houses (as they were commonly known in England) appeared all over Europe.

Much more popular would be the movement begun by Robert de Molesme (1027-1111). A member of a noble family in Champagne, he entered a monastery at age fifteen. Shortly after 1060 he became abbot of a Benedictine monastery in Burgundy, but he failed to reform its greatly relaxed discipline. In 1075 some hermits living in a forest asked to be placed under his direction, and with the approval of the Pope he began a monastery for them at Molesme in Burgundy. The saintly life of this abbot and his monks caused the house to flourish, but increasing wealth and the influx of new members lacking total commitment to reform brought division to the community.

In 1098 Robert and several of his monks left Molesme and founded the monastery of Citeaux, near Dijon, in Burgundy.[2] The Latin name for the French town was *Cistercium*, and this provided the name for the new order, the Cistercians. Cistercians were popularly known as the White Monks, from the color of their habit. The Cistercians demanded a strict observance of the Benedictine Rule, although the new order was not a part of the Benedictine Order. All flesh food was forbidden to the monks, learning was discouraged, and all clothing, buildings, and vessels used in worship were to be plain. The Cistercian life was to be one of secluded communal intercession and adoration. Houses were to be erected only in remote situations. All physically able monks were to apply themselves to manual labor to make the monastery independent of the outside world. Because of this emphasis on manual labor, the Cistercians outshone all other orders in taking over wild, desolate places and making them fertile areas. By draining marshes and clearing forests, they helped to colonize eastern Germany and repopulate northern England. The Cistercians became important agricultural pioneers, particularly playing a notable part in the development of English sheep farming.

The little band grew slowly at first. After eighteen months, the band of monks left at Molesme asked Robert to come back, and he did so. Molesme became the center of a renewed and reformed Benedictine observance. Meanwhile, the new monastery at Citeaux struggled along with only a couple of dozen members. But it had achieved a reputation for strictness and seriousness in observing the monastic regime. Thus it attracted the attention of a young nobleman of Dijon, Bernard (1090-1153). When he decided to enter a monastery in 1113, he decided upon Citeaux. He did not come alone, however. He convinced his brothers and other friends and relatives to accompany him, and thirty men knocked on Citeaux' gates at the same time — more than doubling its size. Later Bernard persuaded his own mother, father and sister into monasteries. Two years after his entrance, the abbot asked him to spearhead a new monastery and choose the location. He selected a wooded area called Bright Valley, *Clara vallis*, or Clairvaux. Here he spent the rest of his life, known to history as Bernard of Clairvaux. By the time of his death there were 700 monks at Clairvaux, and a total of 343 monasteries in the new Order. From his cell Bernard launched the Second Crusade by his impassioned preaching on behalf of the Holy Land. He also gave the advice that led to the selection of popes. In 1128 he served as secretary to the Synod of Troyes, where he obtained a recognition for the Rule of the Knights of Templar, which he is said to have compiled himself. Bernard's austere life of self-mortification complemented his life of mysticism. He was one of the most significant medieval theologians. Beyond a doubt, he was the most influential clergyman of the twelfth century.

The Carmelite Order was founded in 1154 in Palestine, but its members claimed continuity with a band of hermits settled on Mount Carmel from earlier times. They even claimed to be a direct descendant of Elijah and the "sons of the prophets" mentioned in II Kings 2. Their primitive rule adopted in 1209 demanded extreme asceticism. It prescribed absolute poverty, total abstinence from flesh food, and solitude. After the failure of the Crusades, many of its members migrated to Europe, where the order was reorganized on the lines of the mendicant friars. Since the habit of the order was dark brown with a brown scapular and a white mantle, the Carmelites were popularly called "White Friars." A later reform of the Carmelites in the sixteenth century produced the Discalced Carmelites, those following a return to the original severity of the rule, while the others became the Calced Carmelites, who followed a somewhat more relaxed rule. The Discalced Carmelites refused to wear shoes; they wore sandals only.

There were certain clergy that were known as "canons." These were clergy on the official staff of a diocese, usually those aiding in the work of the cathedral church, the seat of the bishop. Normally they were secular clergy, that is clergy "in the world," as opposed to regular clergy, those living "under a rule." But as we noticed earlier in Chapter VI, many bishops in the early church organized their cathedral clergy under a rule, as did Augustine. By the mid-eleventh century, many of these cathedral canons were being organized along monastic lines and were living under a Rule. This was particularly true in southern France and northern Italy. Such canons took the commitment to poverty, celibacy, and obedience. By the early twelfth century, they were known as "regular canons," to distinguish them from the "seculars." Most of them also adopted the recently rediscovered Rule of Augustine and became "Augustinian Canons." They were sometimes also called the Black Canons because of the color of their habit.

During the twelfth century, several independent

Augustinian congregations were established, some of which became famous. One was the Victorines, founded in Paris in 1113 by the scholar William of Champeaux (1070-1121). These were the canons regular of the former abbey dedicated to St. Victor, thus their name. St. Bernard also had some influence in the drafting of their customs. The house was never very large, but it included prestigious scholars in the twelfth century, such as Hugh of St. Victor (1096-1141), Richard of St. Victor (?-1173), and Walter of St. Victor (?-1180).

The Premonstratensians were established in 1120 by St. Norbert (1080-1134) near Laon. They were based on the Rule of Augustine, although Norbert added abstinence from meat. Through Norbert's friendship with Bernard, there were also some Cistercian influences at work. In 1126 the Pope approved the order, and it quickly spread over much of Europe. In England the Premonstratensians were called the White Canons, again from the color of their habit.

Just as the original reform impulse at Cluny came at a needed time, so these reforms came at a needed time in the church. In fact, by the beginning of the twelfth century, even Cluny needed reform. The abbot elected there in 1100 used the financial wealth of the abbey to outfit himself in a retinue of some sixty horses; rich garments clothed his liveried servants. He finally became such a scandal that he was removed and replaced with Peter the Venerable (1092-1156) in 1122. Under Peter, Cluny was quickly reformed.

A whole new development of monasticism in this period was the mendicants. These were begging orders (Latin *mendicare*, to beg), those who made their living entirely on the contributions of faithful supporters. They did not even accept the emphasis of other groups on manual labor, for fear that this too might create pride. As we noticed, the Carmelites were reformed as a mendicant order with the collapse of the Crusades. Technically mendicants are not monks, but are "friars," a Latin word for "brothers." Carmelites were the White Friars, Franciscans became the Gray Friars, and the Dominicans were the Black Friars.

Francis of Assisi (1182-1226) was born to a wealthy businessman and lived a rather dissolute life as a youth. In 1204 he had a conversion experience, and in 1207 he committed himself to a life of religious service. Refusing to accept his father's authority, he also refused his father's possessions. He stood in church before the bishop and stripped off all his clothes since his father had provided them. He returned all his proceeds to his father, stated his intention to serve God alone, and was hastily covered with the bishop's robe.

Repulsed by both wealth and luxury, he preached to the simple people and idolized Lady Poverty. Followers gathered around him, and in 1209 the new order — approved by the Pope in 1210 — emphasized both corporate as well as individual poverty. Earlier monastic orders had emphasized poverty too, but it was an individual poverty, whereby the individual monk owned nothing. However, as long as the monastery was wealthy, individual poverty meant almost nothing. Francis wanted to avoid the problem of corrupting wealth, so he insisted that even collectively the monks could own nothing. The monasteries could accept as gifts nothing but perishable items — food and some clothing. They refused all lands, jewels, gold or silver.[3]

Officially known as the Friars Minor, "Little Brothers," the Franciscans spent much of their time on preaching missions to the poor. In 1212 a wealthy noblewoman of only eighteen years formed the Second Order, the Franciscan nuns soon to be named after her, the "Poor Clares." In 1221 the Third Order (Tertiaries) was established; Tertiaries were lay people not bound to the full monastic rule, but who wished to obey the rule as far as possible while living in the "world." They also supported the First and Second Orders in their works of charity. Francis died in 1226, and he was made a saint only two years later. He is certainly one of the most charming figures in the history of the church. Many are the stories of his ministries and conversations with birds and animals, "Brother Sun," and "Sister Moon." At the time of his death there were about five thousand members of his Order.

Almost at the same time Francis was developing his Order, St. Dominic (1170-1221) was doing the same. Born in Castile, he later was an Augustinian Canon. In 1201 he accompanied his bishop into Albigensian country in southern France to try to convert the heretics, and he became obsessed with the need to help these people. In the process of working in this area, he also saw wealthy papal legates lording it over others. He could not help but notice the contrast between the humble Albigensians and the avaricious papal officials. Thus he too idolized poverty and gathered about him a group of fellow preachers. In 1216 the Pope recognized the Friars Preachers (so designated because of their emphasis on preaching) as a new Order, more commonly known as the Dominicans. Dominic died in Rome in 1221, but his Order spread all over Europe. It was active in the Inquisition and especially in education. Albertus Magnus (1200-1280) and Thomas Aquinas (1225-1274) were Dominicans, and the Order was so fascinated by the new procedures of Aristotelian thinking that they even posthumously baptized Aristotle. The Dominicans, together with the Franciscans, the Carmelites, and the Austin Friars (different from the Augustinian Canons), identified monastic life with the common people with great success, and they helped to make the twelfth century the heyday of monasticism in Europe. Yet within monasticism, the Franciscans and Dominicans were often bitter enemies, particularly in educational disputes in the newly emerging universities.

Nuns were almost as major a part of monasticism as the monks themselves. There were separate convents for women as early as the fourth century, and Benedictine nunneries flourished in Europe ever since Benedict's sister Scholastica (480-543) began one in 530. The Cistercians began their first convent in 1125 and had 700 by 1300. Most of the major monastic orders had Second Orders.

Much has been made of the infractions and moral lapses of the monks and nuns. On the one hand, there is abundant evidence that infractions were common. Many of the nuns were put into convents because their families had no place for them, and they were women of the upper classes. Many widowed queens were put away in monasteries, for fear they would try to take the throne away from the next king. Many orders received infants as oblates (gifts), with the child to be raised as a nun (or monk, as the case may be), and it required a papal dispensation to release the person from his parent's vows. As a result, many of the individuals in convents and monasteries had no calling for the monastic life. They were simply captives in monastic surroundings. Consequently, moral lapses in such places could be expected. Some convents were little more than houses of prostitution, and many monasteries were centers of vice in their communities. One abbot was reckoned as the sire of eighteen illegitimate children in his neighborhood. However, the majority of those who took monastic vows lived exemplary lives. The total sublimation of the sex drive is a difficult thing to do even for those consciously committed to it, and a vow of perpetual silence may be impossible, for men as well as for women.

Monasticism produced most of the influential theologians of the Middle Ages. We have already mentioned Bernard of Clairvaux. Mention should also include Anselm (1033-1109), Abelard (1079-1142), and Thomas Aquinas. Anselm was a native of Lombardy, but he spent thirty years in monasteries in Normandy. He became Archbishop of Canterbury in 1089. He led in the reform of the English church, challenging the kings over investiture. This challenge culminated in the concordat of London in 1107. Anselm's work *Proslogium* was the development of the ontological argument for God: since God is that than which nothing greater can be conceived, this demands that He exist. His words on the Atonement, *Cur Deus Homo?* (Why a God-Man?) developed the satisfaction theory which replaced the ransom theory of the early church fathers.

Peter Abelard had one of the most brilliant minds of

the medieval period. He was both a philosopher and theologian at a time when there was little distinction between the two. Because he challenged the philosophical presuppositions of his day, many significant figures of the church resisted his teachings, including Bernard. Abelard's writings on the Trinity created a significant controversy. His book *Sic et Non* (Yes and No) was a sensation. This work quoted the early church fathers on both sides of most theological issues, indicating there was little unanimity within the church's teachings.

Thomas Aquinas was a Dominican philosopher and theologian. His *Summa Theologica* (Summary of Theology) represented the apex of medieval theological achievement. This massive work harmonized disparate teachings into a synthesis along Aristotelian lines. His work has had a significant influence on the church, although it was several decades before its worth was appreciated. The modern revival of Thomism dates from the encyclical *Aeterni Patris* by Pope Leo XIII (1878-1903) in 1879. This document praised and endorsed Thomistic thought and gave it an official place in Roman Catholicism.

In sum, the monasteries and convents played useful roles in the life of the Middle Ages. Convents were the only places for young women to receive any kind of an education. Often the monasteries were the only places of study in the diocese, and played the part of schools until the rise of universities in the early thirteenth century. Not only did monks clear farm land and teach youngsters, they also built many magnificent abbey churches and produced many handcrafts. The Cistercians alone reclaimed thousands of acres of English grazing land

and developed the sheep industry. In times of famine monasteries often slaughtered some of their own flocks to feed the poor. In Egypt monks came out during the short period of harvest to help gather the grain for the farmers, then returned to the monastery refusing any remuneration. Many convents operated hospitals. The typical monastery offered a Spartan life: four hours of prayer a day, with brief and vegetarian meals. The typical concept of feudal society was that the peasants fed the society, the nobility fought to defend it, and monks prayed to preserve it. They played a significant role in their generation, and on balance, they had a healthy influence for good.

Bibliography for Chapter Thirteen

Boase, Thomas Sherrer Ross. *St. Francis of Assisi.* Bloomington, Indiana: Indiana University Press, 1968.
   A somewhat brief account, but well written and geared to a popular audience.
Godfrey, John. *The Church in Anglo-Saxon England.* Cambridge, England: The University Press, 1962.
   A thorough treatment of the subject, also detailed on the subject of monastic reform in this period.
James, Bruno S. *Saint Bernard of Clairvaux: An Essay in Biography.* New York: Harper & Brothers Publishers, 1957.
   One of many books on this spiritual giant of the twelfth century.
Workman, Herbert B. *The Evolution of the Monastic*

Ideal From the Earliest Times Down to the Coming of the Friars: A Second Chapter in the History of Christian Renunciation. Boston: Beacon Press, 1962 (Reprint of 1913).

Already noted in Chapter Six, Workman carries the story down through the mendicants in an easy-to-read though informative style.

Questions and Projects for Chapter Thirteen

1. Try to locate copies of the Rules for some of the newer monastic orders from this period. How do they compare to the Rule of Benedict?
2. Is it fair to say that the different monastic orders in Catholicism are equivalent to Protestant denominational divisions? Could the cycle of reform, wealth, luxury, and decay also be applied to Protestant denominations?
3. After some additional research, try to compile a list of all Roman Catholic monastic orders now in existence, listing such things as founder, chief leaders, and main characteristics of each.

Notes for Chapter Thirteen

1. For an explanation of "secular canons," see p. 266
2. For the founding and early charter of the order see Petry, pp. 283-288.
3. For the Rule of St. Francis, see Barry, I, pp. 417-421; Petry, pp. 293-296; and Bettenson, pp. 181-187.

Chapter Fourteen
THE AVIGNON PAPACY

Our last extended reference to the papacy was in Chapter Ten, when we surveyed the medieval popes. We ended that treatment with the pontificate of Innocent III, the greatest of the medieval popes in terms of power exercised. He certainly stands above the rest as the most significant pope in that period. Within the half century after his death, the popes continued his struggles to break down the power of the Hohenstaufen dynasty of German Emperors. Through marriage, this dynasty had managed to combine the Empire in Germany and the Norman kingdom of southern Italy. The popes saw the danger of Italy's being consolidated into unified control, thus squeezing out their own domination of the Papal States. That was why the popes fought so hard to break this Hohenstaufen stranglehold and its threat to central Italy. By 1250, with the death of Emperor Frederick II, they had been successful. Within four more years the Hohenstaufen dynasty in Germany died out, and within another decade and a half, French forces brought in with papal approval replaced Hohenstaufens in southern Italy. Throughout the entire century, the papacy seemed to reign supreme.

Boniface VIII (1294-1303) can be considered the last of the medieval popes. He tried to follow the leading of Innocent III, riding the crest of a century of papal domination. Unfortunately for him, however, the European situation was rather different from what it had been under Innocent. His inability to perceive this led to one tragic confrontation after another. Innocent was always able to take advantage of an interior political situation in a country to bend that country's ruler to his wishes. Boniface tried the same thing, but the situations did not provide him the same leverage.

When King Edward I of England (1272-1307) and King Philip IV of France (1285-1314) began to tax the clergy of their respective countries, Boniface protested, and in his famous decree *Clericis laicos* he promised excommunication to any monarch who taxed the clergy without the pope's consent. Edward responded by putting clergy outside the protection of the law and having the sheriffs seize clerical property; Philip forbade the exportation of gold from France to Rome. Under this pressure, Boniface relented, beat a hasty retreat, and returned the taxing initiative to the kings.

In 1301 King Philip arrested a papal legate, on the charge that he was suggesting an insurrection against the king. The legate was convicted of treason, but Boniface demanded that clerics were not under the jurisdiction of secular courts. This distinction had always been observed in the past, but nationalism in France now gave Philip the support to refuse the Pope's demands. Boniface continued his thunderings, and in 1302 he issued the papal decree *Unan Sanctam*, a document which repeats all the high claims to authority made by previous popes, including both Gregory VII and Innocent III. Finally growing tired of Boniface's threats, in 1303 Philip sent a body of men down into Italy who captured the Pope. Boniface was rescued a few days later, but the affair broke his health, and he died within a month. It was obvious that the days of papal domination in the manner of Innocent III were over.

The next pope was Benedict XI (1303-1304), but he was poisoned after only nine months in the office. In this time of political uncertainty, the college of cardinals faced the question of whether to elect a man who would continue Boniface's hard line policy against the monarchs, or elect a man who would take more of a low-profile approach toward the kings. After almost a year they selected Clement V (1305-1314), a Frenchman who was a personal friend to King Philip. In an attempt to maintain good relations with the French king, Clement consented to be crowned pope in France. Because the political climate in Rome was unhealthy, and also in order to keep up good rapport with Philip, Clement delayed going to Rome. Eventually he settled his papal court down in the papal territory of Avignon. Technically Avignon was not in France, but it was on the Rhone River just across from French territory and close to Philip's influence. Here the papacy stayed for about seventy years.

The removal of the papal court from Rome was by itself not a completely novel thing. In the 204 years from 1100 to 1304 the popes spent 122 years outside of Rome, and only 82 in it. What *was* unusual about the Avignon period was that the popes stayed out of Rome for such a long, unbroken period of time, and were so far from Rome. Previously popes had stayed in various Italian cities for a few months, or at most a few years. Italians complained about the Avignon settlement because the papacy's removal meant a great loss of tourists and residents for Rome. Clement V fully intended to return to Rome, after he pacified Philip for a while. He did not intend to settle down in Avignon permanently, and he had no idea that the papacy would remain there for seventy years.

Although Clement was not quite a French puppet on Philip's string, he was certainly under Philip's influence. In fact, this entire Avignon period is characterized by French dominance. Of the seven Avignon popes, all seven of them were French — the longest string of non-Italians ever to hold the office. In addition, under Clement and his successor, John XXII (1316-1334), financial corruption became a major characteristic of the papal court. It became normal for persons who wished to see the pope to give sizeable tips to the groomsmen, doormen, secretaries, and other officials who controlled access to the pope. This graft fostered other forms of corruption as well. Further, both Clement and John took advantage of their positions with large salaries. So many of these individuals were nephews of the pope that our word *nepotism* continues to refer to this kind of familial patronage.

Neither Clement nor John were bad men as such, but they were worldly, and they built up a style of papal court life that became a scandal across Europe. The papal court was wealthy, luxurious, and ostentatious. At a time when fur was expensive and restricted to only top church officials, Clement used up 1220 ermine pelts to trim various articles of clothing: 68 for a hood, 430 for a cape, 310 for a mantle, 30 for a hat, etc. John even had his pillow trimmed with fur. When members of John's family were married, the papacy paid the bill. When his great-niece married in 1324, the wedding party consumed 4,012 loaves of bread, 8-3/4 oxen, 55-1/4 sheep, 8 pigs, 4 boars, 200 capons, 690 chickens, 580 partridges, 270 rabbits, 40 plovers, 37 ducks, 50 pigeons, 4 cranes, 2 pheasants, 2 peacocks, 292 small birds, a large quantity of fish, 302 pounds of cheese, 3,000 eggs, 2,000 apples, pears and other fruits, all washed down by 11 barrels of wine.[1]

To finance all this expense, John became a master at making money for the papacy. In addition to bribes and corruption, he developed new sources of money within the church machinery. He demanded a tithe of all clerical income; he received the first year's income from a new office holder, called the *annates*; he claimed the house and goods of any deceased bishop; there were love offerings from the people, and rents from papal land; he claimed the income of numerous offices when the office was vacant, before a new official could be elected or installed; in addition there was Peter's Pence — one penny per household — expected from England,

Denmark, Sweden, Norway, Bohemia, Poland, Dalmatia, Croatia, Aragon, Portugal, and the lands of the Teutonic Knights. With all this income flowing toward the papal court in Avignon, it is no wonder that there was corruption. And it is also no surprise that many people throughout Europe resented the high living enjoyed by the papal court.

During the years of the Avignon papacy, the city of Rome had been stagnating. Much of the population had moved away, and many of the older buildings had been cannibalized for materials. The people of Rome had been requesting the return of the papacy ever since 1305, but the political upheavals there made Avignon look very comfortable to the popes. By the 1360's, however, southern France was experiencing the disorders of the Hundred Years' War, and central Italy was becoming more stabilized. Finally in 1365 Urban V (1362-1370) began to get plans under way for the return. The Vatican palace was ordered repaired; after not being lived in for some sixty years, doors and windows were either missing or crumbling away, and extensive repairs had to be made to the roof. An embassy from the King of France came to Urban in 1367 to try to get him to change his mind, but he was adamant. He left Avignon that April, sailed from Marseilles in May, and landed on the western Italian coast in June. After some minor disturbances were put down that summer, Urban rode into Rome in October. The Romans were jubilant at his return.

After three years, Urban felt the need to return to Avignon. He wanted to be closer to the continuing conflict between England and France, for he hoped to arbitrate their dispute. He left Italy on September 5 and reached

Avignon before the end of the month. In November he became ill, and he died in December. The cardinals assembled and elected Gregory XI (1370-1378). By 1372 Gregory committed himself to return to Italy. Rebellion in the papal lands delayed him, but he landed in Italy in December of 1376 and reached Rome in January, 1377.

Gregory has the honor of having ended the Avignon papacy, but he did not live long in Rome. His health had always been somewhat delicate, and he died in late March, 1378. The next series of events are among the most dramatic and tragic in the history of the church.

It was a law of the church that the election of a new pope must take place in the same place where the old one died. Since most of the cardinals were French, they wanted to return to Avignon, but they first had to elect a new pope in Rome. There had not been a papal election in Rome for seventy-five years, and the Romans were determined that this one would go their way. The Roman countrymen came down from the hills with their wineskins to watch the proceedings — proceedings in which they could not be uninterested. As the cardinals made their way to the Vatican apartments, the crowd milled around them, shouting that they wanted a Roman, or at least an Italian pope. One person recorded the significant threat, "Give us a Roman pope or we will make your heads redder than your hats." Although the French cardinals numbered 10 out of the total of 16, the local townspeople piled flammable materials under the upper room where they met, and the cardinals realized that the election of another Frenchman would probably initiate a massacre. Under this type of pressure, the cardinals selected an Italian, the Archbishop of Bari, who became Urban VI (1378-1389). That might have been the end of it, but for the character of the new pope.

Urban was a papal bureaucrat, who for years had labored under French domination, which he deeply resented. Having suffered one humiliation after another, the absolute power of the papacy was now his, and it turned him into a tyrant. Some suggested it even unhinged his mind. Urban had an overwhelming desire to put the French cardinals in their place. Instead of building good relations with them, he attacked them individually, accusing them publicly of greed, immorality, simony, and neglect of office. The charges were accurate, but the manner was vicious. These men who were used to being treated as princes, were now insulted publicly and called "liar," "bandit," and other epithets by a man who raved, "I can do anything, I can do anything." Throughout the summer of 1378 his abuse of the cardinals increased, including a physical attack upon one of the French ones. One by one most of the cardinals slipped out of town, claiming the press of other duties, or the need to escape Rome's insufferable summer heat.

By September, the French cardinals assembled in Anagni, to discuss if anything could be done about Urban. They decided that the election was invalid, because the cardinals had not been free to make their own choice. They had, they claimed, been pressured by the Roman mob. Declaring the papal throne vacant, they elected a new pope, a Frenchman who took the title of Clement VII (1378-1394), and returned to Avignon with the French cardinals. Urban retaliated by naming a number of Italian cardinals to replace the defected French ones. All of Europe now chose sides, supporting either the pope in Rome, or the one in Avignon. France, of course, backed the Avignon pope, as did Scotland. England and the German Empire, both traditional enemies of France, supported Urban in Rome. It seems that most nations selected a pope more on the basis of foreign policy than the real question of the legitimacy of Urban's election.

From a modern perspective, it seems clear that the election was conducted under duress; but it is also clear that the cardinals would have accepted the election had Urban proved to be a tractable man. Thus their schism on a technicality suggests that their action was based more on personal considerations than on what was best for the church. Roman Catholicism, of course, considers Clement VII and his successors antipopes. Meanwhile, Urban's regime was a series of butcheries. Because Queen Joanna of Naples had sheltered Clement on his way to the coast to take ship to Avignon, Urban declared war on her, captured her, and had her murdered. When some of his own cardinals plotted against him, he had six out of the seven murdered. When he died in 1389, the schism continued. It became even more scandalous than the Avignon papacy itself.

The schism lasted for forty years, and the issues were complicated. The church's lawyers had a field day with it, arguing cogently on both sides. On the one hand, there was an obviously forced election. But on the other hand, the revolt against Urban was personal. The question that emerged was the difficult one of whether a man's behavior was enough to annul a papal election. Canon law does not provide for such a case, and the tradition of the church, going all the way back to Cyprian in the third century, is that a person's personal unorthodoxy or immorality does not annul the validity of his office.

Both popes hurled anathemas at the other side, excommunicating the supporters of the wrong pope, forbidding the celebration of the sacraments in territory loyal to the other pope. All of Europe was under censure by one Pope or the other. Half of Europe was receiving invalid sacraments, but no one knew for sure which half was right. All of Europe was confused.

There had been appeals for reform of the church even during the Avignon period, but now during the schism, when there were two popes, the need for reform was even greater — but perhaps even less possible. How could the body of the church be reformed when the papal institution could not straighten out its own arrangements? Both sides agreed that the schism ought to be healed, but all efforts failed. When Urban died in 1389, things could have been straightened out if the Roman cardinals had then elected Clement VII to fill the Roman spot. This would have put both sides behind the same man. But the Roman cardinals felt this would be to admit the French cardinals were right in the first place, and they refused. When Clement VII died in 1394, the French could have healed the schism by electing the current Roman pope, but they felt that this would be to admit they were wrong in the first place, and they refused. So both Rome and Avignon continued different lines of popes. After 1390 every cardinal in both camps made the promise that he would heal the schism if elected pope, even if he had to abdicate and throw his support to the other man to do so. But each time one was made a new pope, he evaded the commitment. The schism continued.

"Reform in head and members," was the constant slogan for the reform of the church, but it appeared that the head of the church was helpless in reform. It was left up to the members. The main impetus of this reform drive we will reserve for the next chapter, but even during the time of the Avignon and divided papacy there were individuals leading the way into reform.

John Wyclif (1329-1384) was one of the first outspoken leaders of the fourteenth century to make critical comments on the papacy. France and England were traditional enemies, and the mere fact that the Avignon popes were under French influence made the English leery of the papacy. By mid-century, Parliament was enacting laws restricting papal power in England. There was also a prevalent attitude of anti-clericalism. *The Vision of Piers Plowman* and *Canterbury Tales* both recorded the popular disenchantment with the fat and lazy monks and the immoral clergy.

Wyclif received his education at Oxford, and in the early 1360's he was already offended at the unscrupulous mendicant monks who filched money from the poor on their weak religious pretenses. Prior to the great schism in 1378 he did not completely reject the pope's authority in the church, but he did insist that the financial usurpations should be ended. In this period he wrote, "They blaspheme who extol the pope above all that is called God." To implement his concern for proper spiritual ministry, Wyclif began to train a number of men called "poor preachers." They traveled through the countryside, preached to the people in their vernacular language, read from the Gospels and Epistles, and taught the Ten Commandments and other religious basics. These preachers attracted a great deal of popularity among the people, for they were in great contrast to thc bcgging monks who were offering no spiritual consolation at all. From this group developed the Lollards.

After the beginning of the schism in 1378 Wyclif claimed that it would be better for the sake of Christ and His Church if both popes were deposed. Speaking against both the current church and its abuses, he became more and more radical, and soon he denied transubstantiation. Because this raised fierce opposition, he concluded that the Pope was Antichrist himself, and the papacy was the fulfillment of the apocalyptic prophecies of the Antichrist and his coming. He declared that only elders and deacons were orders of ministry that Christ had established, and all others were the result of the secularization of the church. He also contended that elders were the same as presbyters, priests, and bishops. Toward the end of his life he argued that every believer is a priest. He condemned the cult of the saints, relics, and pilgrimages. He repudiated indulgences and masses for the dead, although he retained belief in purgatory.

He led in the translation of the Bible into the English vernacular, completing the New Testament in 1380. His Lollards used these translations in their travels and preaching. Wyclif was convinced that even simple farmers could understand the Bible and should study it. Though he spent his last years in turmoil, Wyclif died peacefully in his home in 1384 enjoying the protection of powerful nobles. But by that time papal decrees had been enacted against him, and a council in London condemned him in 1382. His bones were not allowed to rest in peace. The Council of Constance passed judgment on 267 of his "errors." It ordered his bones exhumed and burned along with his writings. This was done in 1428, with the ashes cast into a river. Many of Wyclif's ideas resurfaced during the early years of the Protestant Reformation. He is appropriately called "The Morning Star of the Reformation."

Somewhat of a counterpart to Wyclif was John Hus (1373-1415) in Bohemia. King Richard of England married the sister of the King of Bohemia in 1382, and political and cultural ties between the two countries continued. A number of Bohemian students came to Oxford to study, many of them returning to the University of Prague. There is little doubt that they took Wyclif's ideas with them. When Hus entered the University of Prague in 1390, he soon ran across some of Wyclif's writings. Before the end of the decade, Hus had recopied them in his own handwriting. By the turn of the century he was teaching at the university, and in 1402 he became Rector of the Faculty of Arts. Ordained a priest in 1400, he was appointed preacher in the Chapel of the Holy Innocents of Bethlehem in 1402.

From his chapel Hus attracted a great deal of attention, preaching both in Latin and Czech. His Czech sermons stirred up a significant measure of patriotism, although his sermons were not directed to that end as much as to daily Christian living. He denounced the evils of the church, from corrupt parish priests all the way up to the divided papacy. He held that Christ and not Peter was the foundation on which God had founded the Church, and that many popes had been heretics. Through all this, however, he seemed to be more concerned in moral reform than ecclesiastical revolution or radical theological speculation.

His preaching brought attention and opposition. He was popular with the Czech nobility, and the Queen made him her private confessor. Several noble ladies came to his preaching. Hus was in fact repeating many of the ideas of Wyclif, and the whole area of ecclesiastical reform received Prague's attention. Finally in 1410 the Archbishop of Prague obtained a decree from Pope Alexander V prohibiting preaching in private chapels, and ordering Wyclif's books to be burned. Hus, however, refused to be silenced, and he continued preaching, supported as he was by king, queen, university, and town. When Pope John XXIII proclaimed a crusade against Naples and began selling indulgences to raise money for that venture, Hus publicly attacked John's designs. This led to Hus' excommunication in 1412, plus an interdict against Prague as long as Hus remained in the city. To relieve the city from this pressure Hus left and stayed in the rural castles of his noble supporters, continuing to preach from place to place. The Czech people remained constant in their loyalty to him.

In this exile Hus wrote his greatest work, *On the Church*, in 1413, the first ten chapters of it lifted from Wyclif's work. The next year the great Council of Constance convened, to restore the unity of the papacy. The Council summoned Hus to appear before it, and he was granted a safe-conduct pass from the Emperor Sigismund (1411-1437), a strong supporter of the Council. Hus went to Constance, convinced that if he had a chance to talk to the theologians and papal advisors, he could bring them to see his point. He was hopeful that he could be an instrument in elevating the fortunes of the fallen papacy.

Unfortunately, he no sooner reached town than the authorities arrested him and threw him into prison, where he remained for six months. When the Emperor made a mild protest about the safe conduct, he was told that promises made to a heretic were not binding. This council had already condemned Wyclif, and it was obvious what it would do with Hus. The Council tried him without giving him adequate opportunity to speak in his own behalf. He stated he was willing to be informed by the theologians, but he did not expect merely a formal condemnation without the chance to be heard. Nevertheless, he was condemned, defrocked, and turned over to the secular arm for punishment. He was burned at the stake on July 6, 1415, followed a year later by his friend and follower, Jerome of Prague (1370-1416).

The Council saw Hus as a heretic, but to the Bohemians he was a national hero. His followers immediately initiated a civil war with the loyal Catholics. Even while Hus was still in prison, some Hussites began celebrating the communion with both elements. They won some concessions from the Council of Basle in 1436, and about mid-century amalgamated with some Waldensians to form the *Unitas Fratrum*, the United Brethren, or Moravian Brethren. These Moravians were an important factor centuries later in pietistic revitalization in seventeenth century Europe and eighteenth century America.

The Avignon Papacy brought on some interesting developments: increasing corruption in the church, a call for reform of that church, and ultimately a major division between Avignon and Roman popes. Doctrinally, Wyclif and Hus went too far too fast for their generations to follow, even though a minority of people raised them to the status of heroes and proto-reformers. The Protestant Reformation a century later also recognized them as reformers and martyrs. But the majority of the Church in the early fifteenth century would have to follow a slower route to reform. Much of this was bound up with Conciliarism.

Bibliography for Chapter Fourteen

Chamberlin, E.R. *The Bad Popes.* New York: New American Library (Signet Books), 1979.

Mentioned in Chapter Ten, this work also carries information on Boniface VIII and Urban VI.

Chaucer, Geoffrey. *The Canterbury Tales.* Trans. by Nevill Coghill. Baltimore: Penguin Books, 1952.

This is a classic work, representing a late fourteenth century view of life and the church in England.

Langland, William. *Piers the Ploughman.* Trans. by J.F. Goodridge. Harmondsworth, England: Penguin Books, Ltd., 1959.

A work similar in import to that of Chaucer, though it is simply a treatise on life, not told in a series of stories.

Mollat, G. *The Popes at Avignon, 1305-1378.* Trans. by Janet Love. New York: Harper & Row, Publishers, 1963.

The most comprehensive and detailed study of the Avignonese papacy.

Parker, G.H.W. *The Morning Star: Wycliffe and the Dawn of the Reformation.* Grand Rapids: W.B. Eerdmans Publishing Co., 1966.

An excellent and vivid portrayal of the life of Wyclif and his significance as an early reformer.

Spinka, Matthew. *John Hus and the Czech Reform.* Chicago: The University of Chicago Press, 1941.

Done by an outstanding scholar of this period, this brief work captures the significance of Hus as well as his differences from Wyclif.

Questions and Projects for Chapter Fourteen

1. Prepare for a debate on the proposition: "The election of Pope Urban VI in 1378 was an invalid election." Be prepared to argue either side.
2. Which of the Avignon Popes (1305-1377) would you consider "good guys"? Why?
3. After some additional research, compare Wyclif and Hus on their criticisms of the papacy and its doctrines. Wherein do they agree? Wherein do they differ?
4. Analyze some Roman Catholic histories of this period to see how they treat Wyclif and Hus. Prepare a paper on the differences between their presentation and the viewpoint presented in this book.
5. In the same or similar Roman Catholic sources, prepare a brief report on their view toward the Avignon Papacy as a whole, as well as their view toward the Divided Papacy from 1378 to 1415.

Notes for Chapter Fourteen

1. G. Mollat, *The Popes at Avignon, 1305-1378*, trans. Janet Love (New York: Harper & Row, Publishers, 1963), p. 311.

Chapter Fifteen
CONCILIARISM:
RISE AND DISAPPOINTMENT

As covered in the preceding chapter, the late four-teenth century saw a growing demand for reform within the church. The divided papacy was a terrible scandal. There had been many times when there had been an anti-pope, usually supported by the Holy Roman Emperor or some king. But never had Europe been so evenly divided over the question of the rightful pope, or never had there been such confusion as to the rightful claims to the papacy. In addition, there were other problems. Quite often, both popes made appointments to some church positions, so two incumbents showed up for the same job. Two papal courts were being maintained, each with the full complement of cardinals, papal bureaucrats, and overhead expenses. This represented a severe economic drain on the church and the people.

Then there were the reform doctrines of such teachers as Wyclif and Hus. In addition, there were further movements, such as Gerard DeGroot's (1340-1384) Brethren of the Common Life, a semi-monastic group fostering deeper Christian devotion, soon becoming a significant educational mission. Although it was obvious that many people throughout Europe — both clerical leaders as well as leading laymen — wanted reform in the church, it was just as obvious that the papacy was in no position or mindset to initiate any reform. Conciliarism arose at the turn of the century to meet this need. Conciliarism was the idea that the church can be properly governed through ecumenical or general councils.

Conciliary theory had a long background. Marsilius of Padua and William of Ockham were theologian-philosophers of the early fourteenth century who had talked about this idea. They claimed that the hierarchy of the Church — the pope and the bishops — was not founded by Christ, but was the result of a historical process.[1] The real authority of the Church, they contended, was in the Church itself — the "body of the faithful." This body is thus "represented" (rendered present) in the council of bishops, on the understanding that the bishop is the working unit of the pastoral supervision of the church.

Actually these theories went back even earlier. The Dominican John of Paris (d. 1306) stated that the authority of the Church rested not on its head alone but extended also to its members. The canonist Huguccio (d. 1210) of Bologna, one of the teachers of Innocent III, maintained that the pope might err personally, but the Church never. He went further to state that the agency that could prove whether a pope was in error on a matter of faith was a council as the representation of the whole Church. Although most canonists were unwilling to go this far in making the council authoritative over the pope, many did agree that the council could determine that the pope had erred, and in that case an erring pope would cease to be pope. This theory rested on the idea that the pope in expressing matters of faith must rely on the advice of the bishops. If he and the bishops agreed, obviously he could not be in error. This was expressed in the axiom, "The council (with the pope) is greater than the pope (by himself alone)."

In addition to those theories developing in the church, there were parallel developments in the new national governments. The thirteenth and fourteenth centuries were a time of rising nationalism. Edward I called the Model Parliament in 1295 in England, and although the early parliaments were basically controlled by the nobility, there was still the idea of authority derived from the people gathered in a representative body. Shortly thereafter, Philip IV of France gathered strength in his contest with Boniface VIII by calling together the first Estates General in 1303, with representatives from the three estates: the clergy, the nobility, and the townspeople. The Estates General was based on exactly the same theory of representational power. These political happenings paralleled the rise of conciliar thought in the church, and it was easy for church leaders to make the analogous application: just as the power of government in the state rested ultimately upon the people in a representative assembly, so the power of government in the church rested upon the bishops assembled in a council.

The pope may be the head executive of the organization, just as the monarch is for the state, but the source of government lay in the body itself.

These ideas were taken up by various intellectuals, both among the laity and particularly among the church. The center of much of this discussion was at the University of Paris. Shortly after the beginning of the schism in 1378 two Germans teaching there began to speak out on conciliar authority: Henry of Langenstein (1325-1397) and Konrad of Gelnhausen (1320-1390). As early as 1379 they said that a general council was the judge of both popes and the cardinals that elected them. In 1393 the University of Paris formally sent a memorandum to King Charles VI of France stating that if both popes would not simultaneously resign, or if some other means of arbitration could not be achieved, then the schism should be resolved by means of a general council. Shortly after the turn of the century the major voices calling for the council were the Frenchmen Jean Gerson (1363-1429), and Pierre D'Ailly (1350-1420), both theologians at the University of Paris,

This was the situation at the turn of the century. In addition, the French put constant pressure upon the French king to withdraw his allegiance from the Pope in Avignon, Benedict XIII (1394-1422). Benedict was actually a much better man than Clement, his predecessor, but he refused to compromise his validity by resigning. In Rome, Gregory XII (1406-1415) was also a good man, but he refused to resign unless Benedict did at the same time. As long as the two men continued in their positions, it was obvious that nothing would be accomplished.

Things began to happen shortly after the turn of the century. In 1407 the University of Paris formally requested the king to withdraw his allegiance from Benedict. In 1408 four cardinals from each of the two camps, and ultimately a total of thirteen, met at Leghorn in Italy and called for a new council, to meet at Pisa, beginning March 25, 1409. Charles VI (1380-1422) of France gave it his protection and support, even though Emperor Rupert (1400-1410) was opposed. There assembled at Pisa 22 cardinals, 12 archbishops in person and 14 by proxy, 80 bishops in person and 102 by proxy, 87 abbots in person with 200 by proxy, more than 300 theologians, plus other representatives both religious and diplomatic, including ambassadors from England, Poland, France, Portugal, Bohemia, Sicily, and smaller areas. The council summoned both popes: when they refused to come, it declared them obstinate and deposed them on June 5. Twenty-one days later, with the authorization of the council, those cardinals elected a new pope, Alexander V (1409-1410).

Alexander was a learned and pious man, and there was great hope that he might resolve the situation. In fact Benedict was impotent because the French officially withdrew recognition of him. In addition, many of Gregory's sources of strength also supported the Pisan pope. Alexander certainly had more support behind him than either of the other two, and he might gradually have ameliorated the situation, winning over the last supporters, particularly from Gregory, but he died only 10 months after his election. The Council of Pisa was still in session, and it elected another pope, who took the name of John XXIII (1410-1415). But where Alexander was genuinely interested in reform, John was not. According to rumor he was deceitful, cruel, tyrannous, and debauched in his private life. The tragedy of the situation is that he had the support to heal the church, but he only made the conciliarists look bad. For now instead of two popes, there were three. Even though he occupied Rome for a while with military force, driving out Gregory, he was squandering his support and certainly doing nothing to heal the schism. From the official Roman Catholic viewpoint, the Council of Pisa is not one of the legitimate councils, and both Alexander and John are antipopes. (That is why the pope who came to the throne in 1958 and took the name John also took the number XXIII. Officially there was no John XXIII; the one appointed by Pisa does not count.)

Things were now worse than they had been before. There were now three popes, each claiming to be the rightful one, and the aggressions and indefensible behavior of John compromised the support and future of conciliarism. Undaunted, however, the conciliarists pressed for another council to take up the matter. They decided this time to take the council out of Italy and meet at Constance, in Switzerland. In addition, the German Emperor Sigismund (1411-1437) had been won over to the conciliarist cause, and he gave his support to the call for a council. He was able to put pressure on John and get John to endorse the call for the council. Thus the council of Constance, which met from 1414 to 1418, had even more support than Pisa did. Gregory did not officially endorse the council, but he still expressed his willingness to resign if Benedict would, so he did not openly resist the council. Benedict did, but he was virtually ignored.

Lack of support soon forced him out of Avignon, and he spent the remainder of his days on a mountain in Spain, still excommunicating the rest of the world, but in fact reduced to a harmless figure. The Council of Constance reigned supreme.

The Council of Constance was certainly the largest religious assemblage of the entire age. Almost everybody was there. Contemporary estimates are probably too high which state there were 18,000 clergy present, plus 150,000 additional others. Modern estimates suggest a total of somewhere around 15,000-20,000 would be more appropriate, but this is still a goodly sum. The retinue and baggage of Pope John was carried by 1,600 horses, that of Emperor Sigismund required 1,000 horses. John had intended to control the council by packing it with Italians, but this was exactly why the conciliarists had insisted the council be outside of Italy. To further forestall John's control, the council decided to follow the practice of the student bodies in the universities by giving one vote each for the English, the French, the Germans, the Italians, and the cardinals. This way, even if the cardinals and Italians combined, the other three could outvote them.

When John realized in the spring of 1415 that things were not going to go his way, he pleaded illness and left town. Once away he denounced the council and ordered it to break up. Feeling that since Pope John had called it, he could disband it, many of those present began to pack their things. But the conciliarists realized that if the council broke up now, it would be all over. So they persuaded Emperor Sigismund to send soldiers after John and bring him back as a prisoner. In addition, Jean

Gerson preached a sermon in which he pointed out the superiority of the council over the entire church, including the pope. The council stayed in session, and John became their prisoner, literally. Two weeks after Gerson's sermon, the council passed the decree *Sacrosancta*, which states that the council is the assembled Church, deriving its authority directly from Christ, and that even the Pope owed allegiance to it.[2] The council deposed John within a month.

Benedict XIII still clung to his position, but his power was gone. With John and Benedict both removed from the scene, Gregory XII had no authority left either. Technically, he still claimed to be the rightful pope (and official Roman Catholicism still holds this position), but at the fourteenth session of the Council, on July 4, 1415, he submitted his resignation, but only after he had first legitimized the council with a new decree of convocation. Officially, then, this allows Roman Catholicism to call this a genuine council since it was called by one they considered to be the rightful pope, Gregory XII. We have not discussed many of the others, but Constance is the sixteenth ecumenical council in the history of the church.

There were still some technical details in dealing with Benedict, and he was not deposed until July of 1417. In the conciliar discussions, the debate centered on whether the council ought to proceed with the reform measures, or elect a new pope. Their problem at Pisa had been that they elected a new pope, leaving reform matters up to him. John had betrayed them. Could it happen again? Shouldn't they clean up the reform matters first, and then elect a pope that would be loyal to their decisions? Others insisted that the machinery of authority was still invested in the pope, and it was pointless to institute programs for the executive officer; the best thing was to elect a reform-minded pope and then let him use the authority of the office to bring in reform. Ultimately there was a compromise; they would enact a few reform measures, make the new pope promise to respect them, but leave much up to him.

Just to be sure that the impetus of conciliarism would be maintained, the council in October of 1417 passed the decree *Frequens*, which stated that the next two councils would be five and seven years after the conclusion of the previous one; after that there was to be a council every ten years.[3] This would guarantee conciliar watch over the papacy. Nine days after this decree, Gregory XII died. Now there was absolutely no doubt that there was a vacancy in the papacy. Both John and Benedict were discredited, Gregory was dead, and the way was open for a new papal election. On November 8 the cardinals went into conclave, along with six deputies from each of the four national groups at the council. The French hoped to secure the position for D'Ailly, but it went instead to an Italian who took the name of Martin V (1417-1431). Thus finally was the schism of some forty years healed. But it took a reform council to get it done.

The Council of Constance had been called for three reasons: to heal the papal schism, to reform the church in head and members, and to condemn and suppress heresy. We have already seen what they did with Wyclif, Hus, and Jerome of Prague. The papal schism was now healed. The matter of church reform was well begun, but it still had a long way to go. Martin was a good pope, interested in reform, but he was convinced that it ought to be controlled by the papacy and not by a committee of radicals who might try anything next. He really did not believe in the decree *Sacrosancta*, and he was determined that all the controls of the church remain in his hands. Within months after his election, he was able to manipulate the council by appealing to the nationalistic interests of the various groups. He gave each group a few small concessions to keep them from getting into major areas of reform. Thus mollified, the council agreed to its termination on April 22, 1418. A few weeks after the adjournment, Martin declared that it was "unlawful for any one either to appeal from the judgments of the Apostolic See or to reject its decisions in matters of faith." Specifically this meant no appeal from the judgment of the pope to the judgment of the council — which is to say that Martin rejected the council's superiority over the Pope.

Martin was a hard worker. He returned to Rome and rebuilt the authority of the papacy so well that it survived the Renaissance popes, some of the worst in history. He restored order to the turbulent Papal States. But he did little to carry through any of the reforms either proposed or enacted at Constance. He breathed a huge sigh of relief when the Council of Constance was over. He stated later that the very mention of the word "council" evoked terror from him.

Yet the decree *Frequens* had mandated that five years after the conclusion of Constance another council be held. The council's success in healing the papal schism had made it very popular, and pressure from the University of Paris to keep the councils on schedule forced him to action. So in 1423 he called a council for Pavia. The gathering had barely convened, however, when an outbreak of plague forced it to move to Sienna. Even here attendance was slim, owing to war between England and France, and Spanish military expeditions against the Moors. Martin allowed the council to struggle along for a year. Some measures of reform were proposed, but effectively blocked by the Pope's supporters. Martin himself never attended. After a year, Martin dissolved the council. It has never been considered a general, or ecumenical council.

In spite of Martin's interest in reform, he accomplished very little in that direction. The old abuses still continued, and complaints were just as loud as before. Seven years after the disbanding of the Pavia-Sienna council, it was time for another one. Martin tried to delay, but the conciliarists were still strong and there was obvious need for more reform. Martin called the next council for Basle in 1431, but he did so reluctantly, and only under the pressure of threats. Then he had the good fortune of dying, and not having to put up with the council personally. Eugenius IV (1431-1447), a nephew of Gregory XII, was elected four and a half months before the seventeenth ecumenical council convened in Basle.

Eugenius himself was not present, and at the beginning almost nobody else was either. At the opening session there was not a single bishop there. The Council began in July, but attendance picked up only in October. Eugenius issued a decree dissolving the council in December, but the conciliarists refused to obey it. Emperor Sigismund encouraged the conciliarists, and they united their forces against the Pope. In this show-down between council and Pope, the conciliarists won. Eugenius maneuvered for fourteen months, but he finally recognized the Council. In the interim Nicholas of Cusa (1400-1464) wrote his *Concordantia Catholica* in defense of the Council, in which he insisted that the pope was only one member of the church, that the Church alone was infallible but could transfer that pre-rogative to a general council, and that the council was superior to the pope and could depose him.

Things indeed were going badly for Eugenius. The conciliarists were firmly in control of the Council, refus-ing to share presiding duties with the papal legates Eugenius sent. A popular rebellion in Rome even forced Eugenius out of the city for a while. In 1433 Nicholas of Cusa suggested the fraudulent nature of the Donation of Constantine, which had been the basis for many of the doctrines of the papacy about its foundation of power. Almost month by month, Eugenius was losing adher-ents.

Meanwhile, the Council was in the ascendant. It had forced the Pope into apparent submission, and it was making progress in dealing with some of the problems of the church. The Council opened negotiations with the Hussites, concluding them in the *Compactate of Prague*, signed in July of 1436 by legates of the council, Emperor Sigismund, and Bohemian envoys. This pro-vided for the reunion of the Hussites with the Roman Catholics with the provision that they could continue to receive communion in both elements. It also gave them some freedom in preaching and removed some grievances with reference to the holding of church property. To the Pope's chagrin, the Council met with these heretics as equals and granted special privileges to those who had openly defied the authority of the pope.

From the years 1433 to 1436 the council promulgated several reform decrees that would have gone a long way toward eliminating abuses in the church. Some measures prohibited clergy from having concubines, dealt with the abuse of appeals to the Roman papal court, insisted on the regular holding of provincial and diocesan synods, or made changes in the liturgy of the church. Other measures were aimed at limiting the power of the papacy, such as abolishing the payments of annates to Rome as well as some other taxes, instituting controls over the use of the interdict, making new regulations for the election of a pope, and demanding that papal legates give a financial accounting of their revenues to the Council of Basle. Eugenius protested such acts in August of 1435 and again in the spring of 1436, though without any success.

In May of 1438 a national French synod called by King Charles VII (1422-1461) met at Bourges and adopted the reformatory decrees of the council. This synodal action was the famous Pragmatic Sanction of Bourges, which set the tone for church-state relations in France.[4] In its terms was the provision that the council was superior to the pope, that the French church could administer its temporal property independently of the papacy, and that the French cold disallow papal nominations to vacant church positions. Emperor Sigismund was also on the side of the Council. He declared himself neutral on the issues in dispute between the papacy and the Council, but in a pinch he would support the Council.

Then the issue of the Greeks came up, and here the papacy won a complete reversal of its fortunes. The Byzantine Empire was in its death throes with the Ottoman Turks, and it again came requesting military aid from the West. Such requests dating from the time of the Crusades had never helped much, but the Greeks were desperate. Byzantine Emperor John VIII (1423-1448) sought a military alliance with the West, but he rightfully felt that religious reunion with Rome was a prerequisite. So he opened negotiations with both Pope and Council. The Council was not much interested: it was more concerned about internal matters at home. The Council did say, however, that negotiations could be continued at either Basle or Avignon. The Pope suggested negotiations could continue in Florence.

The crisis came over the relatively small issue of where negotiations between the East and West were to continue. Obviously, the Greeks would like a city more geographically convenient to them, for Basle was on the north slope of the Alps, and Avignon meant a lengthy voyage around Italy. When it came to a vote within the council, about 200 voting members chose Avignon, and about 70 preferred the Pope's suggestion of an Italian city. Both sides sent delegates to influence the Greeks, but the Greeks understandably wanted the closest site and chose Italy. The Pope agreed, and he recognized the minority of the Council that agreed with him as the legitimate council. The remainder, actually by far the majority, summoned the Pope to Basle, and when he refused they declared him in contempt of the council's authority. Eugenius dissolved the Council, but those at Basle refused to be dissolved. Those remaining in Basle —

actually the more radical of the conciliarists — grew increasingly volatile in their statements and demands, so much so that even men like Nicholas of Cusa left Basle to join the smaller council in Italy.[5]

While this fight between Pope and Basle continued in the background, the Pope reassembled his "legitimate" council in Ferrara in early 1438, and here they met with the Greek envoys. The Council transferred to Florence in January of 1439, and it was here that most of the discussions with the Greeks took place. All the old issues were brought up again: purgatory, the procession of the Holy Spirit (*filioque*), the use of unleavened bread, and the supremacy of the pope. The most thorny issue was, of course, this latter one. The final statement reads: "We recognize the Pope as Sovereign Pontiff, Vice-Regent and Vicar of Christ, Shepherd of all Christians, Ruler of the Church of God; saving the privileges and rights of the Patriarchs of the East." What these "privileges and rights" were is undefined — intentionally so; otherwise there would have been no union. Each side interpreted it as they desired. The decree proclaiming union was published in July, 1439, signed by 115 men from the West, 33 from the East. On paper, eastern and western churches were reunited almost four centuries after 1054.

Actually, however, the action of the eastern representatives at Florence was immediately repudiated by most Orthodox in the East. Many of these Christians preferred the fez of the Turks to the cardinal's hats belonging to the pope. Patriarchs of Antioch, Alexandria, and Jerusalem all joined in repudiating the union. When Constantinople fell fourteen years later, the Turks of course wanted the eastern Christians to have as little contact as possible with the western Christians, so they encouraged the foes of the union. Thus in 1472 a synod in Constantinople speaking for the Orthodox Church formally repudiated the union and anathematized those who adhered to it. But the papacy continued to have followers in the East. The Armenian Church accepted the papal position in 1439, and in 1442 the Jacobite Church of Syria. These eastern Uniate (accepting the union) churches continued officially under the Roman Catholic umbrella, although they had some independence in matters of liturgy and administration.

Meanwhile, friction between Pope and Council was in its last stages. The death of Sigismund in 1437, and the removal of some of the moderates to the Pope's camp, left Basle in the hands of the radicals. They wished to curb the Pope's power even further, and by the spring of 1439 they proclaimed the supremacy of the council over the pope to be a matter of faith. When Eugenius rejected this claim, they deposed him on charges of heresy in June, 1439.[6] By November they elected a replacement, who took the title Felix V. He is the last antipope in the long history of such figures in Roman Catholicism.

Felix had little support: only a part of Switzerland, Austria, Bavaria, the University of Paris, and a few other schools. Both France and Germany remained neutral in this dispute, waiting for further developments. In its antagonism against the pope the Council overreached itself. Because it was desperate for money, it claimed the right to grant indulgences, which was hardly a step toward reform. The idea of another schism in the church was totally unacceptable to most of Europe. More and more countries rallied behind Eugenius. After the union with the Greeks had been settled, Eugenius dealt with the remnant council still at Basle. He declared them heretic and excommunicated, and in April of 1441 the Florence council affirmed the papal declaration *Etsi non dubitemus* which stated the superiority of the pope over the council, exactly reversing the decree *Sacrosancta* approved at Constance twenty-six years previously. In April of 1442 the Pope's council was moved again, this time to Rome, where it remained completely under the control of Eugenius. He finally dissolved it in 1445. At Basle things went from bad to worse. By 1446 the Germans had declared for the Pope, as did the French in 1449. With shrinking support and no hope for the future, Felix resigned that same year. He was rewarded by being named a cardinal in the court of the Roman pope. The remnant of the council then elected Nicholas V (he had succeeded Eugenius in 1447) as their pope also; with nothing else to do, they disbanded. The final consistent response of the papacy to this conciliar drive came in 1460 when Pope Pius II in his bull *Execrabilis* prohibited any appeal from the pope to a council, and pronounced an anathema upon anyone who dared to do so.[7]

Thus ended the era of conciliarism. It had started out with great promise, but it was wrecked over the problems of dissension and disagreement. The radical conciliarists at Basle had overplayed their hand after their initial easy successes over Eugenius. By making too much out of themselves, and by refusing to discuss seriously union with the Greeks, they allowed Eugenius to assume the offensive and take all their strength away from them. As a result, all the proposals for reform still lay with papal initiative.

Nicholas V was the first of the Renaissance popes, and there was no interest in reform under these pontiffs. Consequently, all the abuses that could have been eliminated remained for another half century to become the grievances that launched the Protestant Reformation in the early sixteenth century. The conciliar idea remained around for some time, and many reformers appealed for a council during the Reformation, but conciliarism had lost its strength and attraction. After 1449 the popes were in control of the Roman Catholic Church, without any exception.

Bibliography for Chapter Fifteen

Flick, Alexander Clarence. *The Decline of the Medieval Church.* (2 vols.) New York: Alfred A. Knopf, 1930.
    A thorough treatment, with extensive coverage both of the papal schism and the Conciliar Movement.
Loomis, Louise Ropes. *The Council of Constance.* New York: Columbia University Press, 1961.
    A comprehensive and detailed look at this extremely important gathering.
Tierney, Brian. *Foundations of the Conciliar Theory.* Cambridge: Cambridge University Press, 1955.
    A careful and thorough study of this important development, by a reputed scholar in the field.

Questions and Projects for Chapter Fifteen

1. Do some additional research on the growth of parlia-

mentary government in England and France in this period. Write a paper comparing these developments to the growth of conciliarism in the church.

2. Make a chart listing the Councils of Pisa, Constance, and Basle, and fill in separate columns under the following headings: date, major personnel, decisions made, and results.

3. Make a list of the cycles of division, reunion, and division that have occurred between eastern and western branches of Christianity up to the year 1500.

4. Consult some Roman Catholic historians and report on how they view the actions and results of the Councils of Pisa, Constance, and Basle.

5. Consult some Eastern Orthodox historians and report on how they view the negotiations that took place at Basle and Florence, as well as the result of them.

Notes for Chapter Fifteen

1. Excerpts from the writings of both Marsilio and Ockham along these lines can be found in Petry, pp. 510-517.

2. The decree *Sacrosancta* can be found in Petry, p. 533; Barry, I, p. 504; and Bettenson, pp. 192, 193.

3. Likewise, *Frequens* can be found in Petry, p. 536; Barry, I, pp. 504, 505; and Bettenson, pp. 193, 194.

4. The Pragmatic Sanction can be found in Barry, I, pp. 513-518.

5. The loss of Cusa was a serious reverse to the rump conciliarists at Basle. He was a firm conciliarist himself, but not a radical like them. The tenor of his writings can be gauged from the excerpts in Petry, pp. 538-543; and Barry, I, pp. 506-510.

6. The decree of deposition is in Barry, I, p. 510.

7. Pius' decree is in Barry, I, pp. 512-513.

Chapter Sixteen
THE RENAISSANCE PAPACY

When Nicholas V (1447-1455) ascended the papal throne, it was the beginning of a new era. He is the first of the Renaissance popes. The Renaissance itself is a difficult thing to date. Some historians say it started in 1250, others say 1300, 1350, or 1400. All such dates are arbitrary, of course. The significant thing is that a cultural revolution had been brewing in Italy for some time. As mentioned in Chapter Twelve, this was one of the long-range results of the Crusades. Increased trade in the luxury goods of the East brought great wealth to the maritime cities of northern Italy; wealth and resultant leisure time allowed patrons to subsidize the bright young artists.

Much of the Renaissance, and indeed also the Reformation, is also connected with the word "humanism." As early as the fourteenth century men began to rediscover ancient manuscripts from classical Rome and Greece. At first this was a literary quest to rediscover the glories of the classical languages. But reading the old manuscripts brought these men to realize the tremendous cultural accomplishments that had taken place in the ancient world. This placed a great deal of emphasis on human achievement, thus "humanism." It is important to distinguish this from the modern connotations of "humanism." The modern form is entirely atheistic and secular. In the Renaissance era, the overwhelming majority of humanists were Christian humanists. They still maintained their faith in Christianity, although they were terribly impressed by the cultural accomplishments of the pagan Greeks and Romans. They sought to duplicate in a Christian context the architecture, the sculpture, the poetry, and the literature that had characterized classical culture. Many of their paintings depicted Christian figures in classical style. The Renaissance popes were those pontiffs who lavishly used the financial and appointive powers of the church to support and encourage these humanist artists.

When Nicholas V came to the throne, he had to be careful so as not to do anything that would give the dying conciliar movement in Basle any reason for existence. He could breathe a big sigh of relief when that assembly finally dispersed in 1449. An event that caused him a great deal of grief was the overthrow and loss of Constantinople in May of 1453. The soldiers that had come from the West were few in number, and on the morning of May 29, 1453, the Turkish soldiers finally poured through the holes in the walls of the battered city. It was the end of the eastern half of the old Roman Empire. The Turks renamed the city Istanbul, the name still in use. One of Nicholas' more dubious accomplishments was to perform the last imperial coronation held in Rome — that of Emperor Frederick III (1440-1493) in March, 1452. Later Holy Roman Emperors were crowned, but never again in Rome. It is ironic that Nicholas' pontificate saw the last antipope, the last imperial coronation in Rome, and the fall of Constantinople. It was getting to be a new age.

But the major thing for which Nicholas is remembered is his patronage of the arts. He conceived the plans for a new Vatican Palace and St. Peter's basilica, though the building of the church was cut short by his death. But some wings of the new palace were erected and Nicholas occupied them before his death. Several painters enjoyed his patronage, leaving behind numerous frescoes. Nicholas sponsored additional construction and renovation of buildings in Rome. He also began the collection of books that became the magnificent Vatican library.

He patronized Lorenzo Valla (1406-1457). Somewhat earlier, in 1439, Valla had written a treatise showing that the Donation of Constantine was a forgery. The Donation had been used as a foundation for papal claims to power in the West, and many Christian leaders were very disturbed to learn of its fraudulent nature. This did not, however, bring about a revocation of papal claims. A typical humanist who gloried in classical Latin, Valla ridiculed the Latin Vulgate, the accepted Bible of the Church, which was written in the language of the common people rather than of the classics. For this he was even called before the Inquisition. Valla also wrote a book *On Pleasure*, a thinly disguised scholarly work on hedonism which was really a manual on what sensual possibilities were available. It was such men as Valla that caused many church leaders to wonder whether the humanists were heathen or Christian.

Calixtus III (1455-1458) was born as Alfonso Borgia, the first Spanish pope since the fourth century, and the first significant representative of the Borgia family that became infamous in papal history. Pope only three years, perhaps his most significant accomplishment was in returning the papacy to the practice of nepotism. Two of his sister's sons were made cardinals, one of them Rodrigo Borgia, whom we will meet again. At the time, Rodrigo was only twenty-five years old. Even while Calixtus was still alive, the Borgia kin made themselves a nuisance in Rome, but Calixtus was either unable or unwilling to do anything about it.

His successor was Pius II (1458-1464), a humanist himself, probably one of the best of his generation. He had two illegitimate children while a young man. Both died young, but it was an indication of the kind of lifestyle that began to permeate the church. In Germany he became the poet laureate to Frederick III. Much of his writing, including two dramas, reflected the low moral tone of many of the Renaissance artists. Humanists rejoiced at his election, and indeed Pius did reflect humanist interests throughout his pontificate. His love of natural beauty and architecture led to numerous wandering trips around Italy, during which he took the opportunity to carefully poke around in old ruins. He also engaged in nepotism, making two of his nephews cardinals. One of them, Francesco Todeschini Piccolomini, briefly reigned as Pius III (1503). Pius spent a great deal of effort trying to organize against the Turks, but nothing much ever materialized.

The humanist Pius II was followed by a reaction under Paul II (1464-1471). He was not a man of culture; in fact he knew no Latin at all. He was suspicious of many of the Renaissance artists and humanists, feeling they were thinly veiled pagans functioning under a Christian veneer. He dismissed many writers and artists from the papal service. Two humanist writers even directed a plot to remove him from the papacy (by death if necessary), though the plot was discovered in time. One of the two survived his arrest and painted a very negative view of Paul, a view which has colored historians' understanding of him down to the present.

Paul encouraged crusades against the Turks, and he continued rebuilding in Rome, though his buildings were practical ones, including some for sanitary purposes. Although Paul wanted to cleanse the church by removing Renaissance humanism from the papacy, he accomplished little in this regard. In fact Paul supported two printers who arrived in Rome from Germany in 1467, and thus he founded the papal publishing house. As important as literature was to the humanist, it is ironic that this anti-humanist pope employed the services of publishers.

His successor, Sixtus IV (1471-1484), epitomized what is both the best and the worst of the Renaissance popes. He used the finances of the papacy to support worthy artists and humanists, and he sponsored much grand art; but he also brought the moral tone of the papacy down into the depths and initiated the worst period of the entire Renaissance papacy. Sixtus himself was of blameless personal life, a scholar, and a distinguished teacher. But the war with the Turks, as well as internicene conflicts in the Italian city-states, kept him distracted from watchful care over the activities of church officials. He needed trusted officers within the church, so he turned to nepotism on a grand scale. He put relatives in positions of authority both in the church and in the Papal States, but what he accomplished was to turn political power in Italy into a free-for-all, with everybody grabbing as much as he could. Sixtus put the church into the business of inter-city warfare for his own family purposes, to establish power bases and spheres of influence. At least six of his nephews were made cardinals, one of them later becoming Pope Julius II. Another nephew received four bishoprics in addition to his cardinal's hat, and he used the income to finance an expensive mistress as well as orgies for his friends.

The activities of his family included the famous Pazzi conspiracy against the Medici family ruling Florence. Sixtus was aware of the plot and approved of it. One Medici was killed in church, but the head of the family escaped. For resisting the assassination attempt Sixtus anathematized the remainder of the Medici family and declared war on them. This action became typical of Renaissance Italy and the worldliness of the families controlling the papacy. The corruption and simony in the papal court brought on a doubling of religious taxes, and the number of offices that could be purchased outright increased. Sixtus also supported numerous painters, and he began many buildings, particularly churches. Often he destroyed ancient temples, arches and tombs to do so. The Sistine Chapel, which was consecrated in 1483 is probably his most famous monument. His pontificate represented a complete secularization of the papal office. He was not interested in spiritual ministry but with monarchy and power politics in Italy, dependent upon simony and venality. Sixtus' cultural contributions by supporting the arts were more than counterbalanced by the evil he did through the papal office.

In the conclave that met soon after the death of Sixtus, there were heavy pressures and bribes to make Rodrigo Borgia the next pope. Giuliano della Rovere was also angling for the position. In the deadlock that ensued, a compromise was struck with the selection of Innocent VIII (1484-1492). Married before he had been ordained, Innocent had a son by his wife, plus other illegitimate children. He is the first pope to openly acknowledge his illegitimate children; previous popes had always passed them off as nephews or nieces when observers noted the family likeness. Sixtus had spent so much money on artists that Innocent found the papal treasury sorely depleted. To get through this emergency, he developed a new science in selling church offices, creating new ones to be sold, and making simony a way of life for the papal court. Before the year was out (he became pope on August 29) he even had to pawn the papal triple tiara for 100,000 ducats. A ring of cardinals developed the new business of forging papal decrees for sale. The Pope's vice-chamberlain was once heard to say, "The Lord desires not the death of a sinner, but that he live and pay."

He appointed only one of his nephews a cardinal, but he used his position as pope to advance the station of his illegitimate children. He paid off political debts by appointing the scions of other powerful men. Giovanni de Medici (later Leo X) had earlier been given a position in the church at age 7 by Sixtus; was made abbot of a monastery at age 8; received two more abbacies (including Monte Cassino) by the time he was 12. Innocent made him a cardinal at age 14. Innocent also patronized several of the great painters of the time, and he had tombs, frescoes, and buildings erected with the monies coming into the church. He was a typical Renaissance pope, using his position for the betterment of his family and the increase of the arts, but there was no spiritual improvement in the life of the church.

The death of Innocent opened up the way for Rodrigo Borgia to again try his hand at buying the papacy, and this time he succeeded. There is irony in the fact that he took the name Alexander VI (1492-1503). Alexander was the greatest conqueror of the pagan world, but the last legitimate Roman pope named Alexander had been Alexander IV. Alexander V was elected by the council of Pisa, was considered an antipope, and therefore did not count. Yet Alexander VI apparently counted him anyway. Perhaps this recognition of illegitimacy is a fitting commentary on this pontiff's reign.

His pontificate was certainly one of the most depraved in the entire history of the church, not only because of his own actions, but also for those he allowed on the part of his relatives. During his days as cardinal he maintained several mistresses in Rome. His favorite, Vanozza de Catanei, he married off successively to three husbands, but he lived with her for years, and she bore him four children, including the infamous Cesare and Lucretia. In 1489 he took as his new mistress a thirteen-year-old girl Giulia Farnese, and she continued as his mistress during his papacy, bearing the Pope sons in 1498 and 1503. The Farnese made no trouble about this, because Alexander had bought them off by making Giulia's brother a cardinal (later he became Pope Paul III). The local gossips in Rome called Giulia "the Bride of Christ." In 1493 Alexander made his illegitimate son Cesare a cardinal at age 18, his illegitimacy having been set aside by Sixtus when the lad was only 4 years old.

Alexander continued the policy of earlier popes of enriching his family out of papal resources. He gave administrative positions in the Papal States to members of his family; sometimes outright gifts of church land provided a power base for further Borgia aggrandizement. When an opposing political family invited French intervention in the sordid affairs of Italy, Alexander negotiated with the Turkish sultan for assistance. The scandal of the Pope dickering with the sultan for aid against a Christian king was a shock to much of Europe. The French occupied Rome, but then suffered a reversal of fortunes. With the French retreating, Alexander turned on the families that had sided with the French, not only for warring against the Church, but for warring against the family of the Pope. The college of cardinals did nothing, since there were eight Borgias ensconced there.

Alexander's eldest son Giovanni was being groomed to become the next link of a Borgia dynasty, but he was murdered in 1497. The evidence pointed to Cesare as the culprit, but nothing was ever proven. When Alexander was conducting dragging operations in the Tiber River to locate his son's body, the local wits observed, "Pope Alexander has truly become a fisher of men." With Giovanni gone, Cesare became the heir apparent. He devised a plan to use French aid against their political enemies in northern Italy, and the French came on a second invasion in 1499. With this assist, Cesare went on to grab a great deal of land in north central Italy, much of it withdrawn from the Papal States to become Borgia family territory. Cesare quickly gained the reputation of a tyrant and monster. Once for diversion he turned some criminals loose in a courtyard of the Vatican and shot them from a window. But his position was tied to that of his father. He was dependent upon papal wealth to pay the bills, and the use of ecclesiastical pressure to force people into line. When Alexander died in 1503, Cesare's position in Italy was also lost. He became a mercenary soldier in Spain and died in battle in 1507.

Thus ended the pontificate of one of the most depraved and ill-disciplined men ever to sit in the papal chair. But he is remembered for being a major patron of the arts, and he issued the Bull of Demarcation in 1494 which separated Portuguese from Spanish possessions in the New World.

Pius III, the nephew of Pius II, ascended to the papacy, but he was already mortally ill at the time. He lasted only twenty-six days. Then Giuliano della Rovere returned from a ten-year exile (obviously it was not safe for him in Rome under Alexander). He was elected quickly as Julius II (1503-1513). He is a curious mixture; he used papal power both to cleanse the church and to build an empire.

After his election he came out in full opposition to the use of simony, promising that any simoniac would receive severe punishment. An Italian himself, he wanted to throw out all French and Spanish from powerful positions in the church, including the Borgias. He was determined to recover the territory they had taken away from the Papal States. Julius was a warrior pope, often leading the papal armies into combat himself. There were numerous paintings and sculptures of him in suits of armor. His most famous campaign was against Bologna, which he conquered finally in 1506. Julius was also a great patron of the arts. Not only did he sponsor Michaelangelo, but he also laid the cornerstone for the new St. Peter's and got that massive building project under way. He assigned Michaelangelo to paint the ceiling of the Sistine Chapel, one of the most noteworthy of the Renaissance pieces of art, at the same time that Raphael was doing his famous frescoes and Bramante was redoing the Vatican palace.

Life was never peaceful very long for Julius. Whenever he finished a victorious campaign, his enemies realigned and came back again. In 1509 Julius used French help to defeat Venice, then he used Venetian help to drive the French out of northern Italy. He appeared to be a strongly patriotic Italian driving all foreigners out of the peninsula, but when some of his supporters went over to the French, Julius had to retreat back to Rome. In 1511 Bologna again fell to his enemies. To celebrate Julius' conquest of the city in 1506, Michaelangelo had made a magnificent bronze statue of Julius on horseback, which was considered one of the most beautiful works of art of the entire Renaissance period. But after his opponents captured Bologna, they melted the statue down and made a cannon out of it.

Also in 1511 five of his cardinals, under French support, convened an illegal council in Pisa. Julius countered by calling a council to meet in Rome in 1512, the Fifth Lateran Council. Its chief accomplishment was to work out a new relationship between the papacy and France, the Concordat of Bologna, which remained the foundation of Franco-papal relations until the time of Napoleon. In response to a recent disturbance, the council also declared the immortality of the human soul. Julius died in 1513, but the council sat until early 1517. It talked of some minor reform issues, but accomplished nothing. It is interesting to note that only a few months after it disbanded, without achieving any significant reform, Martin Luther nailed his theses to the church door in Wittenberg.

The death of Julius in 1513 led to the election of Leo X (1513-1521). While not as corrupt and depraved as some of his predecessors, Leo was also noticeably lacking in the spiritual commitment needed to reform the glaring abuses that clamored for attention in the church. His attitude was perfectly reflected in his famous response to a Venetian diplomat: "God has given us the papacy, let us enjoy it." It is no surprise that the Protestant Reformation began under this pope.

All this is not to say, however, that there was no concern for reform on the part of church leaders. Even if we ignore the platitudes of popes who were obviously not serious about reform, there were still many voices who were genuinely concerned. Some of the voices of concern were those of humanists, both in Italy and elsewhere. There were men like John Colet, who came to Italy in the latter part of the fifteenth century, breathed deeply of the Renaissance spirit, and went back to England to foster a new light of learning and spiritual renewal. Every country had its John Colet. Some of these voices were those of bishops, abbots, and plain monks who were sickened of the continual corruption and immorality in the highest places of the church. They were little circles of light in a dark world, and except for a brief local notice, the world paid them no heed. Many of the rulers were aghast at the immorality practiced in the name of the church, with the result that the church had drastically lessened prestige when the time came for the conflicts with Protestantism in the next century.

Two of the most significant voices were those of Girolamo Savonarola (1452-1498) and Desiderius Erasmus (1466-1536). Savonarola was a Dominican monk from northern Italy who became head of a monastery in Florence in 1491. His fame came mostly through his preaching, which denounced the evils in the current lifestyles of the people. He also had an apocalyptic streak in him and warned of disasters to come. When the first French invasion of 1494 brought killing and pillage, his prophecies seemed to be fulfilled. Popular acclaim in Florence brought him great influence in the city and throughout the northern part of the peninsula.

Many lives were reformed, as well as the entire political structure of Florence. But a reaction against him was inevitable in Renaissance Italy. Alexander VI was disturbed at his political meddling as well as his moral preaching. He tried to bribe him with a cardinal's hat, but Savonarola was not interested. In 1495 Alexander summoned him to Rome, but the friar pleaded ill health and stayed in Florence. In October of that year Alexander commanded him to stop preaching, but by the next spring Savonarola was back in the pulpit. By the spring of 1497 he was boldly attacking the evils and corruption in the church, with thinly veiled allusions to the papacy. Alexander excommunicated him in May, but Savonarola defied the Pope's edict, declaring that Alexander VI was neither a true pope nor even a Christian.

Meanwhile Savonarola's blunt preaching was offending some of the powerful political figures in Florence, and many felt that the preacher was meddling in personal affairs. In the spring of 1498 his political enemies took advantage of the people's disenchantment with him and had him arrested. Fourteen times he was tortured and confessed to various crimes, only to retract the confession later. Finally in May of 1498 he and two of his followers were hanged in the Florence piazza under the watchful eye of two papal commissioners. It was obvious that in the political situation current under such popes as Alexander VI no meaningful reform could be possible.

Erasmus was Dutch, born the illegitimate son of a priest. A brilliant young man, but penniless, he became a cleric in order to have access to additional education. Perceptive of human nature, and also well-read in the writings of the apostles and early church fathers, Erasmus challenged much of the superstition of saints' relics, pilgrimages, and empty ritual that formed so much of a part of the expected lifestyle of a sixteenth century Christian. Brilliant with his pen, he wrote satires in which he gleefully castigated stupid priests and immoral monks. His wit became the rave of Europe, and his scholarship became the envy of all. His edition of the Greek New Testament appeared in 1516, the first one printed in Greek, and he set a whole new trend in biblical research. By that time he was the recognized leader of the liberal reform movement in Europe.

But when Luther tacked up his Ninety-Five Theses, Erasmus could not follow the German's lead. Erasmus tried to stay tactfully neutral in the controversies between Luther and his enemies. He believed in the value of education and quiet study of Scripture, but he was not a leader of men or of movements. He once commented in a letter that the theological positions of Luther were not worth dying for. He was also a pacifist, never a crusader. Thus he could not understand the refusal of the Protestants to negotiate some of their demands. He was never willing to break from the Roman Church; he lived and died a Roman Catholic.

As a result, Erasmus was constantly attacked by both sides. The Catholics attacked him for his satire, for providing the Protestants ammunition to use against the Church. The Protestants attacked him for failing to be consistent in his position and abandon the corrupt Roman church. He was enough of a humanist to argue that man was too good to be totally depraved, but he was not enough of a reformer to challenge people to action. Nine years after his death the Council of Trent branded him a heretic and placed some of his writings on the Index of Prohibited Books. A reformer he may have been, but it took the commitment and leadership of Martin Luther to get a meaningful reform movement under way.

Bibliography for Chapter Sixteen

Cellini, Benvenuto. *The Autobiography of Benvenuto Cellini.* Trans. by John Addington Symonds. Garden City, New York: Garden City Publishing Co., 1927.

A classic autobiography by a renowned artist whose ego is even larger than his fame. Excellent inside look at the artistic world of the era.

Gilmore, Myron P. *The World of Humanism, 1453-1517.* New York: Harper & Row, Publishers, 1962.

A classic work by a renowned historian, adequately summarizing the intellectual developments of this significant period.

Huizinga, Johan. *Erasmus and the Age of Reformation.* New York: Harper & Row, Publishers, 1957.

A standard work on Erasmus by one of the great Renaissance-Reformation scholars.

Spitz, Lewis W. *The Renaissance and Reformation Movements.* Vol. I, *The Renaissance.* Chicago: Rand McNally & Company, 1971.

An historical overview of this period by a well-known American scholar. He sees the era as one of *movement*, with Italy being the source.

Questions and Projects for Chapter Sixteen

1. Prepare a list of popes from 1447 to 1534, arranging them from "best" to "worst." Be prepared to defend the order of your listing.
2. Consult a book on Art History and make a list of the famous works of art (sculpture, paintings, frescoes,

architecture) that were done for the Church during this period. List the artist as well.

3. Consult some Roman Catholic histories of the church to see how they treat the popes from 1447 to 1534. Wherein do they agree or differ from the account in this chapter?

4. Take either Savonarola or Erasmus and compare him to either Wyclif or Hus. Wherein do they agree or differ?

5. Compare the Renaissance popes to those of the Pornocracy. Which popes were "worse"? How does the political context differ? How does the political context influence each of the two situations?

Chapter Seventeen
LUTHER AND THE PROTESTANT REVOLT

As we have mentioned in the last several chapters, concern for reform in the church was a constant factor in the two centuries prior to 1500. Men like Wyclif and Hus caused considerable head shaking throughout the ecclesiastical halls of Europe, but many people found several of their ideas defensible. In addition to this idea revolution, there was a ground swell of dissatisfaction with the status quo in the church.

The Council of Constance healed the divided papacy and promised reform. The unified papacy, however, did not follow through on that reform, and many people — clerical as well as lay, prince as well as commoner — were very disappointed. The idea grew that if the pope did not initiate reform —and with the Renaissance popes that was not hopeful — then other people would have to seize the initiative. People felt frustrated because of this lack of reform, and there was a strong feeling of anti-clericalism throughout most of Europe on the eve of the Reformation. Too many clergy were immoral, particularly the upper clergy of bishops, archbishops, and abbots. The papal court was criticized, not because of its power, but because of the corrupt way that power was used. Large numbers of clergy, particularly the higher clergy, were guilty of absenteeism: they held certain offices, received the income from them, but were not present to do the ministry the position required. Quite often a minor cleric was dispatched to do the bare minimum involved, and this person received only a pittance out of the vast income of the office holder. On the eve of the Reformation in Germany, only about 7% of the parishes had a resident priest. Many such absentee clerics were also guilty of pluralism: holding more than one church position, and receiving income from all such offices he held, even if he did none of the work. Further, large numbers of clergy were poorly trained, if trained at all. Many of the parish priests were simply peasants that the local lord put into the parish church because he did not trust an outsider. Many of the upper clergy were unemployed sons of noblemen who were trained for war and the hunt; it was no surprise that they continued such pursuits rather than serve the diocese over which they were made bishop. Many of the poor priests could not even read enough Latin to get through the Mass.

Thus throughout Europe there was a strong feeling of disenchantment and even resentment against the clergy. The popular literature of the day made constant reference to the "stupid priest." German satire just before the Reformation had great fun with the German words *Affen* and *Pfaffen* — which mean respectively apes and clergymen. When the Reformation got under way, it fed upon this popular anticlericalism. If the common people had not supported the reformers, the Reformation would not have succeeded. This pervasive anticlericalism was an essential ingredient in the entire reform movement. People were sufficiently disenchanted with Roman corruption and inefficiency to risk the transition to new ideas.

Martin Luther (1483-1546) did not start out as a troublemaker. The son of a miner rising into the middle classes, Martin received the best education available in local schools, and in 1501 he went to the University of Erfurt to pursue a legal career. Finishing his MA degree in 1505, he went home for a summer vacation, to return to a full law school program that fall. But thoughts of death preyed on his mind. A friend had recently died of pleurisy, another of the plague. Catholic thinking at the time presented God as a wrathful deity Who delighted in punishing men for their sins. Death was a horrible entrance into a threatening world of judgment, and Luther did not want to die. On his return journey back to the university, Luther was caught by a severe thunderstorm in a dark woods. A lightning bolt hit a nearby tree, knocking him to the ground, and the dagger in his belt (students always went armed) seriously wounded his thigh, barely missing an artery. In desperate agony, Luther cried out to the patron saint of miners, "St. Anne, help me! I will become a monk."

Luther survived the experience but he felt he had committed himself to the monastery. Two weeks later he

REFORMATION EUROPE
HAPSBURG LAND

NORWAY SWEDEN

DENMARK

PRUSSIA

IRELAND

ENGLAND
London

ATLANTIC
OCEAN

Cologne
Aachen
HESSE
HOLY ROMAN
EMPIRE

Warsaw
Wittenberg

POLAND

Paris

FRANCE

Augsburg

Geneva

Genoa

HUNGARY

VENETIAN REPUBLIC

BAVARIA

OTTOMAN EMPIRE

PORTUGAL

Madrid

SPAIN

REPUBLIC
OF GENOA

Rome

PAPAL
STATES

MEDITERRANEAN   SEA

N O R T H   A F R I C A

joined the Augustinian Hermits in Erfurt. As a monk, Luther received further instruction in the sacramental system of the church, and he was told that man must do sufficient good works in life to counteract all his sin, or be sent to purgatory at death to pay out the penalty for his sins. Luther, who had a sensitive sense of sin, felt trapped. He felt God expected perfection out of him but had created him with a human nature that was only too prone to sin. Luther even wondered if he could love God for demanding the impossible of him.

In 1508 Luther went to teach theology at the new University of Wittenberg in Saxony, and his studies led him to realize that the biblical concept of repentance was an emphasis on an attitude of sorrow for sin — not a demand that one do "works of penance." This relieved Luther some, but then he came to the further discovery that God's justice was not found in the condemnation of sinners; instead, it meant that the just man lived by faith. This insight led to Luther's great emphasis on justification by grace through faith.

Luther saw new applications of this idea when indulgence sellers appeared in Germany in 1517. Pope Leo X needed more money to build St. Peter's basilica in Rome, and the Archbishop of Mainz needed income to replace the tremendous expenses he had incurred in securing his position. The two agreed on the sale of a special papal indulgence, one that would give the purchaser complete forgiveness of all sins. The whole indulgence concept contradicted Luther's new insight, so on October 31, 1517, he posted ninety-five theses for debate on the door of the castle church in Wittenberg.[1] This was not a rebellious act; the church door served as the college bulletin board. As a university professor, Luther was simply posting ideas for debate, he was not advocating revolution.

But his famous Ninety-Five Theses challenged the entire salvation system of Roman Catholicism. Pope Leo at first dismissed Luther's questions as "a monkish squabble." But within a year Luther moved beyond the indulgence controversy to the whole matter of papal authority. A meeting with Cardinal Cajetan (1469-1534) in Augsburg in October of 1518 convinced both men that their positions were irreconcilable. A debate with John Eck (1486-1543) in Leipzig the next July forced Luther to admit that some of the views of John Hus were both good and Christian. It was now clear that Luther had withdrawn from the Roman Catholic Church.

In June of 1520 Pope Leo, through the bull *Exsurge Domini*, condemned 41 Lutheran errors and condemned Luther as a heretic, giving him 60 days to recant or be excommunicated.[2] In the meantime Luther turned to writing. In August he wrote the pamphlet, *Address to the German Nobility*, in which he stated that if the church leaders would not reform the church, then the nobility had the obligation to do it. Luther argued that they had the authority to do this because of the priesthood of all believers — a doctrine that remained crucial to the Reformation. In October Luther wrote *The Babylonian Captivity of the Church*, an attack on the seven sacraments of Catholicism. Instead of the traditional seven, Luther said there are only two — baptism and the Lord's Supper. In November Luther wrote *The Freedom of the Christian Man*, in which he argued that man is freed from dependence upon good works; he receives the free grace of God through faith. Luther went on to state that this does not produce license. He insisted that there can be no such thing as faith without works. He agrees completely with James, "Faith without works is dead," by explaining that a faith that does not produce works is not even rightly called faith. However, it is not the works that save. They are only the result of a saving faith; yet they are an essential result, or there is no faith. These three treatises are the heart and kernel of Luther's theology.[3]

Also in November Luther wrote a little pamphlet, *Against the Accursed Bull of the Anti-Christ*, aimed directly at the Pope. In December Luther took a copy of the papal bull *Exsurge Domini* outside the city gates and burned it. In January of 1521 he was officially excommunicated. But a thrill had gone through Germany at the realization that this lone Saxon monk was willing to stand up against the entire Roman Catholic establishment. Luther became a hero, and the Germans were determined he would not suffer the same fate as had John Hus.

In April of 1521 Luther was summoned to the meeting of the German Reichstag at Worms. He thought he would be given an opportunity to defend his views before young Emperor Charles V (1519-1556), but, like Hus, he was simply given the opportunity to recant his heretical views. In a moving scene, Luther said that since his views were a faithful exposition of Holy Scripture, he could not and would not recant. Already excommunicated by the church, Luther was now declared an outlaw by the state, and all who aided him were to share his fate.[4] But Luther had the support of his prince,

Frederick of Saxony, who risked his own position to protect the reformer. Luther lived another twenty-five years, while his ideas spread all over northern Europe.

In the mid-1520's, two major events occurred which had great influence on the Lutheran developments in Germany. The first was the Peasant's Revolt. The social conditions of the time represented a major imposition on the lives and freedoms of the peasant classes. Many of the peasants had heard of Luther's teaching on Christian freedom, and they took this to mean that they had the right to throw off their feudal serfdom. Revolt began in south Germany in 1524, spreading to much of the remainder of the country by the next year. At first Luther sympathized with the peasants' demands (he had come from peasant stock himself), but when the peasants became militant and took up arms, Luther wrote several tracts against them. The princes soon crushed the revolt, and the peasants in southern Germany felt Luther had betrayed them. Lutheranism all but died out in these lands.

The second major event occurred in 1525. Luther took a wife, thus ending not only his celibacy but also what celibacy represented to the Roman clergy. His wife Katie was a former nun, and the Luthers had six children. Katie provided a good home for Luther, watching over his health and improving his diet. The Luther household became the model Protestant parsonage for the next several centuries. Increasingly from this time on, Protestant clergy were more often married than not.

Meanwhile, additional rulers and princes were adopting the Lutheran position, including the kings of the Scandinavian countries — first Denmark, then Sweden and Norway. In Germany the Lutheran princes came to represent a sizeable number. When Emperor Charles tried in 1529 to remove some of their religious privileges, they protested and thus became known as "Protestants." Meeting at the Diet of Augsburg in 1530, these princes refused to sacrifice their new adherence, and they presented the Emperor with their statement of faith, the Augsburg Confession. Charles was greatly irritated. Fearful of the Emperor's designs against them, the Lutheran rulers formed a defensive military alliance. Unfortunately, the Catholic princes did the same, and Germany was soon split up into two armed camps.

But Emperor Charles was not yet able to move against the Protestants. The Turks, who had captured Constantinople the previous century, were pushing their way through Hungary and into Austria, and it was necessary for Charles to give first priority to the Turkish threat. Many of the Lutherans showed their good faith by sending contingents to defend the eastern frontier against the Turks — something many of the Catholic princes were reluctant to do. In addition, Charles had to fight four separate wars with the French who were trying to break up the Hapsburg encirclement around their own country. Finally in 1546, the very year Luther died, Charles was able to concentrate on the Lutheran upstarts. He defeated and captured most of the Lutheran princes, but Charles discovered that the common people still refused to abandon their Lutheran identity. In 1555 he had to agree to the Peace of Augsburg, which allowed every prince to decide which religious view would be allowed in his own territory. Through this arrangement, German Lutherans and German Catholics settled down to a very uneasy truce. But as we shall see in Chapter XIX, this truce was not permanent.

Luther was certainly the most important of the sixteenth century reformers, but he was not the only one. Many historians contend that if Luther had never lived, someone would have initiated reform. But Luther was the man who filled this place in history, and it was Luther's insights and personality that influenced the beginning and early development of the Protestant Reformation.

The pioneer of the reform in Switzerland was Ulrich Zwingli (1484-1531), born just fifty-two days after Luther, into a family of well-to-do farmers. Uncles in the clergy oversaw his education, which included stays at universities in Basle, Berne, and Vienna. In the process Zwingli picked up a strong attachment for humanism, but in the fall of 1506 he interrupted his studies to become a parish priest. He became an avid devotee of Erasmus, opened a school for boys in his community, but also fell to the temptation of fornication.[5] His humanitarian instincts led him to speak out against the common Swiss practice of selling mercenary soldiers to the fighting princes of Europe. Twice Zwingli accompanied contingents of soldiers to northern Italy where they participated in the maelstrom of power politics and military confrontation in that area. In one battle the Swiss suffered 10,000 dead. Partially because of the local friction caused by his resistance to mercenary recruiting, Zwingli went to another position in Einsiedeln in 1516. Determined to shun fornication, his resolve lasted a year, until he (in his words) was seduced by his barber's daughter. By her Zwingli had one illegitimate child.

At Einsiedeln Zwingli began expository preaching, which made him popular with the people who now began to receive something from the sermons. Preaching expositorily, Zwingli began to notice that the church pictured in the New Testament was not the church of his day. By the summer of 1518 Zwingli even attacked a papal indulgence seller in town. His preaching brought him to notice, and in 1519 he began a new position as preacher in the large church in Zurich.

It was apparently late in 1518 that Zwingli first heard of Luther, and by the next year he was enthusiastic over the German. The two had much in common, though it is interesting to note that they became reformers through rather different routes. Luther struggled with acceptance before God and had to cast off the Catholic sacramental system. Zwingli had no struggles with sin (as witnessed by his fornication), but it was his humanistic studies that led him to the documents of the early church and the inevitable comparison with the contemporary church. Luther's was a moral impulse, Zwingli's was a more scholarly one. But once Zwingli got on track, their thrust was much the same.

The developments of the Reformation in various countries usually followed the line of political authority in these countries. In Germany there was no unified overall government; the various German princes each controlled their territory. When a prince became Lutheran, Lutheranism prospered in his territory. Switzerland was different. Although there was no unified Swiss government over all the cantons, several of the larger cantons each had a major city as its capital — Geneva, Berne, Zurich, Basle. These cities were

controlled by a town council. The Reformation developments had to await conversion of a majority of the town
council.

Zwingli, therefore, had to be patient and diplomatic.
Where some of the German reformers, with immediate
support from their prince, could implement changes
quickly, this was rarely the case in Switzerland. It was
only after Zwingli had been preaching the evangelical
doctrines for several years that the town council in
Zurich arranged to hold a disputation at which the
reformers and the Roman Catholics openly debated their
respective positions. Zurich's first disputation was in
January, 1523. Zwingli prepared Sixty-Seven Conclusions which dealt with practical piety rather than abstract
theology, but no one offered any meaningful rebuttal to
his presentation.[6] The town council authorized Zwingli
to continue to preach the Gospel and the Scriptures.
From this beginning things began to move quickly
toward a full reformed position, but Zwingli was careful
to allow the town council to make the final decisions.

As was true elsewhere in the Protestant developments,
much of the controversy revolved around the Catholic
Mass, its practice as a reenactment of the sacrifice of
Christ on Calvary, and the whole concept of transubstantiation. As in Germany, once the Catholic sacramental
system was dismantled, the reformed doctrines were
applied, almost as a matter of course. By 1525 most of
the changes were already being implemented. That same
year the town council in Zurich suppressed the monastic
establishments and turned the buildings over to charita-
ble use. The last Mass in Zurich occurred the Wednes-
day before Easter in 1525. Protestant communion ser-

vices took their place, but the decision was to have the Lord's Supper only four times a year. This usage became common elsewhere as well, influencing many denominations down to the present.

All this progress did not mean that the Catholics in Switzerland were not protesting. The Swiss Confederation divided into Protestant and Catholic cantons. The cantons of Basle and Berne soon joined Protestant Zurich, but the more rural cantons, called the "forest cantons," remained fiercely Catholic. Each side became fearful of military action by the other. The Catholic rural cantons even signed a treaty of alliance with the Swiss archenemy, Hapsburg Austria. The execution of a Protestant preacher in one of the forest cantons in May of 1529 led to declarations of war, but the First War of Kappel was more drama than action. Protestant Swiss troops faced Catholic Swiss troops, but while their leaders hesitated, the common soldiers mingled together and exchanged bread and milk. A peace agreement removed the threat of war, although the issues were not resolved.

But this threat moved some of the Protestants to think of combining forces with the Germans to the north. To have a workable alliance, however, they felt they must come to a common theological understanding. Philip of Hesse, a staunch supporter of Luther, arranged for major leaders from both Lutherans and Zwinglians to gather at his castle at Marburg in October of 1529. Luther and Zwingli were both present, but they failed to reach full agreement. They agreed on all aspects of theology except the Lord's Supper. Even here they agreed on what it was not — it was not a Mass, it was not transubstantiation. But Zwingli insisted that communion was nothing more than a memorial service, while Luther still insisted that the physical body of Christ was present with the elements. At this deadlock the Marburg Colloquy came to nothing.

A year and a half later friction between Protestant and Catholic cantons again created a crisis. Both sides prepared for war, and this time the shooting started. The Catholics outnumbered the Zurichers four to one, and annihilated about one fourth of the Protestant army. Zwingli, with his troops, was killed on the battlefield. The Second Peace of Kappel brought a more lasting truce, but the leadership of Zurich in the Protestant developments suffered from Zwingli's death. The city of Berne now came to prominence and for the next few years directed the expanding Reformation in Switzerland.

Bernese dominance was not to last, however, because of the involvement of an immigrant Frenchman, John Calvin (1509-1564). Calvin was a bright young lad, educated at the University of Paris, and the law schools at Orleans and Bourges. Calvin's major interest seemed to be religion, but his father insisted he be trained in law. In the process Calvin also became a humanist. In the year 1531, Calvin's father died, and this allowed him to follow his own interests.

He relocated in Paris again, making friends with other young humanists. Apparently in 1533 or 1534 he underwent a conversion experience that weaned him from Roman Catholicism and brought him into the new reformed views. For the next couple of years, Calvin led an itinerant life, visiting southern France, northern Italy, and taking trips back home to northeastern France. In

1535 he settled in Basle temporarily, and here he finished writing the first draft of his great work *Institutes of the Christian Religion*.[7] This book went through numerous editions, and the final edition was more than four times the size of the original. This work, in its final form, is still the chief monument to Calvin's theological views.

Calvin's training as a lawyer shows in this treatise. Luther wrote various works over a thirty year period, but he never systematized his theological viewpoint into a cogent system. Calvin, at age twenty-six, put out a systematic theology as his first theological writing. He was an organizer, totally systematic in his procedures and development. It is no wonder that one of his major biographers called him "Organizer of Reformed Protestantism."[8] In the *Institutes*, Calvin emphasized the sovereignty of God, and he saw man as laboring under God's predestination. Calvin did not see this as dehumanizing or inferior, but as God's power, love, and total control over the world. Those who trusted in God and Christ's atoning death would be the elect, saved by the Holy Spirit through the Word of God. Calvinism as a theological system is one of the great achievements of the Protestant Reformation.

The *Institutes* gave Calvin an extensive reputation. A few months after its appearance, he traveled through Geneva on his way to Strasbourg, where he hoped to spend his days as a quiet scholar, poring over manuscripts. But he was recognized and enlisted in the work of organizing the new Reformation there in Geneva. The city had only recently come under Bernese control and been weaned away from Catholicism. Those in charge of the conversion of the city felt they needed someone with a clearer gift of organization, and Calvin fit their bill exactly. This was not the kind of vocation he had in mind, but Calvin yielded to their demands. Except for a three-year exile brought on by political tension, Calvin spent the rest of his life in Geneva.

Under Calvin's leadership, Geneva became the most noted city in the world for Protestant organization — a city totally committed to the evangelical doctrines of the Reformation. It was not always easy. For years Calvin fought with the town council over the question of control of excommunication. Because of the intricate involvement of the church and state, excommunication deprived a citizen of the franchise. The pastors insisted the church alone could control excommunication, but the town fathers were unwilling to have the church decide who voted and who could not. Calvin's struggle on this issue lasted from 1538 to 1555.

Calvin drew up an organization plan for the church (a plan he based on biblical teaching and apostolic preaching) which used four types of church officers: pastors, teachers, elders, and deacons. Probably the most important contribution of his system was the eldership. These were to be laymen, but they were responsible for the visitation of all families in the church. With the pastors (or ministers) they formed the Consistory, and the Consistory heard all cases of church discipline. In the Consistory the lay elders outvoted the ministers. The role of the Consistory was to oversee the lives of Christians, and they went at their task with enthusiasm. Family quarrels, absence from church, playing cards, flippant remarks about the ministers, acts of adultery, wearing of ostentatious apparel — all these were situations that came up before the Consistory. Calvin did not play favorites. Members of his family were disciplined just as private citizens. There was, of course, much complaint about the meddling preachers, but Geneva received the reputation of being an urban model of Christian lifestyle. Protestants from all over Europe came to Geneva to see the system in operation.

So successful were Calvin's operations in Geneva that it quickly achieved the dominant position over all other Swiss Protestant cities. Even the older reformed movement in Zurich joined in. Generally those who followed the Swiss viewpoint were called "the Reformed," which is easily translated into "Calvinists." Later national distinctions, such as French Reformed, Dutch Reformed, German Reformed, Swiss Reformed, Hungarian Reformed, all indicate the Calvinist position. Most of these groups had their own statement of faith, whether it was the Heidelberg Catechism, the Helvetic Confession, or some other, but they all rested on a common Calvinist base.

Going beyond the Lutheran and Reformed Churches, it is necessary to call attention to some of the smaller groups that emerged out of the Protestant Reformation. Most major divisions became state churches in their respective countries, sometimes called the Magisterial Churches because of their cooperation with the rulers. Separate from these were some dissenting groups, previously all called "Anabaptists," but now more commonly grouped as the Radical Reformation, the Left Wing of the Reformation, and by a modern writer, Stepchildren of the Reformation.[9]

All of these groups differed from the main line reformers in several respects. Probably the key one was a distinction between a state-church relationship and a church independent of such relationship. These latter are sometimes called "free churches," "believers' churches," or "confessing churches," all reflecting kindred ideas. These groups were more fundamentalist in their emphasis on "regeneration" rather than on mere "sanctification." They tended to have more of an emphasis on the work of the Holy Spirit. Most of the groups also renounced war and were pacifists. But all of them were definitely different from the main-line Protestant denominations of the day.

Some of these groups can be grouped together as Spiritualists. They insisted on the leading of an "inner light," although they preceded the Quakers by a century. There was little in common between various groups of Spritualists other than some basic attitudes. Usually each group revolved around a personal leader, and few of them coalesced into ongoing organizations of churches. Such diverse men as Thomas Muntzer (1490-1525), Caspar Schwenckfeld (1490-1561), and David Joris (1501-1556) were some of the leaders of the first generation. Most Spiritualist groups did not last much beyond the lifetime of the original leader. The Schwenckfelders are the major exception, for some of these people exist today, including some settlements in Pennsylvania.

A second group, which became more institutionalized, was the Evangelical Rationalists. These people were intellectually oriented, basically around the classic problems of understanding the orthodox concept of the Trinity. Michael Servetus (1511-1553) and Fausto Sozzini

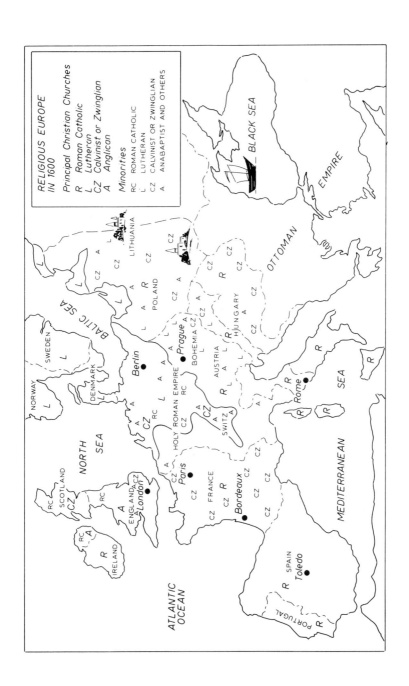

RELIGIOUS EUROPE
IN 1600

Principal Christian Churches

R   Roman Catholic
L   Lutheran
CZ   Calvinist or Zwinglian
A   Anglican

Minorities

RC   ROMAN CATHOLIC
L   LUTHERAN
CZ   CALVINIST OR ZWINGLIAN
A   ANABAPTIST AND OTHERS

BLACK SEA

OTTOMAN EMPIRE

LITHUANIA

POLAND

SWEDEN

NORWAY

DENMARK

BALTIC SEA

HUNGARY

BOHEMIA

Prague

AUSTRIA

Berlin

HOLY ROMAN EMPIRE

SWITZ.

Rome

SEA

NORTH SEA

SCOTLAND

ENGLAND

London

IRELAND

Paris

FRANCE

Bordeaux

MEDITERRANEAN

ATLANTIC OCEAN

SPAIN

Toledo

PORTUGAL

(1539-1604) were the major names in this movement in the sixteenth century. Servetus was burned to death in Geneva by Calvin and his followers, while Sozzini made his way from Italy to Poland where he laid the foundations for the Unitarians. This latter group had significant influence in eastern Europe, and later their ideas permeated the thinking of leading intellectuals in England and the United States, which in turn led to the establishment of the modern Unitarian denomination.

Most numerous of the various left wing groups, and currently enjoying a great deal of historical attention, were the Anabaptists. They began in Zurich under Zwingli. About 1525, when Zwingli was beginning to adopt many reformed positions, several younger men thought he was going too slowly and that the reformers ought not to wait for the approval of the city authorities. They were also convinced that identification with the state was detrimental to the church, and they focused their resentment on infant baptism. They wanted a believers' church, not a church that one was born into by reason of geography. They rebaptized people who had been baptized as infants, thus their name, Anabaptists. At first, most of them were not immersionists. Many of them still practiced sprinkling and pouring.

Zwingli felt the radicalness of these young followers was a threat to the peaceful and wholesale reform he was urging in Zurich, so he fought them. Hounded out of Zurich, these Swiss Brethren were often executed, in Switzerland, southern Germany, and elsewhere. Many found a refuge in tolerant Strasbourg for a while, but it was the Netherlands that gave the most promise in the first couple of decades. At the time the Netherlands was still officially Catholic, and the Catholics tolerated these radicals even less than the Zwinglians in Zurich. As the Anabaptists multiplied, many of these simple Christians were tortured and executed. Under constant harassment, many of them took over the town of Munster in nearby German Westphalia and began a military confrontation of their neighbors. Because of a numerical superiority of women, the leaders instituted polygamy. The religious issues were enough, but this moral issue became too much for the Catholic and Lutheran princes to accept. In 1536 they wiped out the Anabaptists in the city.

A Dutch priest lost a brother at Munster, and he took pity on these zealous but poorly informed folk. Menno Simons (1496-1561) was his name, and for the next quarter of a century (1536 until his death) he gave them direction. Menno was soon converted to their position and became their major leader. His followers, the Mennonites, were still harassed, but they were determined never again to resort to arms. Still today, these Mennonites as well as their splinter groups, the Amish, are pacifist.

Modern Baptists are not directly related to the Anabaptists, but came through English developments. Anabaptist influences came into England from the Netherlands, but it was a small splinter group from the larger Puritans that became the founders of today's English Baptists. Their leader, Robert Browne (1550-1633), emerged in the 1580's to give direction and substance to this following, which ultimately coalesced into the Baptist denomination.

One final note needs to be made about the Continental Reformation. The first generation reformers such as

Luther and Zwingli fought the real issues of the differences between the Reformers and the Catholics. Even a second generation reformer such as Calvin was waging the same battle, although for him it was a matter of organizing the gains made by the first generation, and systematizing the results. Unfortunately the third and fourth generation reformers tended to forget the evangelical impulse of the original reformers, and they concentrated on rounding off the theological systems created by the earlier men. By the latter part of the sixteenth century, the chief issues for the theologians were not matters of preaching the gospel and achieving the salvation of the souls of men, but defending certain theological presumptions. The original reformers had often ridiculed medieval theologians for endless arguments about how many angels could stand on the head of a pin; now their own theological descendants were arguing similar questions.

This happened earliest among the Lutherans. In 1552 the Majoristic Controversy broke out (named after Wittenberg professor Georg Major), which had to do with whether good works were necessary to salvation. In 1555 the Synergistic Controversy erupted over whether man is active in the process of conversion, or completely passive. These and several other disputes split the Lutherans into two camps, the hardline Lutherans (called the "Gnesiolutherans") and the Philippists, named after the leadership of Philip Melancthon (1497-1560), Luther's successor. Harmony was finally accomplished through a Formula of Concord drafted in 1577, and a Book of Concord in 1580. These finally achieved a large measure of Lutheran unity, but only after some fierce fights, and some loss to the Calvinists and others. The victory of these two documents also helps to explain why so many Lutheran seminaries in America are named "Concordia."

The Calvinists also had their problems. The Netherlands finally won their independence from Spain, largely through the aid of the Dutch Reformed who allied religious reformation with political independence. Dutch Reformed Calvinists made their beliefs the state religion there. But in the latter part of the century Jacobus Arminius (1560-1609) questioned many of the Calvinistic presuppositions. He began to doubt the central Calvinist tenet of predestination and its corollary principles. His followers, often known as Arminians, continued the discussion after his death, but their position was finally condemned at the national Synod of Dort in 1618-1619. The Arminians, also known as the Remonstrants, denied (1) predestination, (2) that Christ died only for the elect (called "limited atonement"), and (3) that saints cannot fall from grace.[10] The Counter-Remonstrants, or the orthodox Calvinist group, affirmed all three of these.

The Synod of Dort solidified classical Calvinism with its acrostic of TULIP, which stands for the five basic positions of Calvinism.[11] These are: (1) Total depravity — man can do nothing for his own salvation, he is totally depraved. (2) Unconditional election — man does not deserve to be saved, he is chosen by God for salvation without having met any conditions first. (3) Limited atonement — Christ did not die for all men, only for those who are chosen for salvation. (4) Irresistible grace — if a person is one of the elect, he cannot resist the

Spirit's work upon him, and he will be saved in spite of himself, if necessary. (5) Perseverance of the saints — once a person is saved, he can never be lost. This hardened form of Calvinism became the basic form, and it was particularly prevalent when immigrants brought it to the lands that became the United States.

We have traced Continental Protestantism through its first century. Once a monolithic structure splits, it is inevitable that further splintering will occur. Once Luther severed the façade of Catholic unity into Protestants and Catholics, it was probably inevitable that the Protestants themselves would further break up into different groups. And once the process began, there was no way of stopping it. The Protestant leaders all pleaded for a return to Scripture and biblical Christianity, but different leaders, influenced by different personalities and regional variations in culture and language, all saw the biblical pattern differently. Each tended to institutionalize his own following. This was true on the Continent of Europe, and it was equally true in the British Isles.

Bibliography for Chapter Seventeen

Bainton, Roland. *Here I Stand: A Life of Martin Luther.* Nashville: Abingdon Press, 1950.

   Available in numerous editions, this is still the best biography of Luther available in English.

Calvin, John. *Institutes of the Christian Religion,* ed. John T. McNeill, 2 vols.; Philadelphia: The Westminster Press, 1960, "The Library of Christian Classics."

   All the important aspects of Calvin's theology are

here. This is the edition usually considered to be the best edition available in English.

Chadwick, Owen. *The Reformation.* "The Pelican History of the Church," Vol. III; Harmondsworth, England: Penguin Books, 1964.

This is an excellent overview of the Reformation era by an English historian.

Dillenberger, John, and Claude Welch. *Protestant Christianity Interpreted Through its Development.* New York: Charles Scribner's Sons, 1954.

Not only is this an outstanding text on the beginnings of the Protestant development, but it also carries the development of Protestantism down to the present, providing excellent historical assessment along the way.

Hillerbrand, Hans J. *The Reformation: A Narrative History Related by Contemporary Observers and Participants.* New York: Harper and Row, Publishers, 1964.

An excellent source book of documents during the Reformation Era, enhanced by good selection and probing editorial direction.

McNeill, John T. *The History and Character of Calvinism.* New York: Oxford University Press, 1954.

What Dillenberger and Welch provide for the history of Protestantism, McNeill provides for Calvinism. This is a very helpful and enlightening book.

Potter, G.R. *Zwingli.* New York: Cambridge University Press, 1976.

Written after 25 years of research, this is acclaimed as the definitive, critical biography of this major Swiss Reformer.

Walker, Williston. *John Calvin: The Organizer of*

Reformed Protestantism (1509-1564). New York: Schocken Books, 1969.

An excellent biography of Calvin; although old, it is probably the best still available.

Williams, George H. *The Radical Reformation.* Philadelphia: The Westminster Press, 1962.

This is the most basic and complete book available on the Anabaptists. It has become the standard text on this varied movement.

Questions and Projects for Chapter Seventeen

1. How do the groups of the "Radical Reformation" differ from the groups of the "Magisterial Reformation"?
2. Were the cultural conditions of the sixteenth century as congenial for the Protestant Reformation as the cultural conditions of the first century were for the implementation and spread of apostolic Christianity? Describe both similarities and differences.
3. Prepare a report on the differences between the German and Swiss Reformations, both in terms of theological distinctions and organizational development.
4. Prepare as comprehensive a list as you can of the modern denominations that stem from the "Radical Reformation."
5. "Protestant Scholasticism" is the term given to the theological disputes within the Reformation in the late sixteenth and early seventeenth centuries. How comparable is this to the Christological disputes of the fourth and fifth centuries? Is it fair to state that both represent a loss of the original dynamic of Protestantism/apostolic Christianity?

Notes for Chapter Seventeen

1. The Ninety-Five Theses can be found in *Luther's Ninety-Five Theses*, trans. C.M. Jacobs; rev. Harold J. Grimm (Philadelphia: Fortress Press, 1957). They may also be found in Manschreck, pp. 14-18.
2. The Bull *Exsurge Domini* can be found in Barry, II, pp. 28-34.
3. All three of these pamphlets can be found in Martin Luther, *Three Treatises* (Philadelphia: Fortress Press, 1960).
4. Records of the incidents at Worms can be located in Bettenson, pp. 282-285; Manschreck, pp. 29-33; and Hans J. Hillerbrand, *The Reformation: A Narrative History Related by Contemporary Observers and Participants* (New York: Harper and Row, Publishers, 1964), pp. 88-100.
5. Hillerbrand, pp. 115-117.
6. Manschreck, pp. 67-70.
7. The best edition of the *Institutes* is probably that put out by the Library of Christian Classics series: John Calvin, *Institutes of the Christian Religion* (2 Vols.; Philadelphia: The Westminster Press, 1960).
8. This is the sub-title of Williston Walker's biography *John Calvin: The Organizer of Reformed Protestantism (1509-1564)* (New York: Schocken Books, 1969).
9. Leonard Verduin introduces this title in his book *The Reformers and Their Stepchildren* (Grand Rapids: Baker Book House, 1980).
10. For the articles of the Arminians, see Schaff, III, pp. 545-549.
11. Schaff, III, pp. 581-597.

Chapter Eighteen
PROTESTANTISM IN THE BRITISH ISLES

The development of Protestantism in the British Isles is in many ways similar to that on the Continent, but it is also different in some important particulars. Furthermore, what happens here had tremendous influence on the development of Christianity in modern English-speaking countries. For this reason, we shall give separate consideration to the British situation.

As we mentioned earlier, the new learning of the Renaissance scholars began to penetrate England at the end of the fifteenth century. Men like John Colet (1466-1519) studied in Italy and returned, passing on the new enthusiasm for classical studies. One of the favorite pupils of Colet was William Tyndale (1494-1536). Thomas More (1478-1535) became such a scholar that he could invite Erasmus over for a visit; Erasmus came, was delighted at what he found, and expressed great hope for the future of English learning. Another factor common between England and the Continent was the pervasiveness of anti-clericalism. The heritage of John Wyclif had never been forgotten, and his followers the Lollards were still in evidence. When things began to move against the Roman Catholic church, the common people rarely sought to stop the chain of events.

There was also a factor in the English situation that was very different from the situation which obtained on the Continent, a factor which is absolutely crucial for understanding what happened in England and why. The Tudor dynasty had come to the English throne in the person of Henry VII (1485-1509) after a period of feudal infighting which lasted for about fifty years — the Wars of the Roses. This feudal conflict over succession to the English throne shattered the peace of the country and threw everything into chaos and unrest. Many leaders felt England could not survive another such upheaval. This meant, of course, that the Tudor dynasty would have to lay a firm claim to the throne and guarantee peaceful times by providing a peaceful succession of sons. Henry VII had two sons — which was a good thing, for the first son, Arthur, died in 1502 at age 15. The second son then became the only Tudor link to the throne, and he became Henry VIII in 1509. He was only eighteen years of age at the time, and within a couple of months he married Catherine of Aragon, his brother's widow. Catherine's main job, of course, was to produce sons. In the first fifteen years of their marriage she produced eight or nine children (including at least a couple of sons), but all the children were stillborn or died in infancy except for one daughter, Mary, born in 1516. The fact that King Henry had only a single daughter led into an acute state of dynastic paranoia.

Meanwhile, Lutheran literature began to arrive in England shortly after 1517. As early as 1519 young men at Oxford met regularly to discuss the new doctrines, including William Tyndale. By 1522 Tyndale became enamored with the idea of producing a New Testament in the English language for all people to read, but the Bishop of London refused to allow it. In 1524 Tyndale went to the Continent, completed his first edition in 1526, and began to smuggle copies of his English New Testament back into England. The next decade saw a running battle as the authorities tried to intercept or buy up all the copies they could. Finally, however, Tyndale was betrayed by some friends, arrested in Antwerp, and burned at the stake in Brussels in October of 1536. His efforts represent the growing conviction in England that the ideas of the Reformation had significant value.

Yet Lutheran ideas as such had little support in England. When Luther wrote his *Babylonian Captivity of the Church*, attacking the seven sacraments, King Henry himself rushed to write a refutation, for which he received from the Pope the title "Defender of the Faith." But even through such means as this the people were becoming aware of the issues.

Another factor in England was the foreign policy adventures led by Cardinal Wolsey (1474-1530). From middle class background, Wolsey rose through the ranks of the church to become the Archbishop of York in 1514; through contacts with the King he became

Chancellor of England in 1515. Through Henry's marital ties with the Hapsburgs, England got involved in wars against France: wars that were expensive in terms of money and manpower, but wars that brought no direct benefit to England. Wolsey had received a promise from Emperor Charles V that by bringing England in on the Hapsburg side against France, Charles would do all he could to have Wolsey elected the next pope. But when the time came, Charles supported other candidates, and Wolsey was left out. The mere fact that Wolsey was papal legate, Cardinal, and Archbishop as well as Chancellor, meant that the people's dissatisfaction with his political decisions also increased their resentment against the Church that had rewarded him with high office.

Then, by the mid-1520's, the problem of the dynasty became acute. It became apparent that Catherine's child-bearing days were over, and there was no son. Henry, concerned about the stability of his throne and dynasty, tried to understand the reasons why God was not blessing him with healthy sons. He finally concluded that he had violated the teachings of Leviticus 20:21 — he had taken his brother's wife, and God was displeased. Henry concluded that he was in fact living in incest with his brother's widow, in violation of God's law. Because of Catherine's earlier marriage with Arthur, Pope Julius II had given a special papal dispensation to allow the marriage between Catherine and Henry, and Henry was now convinced that the Pope had done something he had no authority to do: he had given permission to violate one of God's laws, and poor Henry was bearing the burden of it. Henry concluded that he needed an annulment of this incestuous relationship (which, he insisted, never was a real marriage) in order for him to contract a legitimate marriage that would produce needed heirs.

Frankly, it is difficult to take Henry's argument at face value. He did not appear concerned about the legality of the marriage for its first fifteen years. It was only when his dynastic ambition became paramount that he began to question his marriage. Also, he chose to render a literal reading of Leviticus 20:21, but he ignored Deuteronomy 25:5 — that a man should marry his brother's widow to raise up children to him. Thirdly, there is the factor that Henry's eye had been caught by one of the young ladies of the court, the attractive Anne Boleyn. All of this suggests that Henry had much more than religious reasons to be unhappy with his marriage to Catherine.

Henry demanded that the Pope provide an annulment. Unfortunately for him, the Pope at that time was in the power of Emperor Charles V — and Charles V was the nephew of Catherine. Charles would hardly allow the Pope to grant the annulment and thus humiliate Queen Catherine. Pope Clement VII (1523-1534), however, was caught in an uncomfortable situation. To refuse Henry's request might mean disaster for Catholicism in England; but to grant the request would mean virtual confiscation of the papacy by Emperor Charles. So Clement temporized. He appointed a papal court to investigate the situation in England. The court dragged on the investigation and trial as long as it could, but ultimately Clement refused the annulment.

By the late 1520's Henry realized that he would have to take things into his own hands. He first removed

Wolsey, then sent Thomas Cranmer (1489-1556) on a visit to the European universities to ask their opinion on the legality of his marriage. It was a common technique for bolstering support in those days, and many of the universities did side with Henry on the matter. Henry called Parliament together in 1529 and attacked a number of clerical abuses. By 1531 Henry had forced the bishops in England to acknowledge him as the supreme head of the English church "as far as the law of Christ allows." But when the Pope still refused to yield, Henry decided to end all papal authority in England. In January of 1533 he married Anne, who was already one month pregnant. In February Parliament prohibited all appeals to Rome. In March Cranmer was made the new Archbishop of Canterbury, and he declared that Catherine's marriage with Henry was null and void and Henry's marriage with Anne was valid. In July Clement declared the opposite, and excommunicated the King. Henry's reply was to appeal to an ecumenical council. Anne's baby was born in September — a girl, named Elizabeth.

Once the official step was taken to separate England from Rome, Parliament dealt with other pieces of legislation to arrange the newly independent Church of England. All payments to Rome were stopped; the king was given power to appoint all bishops. All dispensations necessary for the operation of the church were to be secured from Canterbury, not from Rome. Elizabeth was declared the rightful heir to the throne, and the older Mary was now declared illegitimate (since she was a child of a non-marriage). All citizens were to swear to accept this succession and the king's supremacy over the church.[1] Several conscientious persons could not do this, including Thomas More and a few bishops. They were executed in 1535.

Henry was now the head of a separate Church. Little had been changed in worship, liturgy, or doctrine. The only change was that the pope had been replaced by a king. It is important to note that in contrast to the Continental Reformations, the upheaval in England had nothing to do with doctrine, indulgences, etc. Originally it was purely a matter of providing a dynasty for the king. But to do that, it was necessary to remove the king's marriage, and to do that it was necessary to remove the authority of the pope. Thus a whole religious reformation became necessary to meet a political need. By 1536 Henry began to move against the monasteries, partially in order to confiscate their property and replenish the royal treasury. Within two years all monasteries in England were suppressed. At this point there was a Catholic uprising in the north of England, although it was not a major threat. Other than this single instance, the changes brought on by Henry were met more with public apathy than by concern.

When after a few more years of marriage Queen Anne showed no signs of a second pregnancy (Henry still desperately wanted a son), the King drummed up charges of adultery against her and had her executed. Shortly after her death he married Jane Seymour, who dutifully gave him a son the next year. Jane died a few days after childbirth, however, and in the next decade Henry had three more wives, all for political reasons. One he divorced because she was too homely for him, another actually committed adultery and was executed, and the sixth outlived him. Much is sometimes made of Henry's serial marriages, but Henry was not the insatiable sexual maniac some writers have made him out to be. His multiple marriages are easily understood as arising out of a variety of dynastic and political needs, not uncommon at the time. But the result was to change the orientation of the church in England.

The history of the last ten years of Henry's reign is a confusing patchwork of religious enactments. The year after Henry allowed Tyndale to be burned, he also allowed an English translation of the Bible. By 1541 every parish in the country was ordered to have an English Bible available for people to read. The concept of transubstantiation was stricken from the Mass in 1536, but put back in by 1539. In fact, things had been slowly drifting in a Protestant direction until 1539 when in the Six Articles Act, Henry reversed himself on several points.[2] This caught numerous reformers too far out in front, and there were a number of executions — of Catholics as well as Lutherans. The King's religious policies were often unclear, first leaning one way, then another. In general, however, the English church retained most of the Catholic concepts although it severed its relationship with Rome. The people seemed apathetic over most of the changes.

In early 1547, as King Henry lay dying, he stated that he wanted the succession to go first to his son Edward, then to Mary, and finally to Elizabeth. It would have followed this rotation even without his request, and Edward (1547-1553) was soon the King. Edward, however, was less than ten years old, and his uncle, Edward Seymour (1506-1552), was made Lord Protector and Duke of Somerset. He was the actual power behind the throne

with the king so young. Somerset was a genuinely committed Protestant, and he wished to simplify the services
and make them more meaningful for the public, as well
as eradicate all elements in the services that seemed to
inculcate false ideas. The result turned the Mass into a
communion service in the English vernacular. The Six
Articles Act of 1539 was rescinded, as well as all heresy
legislation enacted since 1377 — the time of the Wyclif
movement.

There was some radicalism and violence as the
changes were implemented. Images were removed from
churches, vitriolic tracts published. Yet within the year
1547 communion was allowed in both elements, and
celibacy of the clergy was no longer enforced. By 1549
the major accomplishment of the period appeared, the
Book of Common Prayer. This was an attempt to
develop a service ritual that would be common throughout all of England. Basically written by Cranmer, the
Book was a definite Protestant production. The wording
was specifically geared to Protestant interpretations,
while some of the practices could still be susceptible to
Catholic interpretations. Along with the Prayer Book
went an Act of Uniformity demanding that the book be
used in churches throughout the country. When several
bishops with Catholic leanings opposed the uniformity,
the government replaced them with bishops with more
Protestant sympathies.

Things were moving along well until late 1549 when
sociological conditions brought on a palace revolution
on the part of many nobility who felt Somerset was not
dealing firmly with restive elements of the population.
The coup overthrew Somerset and replaced him with

John Dudley (1502-1553), now the Duke of Northumberland. While Somerset was a genuine Protestant, Northumberland was a scheming, corrupt politician who took Protestant guise because he perceived he could get more plunder that way. Once in power he became a tyrant.

Northumberland also became the major influence on the mind of the still-under-age king. Further changes were made in the worship services, and a revised Book of Common Prayer came out in 1552, accompanied by a Second Act of Uniformity. These changes made English services more closely resemble Calvinist services, reflecting the large number of Calvinist refugees now in England, having fled from various persecuting Catholic countries on the Continent. Also in 1552 the Forty-Two Articles appeared, a statement of faith for the new Church of England. Cranmer had the greatest influence on the articles. King Edward signed the Forty-Two Articles in June of 1553, barely a month before he died.

The king's death was not sudden. Those close to the throne saw it coming for months. This posed a problem for those who had actively identified themselves with the Protestants, for now the heir to the throne was Mary, a staunch Catholic. Northumberland in particular tried to impose further restrictions on the Catholics, and even engineered a different succession whereby the heir would be Lady Jane Grey (1537-1554), a distant descendant from Henry VII. Northumberland had his son marry Lady Jane, for he hoped to control the throne in that way. But his efforts were to no avail. When Edward died, Mary was acclaimed by the people, and Northumberland and the other principals in the plot were executed.

It is ironic that Mary came to the throne so peacefully. Henry VIII had feared that a woman coming to the throne would create chaos and civil war in England. Nothing of the sort happened. When one remembers that the major reason for the Protestant development was the king's fear about a woman on the throne, the whole development of events in the preceding twenty years seems terribly ironic.

Mary announced to the population that she was still a Catholic, and intended to remain such, although she also promised not to constrain men's consciences. In the fall of 1553 Parliament declared that the marriage of Catherine and Henry was valid, and that Mary was of legitimate birth. Committed to returning the Church of England to Roman obedience, Mary deposed all Protestant bishops who had not fled the country (many had). Romanist bishops were put back in.

An immediate problem facing Queen Mary was the need for a husband. If she hoped to see England remain under Catholic obedience, she must guarantee her own dynasty. Otherwise Elizabeth would succeed her, and Elizabeth had been raised a Protestant. Mary was already thirty-seven years old, so there was need for haste, for her child-bearing years would soon be over. Most English families had been compromised on the religious issues in the last twenty years, so Mary looked to a foreign prince for her marriage. She decided on Philip of Spain, her first cousin — the son of Emperor Charles. But another Spanish marriage meant tying England again into the dynastic intrigues of the Continental Hapsburgs, and the English resented the idea of foreign domination of England's interests.

This marriage in July, 1554, was a bitter disappointment for Mary. Not only did the English people despise the Spanish in general and Philip in particular, but it was only a marriage of convenience for him. Already once a widower, he would marry twice more after her death. He did not love her; he merely wanted to use England as a base for Spanish operations. Mary wanted a child desperately, and her body played a cruel trick on her. Morning sickness, abdominal swelling, and other indications of pregnancy convinced her that she was about to become a mother. She went into confinement, but after some weeks nothing happened. The swelling went down, and she had to admit she was not pregnant at all. Humiliated, she returned to the court. Philip, rather disgusted by the episode and preferring to be back at his Spanish tasks (he was the heir to the kingdom of Spain, which he would receive in 1556), left England in the summer of 1555, never to return.

Her final disappointment was in the realization that the English people had no interest in returning to Roman Catholicism. Through Parliament Mary reversed all the religious legislation of Edward and her father. By the end of the year 1554 a special papal legate had arrived, and in full court the Queen requested absolution for the disobedience of the kingdom. With the entire Parliament on its knees, as were Mary and Philip, the legate pronounced the absolution and reunited the Church of England to Rome.

But the English people were not in full consent. Priests were lampooned in public; orders from Catholic bishops were refused or disobeyed. By February of 1555 the burnings began. At first singly, they were soon done by the dozen and the score. Several of the Edwardian bishops were burned at Oxford, enlivened by Bishop Latimer's last words to his colleague, "Have faith, Master Ridley; today we shall light a fire which shall illuminate the world." Thomas Cranmer was the last bishop left from the days of Henry, and he was executed in March of 1556. Great pressure was brought on him to recant, and he did so seven times, each time retracting his recantation. As the flames began to finally engulf his body, he leaned over to put his right hand into the fire, saying that the hand that had signed the recantations should die first. The total of executions soon reached three hundred. The Queen was nicknamed "Bloody Mary."

The executions had a reverse effect on England. Previous to Mary, the people saw Protestants as narrow, bigoted fanatics — like Northumberland. Most people regarded the movement with apathy. But the executions under Mary brought great sympathy to the Protestants. Previously, Protestantism was identified with robbery, dissolution, plunder, irreverence and religious anarchy. Now it was identified with virtue, honesty, and resistance to a government half-foreign. The government was burning obviously harmless bishops and simple peasant folk. Queen Mary lost the affections of her people.

As Mary lay dying in the fall of 1558, there was no doubt who was the heir — the Protestant Elizabeth. There was also no doubt that Elizabeth would continue to be Protestant. She was not a fanatic, but she was convinced that the Roman Catholic establishment would have to be replaced. In 1559 Parliament reinstituted the 1552 Prayer Book, though with a few changes which lessened the extreme Protestant stance taken in that edition. A new Act of Uniformity accompanied the Prayer Book.[3] When by that summer the Marian bishops refused to accept the changes, Elizabeth simply replaced them. Two finally gave in, but the others were deposed. None were jailed or tortured, and none were executed. Through such changes, Elizabeth replaced 14 bishops, 12 deans, 15 heads of colleges, and between 200-300 parish clergy. The resulting situation in England came to be referred to as the Elizabeth Settlement. It was definitely Protestant, though not to the extremist form of Northumberland. Elizabeth was not a crusader; she normally delayed decisions until the direction of things became obvious, and then she did whatever would maintain peace, stability, and prosperity. Because so many of the practices and rituals of Catholicism continued in the Church of England, many later Anglicans called themselves Anglo-Catholics; that is, they were part of the Catholic family of churches, but Anglo-Catholic rather than Roman Catholic. That concept, however, came two centuries after Elizabeth. The papacy waited a decade to see how the dust would settle in England before it took a definitive response. Consequently, it was not until 1570 that Pope Pius V excommunicated and deposed Queen Elizabeth in the bull, *Regnans in Excelsis*.[4] The Pope also called upon both France and Spain to carry out this bull of deposition.

There was still a large number of loose ends in the Elizabethan Settlement. The new bishops which replaced the Marian ones demanded some sort of doctrinal standard, and in 1563 they produced the Thirty-Nine Articles. This is the older Forty-Two Articles reworked somewhat. A strongly Calvinist statement, this remains today the basic definitive statement for the Anglican Church.

A further problem that emerged in Elizabethan England was the matter of the Puritans. A number of Protestants felt that Elizabeth's changes had not gone far enough. There were too many vestiges of medieval Catholicism still within the Church of England. The Church needed to be purified of these elements, thus the name "Puritans." One of the early key elements in this dispute had to do with the garments worn by priests/preachers during the worship service. The concerned reformers wanted to get rid of such things as the cassock, the gown, and the chasuble, referring to them as "rags of popery." Others liked the dignity of a formal service, and saw no need to go to the stark simplicity of the "Genevan gown," typical of most Calvinistic reform. This concern over priestly vestments resulted in the Vestiarian Controversy which came up for vote in the House of Commons in 1562. The Vestiarian proposal lost by only two votes — indicating how close were such matters at the time. The minority, in spite of the Act of Uniformity, began to meet privately for worship. The Puritans soon became a semi-organized dissenting church that continued to challenge Anglican practices for the next century.

Meanwhile, there was another Protestant revolution going on to the north. Scotland had been a perennial enemy of England, just as France had been; and for that very reason, the Scots and the French were often in alliance against the English. It was no accident that during the divided papacy both Scotland and France supported the pope in Avignon, while the English and the Germans supported the one in Rome. Trying to wean the Scots away from their French alliance, Henry VII married his eldest daughter to James IV (1488-1513) of Scotland. The result was not commensurate with the goal, however. In 1513 the Scots invaded England, only to be defeated by English troops at Flodden Field. King James IV was among the slain.

James V (1513-1542) was only a year old at the time, but Scottish policy kept this nephew of Henry VIII from any English designs. When James reached marriageable age in the 1530's he was tied into a French alliance. His first wife was the daughter of the King of France; upon her death he married Mary of Guise, a daughter of one of the powerful Catholic families in France. When his troops invaded England in 1542 and were defeated at Solway Moss, James was so shattered he went to bed and died within three weeks. He left behind him a daughter, Mary, Queen of Scots (1542-1567), six days old. At first pro-English factions seemed to gain control of the Scottish government, but within six months the pro-French forces gained the upper hand. They controlled Scotland for the next seventeen years. Increasingly in this struggle, the pro-French were Catholic, while the pro-English identified with Protestantism.

Lutheran ideas made their appearance in Scotland in the 1520's and were taken up by Patrick Hamilton. Turned evangelical preacher, young Hamilton was Scotland's first Protestant martyr, burned at the stake in February of 1528. More executions continued sporadically, but the arrest and execution of George Wishart in March of 1546 galvanized the reformers into action.

David Cardinal Beaton was the prime mover in the opposition to the reformed doctrines, as well as a leader in the pro-French government. Two months after Wishart's death, his friends stormed Beaton's castle and killed the cardinal — with Henry VIII's full knowledge and approval. But they were an island of resistance in a French Catholic sea. They held on to their occupied castle for a year, but they were finally captured by reinforced French troops. Included among the occupants was John Knox (1513-1572), who spent the next nineteen months on a French prison ship.

Knox and the rest of his fellow prisoners were released by English intervention in 1549, and Knox spent the next ten years in England and (after Mary came to the English throne) on the Continent maturing his views in the new Reformed viewpoint. Knox was committed to evangelizing his homeland, and it was while in England that he emphatically prayed, "Lord, give me Scotland or I die!" In 1558, when Elizabeth ascended the English throne, she had to be concerned about events in Scotland, since Mary, Queen of Scots was her first cousin, and next in line to the English throne if Elizabeth had no children. In fact, protesting that Henry's marriage with Anne was invalid, and that therefore Elizabeth was illegitimate, Queen Mary of Scotland claimed that the throne of England was rightfully hers anyway. Thus Elizabeth was almost as concerned with the advancement of Protestantism in Scotland as Knox was. These two figures, so different in so many ways, worked together to get rid of the French influence in Scotland. Knox returned to Scotland in 1559 to aid the organization of the Protestant nobility.

Facing an English fleet supporting an English army, the French finally let go of Scotland in the Treaty of Edinburgh, July of 1560.

Queen Mary was in France at the time, having married the young King of France, Francis II (1559-1560). In her absence, the Scottish parliament enacted measures which rejected papal authority, abolished the Mass, withdrew the spiritual and temporal authority of the bishops, and adopted a confession of faith drawn up by Knox, which became their basic statement until it was replaced by the Westminster Confession of 1646. The local churches were organized into presbyteries, these into provincial synods, and the whole headed up by a General Assembly. Calvinism was firmly planted in the country, and the Presbyterian Church was begun.

Francis II had always been sickly, and he died in 1560, one month before his seventeenth birthday. Mary, Queen of Scots, now a widow at age eighteen, returned to Scotland for a life-and-death struggle with John Knox. Mary was as determined to return her country to papal obedience as her cousin namesake had been in England a few years previously. She was making progress when she foundered on the same problem that had plagued the English Mary — the choice of a husband. Mary of Scotland chose a Scottish husband, and this brought on the feuding instincts of the Scottish clans. In a bizzare series of events, Mary's husband was killed, and then the murderer abducted the queen and forced her to marry himself. The strait-laced Protestant lords convinced themselves that Mary had been involved in adultery with her husband's murderer, and perhaps she had herself even aided the murder. They revolted against her, and captured her; she escaped and fled to cousin Elizabeth for protection.

Elizabeth was in the unusual position of "protecting" the woman who was claiming her throne. Elizabeth put her under house arrest, where she remained for twenty years (1568-1587). Catholic plots to assassinate Elizabeth were constantly forming around Mary, some of which she aided and encouraged. The English lords finally convinced Elizabeth she would have no peace as long as Mary of Scotland was alive. So Mary, Queen of Scots, was executed in 1587, and Philip of Spain launched the Spanish Armada as partial revenge. That attempt was, of course, unsuccessful, and Protestantism rested secure both in England and in Scotland.

Mary's infant son, James VI, reigned in Scotland (1567-1625), with a state church firmly Presbyterian. When Elizabeth of England died in 1603 James succeeded her, and he became James I (1603-1625). The two countries have had joint monarchs ever since. Catholics in England had been laboring under severe harassment, and they felt surely the son of Mary of Scotland would lessen their yoke. He would not, and they turned on him in the famous Gunpowder Plot of 1605. They planned to blow up the chamber of Parliament when he was in it, but the ruse was discovered. This increased the violently anti-papal, anti-Catholic hatred in England.

Presbyterian Puritans were also hopeful that the King of Scotland would ameliorate their position in England, but James refused. He had too many Presbyterian divines in Scotland tell him what to do, and he liked the framework of Anglican bishoprics under his control. In the Hampton Court Conference in 1604 James set them straight. He recognized that political notions in the church have a way of influencing political notions in the state. He argued that if the Puritans wanted to eliminate monarchial control in the church as represented in bishops, they would soon want to eliminate the monarch in the state. "No bishop, no king," James thundered at them. He would not change. And if they continued to resist, "I will harry you out of the land," he promised. Thus the Pilgrims soon went to the Netherlands, from whence in 1620 they would travel to Massachusetts Bay to begin Plymouth Colony in the New World, seeking the religious freedom James I denied them in England. It was at the same Hampton Court Conference in 1604 that James authorized the translation committee that published the justly famous King James Version of the Bible in 1611.

In general, however, James was a weak king. He was often controlled by his advisers, he was a spendthrift, he raised taxes, he got the country in unpopular wars, and he was often at odds with Parliament. Things did not improve under his son, Charles I (1625-1649). He had even less political savvy than his father. While committed to High Church Anglicanism, he married a daughter of the King of France and brought Catholicism back into the country. This inflamed the feelings of many Englishmen, particularly the Puritans. The Puritans were mostly middle class, and they felt the high taxes most directly. They resented Charles' foreign wars, his corrupt political subordinates, and his illegal measures of extortionate taxation. When Parliament refused Charles' taxation demands, he dismissed it in 1629 and ran the country without Parliament for over a decade. In this crucible of political pressure, the Puritans became identified with loyalty to Parliament, political democracy, and patriotism. Those loyal to King Charles were identified with corruption, tyranny, foreign involvements, and suspicion of Catholicism. In addition, William Laud (1573-1645) was made Archbishop of Canterbury in 1633, and Laud was so anti-Puritan that he used measures closely similar to those of the Inquisition to harass dissenting Puritans.

The final tragedy grew out of Charles' and Laud's attempts to impose the Book of Common Prayer on the Scottish Presbyterians. The Scots refused and invaded England, where both Parliament and the Puritans joined with them in a war on the King. This English Civil War raged from 1642 until the King's capture in 1647. Parliament put him on trial for treason to country and the government and had him executed in 1649. James' dictum had been right: the Parliamentary Puritans had moved from "no bishop" to "no king." The Puritan Oliver Cromwell (1599-1658) soon controlled the reins of government in England. His official title was Lord Protector, but he ruled as a king. Although royalists and Catholics were still suspect politically, there was no religious persecution mounted against them.

During the English Civil War, significant developments also occurred with respect to the churches in the country. In 1643 the Scots drafted the Solemn League and Covenant in which they stated their desire to maintain a true, pure, and reformed religion, as well as eliminate government of the church by bishops.[5] In exchange for military assistance in the war against King Charles, Parliament assented to the Covenant in 1644, making it liable upon every Englishman over eighteen years of age. In 1643 an assembly of ministers and theologians convened in the Westminster Assembly to discuss religious measures. Major products from this convention included the Westminster Confession of Faith in 1646, and the Larger Catechism and Shorter Catechism in 1647. These three documents came to be definitive documents for Presbyterians both in Scotland and the English-speaking world.

Cromwell died in September, 1658, succeeded on the Protectoral throne by his son Richard — "Tumbledown Dick" in English history. Richard was an incompetent, and after a year and a half Parliament proclaimed Charles II (1660-1685) the new King of England. This was the son of Charles I, who had spent the interim in exile in France under the protection of his cousin, Louis XIV (1643-1715). This Stuart Restoration met with almost universal rejoicing since most Englishmen were not Puritans. They did not want the tyranny of Charles I, but they were still royalists. Charles II promised toleration, but he still had the "divine right of kings" notions of his father. He was also personally inclined toward Roman Catholicism.

Officially the Church of England enjoyed the return of power, and the government stepped up the pressure on the dissenters. Charles' promises notwithstanding, acts of Parliament restricted the number of persons who could listen to dissenting preachers, prohibited such preachers from coming within five miles of incorporated towns, and disbarred them from teaching school.[6] It was under these penalties that Baptists and other dissenters began large-scale migrations to America. John Bunyon began his *Pilgrim's Progress* while in Bedford jail (he was there for twelve years), and John Milton wrote *Paradise Lost*. Furthermore, the morality of the Restoration period was a scandal. Charles had no children from his wife, but he had a number of others from his many mistresses. Because he had no legitimate children, Charles' heir was his brother James, Duke of York. James had legitimate children, but they were more than outnumbered by his illegitimate ones.

A further problem was the constant Catholic-phobia in England. James converted to Catholicism in 1668. Charles was obviously leaning in that direction, but he did not become an actual Catholic until his deathbed, on February 5, 1685. He died at noon the next day. This elevated James II (1685-1688) to the throne, a professed Roman Catholic. This arrangement was distasteful to most Englishmen, but James had two daughters who had been raised Protestant, and the majority of the English were willing to put up with James and return to normality under his daughters. But then James remarried. His new wife, a Roman Catholic, gave birth to a son on June 10, 1688. Since by English law sons inherit the throne before daughters, irrespective of their ages, this meant the son, who would undoubtedly be raised Catholic, would become king. The English found this totally unacceptable.

James' eldest daughter Mary (1662-1694) was married to William III (1650-1702), the Prince of Orange and ruler of the Netherlands. Both William and Mary were confirmed Protestants. In a quasi-legal move, Parliament offered them the throne. They arrived in England that fall, the English flocked to their standard, and

James II had to flee the country. This "Glorious Revolution" was also called the "Bloodless Revolution," since it was relatively peaceful. But the whole incident showed that the English, while still royalist, had a limit as to what they would tolerate in their monarch. They would brook no tyranny, they insisted on Protestantism, and in a pinch they could still put Parliament against King. And if that king were a Catholic, he hardly stood a chance. The memories of Bloody Mary, the Spanish Armada, and the Gunpowder Plot were too strong. And then there was the Revocation of the Edict of Nantes done by the King's cousin, Louis XIV of France in 1685. By that enactment, Louis had in a single action stripped all Protestants in France of all rights whatsoever. English Protestants would not risk such in England. The development of English Protestantism had been a checkered history, but that England was Protestant there could be no doubt.

Bibliography for Chapter Eighteen

Dickens, A.G. *The English Reformation.* New York: Schocken Books, 1946.

A useful overview of the tumultuous events of this particular phase of the Reformation.

Dickinson, William Croft (ed.). *John Knox's History of the Reformation in Scotland.* 2 vols.; New York: Philosophical Library, 1950.

This is an excellent resource for how Knox saw the situation in Scotland, in a modern, improved edition.

Fraser, Antonia. *Cromwell: The Lord Protector.* New

York: Dell Publishing Co., Inc., 1975.

An excellent and comprehensive biography of the man who emerged as the victorious Puritan during the English Civil War.

_____. *Mary Queen of Scots*. New York: Dell Publishing Co., Inc., 1971.

A stimulating biography of this key person in the Scottish struggle, told with sympathy and insight by a fellow woman.

Haller, William. *The Rise of Puritanism, or The Way to the New Jerusalem As Set Forth in Pulpit and Press from Thomas Cartwright to John Lilburne and John Milton, 1570-1643*. New York: Harper & Brothers, Publishers, 1957.

An excellent study of the rise and development of Puritanism and its ideals.

MacGregor, Geddes. *The Thundering Scot: A Portrait of John Knox*. Philadelphia: The Westminster Press, 1957.

An excellent view of Knox's life and leadership of the Reformation in Scotland, especially his stand-off with Queen Mary.

Mattingly, Garrett. *Catherine of Aragon*. New York: Vintage Books, 1941.

An excellent biography of this English queen, sympathetic to her position vis-a-vis the divorce.

Questions and Projects for Chapter Eighteen

1. In what ways does the political situation in England differ from the situation in Germany? In what ways is

it similar? How influential is it in each case?

2. Construct a continuous graph listing all the rulers of England from Henry VIII to William and Mary. With (1) being fervent Roman Catholic and (10) being fervent Protestant, place each ruler on this continuum. Be able to defend your placement of each ruler.

3. Read some Roman Catholic histories and note how they portray the religious developments in England in the period 1500-1689. How do they compare and/or contrast to the treatment present in this chapter?

4. Doing some extra reading, compare the Reformation development in Scotland to those in the Netherlands or in Switzerland. What differences and/or similarities do you see?

5. What modern denominations in America can be traced to the Puritans? Make a list, giving the approximate date at which each can be identified as a separate denomination, and the major leader(s) of each group.

Notes for Chapter Eighteen

1. Documents pertaining to the English Reformation can be located in all the source books — Bettenson, pp. 308-362; Barry, II, pp. 68-87; Manschreck, pp. 173-213. For the Supremacy Act in particular, see Bettenson, pp. 321-322; Barry, II, pp. 68-69; and Manschreck, pp. 178-179.

2. The Six Articles Act can be found in Bettenson, pp. 330-331; Barry, II, pp. 69-70; and Manschreck, pp. 179-180.

3. The Elizabethan Act of Uniformity can be found in Bettenson, pp. 333-339; and a shortened form in Manschreck, pp. 184-185.

4. The papal bull of deposition can be found in Bettenson, pp. 340-341; Barry, II, pp. 70-72; and Manschreck, pp. 188-189. This was the last time the papacy excommunicated and ordered the deposition of a monarch.

5. The Solemn League and Covenant can be found in Bettenson, pp. 392-396; and in Manschreck, pp. 198-220.

6. These laws can be found in Bettenson, pp. 401-407; the Five-Mile Act in particular is in Manschreck, pp. 207-208.

Chapter Nineteen
THE CATHOLIC COUNTER REFORMATION AND THE THIRTY YEARS' WAR

The loss of virtually all of northern Europe and the British Isles (with the exception of Ireland) was a heavy blow to Roman Catholicism. A response was in order, and it certainly came, although the exact nature of the response is a bit complicated, which is reflected in the dilemma of what to call this Catholic response. As we have seen, there were various elements within Roman Catholicism clamoring for reform long before the revolt of Martin Luther. Therefore, there is a great sense in which the Catholic Reformation is just that — a Catholic response to the need for reform. Yet there is also a sense in which the response is a countermove against the Protestants — a "Counter-Reformation." Some historians merge the two influences and call this development the "Catholic Counter-Reformation." It is an awkward title, but at least it accurately suggests that the move toward reform came from two different impulses.

The best part of the Catholic Reformation is illustrated by a revival of piety in the clergy and laity rooted in Christian humanism, in mysticism, and also in the monastic tradition. We have already seen how concerned many of the humanists were — men such as Erasmus, Thomas More, and scores of others.

Spain was an early center of much of this Catholic Reformation. The Spanish Inquisition was formed in 1480 to ferret out quasi-converts from Judaism and Islam at a time of national fervor when these people were still viewed as threats to the stability of the nation. Thomas Torquemada (1420-1498) became the Grand Inquisitor in 1483 and made his name synonymous with the Inquisition. Cardinal Ximenes (1436-1517) became confessor to Queen Isabella in 1492, and he used both the erection of new colleges and the Inquisition to prepare an educated clergy and reform the national church. Ferdinand and Isabella were strong monarchs, and since they were firmly loyal to the papacy, they could get away with resisting papal appointments to open Spanish bishoprics. When popes sent unqualified or inferior Italian court figures to become bishops in Spain, the monarchs refused to accept them. They appointed their own bishops and saw to it that men were qualified and serious about doing the pastoral work of the office. The result was a strong Spanish church, reforming itself along excellent lines. The Protestant Reformation had no real chance of gaining a foothold in Spain, because a properly trained and functioning clergy was not creating the abuses that brought on anticlericalism that was always the herald of Protestant developments elsewhere in Europe. This was reformation, but a reformation done entirely within the Catholic establishment.

One of the significant Spanish monastic figures in this period was St. Teresa of Avila (1515-1582). She entered a Carmelite convent in 1533 but led a lax life. It was not until 1555 that she had a religious experience which drove her to want a deeper relationship with Christ. She spent much time in spiritual meditation and within a few years experienced her first ecstasy: a feeling that one's soul is absorbed in God and one's exterior senses are suspended. Teresa wrote several books on mystical experiences such as hers, concluding that there were intermediate stages between meditation and ecstasy. She established a number of reformed monasteries, and she was a major influence in uplifting the piety of the common people.

Another major figure coming out of the reformed Spanish church was Ignatius Loyola (1491-1556). He was a military adventurer who was seriously injured in a battle in 1521. The seriousness of his leg injury ended his promising military career, and Loyola resolved to become a soldier for the church. He worked out a technique of religious commitment in his book *Spiritual Exercises*. These exercises were not for devotion, but for spiritual discipline. Loyola soon founded the Society of Jesus, more commonly known as the Jesuits, and these hardy spiritual warriors were often called the "shock troops" of the papacy in the coming ideological conflicts of the Counter Reformation.

Several additional new monastic orders were established

in Italy. The Theatines, founded in 1524, devoted themselves to preaching and administering the sacraments. Their goals were to become models for the clergy and check the spread of heresy. Within the Franciscans, a reformist group split off from the order in 1529 to restore the rigor of the original Rule of St. Francis, even to the point of emulating his four-cornered hood, called a *cappuccio*. These monks were called *cappuccini* (little hooded men) and became the new order of the Capuchins. Their enthusiastic preaching and missionary work among the poor made them highly popular in Italy. The Ursulines were an order of nuns created in 1535 to provide education for girls of all classes. The Oratorians were authorized as a separate order in 1572. They were secular priests who provided afternoon prayer services emphasizing the reading of religious literature and the performing of musical devotional programs. By the seventeenth century such musical programs were called "oratorios," with compositions later written by such men as Handel and Mendelssohn.

In spite of such developments, however, it was obvious that the church could not be reformed without some major changes in the papacy. Leo X was not at all interested in reform. His death brought Adrian VI (1522-1523) to the throne. Supported strongly by Charles V, he might have accomplished much, but for his quick demise. A Dutchman, he was the last non-Italian pope before the election of John Paul II in 1978. Adrian's death brought a cousin of Leo X to the throne, Clement VII. It was Clement that tried to temporize between the conflicting aims of the German and French rulers; it was Clement that had to face the wrath of the angered

Henry VIII. Perhaps because he saw so much chaos around him, Clement feared the end of the world. He commissioned Michaelangelo to do his famous painting "Last Judgement" on the end wall of the Sistine Chapel. When Paul III came to the papal throne (1534-1549), things began to change. He had been a cardinal since 1493, and he had illegitimately sired three sons and a daughter. He was a typical Renaissance cardinal at the time, but by the time he came to the papacy his lifestyle had changed. He was seriously committed to reform, and he is considered the first of the reforming popes. He appointed new cardinals who were also serious proponents of reform, and these men together initiated many of the measures that brought a complete turnaround for the Catholic Church and the papacy in the next few decades.

In 1536 Paul appointed a commission on reform and put the new cardinals on its membership. Their report published in 1537 stated that all the abuses of the papacy stemmed from the secularization of a spiritual office. In twenty-six sections, they listed the evils that needed correcting: the venality of worldly cardinals; excusing clergy of crimes by cash dispensations; laxity among the monastic orders; hawking of indulgences without regard to spiritual considerations; condoning prostitution, especially in Rome; clerical absenteeism. Catholics were shocked, and Protestants used the Catholic information to substantiate the claims they had been making for years. Within months Paul's commission was implementing some of the suggestions in the report, and the worst of the abuses were being corrected.

While Paul authorized the Jesuits as a new monastic

order, he was also willing to negotiate with the Protestants. He authorized Cardinal Contarini (1483-1542) to go to the German Reichstag at Regensburg in 1541 to discuss means of reconciliation with the Lutherans. Contarini worked out a joint statement of justification, and he even agreed that the body of Christ could be understood apart from the pope (therefore admitting that those outside Roman Catholicism could still be considered Christians), though Rome later rejected this. But efforts at Regensburg fell apart on the inability to reconcile differences on transubstantiation.

Cardinal Caraffa (1476-1559) was much more conservative than Contarini, and the latter's failure at Regensburg left the field open to Caraffa. Under Caraffa's urging, Paul established the Congregation of the Holy Office in 1542, the Italian counterpart to the Spanish Inquisition.[1] Caraffa was a determined reformer, but he was also a determined opponent of the Protestant rebels.

The earliest cries for reform included the appeal to an ecumenical council. Luther had expressed this, as did Henry VIII in his differences with the papacy. Even Charles V, a staunch Catholic, joined the appeal, insisting that such a council convene on German territory, to prevent papal manipulation of it. Clement VII refused discussion of the idea, but Paul was willing. Several possible starts were frustrated by warfare between France and Germany, but the council finally convened in Trent in December of 1545. Technically Trent was on German soil — at the time it was part of Austria. But it is on the Italian side of the Alps, which meant the Council was still susceptible to papal control.

Lutherans were invited, but they refused to attend.

Italian bishops were in a majority at the council, so papal control was guaranteed. The Council went through three sittings; 1545-1547; 1551-1552; and 1562-1563. The decrees of this council became the doctrinal definition of Catholicism for the modern period.[2] In fact they did their job so well that there was not another ecumenical council for over three hundred years, the longest gap in the history of the church, even counting the time from Pentecost to Nicaea.

In its first sitting, the Council declared that Scripture and Tradition were equally valid sources of religious truth, and the Church had the sole right to interpret Scripture. The Council further decreed that the Latin translation by Jerome in the fourth century was the authoritative text of scripture. The decree then listed the canonical books in case there was any confusion as to what was Scripture. The significance of this is that the books of the Apocrypha were for the first time in history fully counted as Scripture along with the books of both Old and New Testaments. The council also stated that Christ had instituted seven sacraments, and all are necessary to salvation (with the exception of marriage and ordination, where it was assumed that good Christians will do one, or the other, but not both).

Julius III (1550-1555) reconvened the Council in 1551, and in this second sitting Lutheran representatives arrived. They wanted to open discussion on doctrines already decided, but the Catholics refused. Since the first setting had already decided that Tradition was equal to Scripture, that the church alone can interpret Scripture, that Scripture includes the Apocrypha, and that there are seven sacraments, the Lutherans could not possibly participate. They broke off contact and went home. In this second sitting the council confirmed Transubstantiation and went on to condemn the Lutheran, Calvinist, and Zwinglian doctrines of the Lord's Supper.

Political problems forced the recessing of the Council in 1552, and before it could be reconvened again, Julius died, succeeded by Caraffa as Paul IV (1555-1559). Paul was so violently anti-Protestant he saw no need to bother with the Council and refused to call it into session. The hard line against Protestants moved ahead under his leadership, including the first appearance of the Index of Forbidden Books in 1559.

Pius IV (1559-1565) finally reconvened the council after a lapse of ten years, but by this time all hope for reconciliation with Protestants was gone and the Jesuits were in firm control. A major controversy that came up in this session was the residence of bishops. All agreed that bishops ought to reside in their diocese, but the controversy centered on the authority behind this insistence. Was it a matter of divine law, inherent in the office of bishop, or was it a matter of church rule? If the former, then there could be no changes in it; if the latter, the pope could dispense with it if he saw fit. If the former, the papacy would be curtailed in its use of bishops and also in its claim to authority over bishops. The papal forces were in favor of episcopal residence, but insisted that it was a church rule. After long debate, they won by a slight majority. The office of indulgence seller was also eliminated in this session, and this abuse now disappeared.

The lines had now been laid for the development of the continuing Catholic response to Protestantism. Their doctrine was confirmed, papal authority was made even stronger, and the pope had several new invigorated monastic orders to use in opposition to the Protestants. Catholicism not only reformed itself but began to step up the initiative and aggressively move back into areas that had become Protestant — Bavaria, Austria, Hungary and ultimately even into Poland. In addition, there were the useful provisions of the Peace of Augsburg in Germany: if a ruler converted to Catholicism, that became the official religion for his entire area. There was a real premium on winning the rulers.

Furthermore, the Jesuits began to establish a number of colleges in German lands. Here young men were trained in devout loyalty to the Catholic Church. Many of these men were recruited for the Jesuit ranks. Others were the sons of rulers, and they went back home imbued with a commitment to the Roman Catholic Church. In addition, many Jesuits trained themselves to be experts in diplomacy and finance, so that various rulers in Europe came to rely upon them for decisions of national policy and direction. Eventually, the Jesuits came to exert a tremendous influence in the Catholic countries of Europe: they also were active in converting numerous Protestant areas back to Catholicism.

As a result, the Catholic Church was in a much more healthy position in 1565 than it had been in 1500. The abuses that had brought on the Reformation were virtually over — though the doctrinal disagreements still prevailed. The Roman Catholic Church was reformed in morals and in organization.

The two emperors that followed Charles V in Germany were content to leave religious matters alone, but things changed radically when Rudolf II (1576-1612) came to the throne. He had been educated in Spain, and he was the first emperor to encourage the Counter Reformation and import Jesuits into Austria. This new aggressiveness characterized his long regime. Friction between Catholics and Protestants increased and tensions mounted higher. Typical of the type of incidents heating the atmosphere was that which occurred in Donauworth in Bavaria.

Donauworth was a free imperial city, which meant it was not under any ruler other than its own elected leaders. Bavaria was strongly Catholic but Donauworth was almost entirely Lutheran, including the entire city council. There was also a Benedictine monastery in the city, with a number of monks educated at a Jesuit college. In April of 1606, against orders from the city council, the abbot led a religious procession through the city. On their return to the monastery the marchers were attacked by a mob. Emperor Rudolf gave Duke Maximilian of Bavaria the authority to investigate the incident and protect the Catholic minority. When the city council refused to promise freedom of worship to the small Catholic minority, Maximilian occupied the city, annexed it to Bavaria, and made it Catholic by force in 1607. This was an outright violation of the Peace of Augsburg.

By 1608 the Protestants and Catholics were both forming military alliances, preparing for the worst. Frederick IV, Count Palatine of the Rhine, formed the Protestant Union, consisting of most of the Calvinist and Lutheran princes and cities, with French support. (The French were still anti-Hapsburg.) Duke Maximilian of Bavaria formed the Catholic Union in 1609 consisting of

Catholic rulers, with Spanish support. They had their own army under Count Johannes von Tilly.

With Germany again turned into two armed camps, it only needed a spark to set the area ablaze. The spark almost came when John William, a ruler of five small territories in northwestern Germany, died in 1609 without children. Two of his nephews tried to take over the little principalities, and neighboring princes also tried to get a piece of the territory. The French and Dutch promised to support the Protestants, while the Hapsburgs with Spanish support vowed to resist any military attack. Trying to gain more support for his claim to the principalities, one nephew converted from Lutheranism to Calvinism, and the other converted from Calvinism to Catholicism. Although major war was averted, it was apparent that religion was becoming a tool for power politics.

The storm that finally broke involved the Hussites in Bohemia. For some years the Hapsburgs had been appointing the kings of Bohemia, and the Protestant nobles in the country were concerned that the crown might become totally a Hapsburg hereditary possession. They sent a petition to Emperor Matthias (1612-1619) protesting violation of their constitution. Matthias defended his appointment and declared their resistance illegal. When three imperial ambassadors met with them in May of 1618, the Protestants became so enraged they tossed the imperial representatives out of a castle window. They fell fifty feet into the moat below. Injured, they managed to escape. This incident, called the Defenestration of Prague, was the spark that ignited Europe.

The Protestants in Bohemia set up an insurrectionary

government, banished Jesuits from the kingdom, and declared their independence. They elected a new king, Frederick V, Count Palatine of the Rhine. He was crowned in November of 1619, eight months after Ferdinand II became the new Holy Roman Emperor in Germany (1619-1637). Ferdinand would not tolerate the Bohemian rebellion, nor the involvement of the Calvinist ruler from the Rhineland. The Catholic forces under Count Tilly marched into Bohemia early in 1620 and easily defeated the Protestant troops. Within six months the insurrectionary forces were suppressed, and Frederick chased out of the country. By 1624 the Hapsburgs drove the Protestant clergy out of the country, and deprived all Protestants of both civil and religious rights. By 1627 thirty thousand Protestant families had left the country, many of them becoming known as the Moravian Brethren.

After this Bohemian period, the war transferred to the lands of Frederick along the Rhine. Spanish troops arrived there in 1621. Count Tilly met three separate Protestant armies and defeated all of them. With the help of the Bavarian officials and the ever-present Jesuits, Ferdinand suppressed Lutheranism in the Upper Palatinate, and both Calvinism and Lutheranism in the Lower Palatinate.

By 1625, however, other countries were becoming alarmed about Hapsburg domination of so much of central Europe. England and France now supported the Protestant attempts against the Catholics, aided by the entry of King Christian IV of Denmark (1588-1648) into the war. But although this anti-Hapsburg combination looked good on paper, it failed in practice. English naval forces failed on the Spanish coasts; the English Parliament failed to approve financial subsidies to the Danish; the French refused to allow some undisciplined Protestant troops to march across their territory; and King Christian was no match for the Catholic generals. While Tilly devastated Lower Saxony, von Wallenstein, an Austrian soldier who had risen to prominence in the Bohemian fighting, recruited an army of 20,000 and marched across Germany, smashing opposition around the Baltic. By 1628 the two armies had united and conquered the Baltic coast up to Jutland. King Christian signed a peace treaty the following year.

But now even more dissension broke out in the Catholic camp. Bavaria resented the Hapsburg rise and disputed with Austria over possession of several bishoprics. Various monastic orders disputed with the Jesuits over reclaimed church property. Even Catholic France was interested in checking the Hapsburg growth.

The leading power in the north was now King Gustavus Adolphus of Sweden (1611-1632). He took over all Scandinavia, and in June of 1630 he landed on the south shore of the Baltic. By 1631 numerous German cities had come to his standard, and in September of that year he won a smashing victory over Tilly which brought all Protestant princes to his support. All Germany fell into his hands, down to Bavaria. Tilly was mortally wounded near Munich in early 1632, and Adolphus defeated Wallenstein at Lutzen in November, although he himself was killed in the battle. There was no successor with his ability, so desultory fighting continued for three more years. It was becoming obvious that the Catholic South could not subdue the Protestant

North, nor could the Protestant North subdue the Catholic South.

The Germans were tired of the war, but the French and Swedes continued the struggle. France declared war on Spain in May of 1635, and fighting continued for an additional thirteen years. By now it was no longer a religious war, but a huge political power struggle between major alliances. Germany had already been devastated by years of fighting, but French, Swedish, Spanish and Austrian armies marched back and forth across its territory, attempting to win positions of power. Although negotiations for concluding the fighting had begun in 1640, it was 1648 before the shooting stopped, with the peace of Westphalia.

The treaty ended the religious issue once and for all. Westphalia reaffirmed the Peace of Augsburg (all that fighting, and they simply returned to an earlier agreement!), with the provisions extended to include Calvinist rulers. The right for rulers to change religion was granted, but the rights of religious minorities were also guaranteed, though not in the lands of the Hapsburgs, where no toleration was granted to Protestants at all. Territorially several significant changes occurred. Sweden received land on the southern shore of the Baltic, while the German territory of Brandenburg was enlarged — soon to be known as Prussia. France received several bishoprics along the Rhine (Metz, Toul, Verdun) and much of Alsace, but not Strassburg. Finally, all signatories agreed to recognize the independence of the Netherlands and Switzerland, countries that had been independent for some time, but never with legal recognition.

We have said nothing about the Reformation in

France, and perhaps here is the best place to make up for that omission. Lutheran ideas began to make headway in France as early as the 1520's, although usually the French kings persecuted any Protestants that came to their attention. However, King Francis I (1515-1547) was constantly battling Emperor Charles of Germany, and he was willing to tolerate Protestantism at brief intervals and succor the German Protestants if it would hinder Charles. In general, however, the first half of the century was a dangerous time for Protestantism in France. For this reason John Calvin left France to take up residence in Strassburg, although he wound up spending most of his life in Geneva, Switzerland.

Henry II (1547-1559) was even more violently anti-Protestant, but it was under his rule that the French Protestant Church grew considerably. The reformers organized a church in Paris in 1555, and in 1559 they held a national synod of French Protestants there, representing some fifteen churches throughout the country. They drafted a confession of faith and a book of discipline, both of course Calvinistic. In that same decade the Protestant faith was also spreading through the nobility.

Charles IX came to the throne in 1560 (1560-1574), but he was only ten years old. The Queen Mother, Catherine de Medici, was the Regent, and she agreed to a meeting with Protestants, the Colloquy of Poissy, in July of 1561. Poissy accomplished no reconciliation, but Catherine agreed to give the legal right to meet for worship outside of walled towns. But when the Duke of Guise (the brother of Mary of Guise, who was married to James V of Scotland) found some Protestants worshiping in a town in early 1562, violence broke out and led to warfare. The Protestants, now usually called the Huguenots, fought a series of eight wars from 1562 to 1595. Each conflict lasted a year or two, followed by a peace of a few years' duration. In spite of such disasters as St. Bartholomew's Massacre, in which some 70,000 Huguenots were killed in 1572, the Protestants held on, particularly in the middle classes.[3] The Huguenots gradually expanded their numbers, but they clustered in southern and western France, particularly in the towns along the Bay of Biscay. Their strongest center was La Rochelle.

Henry of Navarre, a distant cousin to the King, was the nominal leader of the Huguenots, and in his dashing way he was their unquestioned leader on the battlefield. Through a series of circumstances three kings in succession died without sons, finally leaving Henry of Navarre as the claimant to the throne in 1589. But Catholic Paris refused to accept him. For four more years he fought, until he concluded that France needed peace more than the Huguenots needed a king. He probably did not say what has been attributed to him, that "Paris is worth a mass," but it did represent his response. He took instruction, and in 1593 he officially converted to Catholicism, becoming Henry IV (1589-1610).

His Huguenot colleagues were stunned and felt betrayed. But Henry also felt a keen obligation to them, and in 1598 he granted the Edict of Nantes, giving them liberties and privileges which they had lacked under the earlier Catholic kings. They could worship freely virtually throughout the country, although not in Paris. He guaranteed them full civil and political rights. As further insurance that the state would not threaten their people,

they were allowed to hold two hundred fortified garrisons throughout the country, with the troops paid by
the king.[4]

Henry saw to it that the Edict of Nantes was observed
during his life. Two Jesuit assassination attempts on his
life were foiled in 1594 and 1595, but a demented monk
succeeded in 1610. His son, Louis XIII (1610-1643),
was raised a Roman Catholic, and in 1621 Louis began
to take away some of the privileges of the Edict of
Nantes. The Huguenots resisted and fought three more
wars until peace was restored in 1629. King Louis
stripped the Huguenots of their independent fortified
garrisons, as well as their political and military rights,
but they still retained their civil and religious rights.
Having removed this Huguenot threat at home, the
French could contribute to the anti-Hapsburg efforts of
the Thirty Years' War. The French effort was definitely
anti-Hapsburg, not anti-Catholic.

The prime ministers of France in this period, Cardinals Richelieu and Mazarin, were determined to maintain the Huguenot privileges. Although they both were
cardinals in the Roman Catholic Church, they were not
interested in a policy of religious persecution. When
Mazarin died in 1661, King Louis XIV (1643-1715)
began to make his own decisions. Huguenot strength,
never more than 10-15% of the population, now stood at
about 9%. But Catholics were affronted by the Huguenot
presence. Beginning immediately after the death of
Mazarin, Louis XIV began to make inroads on the
promises made to the Huguenots. Each year brought
more pressure. In 1666 a royal edict listed sixty clauses
by which Huguenots could be harassed. The government

closed their hospitals, schools, and colleges, the endowment monies turned over to the Catholic institutions. Many church buildings were destroyed. On the pretext that the youngsters wished to convert to Catholicism, many Huguenot children were abducted and raised as Catholics.

As a result, many Huguenots fled the country. The climax came in 1685 when Louis simply revoked the Edict of Nantes completely.[5] When other governments tried to intervene, Louis explained that the edict was a dead letter since there were no Huguenots left in France anyway. Inconsistently, he then had thousands of Huguenots sent to the galleys for resisting Catholic conversion. Ministers were exiled, but the people were forbidden to leave the country. Yet approximately 250,000 did leave. Skillful craftsmen, trained professionals, and thrifty merchants, they became a healthy addition to the economies of Prussia, England, and the new colonies in America. The Revocation of the Edict of Nantes spread terror through much of the Protestant parts of Europe.

In spite of such incidents as this in France, however, the Peace of Westphalia ended religion as an issue in international conflict in Europe. Some countries still had repercussions with official policies toward religious minorities, but Westphalia at least brought peace to a great deal of Europe. It was a Europe becoming secularized. Secularization of life increasingly marked the movement of Europe into the modern period.

Bibliography for Chapter Nineteen

Gray, Janet Glenn. *The French Huguenots: Anatomy of*

Courage. Grand Rapids: Baker Book House, 1981.

An excellent overview of the rise, troubles, and history of Huguenots in France during the period of the Reformation.

Janelle, Pierre. *The Catholic Reformation.* Milwaukee: The Bruce Publishing Company, 1963.

Written by a Roman Catholic, a very favorable account of this development, and sympathetic to the Jesuits.

Olin, John C. (ed.) *The Autobiography of St. Ignatius Loyola, with Related Documents.* Trans. Joseph F. O'Callaghan. New York: Harper and Row, Publishers, 1974.

An excellent and informative look into the life of this founder of the Jesuits.

_____. *The Catholic Reformation: Savonarola to Ignatius Loyola; Reform in the Church, 1495-1540.* Westminster, Maryland: Christian Classics, Inc., 1969.

Written by a Roman Catholic historian, this book also contains numerous source documents of the development of the movement.

Questions and Projects for Chapter Nineteen

1. Why would the Protestant Reformation succeed in certain countries of Europe and not succeed in other countries?
2. Analyze the popes of the sixteenth century and determine how much each of them was interested in meaningful reform.

3. Contrast the Council of Trent with the Councils of Constance and Basle. Which did the most for reform? In what way?
4. The sixteenth century saw the creation of a large number of new monastic orders. Why were they begun? Contrast this to the monastic orders already in existence — why were they begun?
5. Compare and/or contrast the church history of Spain to that of France in the period 1490-1650.
6. Which was the most important factor in the Thirty Years' War — religion or international politics? Be able to defend your answer.

Notes for Chapter Nineteen

1. For a condensed translation of the papal order establishing the Roman Inquisition by Pope Paul III, see Manschreck, p. 140.
2. The canons and decrees of Trent can be found in Schaff, II, pp. 76-210.
3. For a statement and eye-witness description of St. Bartholomew's Massacre, see Manschreck, pp. 141-145.
4. The Edict of Nantes is given in Manschreck, pp. 145-146.
5. The Revocation of the Edict of Nantes is included in Manschreck, pp. 146-148.

Chapter Twenty
REVIVAL AND RATIONALISM

At the end of the Reformation Era in Europe, the monolithic picture of Christendom was a thing of the past. There was the basic division between Catholics and Protestants, and then the major state churches within the Protestant camp: Presbyterians in Scotland, Anglicans in England, Lutherans in Germany and the Scandinavian countries, Calvinists in the Netherlands and Switzerland. In addition there were minorities of many of these groups scattered through various countries. Finally, there were the dissident churches, most of which (but not all) lined up on the left wing of the Reformation. After the wars of religion were over in Europe by approximately mid-century (although internal religious differences caused difficulty within both England and France in the

1680's), Europe pretty much settled down to a *modus vivendi*, accepting the current religious differences.

But for most people, the vitality of religion had disappeared. The original evangelical commitment of the reformers was replaced by scholastic wrangling by the theologians, but by the late seventeenth century, it was replaced by religious apathy. "Conversion experiences" as such were becoming unknown, even among the clergy. Since virtually all of Europe was covered by state churches, people were members of churches because of their birth in a Christian country, but it was an empty religion. Preaching was very formal, usually dealing with theological minutiae. It was not at all uncommon for people to walk around during church services, gossiping during the prayers and hymns. Complicated sermons on hair-splitting doctrines put many people to sleep — one theologian was even praised in his eulogy for never having slept in church.

Things in Germany began to change under Philip Jacob Spener (1635-1705). As a young lad Spener was influenced by German devotional literature, and he became a Lutheran pastor. After he became a minister in Frankfurt he realized that most people needed to deepen their spiritual lives. He encouraged lay people to meet together in groups to discuss religious or devotional literature. Later, the discussions centered on Bible passages. In 1675 he wrote a little book in which he pointed out the shortcomings of the church in his time and how the church could be reformed. The book, *Pia Desideria*, or "Pious Wishes," gave its name to this movement, called Pietism.

Spener listed six concrete proposals: (1) Use God's

Word to enhance personal devotions. (2) Encourage all Christians to exercise their spiritual priesthood. (3) Cultivate a practice of brotherly love, not just a knowledge of the Christian faith. (4) Conduct religious controversy only to win the heart of the other person, not to beat him in argument. (5) Train ministers in piety as well as in scholarship. (6) Direct sermons toward Christian edification in faith and its fruits.[1] The major medium for the dissemination of Pietism was the home Bible meetings, what are sometimes called cottage prayer meetings, called by Spener the *collegia pietatis*, the "groups of piety."

Pietism at first met resistance on the part of many Lutheran clergy, but it was soon adopted and became pervasive throughout almost all German Lutheranism. There was occasional trouble with some pietist groups who drew up lists of moral rules for the regulation of their members, and some groups became sectarian and separatist. But on the whole Pietism revitalized the life of Lutheran churches.

The major leader after Spener was August Herman Francke (1663-1727), a professor at Leipzig. In his first enthusiasm for the movement, he went too much the other way, insisting that ministerial training ought to emphasize piety at the expense of academic preparation. After a few more years, he became more balanced in his approach, and from his position at the University of Halle he built that school into a Pietistic center whose alumni influenced developments in India, England, and America, as well as planted the movement firmly within Germany. Count Nicolaus Zinzendorf (1700-1760) was born of Pietist parents and educated at Halle. In 1722 he welcomed the persecuted Moravians onto his estates, became a Moravian himself, and through his and their influence, he planted strong Pietist colonies in the American colonies and elsewhere. We will note again the Pietist influence in America in Chapter XXIII.

The religious situation in France in the latter part of the seventeenth century was a rather complex one. On the one hand there was the official persecution of the Huguenots, as we have noted already. This was strictly a Catholic vs. Protestant affair. At the same time, however, there was a strong movement within France to mark the limits of papal authority. At various times throughout history the French church was zealous of maintaining its independence from papal interference. This had already been demonstrated in 1438 in the Pragmatic Sanction of Bourges, and the 1516 Concordat of Bologna. The Pragmatic Sanction allowed the French Church to administer its property without interference by the papacy, and it also kept the pope from interfering with the appointment of French bishoprics.[2] The Concordat accepted papal primacy but placed in the hands of the French king the right to nominate all bishops and archbishops in the Kingdom.[3] This desire for French internal control is usually known as "Gallicanism." Louis XIV, who was responsible for the Revocation of the Edict of Nantes, was also responsible for fostering a new upsurge of Gallicanism.

Louis was not particularly a pious Catholic, but he was committed to being an absolute ruler, and the idea that the French church could be controlled from outside France was unacceptable to him. But the Jesuits were just as firmly committed to papal supremacy. There were a number of instances where Jesuits and royalists locked horns on these issues. J.B. Bossuet (1627-1704), after 1681 the Bishop of Meaux, in 1682 drew up a document known as the Gallican Articles, approved by a synod of clergy in Paris that same year. It consisted of four articles, the thrust of which was to reassert that popes were inferior to ecumenical councils, and that kings were not subject to the papacy in temporal matters.[4] Officially the Gallican Articles were revoked in 1693 in an agreement with the papacy, although in fact they were still taught in French seminaries for another century.

Causing similar reverberations in France was the Jansenist movement. Cornelius Jansen (1585-1638) was a Dutch Roman Catholic theologian who completed much of his education in France. He began to write his major work, *The Augustinus,* in 1628, but it was not published until 1640, two years after his death. In many ways Jansen was a Catholic Calvin — based of course on Augustine. Although he strenuously resisted Protestantism, he thought current Catholic teaching made man too self-sufficient, reducing man's utter dependence upon God.

The item that caused the most difficulty was Jansen's opposition to a theory of moral theology known as "probabilism." Probabilism allows the justification of a moral action if *any* kind of a reason can be produced to defend it, even if the reason is highly unlikely or questionable: a heretic can be assassinated to prevent false teaching; a person may lie to save a friend; a priest can engage in fornication to show he is human; a businessman can cheat if it allows him to give more money to the church. Probabilism tended to produce a lax standard of moral conduct which the Jansenists felt encouraged sin. The Jesuits defended the idea of Probabilism and the moral casuistry involved. In fact "casuistry" today usually carries the connotation of a line of argument that proves that immoral acts are good.

Jansenism never became a majority movement in France, although a number of thinkers and pious Catholics defended it. Blaise Pascal (1623-1662) became its most noted voice. In spite of its minority status, Jansenism was attractive because it took some of the wind out of the sails of the Protestants (particularly Calvinists), it attacked the Jesuits, and it supported Gallicanism by resisting papal interference in French affairs. The Pope condemned Jansenist ideas in the Bull *Unigenitus* in 1713, but Jansenism survived both in France and in the Low Countries. In 1724 the Dutch Jansenists split off from Roman Catholicism and formed a branch of the Old Catholic Church. They continue down to the present. The Jansenist ideas were also a factor in the eighteenth century rationalistic revolt against the Catholic church spearheaded by such men as Voltaire and Diderot, which we shall come to shortly.

The struggle in England for religious peace in the latter part of the seventeenth century produced its own reaction. Many people were fed up with the wrangling over doctrine. The theological fighting produced theological apathy. This sapped the strength of the Anglican Church in the latter seventeenth and early eighteenth centuries. To avoid the theological disputes, many people turned to a natural religion, which resulted in the wave of Deism.

Edward Herbert (1583-1648), raised to the peerage in

1629 and thereafter known as Lord Herbert of Cherbury, is considered the founder of Deism. In 1624, Herbert wrote *De veritate*, a book of rational theology. His position is usually summarized in five points: (1) there is a God; (2) He ought to be worshiped; (3) virtue is the chief element in this worship; (4) repentance for sin is a duty; and (5) there is another life of rewards and punishments. Herbert considered himself a Christian, and he believed Christianity reflected these elements better than any other religion. Implicit in this position was the superiority of virtue over theological controversy.

Accelerating the attractiveness of the development of Deism was the new world view of the late seventeenth century. This was the century of the giants of physics, mathematics, mechanics, and cosmology — Kepler, Galileo, Descartes, and Newton. Most of these men were sincere Christians who had no desire to attack the faith, but they also emphasized the place of reason in understanding the world. New understandings of physics and astronomy opened the doors to understanding more and more of nature. Natural theology enjoyed a big resurgence. Increasingly, however, the new views of cosmology raised questions about some of the apparent worldview of the Scriptures. Miracles now stood out as irrational. Time and space had exploded to such vastness that the story of salvation from Eden to Judgment seemed an extremely small part of cosmic history.

Partially to counter some of these ideals John Locke (1632-1704) wrote his *Reasonableness of Christianity* in 1695. He was a committed Christian, interested in presenting a good apologetic, and he pointed out that Christianity was reasonable, not irrational. Deism entered a new phase in 1696 when John Toland (1670-1722) wrote his book *Christianity Not Mysterious* in which he argued that revelation must operate in a sphere governed by rational considerations, which meant that Christianity could not contain anything contrary to reason or above it. Mystery must be banished from Christian thought — this eliminated the miracles. This second generation of the Deists attacked the Scriptures by applying the new laws of the universe to the biblical material, and miracles and the supernatural came under heavy attack.

The next several decades were filled with the Deist attack and the orthodox response. Many works of apologetics were published, from Charles Leslie's *A Short and Easy Method with the Deists* in 1698, to Bishop Butler's *Analogy of Religion* in 1736. One development coming out of this conflict was the Latitudinarians, a party among the Anglican clergy who placed little importance on matters of dogmatic truth, ecclesiastical organization, or liturgical practice. They were in reaction not only to the Deists but also to the Christian apologists who were responding to them. Latitudinarians were willing to set creeds and confessions aside as things indifferent, and accept the construction of Christianity on the arguments of natural religion, fortified by the testimony of the prophecies and miracles. The gospel of reasonableness was the theme of the Latitudinarian preacher.[5]

It is against this background that the Evangelical Revival took place. The Anglican Church had become formal, and rational, but doctrinally sterile. The Puritan dissenters had been weeded out during the Restoration days, and there was little evangelicalism left in the Church of England. It was not entirely absent, as will be seen in the revival. But the Anglican Church of the early 1700's had become stiff, apathetic, rational, and virtually secularized.

The Evangelical Revival of the eighteenth century is far broader than John Wesley. He was the preeminent leader in the movement for the entire century, but it is unfair to simply call the movement the Wesleyan Revival. The revival represents far more than merely the beginning of the Methodists. There were still evangelicals among the Anglican clergy. In addition there were the Moravians, already Pietistic, who settled in London early in the century. They had a particularly significant impact on the life of John Wesley.

Wesley (1703-1791) was born into a parsonage family, with both grandfathers and one great-grandfather identified as preachers. Two generations back the grandfathers had been nonconformists, but John's father was satisfied to remain within the establishment. John and his brother Charles (1707-1788) went to Oxford, the fourth generation of their family to do so. While John decided to study for the ministry and was helping his father in parish work, it was Charles who organized the Holy Club about 1728. After John returned to Oxford he became its central leader. The group was also called the Bible Moths, the Bible Bigots, Supererogation Men, and, because of their methodical means of Bible study, Methodists.

In 1735 John Wesley went to the new American colony of Georgia where he met some Moravians. He was impressed with their calm faith and their pietistic convictions. Back in England by 1738, within a few months he made more contacts with Moravians in

London. It was these contacts with Pietism that prepared Wesley for his life-changing experience. At a devotional gathering on May 24 he had his famous conversion. Someone was reading from the Preface to Luther's commentary on Romans, and

> about a quarter to nine, while he was describing the change which God works in the heart through faith in Christ, I felt my heart strangely warmed. I felt that I did trust in Christ, Christ alone, for salvation; and an assurance was given me that he had taken away *my* sins, even *mine*, and saved me from the law of sin and death.[6]

This conversion stripped away from Wesley his emphasis on ceremonies and the ritual of the Anglican church, replacing it with a heartfelt revivalistic evangelism. By the next year he and his co-laborer George Whitefield (1714-1770) began the practice of field preaching when churches were closed against them. Reaching now the poor of the towns and countryside, the revival swept through the entire length and breadth of England. Charles Wesley was also an itinerant preacher, but he made his greatest contribution through his hymns, writing some 6,500 in all, most of them paraphrasing biblical language. His most famous ones include *Christ the Lord is Risen Today; Love Divine, All Loves Excelling; Hark the Herald Angels Sing; Jesus Lover of My Soul;* and *O For a Thousand Tongues to Sing.*

The major creation that John Wesley left behind was the Methodist organization. Whitefield was a far greater orator, but Wesley was the organizer. His Methodist classes grew into nonconformist churches. Wesley and

Whitefield both remained within the Anglican Church, refusing to break away from it. After Wesley's death, however, the ministers into whose hands he left his following soon organized the separate Methodist Church.[7]

Another aspect of the Evangelical Revival was the part played by clergymen who worked from within the Anglican Church. These Anglican Evangelicals retained all the Anglican liturgy and church laws: they also accepted the parish system and the idea of episcopal authority and jurisdiction. Theirs was not the itinerant preaching that marked the Wesleyan preaching. Nor did they approve of unordained evangelists. Most well-known among these Anglican Evangelicals was John Newton, the former slave trader who wrote the popular hymn *Amazing Grace*. A number of laymen supported this Anglican Evangelical movement, including several members of Parliament. The most noted was William Wilberforce (1759-1833), who led the fight for the abolition of slavery in the British Empire, achieved the very year of his death.

Some historians credit the Evangelical Revival with helping to prevent the French Revolution from happening in England by meeting the needs of England's poorer classes. Not only did the revival give them religion to get their minds off their social problems, but it also brought more of the establishment into tune with lower class needs.

It may be hard to prove that this revival stayed revolution in England, but it is obvious that English society was stable in this century while the French went through a heady period of rationalism, militant anti-religious development, and revolution. The rationalism that climaxed in France had its beginning in Germany. Christian Wolff (1679-1754) taught at the Pietistic University of Halle. Wolff worked out a defense of the Christian faith, but his arguments were so based on reason that his methods antagonized the Pietists. Much of Wolff's thinking was foundational for the work of Immanuel Kant.

Kant (1724-1804) saw himself as a convinced Christian, even though his philosophical writings were used by numerous others as an attack on the Christian faith. He attempted to reconcile the rationalism that was becoming impressed with scientific developments with the moral obligations that man experienced only in a religious system. Kant became the king of philosophers for much of the nineteenth century, but his work is not essentially anti-Christian. His *Critique of Pure Reason* pointed out that reason is filtered through our minds; therefore even the evidence for natural religion can never be apprehended by our knowledge in a pure state, since it is always interpreted through our minds, through which pure objectivity is never possible. This completely cut the ground out from under the Deists, but it also devastated the traditional arguments for the existence of God.

These ideas had no immediate shocking application in Germany. Such ideas in Germany were still being applied through the church. It was not until the nineteenth century that Kant's ideas fed German secularism. Eighteenth century France, however, was in a far more secular mood. For one thing, the Jansenist controversy was still simmering. Many French, including large numbers of the clergy, resented the Pope's anti-Jansenist interference with French internal affairs. The Jesuits, loyal to the papacy, also got the ear of King Louis XV (1715-1774) and accelerated the struggle. In 1730 Louis declared the *Unigenitus* was part of French law, but the French law courts refused to enforce the King's decree. When the King exiled the court to Paris for disobedience, the populace blamed this on the meddling of the Jesuits and stepped up their own anticlerical attack. Through all this struggle, the Jesuits and the French Church became identified with intolerance, persecution, and harassment.

Another background theme to French Rationalism was the decline in the level of French religious fervor. The French church was rich, powerful, and influential. It had a monopoly over the record of all births, deaths, and marriages. The church was also immune from most of the taxes the people had to pay. Many of the bishops were nonresident, and many of the monasteries were closing for lack of inhabitants. As a result the monasteries and the upper clergy were generally detested in France. The parish priests were often the devoted pastors of souls, much loved by the people, but their superiors failed to carry the same popular respect.

Just as Erasmus had been able to use satire against the glaring abuses of the Renaissance Church, so the witty intelligentsia among the French rationalists were able to point out the foibles of a wealthy, corrupt church establishment fattening off the peasantry who were living on the bare level of subsistence. Denis Diderot (1713-1784) was a materialist who became the head of a project to put out a new encyclopedia. He published this work in thirty-five volumes between 1751 and 1780. It was a complete review of the arts and sciences of the day, written mostly by men of a naturalist inclination. Those involved in the production, and those who identified with it, were called the *encyclopedists*. As a class they were antireligious, and even beginning to suspect the rights of an absolutist monarchy. The *encyclopedists* advocated toleration and democracy, and they attacked the Church for its intellectual and spiritual tyranny. Diderot himself wrote the article on "Christianity," in which he expressed respect for the transcendent religion of Jesus, but contempt for its social morality. The *encyclopedists* were also often known as *philosophes* — free thinkers who cut themselves off from the corruption of the Church and similar problems in the State.

Jean-Jacques Rousseau (1712-1778) was somewhat of a reaction to the emphasis on reason and rationalism. Stating that logic alone could not satisfy the heart of man, he emphasized a simple religion of reverence for God and love for mankind. He taught that Nature was fundamentally good, but that men had been corrupted through the evils of society. His religion was mostly just Deism with emotional enthusiasm included.

The final stage in the development of French rationalism was represented in the most noted of them all, Voltaire (1694-1778). He advocated the complete denial of God, and in the name of humanity and reason he declared war on the Jesuits and what the French Church stood for. He ridiculed the beliefs and superstitions of the French people. Increasingly violent and bitter as he grew older, he led the *philosophes* in denouncing the Church. In his famous phrase *Ecrasez l'infame!* ("Crush the infamous thing!") he referred not to God, Christ,

Christianity, or even Catholicism, but the whole structure of privileged and persecuting orthodoxy.

The *philosophes* laid the groundwork for the anticlericalism of the French Revolution, but they also harbored beliefs and aspirations which can only be called religious. They believed in the Deist God and emphasized the value of ethics. They believed in the innate goodness of man, and that man with proper training could live the good life (the "enlightened" man, living in the period of the "enlightenment," as this period of reason is also called). The combination of all these trends undermined the authority of the Church in France. For too long the French Church had allowed Gallicanism to tie it to the fortunes of the state. Thus when the Revolutionaries turned against the *"ancien regime,"* they also attacked the Church. Anticlericalism was as much a part of the French Revolution as the resentment against the tyrannical monarchy.

It is hard not to see the falling fortunes of the church in France in terms of the impending French Revolution. But what was happening in France was not entirely unique in Europe. Other Catholic countries as well were experiencing restive nationalism, and popular antagonism toward established Catholic institutions. The best illustration of this can be seen in the history of the Jesuit order in the late eighteenth century. The Jesuits had an international reputation for dabbling in intrigue, and their questionable moral probabilism opened them up to attack. In France, not only the Gallicans, but the Jansenists, the *philosophes*, and the local courts were all waiting for the moment to strike.

This anti-Jesuit feeling in France was aided by developments in Portugal. The Prime Minister there, Pombal, accused the Jesuits of usurping royal prerogatives in the colonies, and when there was an assassination attempt on the King, Pombal blamed the Jesuits. In 1759 the Order was driven from Portugal. Such feelings transferred easily to France, where the financial collapse of a Jesuit speculator created the charge that the Jesuits as a whole were responsible. Other proceedings against them multiplied, and under popular excitement the government closed their schools and confiscated much of their property. Finally, under intense public opinion in 1764, Louis XV issued the edict which banned the Society from France. The King of Spain, Charles III (1759-1788), a relative of the French monarch, also distrusted them because of their intrigues. His prime minister persuaded him that the Jesuits were planning his assassination, and in 1767 Charles suppressed the Jesuit Society in all Spanish territory, including missions in the New World.

With the Jesuits suppressed both in Spain and in France, and exiled from Portugal, the papacy came under additional pressure to dissolve the order. Even within the papacy the Jesuits were under suspicion, because of continued defiance of stringent regulations on probabilism and attempts by Jesuit missionaries to accommodate Catholic teachings to local customs in Oriental countries. Bowing to the tremendous pressure brought by both France and Spain, Pope Clement XIV (1769-1774) decided that for the sake of peace and to avoid even greater evils, it was necessary to dissolve the Order. This he did in 1773 with the Bull *Dominus ac redemptor noster*, suppressing the order "forever."[8]

But this was not the end of Rome's difficulties. A German form of Gallicanism came to light through the writings of Justinus Febronius, the penname of the auxiliary bishop of Trier. The basic tenets of "Febronianism," as it came to be called, were that although the pope was necessary to unity, he was only the *primus inter pares* and he must be subordinate to the church as a whole. Febronius argued that church affairs should be put into the hands of bishops and the civil authorities, thus stripping the papacy of its traditional power and prerogatives. Febronius wrote his major book *On the State of the Church* in 1763, and the papacy placed it on the Index of Forbidden Books the following year. Febronianism did not survive the Napoleonic incursion into the Rhineland, but it represented an interesting corollary to what was happening outside of France with regard to ideas similar to Gallicanism.

A further illustration of this was seen in the Hapsburg homeland itself, Austria. Empress Maria Theresa (1717-1780) and her son Joseph II, Holy Roman Emperor (1765-1790), considered themselves Catholics, but they shared many of the same ideas as Gallicanism and Febronianism. In Austria it was called Josephism. The state confiscated numerous church lands, suppressed some religious orders, put the training of priests under state control, and denied papal publications that did not secure prior royal permission. In 1781 Joseph passed an Edict of Toleration which allowed full religious toleration to all religious bodies, including Protestantism.

Joseph's brother Leopold was the ruler in Tuscany in northern Italy, and he was developing similar policies. A synod here in 1786 was a virtual elaboration of Jansenist views. Leopold succeeded his brother as Holy Roman Emperor (1790-1792), but his short reign resulted in the quick collapse of Josephism. However, the combination of all these developments seriously hindered the strength of the Roman Catholic Church to face Napoleon. The result was a very weak papacy by the end of the eighteenth century.

The Evangelical Revival had strengthened much of Protestantism, but Catholicism suffered seriously from the new intellectual climate merged with renewed nationalism. The early nineteenth century saw the Catholic Church at an all-time low, but its very humiliation brought it the sympathy to rise to prominence again. By contrast, in the nineteenth century the Protestant churches suffered under new intellectual challenges.

Bibliography for Chapter Twenty

Brown, Dale W. *Understanding Pietism*. Grand Rapids: William B. Eerdmans Publishing Company, 1978.

A succinct presentation of the major points of Pietism, giving also an assessment of its potential problems.

Caillet, Emile. *Pascal: The Emergence of Genius*. New York: Harper & Brothers, Publishers, 1961.

An excellent intellectual biography of the man who came to present many of the virtues of the Jansenists in seventeenth century France.

Henry, Stuart C. *Whitefield: Wayfaring Witness*. New York: Abingdon Press, 1957.

An excellent introduction to the life of this stimulating evangelist who typified much of the eighteenth century revival in England and America.

Irwin, Grace. *Servant of Slaves: A Biographical Novel of John Newton.* Grand Rapids: William B. Eerdmans Publishing Co., 1961.

Although told in novel form, this is an excellent overview of the life of Newton, one-time slave dealer, later famous evangelical preacher.

Newton, John. *Letters of a Slave Trader Freed by God's Grace: An Autobiography.* Moody Press, n.d.

First published in 1764, these letters portray the inner history of this great evangelical preacher who wrote *Amazing Grace.*

Nicholas, James Hastings. *History of Christianity, 1650-1950: Secularization of the West.* New York: The Ronald Press Company, 1957.

The best textbook approach to the history of Christianity in the modern period. Dry in reading, but comprehensive in scope.

Spener, Philip Jacob. *Pia Desideria.* Translated, edited, and with an Introduction by Theodore G. Tappert. Philadelphia: Fortress Press, 1964.

This is the book that began the Pietist revolution. It is still provocative reading.

Tuttle, Robert G., Jr. *John Wesley: His Life and Theology.* Grand Rapids: Zondervan Publishing House, 1978.

One of the excellent overviews of John Wesley, his life and influence.

Questions and Projects for Chapter Twenty

1. Explain what happened to Lutheranism in the century

after the death of Luther so that it became so lifeless. How do you account for this?

2. Are Pietism and the Evangelical Revival represented by the Wesleys' revivals of original Protestantism, or are they significantly new developments? Does every reformation need periodic revival?

3. Explain what happened to the Jesuits which led from their being the "shock troops of the papacy" to their dissolution by papal order. How would you compare their experience to that of Lutheranism?

4. Analyze the place of the Jansenists in Catholicism in general, and French Catholicism in particular. Would anything be different if the Jansenists had never developed?

5. How different is Gallicanism from the development of Anglicanism in England? How far can you push the similarities?

Notes for Chapter Twenty

1. Philip Jacob Spener, *Pia Desiderata* (Philadelphia: Fortress Press, 1964), pp. 87-122.

2. The Pragmatic Sanction is given in Barry, I, pp. 513-518.

3. The Concordat of Bologna is given in Barry, I, pp. 518-523.

4. Bousset's four Gallican Articles are given in Bettenson, pp. 378-380, and in Barry, II, pp. 241-242.

5. When Thomas Campbell wrote the *Declaration and Address* in America in 1809, he argued for the setting aside of the creeds and confessions, but he did not want to be classed with the Latitudinarians. See his comments on pp. 146-147 of Charles Alexander Young (ed.), *Historical Documents Advocating Christian Union* (Chicago: The Christian Century Company, 1904 [reprinted by Old Paths Book Club, 1955]).

6. Wesley himself saw this conversion experience as the result of a long process of spiritual development. See his comments in Manschreck, pp. 284-288.

7. For the documents concerning Wesley's "Deed of Declaration" and the organization of his followers in spite of his wishes, see Bettenson, pp. 359-362.

8. The papal bull of dissolution is found in Barry, II, pp. 264-272.

Chapter Twenty-One
REVOLUTION, ROMANTICISM, AND REACTION

History rarely falls into nicely divided blocks. Beginning and ending dates are often chosen somewhat arbitrarily, though they usually do represent significant times or events of transition. The nineteenth century is such a time. Obviously the years 1800 and 1900 represent artificial division, since nothing important occurred in these century years. For this reason many historians discuss the period 1789-1914 as the nineteenth century. Actually, of course, it is a century and a quarter. But the French Revolution on the one end effectively initiates a period radically distinct from its preceding era, and the outbreak of World War I just as effectively heralds a new transition. We shall use this same chronological period as the focus of the present chapter.

As we saw in the last chapter, events in France had been moving toward some sort of climax for some time. The religious developments in and of themselves were not overwhelmingly significant, but they were also reflections of what was going on in the society in general. The rationalists' attack upon French Catholicism paralleled their similar attack on the French monarchy. Since church and state were so closely tied together in France, it was almost impossible to attack one without attacking the other.

The immediate cause of the beginning of the French Revolution was the bankruptcy of the state. Financial mismanagement had been an unresolved problem in France for some time, and the numerous expenses the French incurred on behalf of the American patriots did not help their solvency any. In order to get new taxes, in 1789 Louis XVI (1774-1792) had to call the Estates-General into session. Since it had not met since 1614 — a full 175 years — the people had plenty of complaints against the government, chief of which was that the nobility and the clergy were escaping most of the taxes. Most of the parish priests were taken from the peasantry and identified with the people, and they too were discontented with the higher clergy. Among the deputies representing the clergy, the priests outnumbered the bishops by more than four-to-one. When the deputies of the people began to make demands for reform, the priests shifted their vote in the same direction. When the King tried to dismiss the Assembly, most of its members took an oath not to separate until the constitution of the kingdom had been overhauled. Louis XVI gave in, and the Revolution was on.

While the Assembly began to restructure the tax and social structure of the country, the mob stormed the Bastille on July 14. By August 4 the entire feudal structure of France, with special privileges enjoyed by aristocracy and clergy, was demolished. On August 27 the Assembly passed the Declaration of the Rights of Man, giving full freedom for Protestants.[1] On November 2 the Assembly confiscated the lands of the Church. By February of 1790 monastic vows lost official recognition, with the result that most monks left their monasteries, although most nuns stayed. Alarmed, Pope Pius VI (1775-1799) condemned the Declaration of the Rights of Man, with its assertion of full religious freedom. Unfortunately, this had the effect of presenting the Church as the foe of all social progress.

Pressure increased for the document then being drafted, the Civil Constitution of The Clergy, which completely rearranged church-state relationships.[2] A salary scale was worked out for all clergy, ending the horrible disparity between salaries of priests and bishops. Further, both priests and bishops were to be elected by the people, rather than appointed by the Church. The French thought that the Pope would approve these measures rather than face a schism. Pius temporized as long as he could, but finally in March of 1791, he disapproved of the Civil Constitution. This split the French Church into the Constitutional Church and the Non-jurors, those who would not swear to the new arrangement. The Assembly labeled the Non-jurors as "traitors," and expelled 40,000 of them from the country.

When war erupted between France and Austria in 1792, Prussia soon joined Austria, and England did the same the following year. This created a war psychology on the part of the Assembly, making them even more radical. The Assembly abolished the monarchy by fall, and executed King Louis in January, 1794. Since the Church was opposed to the revolutionary reforms, and since most of the deputies were Deists anyway, church and state drifted further apart. The Deists and *philosophes* began to convert the churches into "temples of reason." In the famous cathedral of Notre Dame in November of 1793 the statue of the Virgin Mary was replaced by that of an actress (some said that of a prostitute, but morally speaking there may have been little difference), and to her was addressed the hymn glorifying Holy Liberty. In June of 1794 — the same day as Pentecost — Robespierre led in the celebration called the Festival of the Supreme Being. Fifty days later (another pentecost?) he went to the guillotine, and the Cult of the Supreme Being died shortly thereafter.

Things went from bad to worse for the Church. Any cleric that had six people testify against him could be deported. To save their lives, thousands of priests abdicated their office and many of them married. The state annexed Avignon without recompense to the papacy. French troops conquered the Papal States and brought Pius back to France a virtual prisoner. He died in 1799. The fortunes of the Roman Church had not been so low in centuries.

The one figure who emerged out of the entire Revolution was Napoleon Bonaparte (1769-1821). He entered a military school at age ten, joined the army at age sixteen, and was a rising young officer just when the fighting broke out. The Italian campaign particularly made him a national hero. He conquered northern Italy, advanced into the Papal States, and set up the capture of Rome. By November of 1799 Napoleon's coup d'etat put him in charge of the government, and in 1804 he was made Emperor of France.

Napoleon saw that France needed stability, but he reasoned that it would never happen as long as the state and the church were at odds. Religion was merely a matter of convenience to him, but he knew that most of the French people still identified with Catholicism. Napoleon felt he had to come to a rapprochement with the papacy. The new Pope, Pius VII (1800-1823), agreed on the wisdom of reconciliation. The result was the Concordat of 1801.[3] The papacy conceded that Catholicism could be recognized as "the religion of the great majority of the French citizens," which was less than saying it was the official religion of the state. The papacy also acknowledged the loss of the church's estates, although the state now took over the matter of clerical salaries. The schism between Constitutional Church and Nonjurors was healed, but Protestants still had freedom of worship. The Papal States were restored to the Pope, but papal territory in northern Italy was not.

Another major event which took place under Napoleon's guidance occurred in western Germany. France seized all land west of the Rhine, and the rulers who lost these areas were compensated by receiving ecclesiastical territories east of the Rhine. By this single stroke 112 ecclesiastical states disappeared; only Mainz remained, and it was severely reduced. Of 50 free cities, only 6 remained. Prussia and Bavaria gained the most from this shift, and Austria was a relative loser. In 1806

Napoleon announced the Confederation of the Rhine, a union of fifteen German states; later this union was extended to include virtually every German state except Prussia and Austria. By August of 1806 Napoleon announced the end of the Holy Roman Empire. When the fifteen German rulers of the Confederation announced that they no longer recognized the Empire, Emperor Francis II (1792-1806) was forced to accept the situation. He became merely the ruler of Austria (1792-1835), and the entity that Charlemagne had forged over a millennium previously was no more.

Later political developments led to increased friction between the Pope and Emperor Napoleon. By 1809 the Papal States were again incorporated into the French Empire. Pius excommunicated those responsible for such an action, and for this he was arrested and taken to southern France. He spent the next five years under Napoleonic pressure, but in the process he gained the sympathy and popularity of all of Catholic Europe. Just as Prussia gained the political sympathy of much of Europe because of her resistance to Napoleon, so did the Pope receive the spiritual sympathy. As a result, after the fall of Napoleon, both Prussia and the papacy emerged as powerful institutions in post-Napoleonic Europe.

Any events as major as the French Revolution and the Napoleonic Era are certain to bring reactions. Part of the reaction which occurred in nineteenth century Europe is intellectual, and part is institutional. It is difficult to isolate these, for chronologically they occurred at the same time, and they were often mutually influencing. But in order to give some structure and clarity to the developments, it will be necessary to treat these two differently.

First, the intellectual developments.

The bitter anticlericalism of the rationalists brought reaction even during the Revolution itself. As early as 1795 there was a Catholic resurgence when the state church was briefly dissolved under the radicals. There was also a religious revival which characterized the first half of the nineteenth century. This revival represented a conservative change from the liberalism of the Revolution.

The same feelings of reaction and disillusionment with the revolution lapped over into religious concepts. Part of this reaction was against the Enlightenment in general, and it was prefigured in the writing of Kant. In his works *Critique of Practical Reason* (1788) and *Religion Within the Limits of Pure Reason* (1792), Kant placed the ground for religious belief in the moral consciousness — not in reason — and thus he put it out of reach of the rationalists' attacks. He helped to develop the Philosophy of Religion as a fit discipline for study.

This soon led to F.D.E. Schleiermacher (1768-1844). The son of a German Reformed minister (and army chaplain), Schleiermacher was early sent to a Moravian school. Educated for the ministry, Schleiermacher became a tutor, minister, hospital chaplain, and ultimately a university professor. In 1799 he shot into fame with his little book *On Religion: Speeches to its Cultured Despisers* where he began the reformation of all Protestant theology. Previously theology had been torn between the two tendencies of orthodoxy (rational scholasticism) and pietism (anti-intellectual and mystical). Both had become sterile in the late eighteenth century in the Enlightenment and the Revolution.

Sophisticated despisers of religion were attacking both. Schleiermacher pointed out that they were right in attacking both, but neither one was true religion. Religion is neither dogma nor piety, Schleiermacher insisted; instead it is a "feeling of dependence upon the Infinite." This emphasis on feeling dominated much of nineteenth century German theology, and from that base it influenced much of theology in Christian Europe and America.

This emphasis on "feeling" also characterized the Romantics of this century, as did emphases on melancholy, imagination, and sensitivity. A partial reaction to this Romanticism was Soren Kierkegaard (1813-1855), who stated that the essence of reality was not in the feelings, but in one's personal commitment. This commitment, in turn, led to frustration and despair, which led to the leap of faith into religious certainty. This combination of decision and commitment is usually known today as "existentialism," and it was rediscovered by the neo-orthodox reaction to the Romantic theologians in the early twentieth century, led by Barth and Brunner. But of this, more later.

A contemporary of Schleiermacher's, and a person with perhaps just as much influence, was Georg W.F. Hegel (1770-1831). He saw the dialectical process as the key to understanding both philosophy and history. Disagreeing with those philosophers who saw everything in terms of contradiction or polarization, Hegel saw principles as being in dialogue, working out compromise solutions. He used the basic triad of thesis, antithesis, and resolution into a synthesis; the synthesis became the new thesis, ultimately was opposed by an antithesis, and the whole process began all over again.

David Friedrick Strauss (1808-1874) was a pupil of both Hegel and Schleiermacher. He was a faithful Hegelian in that he saw Christianity as an expression of eternal truths, with the historical setting of secondary importance. Thus Christ was important not as a person, but because He stood for the idea of humanity moving towards perfection. He wrote his famous book *Leben Jesu (Life of Christ)* in 1835 when he was only twenty-seven years old. He saw Jesus as a purely human person who came to believe in Himself as the fulfillment of the Messianic hopes. His followers were so impressed that their imagination transformed Jesus into the divine and supernatural Christ. Eliminating many of the incidents of the Gospel accounts as myth, he threw out the miracles (including the virgin birth and resurrection) and the detailed accounts of the Crucifixion. Ultimately he broke completely with Christianity and became a pessimist and materialist.

Another student of Hegel was F.C. Baur (1792-1860). He applied the Hegelian philosophy to the New Testament and the history of the early church. He felt Strauss had ignored the historical records, which he felt proved that dialectic was the life-blood of the early church. In typical Hegelian style, Baur postulated that the original form of Christianity was that of the Judaizers, and this was "thesis." Paul led the opposition, the "antithesis." Baur saw this conflict as the most significant event in the first century of Christianity. Ultimately the conflict became synthesis by mid second century. Baur used this theory as the framework for dating various New Testament books. Any books which showed strife between Judaizers and Paul were early; any books which showed the strife compromised and peace restored were late — thus Acts and the Pastoral Epistles are second century products. Baur accepted as genuinely Pauline only I and II Corinthians, Galatians, and Romans. The synthesis then became a thesis, to be challenged by the new Hellenistic thinking as applied to the nature of the Trinity and the nature of Christ. Thus the ecumenical councils of the fourth and fifth centuries provided another synthesis. Baur's theory was provocative and his persuasion convincing, but by the end of the century further research into the New Testament documents proved that Baur went too far. His theory is no longer accepted today, though in the meantime, it convinced many people that the New Testament sources could not be trusted.

Charles Darwin (1809-1882) represented the increasing influence of science in religious questions in the nineteenth century. His work *The Origin of Species by Natural Selection* (1859) ushered in the controversy over evolution that is still going on. Darwin was originally planning on becoming a country parson, but his interest in naturalism led him into other directions, including his participation on the voyages which brought him to his evolutionist conclusions. Darwinism became bigger than Darwin himself, and the implications for the church were awesome. Scientists now discounted the creation accounts in the early chapters of Genesis, and they discarded other miracle narratives in Scripture. Science and religion reached a new stage of hostility as a result of growing Darwinism.

Albrecht Ritschl (1822-1889) was influenced by most of the philosophical and theological currents floating around Germany by mid-century. Influenced by Kant, Ritschl accepted the close identification between religion and morality. He believed that religion was essentially a practical affair, concerned with the victory of spirit over nature in human life. From this matrix, Ritschl sought to restore the historical Jesus as the center of theology. He wanted to separate the historical core of Christianity from the Hegelian philosophy, saving it from the theologizing process to which it had been subjected down through the centuries.

His major emphasis was on the "Kingdom of God," which he saw as the central point in Jesus' teaching. Ritschl believed the purpose of God in the world was to build up a kingdom of free spirits of every race who were bound together in a moral community and in brotherly love. The Kingdom of God had an ethical responsibility, and this brought in the social gospel. Ritschl is rightly considered the father of the social gospel movement. The Church's purpose was to attack social injustice and establish the brotherhood of man, not just work for the pious devotion of individual souls. This concern for ethics and the optimism that man can improve his social situation became central tenets to later liberal theology.

Adolf Harnack (1851-1930), a disciple of Ritschl, became the most outstanding scholar of patristic literature in his generation. His extensive *History of Dogma* (published in seven volumes, 1886-1889) remains a classic. He stressed the influence of historical causes on the development of doctrine in the early Christian centuries, particularly from Hellenism. Greek metaphysics he regarded as elements alien to the simple Christian message. Thus he could reject the classical creeds of the ecumenical councils because they were based in Greek philosophy. All formulations reflecting Greek philosophy he rejected as foreign to the spirit of original New Testament Christianity.

Parallel to the development of these theological trends were new developments in biblical studies. Julius Wellhausen (1844-1918) saw the Old Testament as a development in stages from a crude belief in a tribal deity to a more ethical and universal creed as the Israelites made the transition from a nomadic, pastoral people to a settled, urbanized society with social prophets like Amos and Isaiah. Probably the two most noted controversies in the Old Testament in this era were the Documentary Hypothesis with its JEPD fragments edited into the Pentateuch (often called the Graf-Wellhausen theory) and the concept of Deutero-Isaiah: the belief that this Old Testament book of prophecy is really two different works, divided at chapter 40, written by two different men centuries apart.

F.C. Baur spent most of his active teaching career at the University of Tubingen, and there he developed his views of the New Testament in what has come to be called the "Tübingen school." This shifted attention to the New Testament and the alleged strife between Pauline and Petrine factions within Christianity. Even more of the attention of nineteenth century studies was in the attempt to reconstruct the life of Jesus in human terms. Strauss' *Leben Jesu* was only the first, but numerous others followed his example. By the end of the century, almost every biblical scholar felt he had to write a new biography of Jesus.

In 1899-1900 Harnack gave a series of lectures at the University of Berlin which became the book *What Is Christianity?*, one of the classic expressions of liberal Protestantism. Harnack stressed that one must get behind the message of Paul to the original teaching of Christ Himself. Even here, one must sift through the husks of Jesus' message to the very kernel. Harnack insisted that Jesus put his message in eschatological language, but this was not to be confused with the real kernel of the message. This kernel, Harnack insisted, is threefold: (1) the kingdom of God and its coming; (2) God the Father and the infinite value of the human soul; and (3) the higher righteousness and the commandments of love. The Gospel, therefore, is an ethical message, teaching the law of love and human brotherhood.

Albert Schweitzer (1875-1965) is significant for his book published in 1906, *The Quest for the Historical Jesus*. This was a review of various modern attempts to understand the life of Christ, all of which he held to be inadequate. He disagreed with Harnack in that Schweitzer considered the eschatological message of Jesus to be central to his message — Jesus expected the speedy conclusion of the world, and when this proved to be a mistake, He decided that He Himself must suffer in order to save His people from the tribulations preceding the last days. An interesting observation that Schweitzer made in his historical overview was that all of these scholars writing the life of Christ were like so many men looking down into a well — they saw themselves reflected there. The scholars looking for the real picture of Jesus saw reflected their own concept of what Jesus ought to have been.

Capping this whole development in biblical studies in Germany was the development of Form Criticism. Martin Dibelius (1883-1947) and Rudolf Bultmann (1884-1976) were probably the most significant of the founders of this school. Form Criticism lays stress upon the Gospel accounts as collections of sayings, miracle stories, and one-liner anecdotes of the life and ministry of Jesus. These types of literature about Jesus were standardized in first and second century sermons, but based on authentic incidents carried through oral tradition. Form Criticism is therefore an attempt to get behind the forms to the historical content. The result, again, is to deny the historicity of the Gospels as such and lay emphasis upon views in tune with modern liberalism.

While all this was going on in the Protestant world the Catholics were not as much affected, but one significant exception was Alfred Loisy (1857-1940). A professor at a Catholic school in Paris, Loisy raised questions in 1892 in his lectures on Genesis that created considerable suspicion towards him. In 1902 Loisy attacked Harnack in print, but in the process he also rejected biblical inerrancy and the accepted orthodoxy of the Catholic Church. By 1903 five of Loisy's books were on the Index. By 1907 the papacy had condemned fifty propositions drawn from the works of Loisy.

Thus romanticism's reaction to the events of the French Revolution led Christianity into a departure from the accepted orthodoxy of the centuries. This paved the way for liberalism, and a denigration of the biblical sources of Christianity. But at the same time that these events were occurring in the intellectual arena, institutional Roman Catholicism was undergoing a significant transition. To a certain extent this was an attempt to meet the threat from the compromising position of romanticism and liberalism; from a different perspective, however, it overshot the mark and created as many problems as it hoped to resolve.

We have mentioned that in the aftermath of the downfall of Napoleon, Pius VII enjoyed a renewal of sympathy and support throughout Europe. After the heyday of Napoleonic liberalism, much of Europe was ready for a return to former stability. The Bourbon monarchs returned to the throne in France; Pius VII returned to Rome in 1814, and one of the first things he did was to revive the Jesuit order. They were soon to recover their strength and prestige and again be a major factor in the activities of the Church. Also, as a result of the Congress of Vienna at which politicians redrew the map of Europe, the papacy received back most of the Papal States.

Romanticism itself is a somewhat difficult word to define, even though it is a significant aspect of the nineteenth century. Basically it is a literary, artistic, and philosophical movement characterized by an emphasis on the imagination and the emotions. In literature this became an inclination for figures wrapped in melancholy. There is an inclusion of themes on the common man, an exaltation of primitive ages, and thus an emphasis on history — an appreciation for older glorious moments of aesthetic accomplishment. Thus Victor Hugo with his *Hunchback of Notre Dame* (1831) went into rhapsody about the architectural accomplishment of the great cathedral, though the book concluded with the tragic death of the dancing Esmeralda and the faithful Quasimodo — more melancholy.

In the Anglican Church this romanticism took a unique turn in the development of the Oxford Movement. This stemmed from some young intellectuals about Oxford University who were drawn to an appreciation of the church in past ages, in contrast to the pervasive secularism taking over the nineteenth century. This glorification of the church led a number of these men to convert to Roman Catholicism — the essence of glorified medieval church history. The most famous of such converts was John Henry Newman (1801-1890), who converted in 1845. Pope Leo XIII made him a cardinal in 1879. Although the Oxford Movement was a minority development in the total Anglican Church, it represented some of the major tendencies of Romanticism. It also began the development of the Anglo-Catholic party within the Church of England.

Meanwhile, the French Church had to accommodate itself to the realization that the state controlled the former church lands and paid the salaries of the clergy. The removal of their lands made the bishops less of a threat to the papacy; putting them on state salary made them dependent upon the state. The recent experience under Napoleon made them realize this left them in a defenseless position. They concluded that the only agency that could help them was a strong papacy. So they looked to a reinvigorated papacy for help. This movement was known as "ultramontanism," since it looked "beyond the mountains." Thus the political situation in France, allied with the increased sympathy now directed toward Pius VII, made for a situation in which much of Catholic Europe was desirous of a stronger papacy. The ultramontanist movement in the first half of the nineteenth century put the papacy in a position of leadership that it had lacked at the end of the eighteenth century. Pius IX (1846-1878) combined this ultramontanism with a strongly conservative papacy. His pontificate is the crowning achievement of nineteenth century church politics.

Pius' thirty-two-year pontificate is the longest in Roman Catholic history. According to tradition, Peter was Bishop of Rome for twenty-five years, and Pius IX was the first figure to break that record. When he was elected in 1846, he held the reputation of being slightly liberal. He was pro-Italian, anti-Austrian, and he did some things that indicated a liberal political orientation. As pope, he provided amnesty to political prisoners in the Papal States, instituted a citizen militia, and fostered economic improvements. Late in 1847 he established an elective consultative assembly and a council of ministers which included laymen.

Then the revolutions of 1848 hit. Major revolutions wracked France, Germany, Austria, Hungary, and Italy. One of Pius' ministers was assassinated in Rome, Pius himself was besieged in one of his castles, and for a year he had to take refuge in Naples. In response to his plea, troops from France and Austria came to Rome to put down the rebellious mob and restore Pius to his territory. Whatever might have been his political orientation earlier, he was now dependent upon outside military protection, and he took advantage of all the ultramontanist buildup. He instituted an absolutist regime in the Papal States and became one of the most innovative but conservative popes in modern times.

In addition to these political implications, he showed

this innovation and commitment to tradition at the same time in doctrinal pronouncements. In 1854 he proclaimed the dogma of the Immaculate Conception of the Blessed Virgin Mary. This states that Mary was kept free from all stain of original sin from the very moment of her conception because of the singular grace of God and in view of the merits of Christ.[4] The idea goes all the way back to the second century, yet many significant theologians through the centuries had opposed the idea. Part of the significance of Pius' pronouncement is that this is the first time a pope had issued such a dogma without the concurrence of a Council, or the support of Scripture or tradition.

Political events continued to gain attention in Italy. There was a major movement for Italian reunification called the *Resorgimento*, "the Resurgence." Fearing that such a move would again deprive him of the Papal States, Pius fought it. The King of Sardinia put himself at the head of the political unification, and with the aid of the patriot Garibaldi (1807-1882) achieved significant success. By 1860 most of the peninsula was united, with the exception of Venice and the papal territory immediately around Rome. Garibaldi occupied most of the Papal States, and popular plebiscites favored union into a new Italy.

Pius denounced his despoilers, excommunicated Victor Emmanuel, the new King of Italy (1861-1878), and kept Rome only because of the presence of French troops. Taking the offensive, Pius in 1864 promulgated the Syllabus of Errors, in which he condemned eighty propositions reflecting political and economic liberalism. He condemned such ideas as democracy and the separation of church and state.[5] The publication of the Syllabus raised a storm of protest across the western world, in Catholic as well as in Protestant countries. But Pius would not back down.

His next achievement was the convening of the Vatican council (at first it had no number, but since Vatican II this one is referred to as Vatican I). There had been no ecumenical council for the Church in over three hundred years, and Vatican I was the best attended council up to this point. Many liberals hoped the council would soften down the tone of the Syllabus, but Pius focused attention on the doctrine of papal infallibility. One of the major items of the debate was the "Question of Honorius" who seemed to endorse Monothelitism back in the seventh century. The infallibilists, however, explained that Honorius was guilty of an indiscreet personal letter; it was not a case of official papal teaching. When the issue came up for final vote, the bishops voted 533 to 2 in favor of papal infallibility, with the two bishops in the minority immediately changing their vote after the official tabulation. The decree states that the pope is infallible when he speaks *ex cathedra* ("from the chair," that is, officially) in the areas of faith and morals.[6] There has been much misunderstanding on this issue, particularly by Protestants. This is not to say that the pope is personally without sin. It has nothing to do with his personal character and actions. It only states that when he speaks officially in the realm of morals and doctrine, his pronouncements are without error. All the bishops of Catholicism yielded to the decree, but some intellectuals refused. They knew the question of Honorius could not be waived, and they felt that any statement on papal infallibility was dishonest, not to mention unauthorized. The church historian Döllinger (1799-1890) of Germany led the opposition, and when he was excommunicated in 1871 the anti-infallible party in Germany set up the Old Catholic Church.

Two days after the decree of papal infallibility, France declared war on Prussia. The Franco-Prussian War meant that all French military contingents were needed at home, and France could no longer afford to leave some in Rome for the protection of the Pope. These troops were withdrawn, and Italian forces soon marched in. The Kingdom of Italy absorbed the state and city of Rome, and the temporal power of the pope, achieved by the Donation of Pepin in 756, went the way of the Holy Roman Empire. Pius refused to accept this. He demanded that the Catholic states of Europe send troops to reclaim his land, but none responded. Pius refused to negotiate the situation with the new Italian government, and he proclaimed himself the "Prisoner of the Vatican." He never left the Vatican grounds again. All later popes maintained his precedent until the issue was finally resolved in 1929.

The pontificate of Pius marked a strange transition in the papacy. He had gathered more popular acclaim than any pope in centuries, yet when he died he was more out of step with the feelings of the Catholic people in Europe than any pope had been for centuries. Pius rode the crest of ultramontanism to new heights, and he took advantage of this support to define Catholic dogma in areas that were under unresolved discussion for seventeen centuries. In spite of his refusal to aid Italian reunification, Pius remained popular. In fact he started a trend of popular adulation that all his successors have also enjoyed. For all these reasons, he is certainly a significant churchman of the nineteenth century.

The decree on papal infallibility and the resultant creation of the Old Catholic Church in Germany created a further headache for Pius and the German government. Germany still had a state church, and Catholic professors were on the faculties of major universities. The Catholic Church in Germany excommunicated and suspended from their teaching responsibilities all Catholic professors who refused the decree on papal infallibility. The German Imperial government, headed by Chancellor Bismarck (1815-1898) was concerned about these implications. Did this mean that the Catholic Church, headed by a foreign pope, could influence, even control, German education? Bismarck supported the Old Catholics in their struggle with the papacy.

In 1872 Bismarck appointed a new Minister of Education, Paul Falk (1827-1900), with instructions to defend the rights of the state against the church. Several laws passed in 1873 were known as the Falk Laws, and they had to do with regulating the education of Catholic seminarians, licensing regulations, and the appointment of pastors and bishops. Catholics were upset, but the secularists insisted it was only proper in a state-church situation. In 1878 Pius IX stated the Falk Laws were invalid. Germans saw this as a rejection of German sovereignty, and the state put further pressure on the entire Catholic Church. This struggle was known as the *Kulturkampf*, which means "struggle for civilization." Each side felt it was exactly that. Catholics saw themselves as battling for religious freedom; German politicians saw themselves as fighting for German sovereignty freed from foreign interference. Things got much worse before they got better. Most Catholic clergy refused to knuckle under to the Chancellor's demands, and by 1878 nine bishoprics were vacant, 2,000 priests had been fired, half a million Roman Catholics were without pastoral care, many schools and colleges had been suppressed, disrespect for religion had spread, and disorder was becoming a problem for the country. After the death of Pius, Bismarck was weary of the strife, and for political reasons of his own he felt it was necessary to end the struggle. Under official encouragement from both sides the explosive issues were defused, and by 1886 the Falk Laws were formally rescinded.

Historians are still arguing who won this "Battle for Civilization." The Catholics came out of the struggle with renewed strength, but Bismarck had achieved most of his goals in the short run. Bismarck had saved the newly created German Empire, and the Vatican had learned there was a limit to what it could achieve in the new secular states. In some ways it set the stage for similar problems in France.

When Louis Napoleon came to power in France in 1852 as the new Emperor, he encouraged a strong relationship with Catholicism. Religious life in the country again seemed to flourish. But the French experienced major disaster in their war with Prussia. The French armies were wiped out in a matter of weeks, and Paris had to withstand a siege through a bitter winter. The new government which followed was another republic, and a new wave of anticlericalism swept through France. Most of the intelligentsia — particularly politicians — were anticlerical. Many were from Protestant backgrounds and bitterly anti-Jesuit.

By 1879 the Republicans in France had gained clear control over all the elements of government, and they began to move along lines consistent with their anticlericalism. Jules Ferry (1832-1893) became Minister of Education, and he proposed laws to secularize all education in the country, removing unauthorized parochial schools and colleges from the educational process. Additional laws in 1883-1885 allowed Sunday work, discontinued public prayers at the opening of the parliamentary session, and restored divorce to the Civil Code.

Catholic resistance to these measures was never fully organized and supported, and what little support it had was shattered by the Dreyfus Affair. In 1894 Alfred Dreyfus, an Army captain, was accused of providing secret information to the Germans. Dreyfus was also a Jew, and his unfair trial became a platform for a great deal of antisemitism on the part of the church, enunciated by those who wished to show corruption in the state which harbored such a spy. The "Affair" dominated the political life of France for a decade, but the result showed that the Church had made a shallow attack on the state. The clergy's intransigent unwillingness to review the case objectively increased the anticlericalism of most politicians. After Dreyfus was exonerated, many drew the lesson that the Church put expediency before truth or justice.

Emile Combes (1835-1921) became premier of France in 1902 at the head of a Radical coalition supported by the anticlericals. A former seminarian and professor of theology, he had a renegade's hatred of his former alliances, and he was ruthless in enforcing anti-clerical legislation. Some 3,000 parochial local schools were closed for failing to comply with government regulations. In November of 1904 Combes introduced a bill into the Assembly which called for the full separation of Church and State in France. Although he fell from power early the next year, the bill proceeded under the new government anyway. When it came to vote in 1905, it passed 314 to 233. The law guaranteed full freedom of worship, without recognizing or subsidizing any form of worship. There was an end to the Ministry of Worship in the government.[7] The Pope condemned the new law, though this probably encouraged more Frenchmen to accept it.[8] Although in the long run this disestablishment was probably a good thing for both church and state, it represented a further development of secularization in Europe. The old props of religion in Europe were falling. The churches were entering the twentieth century with probably less civil support than at any time since the Roman persecutions.

Bibliography for Chapter Twenty-One

Altholz, Josef L. *The Churches in the Nineteenth Century.* Indianapolis: The Bobbs-Merrill Company, 1967.
   An excellent overview of the churches in this century, going from 1789 to 1914.
Bury, J.B. *History of the Papacy in the 19th Century: Liberty and Authority in the Roman Catholic Church.* Edited by R.H. Murray. New York: Schocken Books, 1964.

An excellent insight into the papal developments of the mid-nineteenth century, represented in the pontificate of Pius IX.

Church, R.W. *The Oxford Movement: Twelve Years, 1833-1845.* Edited and with an Introduction by Geoffrey Best. Chicago: University of Chicago Press, 1970.

A reprint of an 1891 work, but an excellent portrayal of the major themes and detail of the Oxford Movement.

Harnack, Adolf. *What Is Christianity?* Trans. Thomas Bailey Saunders. New York: Harper & Row, Publishers, 1957.

A useful and modern translation of Harnack's key essay.

McManners, John. *Church and State in France, 1870-1914.* New York: Harper & Row, Publishers, 1973.

A penetrating analysis of the development of disestablishment in France.

_____. *The French Revolution & the Church.* New York: Harper & Row, Publishers, 1969.

A significant appraisal and investigation of what was done by and done to the Church in France during the Revolution.

Newman, John Henry. *An Essay on the Development of Christian Doctrine.* Edited with an introduction by J.M. Cameron. Harmondsworth, England: Penguin Books, 1974.

First printed in 1845, this represents Newman's thinking which led him to Rome — the Church can change doctrine according to laws of development.

Schleiermacher, Friedrich. *On Religion: Speeches to its Cultured Despisers.* Trans. John Oman, with an introduction by Rudolf Otto. New York: Harper & Row, Publishers, 1958.

A good translation and edition of Schleiermacher's pivotal essay.

Questions and Projects for Chapter Twenty-One

1. Prepare an outline of the history of French Catholicism from 1789 to 1914. What similarities and differences exist between the Revolution and the 1905 disestablishment?
2. Which of the German theologians mentioned in this chapter had the most influence in shaping modern Christianity? Be able to defend your answer.
3. Would you have expected a monastic revival to accompany Romanticism? What do you think major medieval figures would have thought about Romanticism?
4. Compare and/or contrast the *Kulturkampf* to the Investiture Contest of the Middle Ages. How would Otto I and Henry IV have responded to Bismarck?
5. Compare and/or contrast Pius IX to some of the major medieval popes. What are the crucial cultural factors involved?
6. Assess the influence of the Papal States on the history of the popes and on Roman Catholicism since their creation by Pepin.

Notes for Chapter Twenty-one

1. The declaration of the Rights of Man is in Manschreck, II, pp. 327-329.

2. Excerpts from the Civil Constitution of the Clergy are in Manschreck, pp. 329-331, and in Barry, III, pp. 7-13.

3. The Concordat is given both in Manschreck, pp. 333-334, and in Barry, III, pp. 13-15.

4. The decree by Pius can be found in Manschreck, pp. 371-372.

5. The Syllabus of Errors is given with some deletions in Barry, III, pp. 70-74; an even shorter listing is in Manschreck, pp. 372-374.

6. The Vatican decree on papal infallibility is given in Barry, III, pp. 74-79; a shorter version is in Manschreck, pp. 374-375.

7. The law on disestablishment is in Barry, III, pp. 49-58.

8. The Pope's response is given in Manschreck, pp. 390-392.

Chapter Twenty-Two
THE EASTERN CHURCHES
SINCE THE REFORMATION

Most of us are so used to the tripartite division suggested by Will Herberg in his famous book *Protestant-Catholic-Jew*, that we tend to forget that there are other major religious options. In America we are so used to dividing Christians into Protestants and Catholics that we often have to stop and remember that the Eastern Orthodox Churches represent another major branch of Christianity. First of all, note the phrase, "Eastern Orthodox." There has been a tendency in the past to call them "Greek Orthodox" Churches. This is too limiting. There are a number of Orthodox churches, and the Greek Church is only one of them. The overall term is Orthodox Churches, or Eastern Orthodox Churches.

The phrase "Greek Orthodox Church" had some

meaning until 1453 when Constantinople finally fell to the Turks, after having fought off the Muslims for over seven hundred years. The Patriarch of Constantinople had been the head of the Orthodox Churches (unrivaled since Alexandria, Jerusalem, and Antioch had all been conquered by the Muslims in the seventh century) up to this time, but after 1453 he came under the dominance of the Turkish sultan. The Turks allowed the church structure to survive, but the hierarchy became servants of the Turkish government.

The Christians were organized as a semiautonomous community, called the Rum Millet ("the Roman nation"), and the clergy was responsible for them. This may have increased the clergy's power, but it also made them responsible for the collection of extortionate taxation and the famous Janissaries. Every four years the Muslims took the choicest of the Christian boys to be brought up in Muslim military schools. Not only did they emerge as committed Muslims, but they also formed the crack Janissary regiments, the elite of the Sultan's armed forces. They were roughly the equivalent of the Praetorian Guard in the days of the Caesars.

Under the Sultans the Christians became second class citizens. They paid higher taxes than their Muslim neighbors, wore distinctive dress, could not serve in the army, and could not marry Muslim women. The Church was not allowed to undertake missionary work, and it was a crime to convert a Muslim to Christianity. There was no militant persecution of Christians, but there was every inducement for the Christians to become Muslim. As we saw in Chapter Eight, this became the pattern from Syria to Spain. But in southeastern Europe, only the native Albanians converted to Islam in large numbers. They remain today one of only two nations in Europe that are predominantly Muslim.

Most exercises of Christian worship were threatened by the Turks. Most church buildings were converted to mosques, and no new ones could be erected. Monasteries were virtually the only effective centers of Christianity. The Greeks in Constantinople in particular became willing parasites for the Turks. Unfortunately, under these pressures and inducements, the Church's higher administration was caught up in a web of corruption and simony. It has been said that during the Turkish control of the Patriarchate, everything in the church was available for sale, including the patriarchal throne itself. Few men held that office for very long.

The continuation of the *millet*, however, insured that as long as the Christians maintained a separate existence, their Christianity took on the flavor of nationalistic fervor. Christianity and patriotism were merged, and not always to the improvement of Christianity. Even under the degrading situation of the Turkish control, Christianity survived, in some cases for more than four centuries. But the corruption of the Greek patriarchate in Constantinople created a situation that when independence for the Balkans did come in the nineteenth century, most areas not only threw off the Turkish political yoke, but they also refused Greek religious leadership. In the meantime the leadership of Orthodoxy passed into the hands of the Russians.

At about the time that Constantinople fell, the leadership of the Russians was passing from the hands of the Grand Dukes of Kiev to the princes of Moscow. Ivan IV (the Terrible, 1530-1584) established much of the power of this line, and in 1547 he appropriated the title of Tsar (a Slavic corruption of the word Caesar, as is the German word Kaiser). Even before this, however, Moscow had begun to call itself the Third Rome. With the building of Constantinople in the fourth century, that city became the eastern capital of the Empire, and by 381 it was called "New Rome." Now that Constantinople in its turn had fallen, Moscow saw itself as the heir to the leadership of the Orthodox Churches, thus "third Rome." In 1589 the Metropolitan of Moscow received the title "Patriarch of Moscow" from the Patriarch of Constantinople. Again this followed the rule of the religious status of a city following its political status. By this time the prince of Moscow had unquestioned dominance over all the Russians, and the Metropolitan's new title of Patriarch signified that he had equally unquestioned leadership over Russian Orthodoxy.

While all this was going on, however, Roman Catholic forces were also active in the east, particularly during the time of the Catholic Counter Reformation. Poland had been Orthodox under the leadership of Kiev when Jesuits arrived in 1564 and began to negotiate secretly with the Orthodox bishops. These bishops were most willing to cooperate in dealings with Rome: one must remember they were appointed by a Catholic monarch. In 1596 a council summoned for Brest-Litovsk proclaimed a union. Six out of eight Orthodox bishops supported the union, including the Metropolitan of Kiev, but two other bishops refused. They desired to remain members of the Orthodox Church. The two sides concluded by excommunicating and anathematizing each other.

Thus there came into existence in Poland a "Uniate" Church whose members were called "Catholics of the Eastern Rite." These Uniates recognized the supremacy of the pope, but they were allowed to keep their traditional practices (including a married clergy) and the worship service in their own language. In the course of time more and more Roman elements came in, but at first there was little to distinguish Uniates from Orthodox. The Polish government recognized only the majority decision at Brest-Litovsk, and in its eyes the Polish Orthodox Church no longer existed. Those who wished to remain Polish Orthodox were persecuted. Their church property was seized and given to the Uniates, sometimes rented back to them for high fees.

The story of the Uniate Church in Poland may have been a triumph for the West, but it was a tragedy for the East. They saw the Jesuits begin in deceit and conclude with violence. The repercussions of the decision of 1596 are still irritants with Eastern Orthodox down to the present. Orthodox in other lands saw what was happening in Poland and decided they would rather have Muslim rulers than Roman Catholic ones. Other Uniate churches did develop, however, particularly in the Ukraine, and even as far away as Lebanon. As far as the remainder of the Orthodox were concerned, the result was the same as with those who became Roman Catholic outright — these people were lost to Orthodox identification and strength.

Except for such developments, the story of the Orthodox Churches is pretty much the story of the Russians. In 1598 the Tsar Fedor (Theodore) died without children, plunging Russia into a period known as the "Time of Trouble." Social unrest, a disputed succession, and intervention and invasion by foreign powers all added to a period of chaos and disorder. A Polish army occupied Moscow, and the Jesuits attempted to secure the submission of the Russian Church to Rome. A Swedish army held Novgorod. But throughout this period the Church under its Patriarch Hermogen provided leadership for the Russians and acted as a rallying center against the foreign powers and the presumptuousness of Rome. Ultimately Hermogen was thrown into prison by the Poles where he died. Shortly thereafter a combination of patriotic forces retook Moscow, expelled the Poles, and called a representative assembly of the people to restore order. In 1613 they elected Michael Romanov as tsar, although he was only sixteen years old. His dynasty lasted until the 1917 revolutions. Michael's father, Philaret, had earlier been forced into a monastery for political reasons, but he was now made Patriarch of Moscow. Together this father and son team restored order in the history of the Russian Church.

The next major event in the history of the Russian Church came under Patriarch Nikon (1605-1681). Even as a lad he showed a commitment both to scholarship and asceticism, and he became a novitiate monk. Relatives convinced him to marry, however, so he did and served as a parish priest, in Moscow. But by the time he was thirty, all his children had died, he talked his wife into joining a convent, and he joined a monastery. Soon he came to the attention of the Tsar, became Metropolitan of Novgorod in 1649, and Patriarch of Moscow in 1652.

Nikon accepted the post somewhat unwillingly, but he

insisted that the tsar and the assembly were to obey him in everything. Nikon had a lofty vision of the power of the Patriarch, wishing to carry on in the tradition of Hermogen and Philaret. There was sure to be resistance, but Nikon plowed on ahead. The issue that tripped him up was a petty one, but it became symbolic. It was necessary to head up a project to modernize the translations of the service books used in worship. One item was the Epiphany rite asking for blessing "by the Holy Spirit and by fire." No proper Greek basis for this passage could be found, so Nikon made the decision to delete the "fire" part, in spite of the ancient and widely-believed concept that the Holy Spirit was composed of fire. In addition Nikon adopted the practice of using three fingers to make the sign of the cross rather than just two, in spite of the fact that a Russian Council had condemned this Greek usage in 1551. In the worship service a triple "Hallelujah" was to be used rather than just a double one, even though this was popularly regarded as a "Latin heresy." People transferring membership from Roman Catholic churches were not to be rebaptized, even though most Russians considered Catholicism so heretical that its baptism was invalid. The Tsar supported the innovations, but they generated a great deal of religious unrest throughout Russia.

The Tsar also became tired of the way in which the Patriarch was dominating him, so in 1658 he quit going to services where Nikon was officiating. In protest Nikon withdrew from Moscow, retreating to various monasteries in the countryside. He still regarded himself as the Patriarch, but he was deposed by a council in Moscow in 1666 and exiled. The unfortunate result of all this was to create a schism that ran deep through the Russian Church. Many of the people — particularly the lower peasants — refused to accept the new changes Nikon had fashioned. They split off and were called the Old Believers. They believed that Rome was apostate. Constantinople had been punished for its apostasy, and now even Moscow was losing the faith. The Old Believers numbered about one-sixth of the entire population, even though they soon split up into two camps. One group was the *Popovsty* (the priests), and the other was the *Bespopovsty* (without priests). The *Popovsty* at first used the clergy that seceded with them; later they used state clergy who sided with them for various reasons, Uniate clergy, and in the nineteenth century some Greek Orthodox clergy. But they always insisted on using the prayer book as it existed before Nikon's reforms. The *Bespopovsty* soon divided into various groups, as might be guessed from the fact that they had no learned clergy to guide them. Most of the Old Believers were peasants. This was probably the most significant schism the Russian Orthodox Church ever suffered.

Peter the Great (1682-1725) came to the Russian throne at the age of ten, but when he reached the age of majority in 1689 he dismissed his sister who had acted as Regent, and he took charge himself. He had journeyed in western Europe, saw the advantages of developed civilization, and incorporated many of its tendencies in his rule, including building a new capital at St. Petersburg on the Baltic. Peter also insisted on the subjection of the Patriarch to the Tsar, and when the Patriarch died in 1700, no one was appointed to succeed him. Instead, in 1721 a substitute was developed: a spiritual college, later called the Holy Synod, was put in charge of the church. Peter was inclined to be lenient to the Old Believers, but they saw his westernizing trends as further indication of the apostasy of the Russian Church. Because of their continued resistance, he finally resorted to forceful methods and fulfilled their picture of him as the Antichrist. Thousands of the Old Believers were executed, and thousands of others committed suicide in various ways, including burning themselves to death. In spite of official attempts, the Old Believers could not be eliminated.

On the fringe of the Old Believers, but akin to them in various ways, were other sect types. In the 1690's there emerged the *Khlysty*, a spiritualist, ecstatic group founded by a peasant, Daniel Filippov. Their tradition had it that the Spirit of God came down and inhabited Daniel who thus became the living God. They were total abstainers from liquor, sex, stealing, and profanity. They spoke in tongues and often flagellated themselves. The *Skroptsy* ("castrated") were a spinoff from them. Andrei Ivanov discovered that some of the Khlysty were unable to maintain sexual abstinence, so he castrated himself, induced others to do likewise, and attracted a wide following. The *Dukhobors* ("Wrestlers by the Spirit") were somewhat Gnostic in their views of the flesh, though they practiced communism and engaged in free love and nudity, even after many of them migrated to Canada in the late nineteenth century. The *Molokans* reacted to the nebulous biblical basis of the *Dukhobors*, taking the Bible much more seriously, though they did not accept the historical sacraments. They were pacifists and nonviolent, and their worship services consisted of

Scriptural readings and prayers. Eventually both the *Dukhobors* and *Molokans* split into smaller sects. In the nineteenth century, several developments occurred which affected the Orthodox churches. A series of successful nationalistic revolts took considerable territory out of Ottoman control. For some time the Ottoman Empire had been known as the "sick man of Europe." Revolt broke out among the Serbs in 1804, resulting in virtual political autonomy in 1817, although they remained under the nominal sovereignty of the Sultan. A Russian invasion in 1828-1829 resulted in the recognition of Serbian independence, and in 1879 the Serbian Orthodox Church became completely free from the Ecumenical Patriarch of Constantinople.

In 1821 a Greek uprising in the Peloponnesus started their war of independence. The local Muslim population of ten to fifteen thousand was massacred, and the Sultan retaliated by taking the Patriarch in his vestments and hanging him outside the door of the patriarchal church. Three days later the body was turned over to the mob who dragged it through the streets before throwing it into the sea. The Greeks finally secured their freedom in the naval Battle of Navarino in 1827 when an allied fleet of British, French, and Russians defeated a fleet of Turkish and Egyptian ships. In 1833 the Greek parliament set up the Greek Church as autocephalous (self-governing) under no head but Christ, but they established a Holy Synod to govern the church. The Patriarch of Constantinople did not accept this situation until 1850.

Rumania achieved statehood in 1862 with an autocephalous church, although the Patriarch did not recognize this until 1885. Bulgaria received autonomy for its

Church in 1870 from the Sultan, although the Patriarch of Constantinople did not finally accept that situation until 1945. All these autonomous Orthodox Churches accept the nominal leadership of the Patriarch, although he has direct control only over four metropolitans in Turkey, and the Orthodox of the dispersion, particularly in America, where half his strength lies. He is accorded primacy of honor by the other Orthodox Churches, although they are not directly under his jurisdiction.

Another influential development, particularly in Russian Orthodoxy, was the rise of the *startzi* (elders). The *staretz* did not necessarily hold an ecclesiastical office, but he was usually a monk. He achieved a reputation as a holy man, and people from all over came to him to confess sins and crimes, to be healed of diseases, and to ask advice on practical decisions. Some of the more famous ones consulted with thousands in a single day. Probably the most well-known image is that of Father Zossima in Dostoyevsky's *Brothers Karamazov*. Such men produced a revival of the spirit, but much more quietist than activist. Many of the *startzi* also were deeply steeped in the study of the early fathers, and they collected their writings on the life of the Spirit in the *Philokalia*, which won great popularity.

Another element which had great significance was the ongoing struggle in the Russian Church between the "Westernizers" and the "Slavophiles." On the one hand were those influenced by the social developments and democracy of Protestant Europe. On the other hand were those committed to retaining their own inner resources in Orthodoxy, particularly within the history and development of Slavic Orthodoxy. This struggle had more than simply religious connotations, for much of the Russian leadership felt the same pull. Basically, the Slavophiles were the more dominant party. This is why in the nineteenth century Russia became much more involved in the emerging countries of eastern Europe. Russia took up the burden in several of the fights for independence experienced by her Balkan neighbors, particularly those of Slavic background. This was to be a factor in the coming of World War I: Russia supported Serbia against the demands of Austria.

There has always been a deep religious reservoir among the Russian people. Most of the peasants may have been illiterate, but they firmly believed in the doctrines of Orthodoxy. Throughout the nineteenth century there was a combination of both political and religious conservatism in Russia. Tsar Alexander I (1801-1825) proposed the Holy Alliance in the conclusion of the Napoleonic Wars, and he intended that the adjective be meaningful. The Russian rulers maintained the place of the church, and they were almost venerated by the people themselves. Even in World War I Russian troops carried icons into battle. This depth of religious feeling posed grave problems after the Bolshevik Revolution, and the implications of it remain down to the present. The elderly people of Russia still retain some of that religious commitment they knew as children.

For most of the nineteenth century, the leaders of Russian religious thought were not the clergy, but the laity. Perhaps the most notable exception were the *startzi*, but other than them, hardly any clergyman received any attention outside Russia. Those who upheld religious devotion were laymen, particularly writers. Fyodor Dos-

THE EASTERN CHURCHES SINCE THE REFORMATION

toyevsky (1821-1881) was typical of such writers, reflecting Christian virtues, struggling for answers to social problems, and reducing the problem of social improvement to the moral problems of individual regeneration. Even more significant was the life and career of Leo Tolstoy (1828-1910).

A Count in the Russian nobility, Tolstoy was a prosperous farmer and novelist as well as a playwright, but in middle life he felt religious discomfort. He tried to find happiness in science, but he could find no meaning. Then he discovered that the peasants, though their life was hard, found meaning in their religion. Dostoyevsky had gone through a similar crisis: both he and Tolstoy were brought to a new religious sensitivity through the deep faith of the Russian peasants. After studying the teachings of Christ, Tolstoy decided to be a pacifist and practice love. He felt the concept of private property was at the core of the problem of sin in the lives of men, so he sold his large estates, dividing the money between his wife and children. He lived as a vegetarian, stopped using alcohol and tobacco, and did manual work. His wife detested these changes, and he was forced to live off her charity and that of his son. Tolstoy had few followers in his own country, but he became a symbol of the quest of the Russian religious spirit. Particularly outside the country, he had a great influence. His writings achieved worldwide circulation, and he probably had more readers than any other writer had ever reached during his own lifetime.

World War I brought drastic change to the Russian Orthodox Church. A Russian revolution in 1905 brought the promise of reform, but this was slow in coming.

Involvement in the World War brought disaster to Russia's army, due to inept generalship and even worse leadership at the highest levels of the government. In February of 1917 a revolution overthrew the tsar and instituted a Provisional Government. One of its policies was to restore religious liberty, but some of the clergy, particularly the higher placed bishops and archbishops, really desired a return to the monarchy. The assembly of the Russian clergy, The Sobor, was debating the proposal to restore the patriarchate of Moscow (vacant since Peter the Great) when the Bolshevik Revolution of November occurred. The Sobor elected Tikhon (1865-1925), Metropolitan of Moscow, to be the new Patriarch, but political power in Russia had now fallen into the hands of the Bolsheviks.

At first they had no definite antireligious policy, but over the first few months it became obvious that they intended to eliminate Russian Christianity completely. The Bolsheviks confiscated church lands and buildings without compensation to the Church, enforced civil marriage and birth registration, and forbade religious instruction in both private and public schools. Patriarch Tikhon fought these developments, but there was little he could accomplish. The Russian civil war of 1918-1920 only hardened the Bolsheviks as they saw foreign powers intervene in Russia. When Tikhon died in 1925 the government would not permit a new election.

By 1922 the Communists organized an Atheist Publishing Company, and in 1925 a Militant Atheists' League which declared that religion was disloyal, superstitious, and exploitative. In 1922-1923 sensational trials led to the execution of twenty-eight bishops and over one thousand priests. When the government introduced the first Five-Year-Plan in 1928, one of its aims was to wipe out Christianity. Thousands of priests were exiled or executed, and one hundred fifty bishops were imprisoned. The Bolsheviks introduced a six-day week to preclude Sunday worship, and in 1929 closed over a thousand churches, often with violence. Systematic antireligious education was introduced into the school system.

As Hitler came to power in Germany, Stalin saw the need for political bridge-building, and the persecution eased. But in the great Purge which followed the fall of Trotsky in 1937 large numbers of clergy were again arrested. Ten thousand religious associations were taxed out of existence in 1937-1938 alone. Yet a census taken in 1937 showed that in a country where belief in God brought bloody oppression, approximately 45% of the population still declared themselves as believers. Because of the needs of restoring morale and preparing for war, great changes came in the advance and the process of World War II. The seven-day week was restored, chaplains were used in the army, antireligious museums were closed. A restored patriarchate in Moscow began in 1943. Yet Christians in the occupied countries of Eastern Europe were terribly persecuted when the Red armies overran their territory. And none of the concessions given to religions within the country changed the official ban on giving religious instruction to anyone under eighteen.

In the wake of World War II, the same shifting policy continued. For political reasons, sometimes concessions were granted to the Christians, but they could be removed just as easily. The years of Kruschev's government, from 1953-1964, were years of persecution for the Christians. Ten thousand churches were closed. By the late 1960's, the Communists had complete control over the Russian Orthodox Church. In 1973 its Patriarch defended Soviet society and claimed authority over expatriate groups, including the large organization of the Russian Orthodox in America.

Yet Christianity survived; and since the breakup of the Soviet Union in 1989, Christians are experiencing new opportunities for evangelism and expansion. One authority estimates that at least ten percent of the population of Russia worships weekly — a higher percentage than in western Europe.[1] Young people in large numbers were still turning to Christianity at the end of the Soviet system, since they found secular existence under the Communists rather meaningless. The Baptists grew rapidly during the period of repression in the 1920's, and today they number in the millions. Because they were not part of the Orthodox Church, they were unregistered churches, and therefore had even fewer protections than the Orthodox. Their leaders were harassed, persecuted, and jailed, but their churches survived. The church fathers of the early centuries would certainly have been able to identify with the Soviet Russian Christians.

Bibliography for Chapter Twenty-Two

Ware, Timothy. *The Orthodox Church.* Baltimore: Penguin Books, 1963.
  Referred to earlier in Chapter Eleven, Ware's work

treats both the history and the practices of orthodoxy. An excellent introduction to the topic.

Questions and Projects for Chapter Twenty-Two

1. Locate on a map the areas of the world where Eastern Orthodoxy is still a dominant form of religion. Other than immigration to North America, have Orthodox missions had any successes in the last thousand years?
2. How do the small Russian sects compare to the sectarian groups that split off from Protestantism? Are the formative factors very different?
3. How do the church-state struggles in Russia compare to the situation elsewhere in Europe? How different was the situation after the Bolshevik Revolution compared to that before the Revolution?
4. How many branches of the Orthodox Church currently exist in America? Is nationalism more of a cause for division among the Orthodox than among Protestants?
5. Why was Islam so successful in converting the native population of Albania, but nowhere else in the Balkans?
6. Analyze what religious changes have come to Eastern Europe because of the fall of the Iron Curtain and the breakup of the Soviet Union.

Notes for Chapter Twenty-Two

1. Timothy Ware, *The Orthodox Church* (Baltimore: Penguin Books, 1963), p. 170.

Chapter Twenty-Three
RELIGION IN EARLY AMERICA

Every youngster in school learns that "in fourteen
hundred and ninety-two, Columbus sailed the ocean
blue." In the next century and a half, thousands of
colonists from various countries in Europe came to the
New World. Spain reaped the largest harvest of empire,
with virtually uncontested control over Central and
South America, although Portugal received Brazil.
France, England, Sweden, and the Netherlands sent
colonists to North America, precipitating a series of battles for empire that took still another century and a half.
The founding of colonies and the fortunes of empire do
not concern us directly, except as they relate to the story
of the religious development in the new lands across the
Atlantic.

Columbus sailed under the Spanish flag, and the Spanish were the first to seize upon the possibilities for empire. On Columbus' second voyage to America, a priest accompanied the sailors and colonists, and the planting of the Spanish form of Roman Catholicism began in earnest. Because it was often very difficult to secure enough priests to work the new country, monastic establishments were usually invited to take over a large area — providing for the pastoral needs of the settlers, as well as evangelizing the native Indians. Dominicans were active in Central America, the Franciscans planted the famous twenty-one missions in California, and French Jesuits were busy in French Canada.

Roman Catholicism retained a firm hold in the areas settled by the Spanish, Portuguese, and the French. In some places Catholicism later slipped into a minority status, but that was because of massive Protestant immigration, not Catholicism's failure to plant its seeds well. In Spanish territory, there was a tight intermingling of church and state. The church profited from state protection and support and loyalty. From Mexico all the way through South America, Catholicism was virtually unchallenged and unquestioned. Some countries remain that way in the present, though Protestant missionaries have worked with some success in many of these countries for a century or more.

After some unfortunate initial attempts, real French activity in the New World can be dated from Samuel de Champlain's work in Canada beginning in 1604. The first permanent colony was established at Quebec in 1608. The Franciscan Recollets received a spiritual monopoly over the land, but they were overawed by the magnitude of the task and called in help from the Jesuits. Jesuits were never intimidated by anything, and they immediately set to work in the Canadian wilderness, particularly working as missionaries among the Indians. It was often difficult to separate the issues of religion and nationalism (Spanish Franciscans bitterly opposed French Franciscans in the lower Mississippi Valley), and often the Jesuits stirred up the evangelized natives against the Protestant English and Dutch for nationalistic reasons, under the guise of religion. In King William's War in the 1690's some Indians captured in Maine by Massachusetts troops claimed that the Jesuits had told them that Mary was a Frenchwoman, that her son Jesus was killed by an Englishman, but that he had risen to heaven; therefore all who wished to win his favor must avenge his death by killing Englishmen.[1]

The story of religious development in the early British colonies of North America is not nearly as monolithic. In some of its colonies England planted its official church, the Church of England (Anglican), but in other colonies dissenting groups planted their own churches — Congregationalists in New England, Presbyterians in New York, Quakers in Pennsylvania, even Catholics in Maryland. This variety was further diversified by earlier colonies that were taken over by the English, leaving a significant residue of Dutch Reformed in New York, and a few Swedish Lutherans in Delaware. The truth that emerges from this is that the New World is not the Old World. All the transplants soon showed the tendency to adapt to conditions of the New World, often significantly altering the details of the original transplant. This was the dominant pattern of early American religion: direct

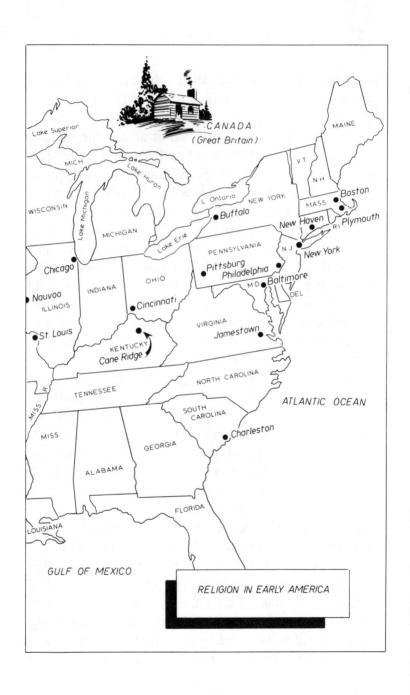

RELIGION IN EARLY AMERICA

transplants from Europe, then cultural adaptation to colonial realities.

The Anglican Church was the state church in the southern colonies of British North America: Virginia, both Carolinas, and Georgia. Anglicans were nominally under the jurisdiction of the Bishop of London, but he was three thousand miles away. As a result, two significant changes began to occur in colonial American Anglicanism, both of them heightened in Virginia, the largest Anglican concentration.

One change had to do with the vestries. The vestry is an organization of Anglican laymen given control of the church property, closely resembling a board of trustees. In the normal Anglican pattern, the vestry is concerned only with temporal affairs, but with religious authorities so far removed, the local vestries were soon on their own. They even controlled appointment of Anglican priests and their salaries. Vestrymen were elected by the church members, but they usually came from the landed gentry class — the same class that provided most representatives in the Virginia House of Burgesses. In effect, the Virginia vestries were becoming far more democratic than their counterparts elsewhere in the Church of England. It should come as no surprise that virtually all Anglican laymen in Virginia supported the patriotic cause during the American Revolution.

Another casualty of the Anglican system by mid-seventeenth century was the parish concept. The English countryside was dotted with small towns and villages, each with its church and priest. The priest of the village was responsible for the spiritual welfare of all those who resided in his area, an area never more than a few miles from the church building. But the Virginia countryside was far different from the English. Virginia had many rivers running in a generally easterly direction toward the coast; these were the major highways of the colony, and in between the rivers was dense forest. A typical Virginia parish consisted of the land on both banks of a river. Instead of being a compact square, it was a long rectangle, sometimes a hundred miles or more. Parish visitation was a major difficulty for the clergy, as was regular attendance by those who resided at the extremes of the area. All of this eroded tight ecclesiastical control which England was experiencing at the time. The result produced an American Anglican Church much more loose and democratic than its English model.

The Puritans established their colonies in New England, based on a full commitment to Calvinism. Because their churches were congregational in government they were called Congregationalists. Originally they were convinced that church membership belonged only to the regenerated, the converted. Calvinistic concepts of conversion demanded a traumatic experience to certify God's election of the saved. Sailing to the New World and creating a new life out of the New England wilderness provided most people with the experiences that could be fashioned into an acceptable certification of salvation. But within a generation or two New England became more stable and refined, and most people were no longer having such experiences.

Only those people who testified to a traumatic saving experience could hold church membership. Only those people who held church membership could have their children baptized. The decline in conversion experiences meant that fewer families could qualify to have their children baptized. This threatened serious consequences to the continuity of the New England Church. The Half Way Covenant of 1657 and 1662 allowed individuals who had been baptized as children to have *their* children baptized, whether or not conversion experiences had occurred. This was far different from the practice of the Puritan founding fathers. It created a nominal church membership, and it helped bring on the great colonial revival, the Great Awakening.

The Congregationalist Church enjoyed the recognition of being a state supported church in New England, just as the Anglicans did in the southern colonies. The Dutch Reformed started out the same way in New Netherlands, but when the English took over the colony in 1664, making it New York, the Anglicans competed for supremacy, particularly around New York City.

Maryland began as a haven for harassed English Roman Catholics, but even here there was adaptation. Begun in 1632, the colony had the services of two Jesuit priests. They were soon converting many of the nominal Protestants who had come along with the original Catholic settlers. The proprietor of the colony, Lord Baltimore, knew that in England Catholics were still feared, and he felt that if Maryland got the reputation of being an aggressive Catholic colony, the English authorities would take it over, and it would lose its purpose as a haven for English Catholics. Thus he demanded a policy of religious toleration in the colony, even to the point of restricting Jesuit activity. In 1649 Baltimore appointed a Protestant governor of the colony, William Stone (a direct ancestor of the later Restoration figure, B.W.

Stone). Under Governor Stone, Maryland passed a special Act Concerning Toleration, the first American colony to do so. When the Baltimore family converted to Anglicanism at the turn of the century, Anglicanism became the state church in Maryland.

Other colonies enjoyed religious toleration from the very beginning. Dissenters expelled from Massachusetts formed Rhode Island, and these leaders were committed to religious freedom, particularly Roger Williams. New Jersey came under dominant Quaker control in the late seventeenth century, and Quakers allowed religious freedom. Then in 1681 William Penn began his "Holy Experiment" in Pennsylvania, firmly believing that members of various Christian groups could in fact live together in peace and harmony if they were religiously free. He intended his colony to be a haven for Quakers, but when he learned that various splinter groups in Germany were experiencing significant religious persecution, he invited thousands of them to sail to Pennsylvania. They came in large numbers, becoming the basis for the later inaccurately called "Pennsylvania Dutch," who are, of course, really Germans.

The religious pattern that emerged by the early eighteenth century was significant. The established churches in the North (Congregationalists) and South (Anglicans) were forced to accommodate themselves to the new freedoms of the American situation, and the states enjoying full religious freedom in the middle colonies set the example that was later adopted nationwide. Transplanted European state churches were being transformed into American denominations.

Probably the most significant single event in the religious life of the colonial period was the Great Awakening. It started from local revivals and then later broke out into an intercolonial contagion of religious interest. Theodore J. Frelinghuysen (1691-1747) was a Dutch Reformed preacher who had been reared in Pietism in Europe. Through him, the Lutheran Muehlenberg, the Moravians, and others, Pietism played a significant role in religious development in eighteenth century America. When Frelinghuysen settled in some Dutch Reformed communities in New Jersey in 1720 he planted the seeds of revivalism that sprouted in 1726. That same year Gilbert Tennent (1703-1764), a young Presbyterian minister, moved into the same area. Influenced by Frelinghuysen, Tennent spread revivalism among the Presbyterians. Jonathan Edwards (1703-1758), a Congregationalist preacher in western Massachusetts and probably the most famous clergyman of the colonial period, witnessed a revival in his parish in 1734-1735.

All of these sparks of revival were localized, but the individual sparks were joined into a consuming flame when George Whitefield came to the colonies in 1740 on a preaching tour. Fresh from the revivalistic awakening then affecting England and the Wesleys, Whitefield was a masterful orator and a spellbinding preacher. From Georgia to New England, Whitefield left a string of converts behind him, and under local leaders revival burned brightly, particularly in New England. Thousands of people expressed conversion, churches multiplied, and religion became the dominant topic of conversation. Several denominations grew so well and needed additional clergy that they began their own colleges: the Presbyterians started Princeton in 1745, the Anglicans began Columbia in 1754, the Baptists opened Brown in 1764, and the Dutch Reformed had Rutgers in 1766.

But not all was sweetness and light as a result of the revival. Many of the revivalistic ministers were uncouth and radical, and they antagonized more than they uplifted. Many prominent church members, genuinely unmoved by the revival and suspicious of the motives of itinerant evangelists, were angered by being called "unconverted" by those same itinerants. Many of the younger revivalistic ministers violated traditional ministerial ethics and decorum, which helped put their cause in a bad light. Bitter divisions afflicted the Presbyterians, the Congregationalists, and the Dutch Reformed. Within a decade or two most of the divisions had healed, but there remained a residual suspicion of frenetic revivalism.

In the American Revolution, most churches supported the patriotic cause and the new national government. Many of the major denominations in America had been dissenters back in England and had suffered under Anglican pressures. These were guaranteed to be unanimously in favor of political freedom: the Congregationalists, the Presbyterians, and the Baptists. The Quakers were committed to pacifism, and so they were regarded as untrustworthy by both sides. The same could be said of many of the small German groups in Pennsylvania who were just as equally committed to nonviolence and the separation of church and state, which they extended to a separation of the Christian from the state. They paid their taxes and allowed the authorities to confiscate some of their property to pay the special war taxes, but they tried to remain aloof as much as they could from the issues and decisions.

As could be expected, the Anglicans came the closest to supporting the British side in the war. Virtually all the Anglican clergy sided with the home government, partially because there were very few home-grown Anglican clergy: almost all of them were from Britain. As mentioned earlier almost all of the southern laity supported the patriotic cause, although many of the northern laity were Loyalists. George Washington was typical of the former, Alexander Hamilton an exception to the latter.

One group that had almost as many difficulties as the pacifists was the Lutherans. Henry Melchior Muehlenberg (1711-1787) was the acknowledged patriarch of the Lutherans in America, but he was originally from Hanover, the principality that had supplied George I to the British crown. English kings still wore the title of Elector of Hanover, and for this double reason Muehlenberg felt it was wrong to revolt against George III (1760-1820). He said war was a sin and to praise God for a military victory in the Revolution was like doing the same after committing adultery without getting caught. In spite of his stance, four of his sons, Lutheran ministers all, identified with the Patriots. Peter joined the army, recruited soldiers from his own congregation, became a general, and served throughout the war. Frederick was a member of the Continental Congress, in 1779 and 1780, and he later became the first Speaker of the U.S. House of Representatives in 1789.

The colonies entered the war with eight colonies having a state church — five were Anglican, three were Congregationalist. This does not count New York, where Anglicanism was established in New York City and three adjacent counties. In 1776, after the Declaration of

Independence, the Continental Congress requested the various states to write new state constitutions to provide an effective legal replacement for the now outmoded colonial charters. In the process of rewriting constitutions, the question of religious establishment inevitably came up.

The southern states were the first to do away with their religious establishments. Maryland did so in 1776, as did North Carolina. Georgia did it in 1777. South Carolina's 1778 constitution created a vague Protestant establishment, but even this was removed with a new constitution in 1790. The real struggle, however, came in Virginia, where the Anglicans were the strongest, and where they were determined to hold on. Virginia wrote a new constitution in 1776, but it continued the establishment. Certain privileges were taken away piecemeal in the next few years, but the real breakthrough came in 1779 when Thomas Jefferson presented his Bill to Establish Religious Freedom. Even so, it took six years of debate to get it through the legislature, and in 1784 it was almost lost behind a compromise bill which drew the favor of both Patrick Henry and George Washington. The Deist Benjamin Franklin spoke for more than himself when he stated, "A religion that cannot support itself is not worth supporting." Jefferson's bill was finally passed late in 1785, and it provided complete religious freedom for all.

But in the north, it was a different story. Congregationalism had a much more positive image because of its ardent support of the war effort, and the new constitutions in New Hampshire, Massachusetts, and Connecticut all continued their state church. It was an additional forty years before disestablishment won in New England. New Hampshire finally voted her state church away in 1817, Connecticut in 1818, and Massachusetts in 1833.

All this was on the state level. On the national level, for a long time there was no action. The Articles of Confederation did not even mention the religion issue, although it did come up at the Constitutional Convention in 1787. It was Charles Pinckney of South Carolina who proposed that "no religious test shall ever be required as a qualification to any office or public trust under the United States," a clause which was added to Article VI of the Constitution. He also proposed that all elected officials be bound to their duties either by "oath or affirmation," a provision which enabled Quakers to participate fully in the new government. They would not take oaths, although they had no objection to giving an affirmation.

At first the convention totally ignored the possibility of a church establishment on the national level. Everyone realized that only the Congregationalists and Anglicans were in a position to argue for establishment, but obviously neither would accept the other. There thus being no contenders in the field, why should the Constitution even deal with the possibility? The only option available to the convention was to grant full religious toleration to all. Historian Philip Schaff made the observation that the government was "shut up" to this conclusion, there being no viable alternative. As a result, the religious pattern of toleration which developed in the middle colonies, neither Anglican nor Congregationalist establishment, became the national model.

Yet a number of states still clamored for a fuller statement for religious freedom. Those most in favor of civil liberties wanted a statement in the constitution that the government had no power to set up a national religion; others argued that the Constitution nowhere claimed this right; therefore a prohibition of it was unnecessary. But the former group contended that an assumed negative was not enough — something explicit was needed. One of the first duties the new U.S. Congress faced when it convened was to prepare a Bill of Rights on this and other items. They became the first ten amendments to the Constitution.

Among other things, the First Amendment states, "Congress shall make no law respecting an establishment of religion, nor prohibiting the free exercise thereof." Those few (16) words have been the subject of a tremendous amount of controversy ever since. They apply, by the way, only to the federal government: "*Congress* shall make no law...." This allowed the three New England states to keep their state churches. But those three states within a few decades gave up their state churches anyway, thus making uniform the American practice of eliminating religious establishments. In the early twentieth century a U.S. Supreme Court decision with respect to an entirely different issue said that powers denied to the federal government were also denied to the states, thus effectively preventing the later religious establishment on the state level. On the whole, Americans have been pleased and proud of this enactment, although modern secularists have tried to push the meaning of the Amendment far beyond what was first intended. Its backers in 1790 certainly had no idea of resisting military chaplains, eliminating Bible reading and prayer in public schools, or considering Muslim and Buddhist chaplains in the armed forces.

The First Amendment meant that America would continue to be a country of religious pluralism. No one religious group (other than Christian in general) would be dominant; instead there would be numerous Christian denominations vying for increased membership. At the time, there were certainly enough prospects to go around. The best estimates place church membership in the late eighteenth century at about 10% of the entire national population. Many of the other 90% were believers, or church attenders, but they were not members of any church. This pool of unchurched constituted a significant challenge to the churches as they entered the new century. The story of the next half century in American religious history was the development of various attempts to evangelize this vast pool of unchurched Americans.

Revivalism was a major tool. The Great Awakening had been extremely successful in the late colonial period, and revivalism came again to the fore just before the turn of the century. Following the turmoil of the Revolution, the situation of religion in America seemed desperate. Many churches were floundering for lack of leadership, and even in the church-sponsored colleges there were few Christians in the student body. Ministers in Connecticut formed the Missionary Society of Connecticut in 1798, and revivals began to occur within a few weeks. They soon spread throughout New England, influenced Yale and other colleges, and then went on to other areas in the East. Lyman Beecher (1775-1863) and

Nathaniel W. Taylor (1786-1858) were some of the notable leaders of this expanding revival.[2]

About the same time that revival was getting under way in the East, it was exploding in the West. There it took the form of camp meetings on the frontier. People came from miles distant, with provisions in a wagon, and camped out for several days whenever there was promise of a religious meeting. These meetings drew thousands of listeners, and the biggest was held at Cane Ridge with B.W. Stone (1772-1844) in August of 1801. Attendance was estimated at between twenty and thirty thousand, there were always half a dozen preachers going day and night, and the "religious exercises" were prevalent throughout the meeting. These exercises made people jerk, dance, run, bark, or faint. The people affected could not control their actions, and many of those who witnessed the events attributed them to the powerful working of the Holy Spirit. B.W. Stone himself saw that however the exercises might be explained, through them people were being converted by the hundreds.[3] This combination of revivalism in the East and West (although that in the East was certainly not the frenetic type in the West) is called the Second Great Awakening, sometimes the Wave of 1800. Revivalism became a lasting component of many American denominations.

With the push of population west of the Appalachian Mountains, it was soon apparent that this area held the key to the future of the country. The churches geared up to take advantage of the opportunities. The denominations that were most successful on the American frontier were the ones that attained the largest membership in the country. The leaders in this move were the Presbyterians, the Baptists, and the Methodists.

The Presbyterians were the best organized of the three, and they had a dozen churches in Kentucky by 1785. In 1801 the Presbyterians joined the Congregationalists in a Plan of Union whereby they cooperated in planting churches in the western territories. The Presbyterians were very similar in doctrine to this older church, but they were much more aggressive. They reaped the lion's share of the benefits, even converting about a thousand Congregational churches into Presbyterian ones. Presbyterians normally did not achieve any areas of absolute dominance, but they were prevalent everywhere, particularly among the better educated classes of people.

Even more successful than the Presbyterians in terms of converting people on the frontier were the Baptists. Most Baptist preachers doubled as farmers to make their living, and they could identify with the frontier people themselves. Baptists also used lay exhorters in addition to their ordained preachers. Baptists were basically congregational in government, and they could appeal to the incipient democracy of the western areas. Their emphasis on baptism by immersion as the practice of the New Testament church also appealed to the people who wanted to read the Bible for themselves and were willing to trust their own thinking.

But if the Baptists were more successful than the Presbyterians, even they were outdone by the Methodists. Methodist preaching as such did not occur in America until 1765, and the Methodists did not organize themselves until 1784. They were an episcopal group — that is, organized under a bishop — and the bishop put all Methodist preachers on a circuit of preaching points. These circuit riders were easily adapted to the needs of the western territories. Trained in the needs of local organization, these circuit riders traversed a wide territory, but they left local affairs in the hands of a lay leader to watch over the spiritual needs of the Methodist society until the preacher's return. Methodists also went the furthest in adopting the techniques of the camp meeting for their large meetings, thus appropriating the impetus this development had created. By mid-nineteenth century, the Methodists had become the largest Protestant denomination in America.

The people in frontier America were attracted to simplicity. Most of them were democrats of the Jeffersonian and Jacksonian type, wanting home rule and local control. They fervently believed in the equality of men and man's basic ability to understand his own situation and make his own decisions. They eschewed the corruptions of decadent European civilization; these yeoman farmers also despised the artificialities of life in the urban centers. They wanted to return to the primitive simplicity of former times — the Greek democratic city-states, and the Roman Republic. Western towns emblazoned such names as Rome, Corinth, Syracuse, Athens, Argos, Sparta, and Milan.

When the Restoration Movement began under B.W. Stone and the Campbells (Thomas [1763-1854] and his son Alexander [1788-1866]), their ideas found a ready field in the western culture. Stone and the Campbells wished a return to the primitive simplicity of the New Testament church, abandoning denominational distinctions and divisions and identified only as Christians. They emphasized congregational autonomy, believer's immersion, the pattern of the New Testament organization of elders and deacons, no distinction between clergy and laity, and above all the Bible as the only sourcebook of Christian belief and practice. All of these emphases coincided with the mental outlook that was predominant on the frontier, and the Restoration Movement scored impressive early gains. By the middle of the nineteenth century, the Movement had become the sixth largest religious group in the nation.

Other groups saw some of the same attraction, and pursued it in other directions. In 1827 Joseph Smith (1805-1844) in frontier New York claimed to have received directions to discover some buried golden plates which recorded the history of pre-Columbian America. Translated as the *Book of Mormon* in 1830, these documents became the foundation for the rise of a new sect that could appeal to the frontiersman's quest for simplicity and primitive sources. Quite probably Smith was aided in this venture by the defection of Sidney Rigdon, a significant leader of the Campbell movement in northeastern Ohio. Rigdon became an important leader in the early Mormons, and the many similarities between the Mormon claim and the Restoration plea can be explained by his transition from one group to the other.

In addition to such groups claiming a return to the original sources of true religion there were the Unitarians and Universalists. Although later Unitarians dispensed with the New Testament as a reliable source for religion, early Unitarians still claimed to revere it and its teachings. In fact they wanted to separate the New Testament from the creeds of the early church that were hammered out in the Christological controversies of the fourth and fifth centuries. They claimed that original Christianity was more Unitarian than Trinitarian. Their approach appealed more to intellectual rationalists along the eastern seaboard, and their center was in Boston and Harvard College. In 1825 they formed the American Unitarian Association which soon captured 75 of the 100 oldest churches in Massachusetts.

The lower class counterpart of Unitarianism was Universalism. Its strength was more in rural areas, although it was just as rationalistic. It has been said that the Unitarians believed God was too good to damn men; the Universalists believed that man was too good to be damned. They believed that ultimately all people in the universe (hence their name) would be saved — there would be no eternal Hell.

At the same time that these innovations were developing, revivalism was going through another burst of activity, not only in the activities of Lyman Beecher, first in Boston and then later in Cincinnati, but even more so in the preaching of C.G. Finney (1792-1875). Finney's style of revivalism, a softened version of the frontier emphasis, swept the eastern cities in the 1830's, and followers of his style became leaders in religious developments for decades. His emphasis on piety and reform was a major influence in the abolitionist movement; many of his disciples committed themselves to that cause.

Thus by the first third of the nineteenth century, religion in America was under a full head of steam that continued to build for the next century or more. The land practiced full religious freedom, marked by the pattern of religious pluralism. This put all the emphasis on the individual churches and their willingness to go out and compete for the souls of men. Religion in America became much more lay-oriented and activist than its European counterparts, another indication of the tremendous transitions that occurred in these transplanted denominations.

Bibliography for Chapter Twenty-Three

Ahlstrom, Sydney E. *A Religious History of the American People*. New Haven: Yale University Press, 1972.
  Winner of a National Book Award — a rare accomplishment for a textbook — this tome (1158 pages) is a comprehensive survey of American church history written by an outstanding scholar in the field.
Baldwin, Alice Mary. *The New England Clergy and The American Revolution*. Durham, North Carolina: Duke University Press, 1928.
  The classic study of the clergy and the war, focusing on the interrelationships between ideals of government and religion.
Brodie, Fawn M. *No Man Knows My History: The Life of Joseph Smith, The Mormon Prophet*. New York: Alfred A. Knopf, 1960.
  The definitive history of Smith; for this work Brodie was excommunicated from the Mormons.
Cartwright, Peter. *Autobiography of Peter Cartwright*. New York: Abingdon Press, 1956.

The classic story of a Methodist pioneer circuit rider on the frontier for fifty-six years; typifies much of frontier religion.

Gaustad, Edwin Scott. *The Great Awakening in New England.* New York: Harper & Brothers, 1957.
A stimulating and penetrating study of the great revival in the New England colonies. Essential reading for understanding this phenomenon.

Hudson, Winthrop S. *Religion in America: An Historical Account of the Development of American Religious Life.* Second Edition. New York: Charles Scribner's Sons, 1973.
An excellent textbook overview, smaller in compass than Ahlstrom's but lacks nothing in quality.

Miller, Perry. *The New England Mind:* Vol. I, *The Seventeenth Century;* Vol. II, *From Colony to Province.* Boston: Beacon Press, 1953.
All the works by Perry Miller are good for their evaluation of the New England Puritans; this set is his most comprehensive presentation of American Puritan thinking.

Noll, Mark A. *Christians in the American Revolution.* Washington, D.C.: Christian University Press, 1977.
A penetrating analysis of the types of responses Christians gave to the Revolutionary War.

Rudolph, L.C. *Francis Asbury.* Nashville: Abingdon Press, 1966.
The biography of the man who did the most to develop the Methodists in early America.

Sweet, William Warren. *Religion in Colonial America.* New York: Cooper Square Publishers, Inc., 1965.
A reprint of a 1942 publication, Sweet comprehen-

sively studies the colonial situation of religion in America.

Weisberger, Bernard A. *They Gathered at the River: The Story of the Great Revivalists and Their Impact Upon Religion in America*. Boston: Little, Brown and Company, 1958.

An analysis of American revivalism from the Second Great Awakening through Billy Sunday. Thorough and objective.

Questions and Projects for Chapter Twenty-Three

1. What effect did European empire-building have on the establishment of churches in America?
2. Prepare a map of the colonial United States, color coding denominational representation. What patterns emerge?
3. How does toleration in America compare to the situation in Europe at the same time? How much of a factor is American pluralism?
4. How do the Great Awakening and the Second Great Awakening compare to Pietism in Germany and the Evangelical Revival of the eighteenth century in England?
5. Analyze the place of revivalism on the American frontier. Why has revivalism remained such a major theme in American religious history?

Notes for Chapter Twenty-Three

1. This interesting episode is related in Howard H. Peckham, *The Colonial Wars, 1689-1762* ("The Chicago History of American Civilization,"

Chicago: The University of Chicago Press, 1964), p. 48.

2. The older view of historians was to see this revival initiating in the work of Timothy Dwight at Yale. This view has been ably challenged by Richard D. Shiels in "The Second Great Awakening in Connecticut: Critique of the Traditional Interpretation," *Church History* (December, 1980), pp. 401-415.

3. For Stone's approval of the activity, see his comments in "The Biography of Eld. Barton Warren Stone, Written by Himself," which appears in Hoke S. Dickinson (ed.), *The Cane Ridge Reader* (n.p., n.d.), p. 35.

Chapter Twenty-Four
MISSIONARY EXPANSION
IN THE MODERN WORLD

Depending upon how one defines the term, "missions" has always been the interest of the church. If by "missions" we include all kinds of evangelism and outreach, then missions has certainly been one of the major ingredients in the life of the church ever since its founding. If by "missions," however, we restrict ourselves to the concept of taking the gospel to "foreigners," then the activity becomes much more sporadic. Even so, the church has been engaged in missions of this type for most of its history. The purpose of this chapter is to point out the significant missionary activity that has occurred in the last few centuries. It might also be well for us to remind ourselves of some of the major missionary activities that occurred even in earlier periods.

At the very beginning of the book we talked about the spread of the faith in the first century so that it began to touch every corner of the Roman Empire. Many of those who transported Christianity were unknown travelers of one kind or another. These, true missionaries in any sense, provided the solid core of expansion in the first century church, the work and travels of the apostles notwithstanding.

Ulfilas was a significant missionary of the fourth century. Though it was an Arian form of Christianity which he carried to the Gothic tribes, his accomplishment must rank as one of the most significant missionary ventures in the annals of the church. Through his efforts, at first virtually singlehandedly, not only the Goths, but several other tribes as well were won to Christianity. This had negative impact also, for they then later had to be won over to Catholic Christianity.

Another event of lasting significance was Augustine and his mission to England in 597. Augustine's enterprise converted Anglo-Saxon tribes, brought back all of Britain to Roman Christianity, and sounded the death knell of Celtic Christianity. As we have mentioned previously, the success of this English mission had a direct bearing on events in the next several centuries. Not only were the British deeply devoted to Roman Christianity, but the work of Anglo-Saxon missionaries on the continent of Europe within a century carried that impact even further. Such men as Wilfred, Willibrord, and Boniface were as significant in the evangelization of the Netherlands and of Germany as Augustine himself was to Britain.

Lesser known mission ventures of the medieval

period represent just as much heroism and drama. German Christians carried their faith north into Scandinavia, and east into the Slavic countries. The Slavs in particular often bitterly resisted Christian advances, for they saw Christianity (not altogether erroneously) as the enticing trap of German imperialism. This has continued to be a crippling liability of Christian missions down into our own time. Nestorian missionaries were in India and China in the ninth centuries. In China they came close to spectacular success, but a Buddhist reaction wiped out most of the Christian gains. In all of these situations the missionaries involved showed the same depth of conviction and self-sacrifice that have typified missions personnel since Stephen first argued the claims of Christ in the synagogues of the Hellenistic Jews. Most of these ventures have not received much attention. Sometimes this has been because the English-speaking world is not in the cultural debt of Scandinavia and eastern Europe; sometimes it is because the mission ventures realized only small gains and thus are easy to overlook.

In the period of the Protestant Reformation most Europeans were so engrossed in the immediate interplay between Catholics and Protestants that they had no time or interest to consider new missionary responsibilities. Some Roman Catholic ventures, however, were significant exceptions. Much of this was tied in with the voyages of discovery and exploration, but not entirely. All Protestant missionary activity in this period was directly related to the planting of colonies, mostly in the New World of North America by the English, the Dutch, and the Swedish. These colonies initiated missions to the American Indians, but only on a limited scale. Early experiences with "hostile" Indians led the white colonists to expect little in the way of Indian conversion to Christianity. Puritan attempts in early colonial Massachusetts, and Quaker-Moravian efforts in Pennsylvania and Ohio achieved some success, but nothing lasting. Protestant missions in this period were minimal, and the success ratio was poor.

The Roman Catholics, however, were far more ambitious and successful. Well-known, of course, are the monastic missions in the New World, both by French and Spanish, which have already been mentioned. Even more promising, however, were Catholic endeavors in the Orient. Portuguese development around Goa, India very early in the sixteenth century brought them in contact with the Mar Thomas Christians, undoubtedly Nestorians who had remained in cultural and religious isolation for some centuries. The Portuguese worked with these people and brought many of them under a Roman Catholic umbrella by the end of the century.

The most significant and challenging of the ventures in this period was the Jesuit mission to the Orient. The Spaniard Francis Xavier (1506-1552) was one of the first companions of Ignatius Loyola and one of the first members of the Jesuit band. In 1542 he went to India not just as a missionary, but as the representative of the King of Portugal. He first went to Goa, then down the coast to South India where he was soon working with a caste of fishermen. Ten thousand of these people had been baptized prior to his arrival and then abandoned. Xavier worked among them for a few years, successfully organizing them into local churches.

His attention was soon called onward to Japan, where

he arrived in 1549. He stayed here twenty-seven months, leaving three bands of converts behind. Further Jesuits arrived (until 1593 the evangelization of Japan was entirely in Jesuit hands), and by 1563 various *daimyo*, local rulers, began to accept Christianity. Often the conversion of the *daimyo* led to the conversion of all his subjects. Japanese priests were ordained in 1601, but local persecution developed and by 1630 Christianity in the islands had been destroyed. Tortures and executions of both Japanese and European missionaries were mixed with numerous apostasies of native Christians. About two thousand Christians died in these troubles, and it was another two centuries before Christianity returned to Japan.

Meanwhile, Christianity came to China again through Matthew Ricci (1552-1610). Another Jesuit missionary, Ricci arrived in Goa in 1578, landed in China in 1583, and came to the capital at Peking in 1601. Success came slowly, and he created a storm of controversy by some of his methods. He reasoned that it was necessary to approach the Chinese as the heirs of a classic civilization that had to be treated with respect. Rather than insisting on using approved Latin terms for God, he used Chinese words, which brought the charge that he was misrepresenting the Gospel. Convinced that Confucianism was basically a system of family respect, he felt Chinese Christians could continue many of the Confucian rites. Later these procedures were heartily condemned in Rome, and there is no doubt that some of the bitterness was simply anti-Jesuit jealousy on the part of Dominicans and Franciscans.

In the seventeenth century, Roman Catholic missions

continued to enjoy a burst of energy and enthusiasm. These particular developments accelerated this growth: (1) Primary was the growing concern that the various monastic orders were engaging in interorder feuding that was not in the best interests of the church as a whole. The papal authorities decided that it was time to take away the independent status of the various orders in their missionary activities; the papacy itself would give central direction and authority to missions work. This was done through the agency of the Sacred Congregation for the Propagation of the Faith, usually simply known as the Propaganda, established by Pope Gregory XV (1621-1623) in 1622.

(2) A further development was the creation in Paris of the seminary called the Society of Foreign Missions in 1663. By the latter part of the seventeenth century, with the continuing decline of Spain and Portugal as world powers, France was becoming more powerful, and it emerged as the most active Roman Catholic missionary nation. France continued to dominate Catholic mission activity throughout the world through the nineteenth century.

(3) A final development that aided Catholic missions was the decision to increase the number of bishops overseas. Continuing to allow missions to be just missions was an inhibiting factor. Training the local leadership and challenging the local leaders to fill positions of responsibility and leadership created an attitude of growth and optimism. The appointment of vicars apostolic paved the way for local bishops and eased the interim in the shift between supervision by monastic missionaries and the secular clergy that was being

increasingly sent from abroad as well as developed in the new fields.

In one field after another, Catholic missions prospered. This was true in India, China, Vietnam, Canada, Latin America, and Africa. Things began to change, however, by mid-eighteenth century. Changes in the race for imperialism put France and England in the lead. Spain and Portugal fell further behind, limiting the influence of these two Catholic nations. In 1742 Benedict XIV (1740-1758) in his papal bull *Ex quo singulari* condemned the accommodations the missionaries in China had made to Confucian practices. This led to a distinct reversal in China. Jesuits had been trusted; the disapproval of their methods spurred nativist reactions against the other missionaries as they feared non-Jesuit missionaries were bent on destroying Chinese customs and cultures. Persecution followed and within the century wiped out most of Christianity in China. The dissolution of the Jesuit Order in 1773 was an additional tragic blow to Catholic missions. In spite of their intrigues in many of the European courts, the Jesuits were the mainstay of mission endeavor in a number of countries, and their dissolution meant a virtual abandonment of those fields.

By the end of the eighteenth century, Catholic missions stood in a sad state of disrepair. In many countries, persecutions had taken away the early Christian gains. In other countries there was too much reliance upon foreigners rather than developing indigenous priests. Worst of all was the tendency to insist upon the transplanting of completely Romanized Christianity — including the use of Latin in the mass as well as insistence upon a celibate clergy — in a different culture. All of these factors combined meant that at the end of two centuries of heroic labor, Catholic missions had relatively little to display. Yet all was not lost. In each of the countries affected, there remained a Christian outpost, a foundation to build upon later.

For the Protestant world in the two centuries following the Reformation, missions was a low priority. Protestants were extremely busy in setting their own houses in order. Those countries which were establishing colonies — such as England and the Netherlands in particular — were too busy meeting the economic and spiritual needs of their own vested interests to be able to assume much responsibility for the rest of the world.

But they were not missing altogether. When the King of Denmark became concerned about the spiritual climate of his little colony in southeast India, he turned to the Pietist school of Halle for help. Lutheran missionaries arrived in India in the Danish work in 1706 and began a flourishing mission that later enjoyed British support and involvement. One of the emphases of this mission was also picked up by most later Protestant missionaries: an emphasis on education so that the converts would be able to read the Word of God in their own language. Missionaries and schools have been closely intertwined in the modern period.

A second Danish mission in this period began in Greenland in 1722. This one also received outside help, in the form of Moravian missionaries who began to arrive in 1733. The only other Protestant missionary ventures were done by English colonists with the American Indians, which we have already referred to. A further source of missionary activity, though not really done by Protestants, was the expansion of the Russian Orthodox Church. This included extensions into the Volga Valley, Siberia, and even into North America. The Russians claimed Alaska, and their missions went down the coast into central California. The Russian River above San Francisco still bears witness to their presence.

In spite of all the missionary activity that we have detailed up to this point, however, it was the nineteenth century that marked the great rise of missionary interest and expansion. For some time mission historians have called this century (usually dated from 1789 to 1914) "the Great Century." It was a century of both Protestant and Roman Catholic missionary activity, although it was the Protestants who were the most active. Not only so, but it was English-speaking Protestants who carried the lion's share of the burden. In 1900 there were some 13,600 foreign missionaries in the world — 5,900 were British and 4,100 were American — about 75% of the total; of the non-Roman missionaries, fully 80% were English or American.

There were several important factors that gave aid and impetus to this great missionary expansion. (1) New developments in travel, transportation, and communication revolutionized many areas and opened them up for the first time. It is important to note that Napoleon could not travel across Europe any faster than Caesar. A fast horse in 45 BC was not different from its counterpart in 1800. It could still take six months to sail from England to India; the great cities in India were separated by more than a month's journey by land. Yet the development of steam engines and the later internal combustion engine completely revolutionized travel. Railroads and steamships drastically reduced transportation time. Communication was hastened just as much, and improved even more with the development of the telegraph and later the telephone. This created a whole new world of transportation and communication possibilities.

(2) Another factor was the significant period of peace that followed the end of the Napoleonic era. The early church was able to spread quickly and easily under the benefits of the *Pax Romana*; in the 19th century it was the same thing under the *Pax Brittanica*. Peace in Europe meant that countries were not diverted into military activity against each other except for a few short-term conflicts. They could allow their altruistic energies to be directed to the cause of foreign missions. Brittania ruled the waves, and she carried a stick big enough that the new developing areas of the world allowed foreign missionaries to enter with their message.

(3) This was also a period of colonial expansion. As the major European countries added to their colonial empires in Asia and Africa, missionaries were also drawn to these continents in greater numbers. There were both positive and negative results of this.

(4) Another aspect was the Industrial Revolution, already reflected in the advances in transportation and communication. Another factor involved was that those countries experiencing the Industrial Revolution were building up national strength and activity that needed an outlet, and this often took the form of foreign missions. By contrast, many of the Catholic countries did not get into the Industrial Revolution, and they also fell behind in missions activity. Active in earlier periods, they now declined.

There was often a combination of these latter two items. Missionaries who followed their flag could usually count on their country's protection. Countries building their imperial holdings were often countries engaged in the Industrial Revolution. They were seeking new markets for their goods, new sources of raw materials. Merchants and developers were drawn to some of their countries' new colonies. Christians at home became concerned about the religious status of the people in their new colonies, particularly when word came back of their heathenism. The missionaries came out in the wake of the flag.

Most countries not only wanted to add these regions as colonies, but they also felt some genuine concern for the humanitarian uplift of these people. They wanted to raise their civilization level, which usually meant establishing schools to raise their rate of literacy. Protestantism was considered the religion of the Book, and Protestant missionaries in particular felt that they could not be successful unless the local people were able to read the Bible in their own language. Inevitably this meant Protestant missionaries establishing schools. A great deal of missionary activity was accomplished as a partner of this new imperialism.

As suggested, however, sometimes there were also negative aspects of this confluence of interests. Some governments acted with a tinge of sinister manipulation. A classic case occurred in China in the 1890's, but it was typical of many others. The Germans wanted to carve out a sphere of economic interest in China, but they had no pretext to do so. They allowed German missionaries to go into northeastern China, an area they knew to be unstable and unsafe, but they hoped the presence of the Christian missionaries would provoke an incident which they could then use to their advantage. It did, for in 1895 two German missionaries were killed in a local reaction. The Germans claimed that the Chinese government was unable to establish law and order, and that the area needed external control and policing, so the Germans moved in and took it over. The missionaries were merely a tool (unknowingly, to be sure) of German imperialism. A number of such incidents convinced local natives that Christian missionaries were merely the vanguard of imperialistic conquest. As a natural result, they often resisted the Christian message.

The real beginning of nineteenth century missionary endeavor is usually dated from the departure of William Carey (1761-1834) for India in 1793. He was a Baptist youth who had read *The Last Voyage of Captain Cook* and became interested in missionary work. He also read Jonathan Edward's *Life and Diary of David Brainerd*, a missionary among North American Indians in the 1740's; Carey also read about John Eliot's work among the Massachusetts Indians in the seventeenth century and the Danish-Halle mission in India begun early in the eighteenth century. In 1792 he published an 87-page book entitled, *An Enquiry into the Obligations of Christians to Use Means for the Conversion of the Heathen.* This was a direct response to those who told him that if God wanted to convert the heathen, He could do it without his help. On May 30, 1792, Carey preached his famous sermon on Isaiah 54:2,3 ("enlarge thy tent, lengthen thy cords") and coined the famous slogan, "Expect great things from God; attempt great things for

God." Carey organized the Baptist Missionary Society, and four months later he sailed for India where he began a fruitful labor of forty years.

The beginning in America is usually traced to a number of students at Williams College in Williamstown, Massachusetts. Seeking shelter from a sudden summer shower one day in 1806, they dove into a haystack; while waiting for the shower to pass, they committed themselves to the cause of foreign missions. As a result of this famous "Haystack Prayer Meeting," four years later they organized the American Board of Commissioners for Foreign Missions among New England Congregationalists. Two years after that Adoniram Judson (1788-1850) went to India and Burma where he began a lifelong term of service.

The ABCFM became the vanguard of a whole series of missionary organizations among North American Protestants. Meanwhile, Carey's actions in England galvanized English support for missions and precipitated a similar sprouting of missionary organizations. The year 1795 saw the creation of the London Missionary Society, a combination of various evangelicals, but largely Congregationalists. In 1799 Anglican Evangelicals organized the Church Missionary Society and the British and Foreign Bible Society in 1804. By 1800 Scotland had both the Scottish Missionary Society and the Glasgow Missionary Society. The Netherlands Missionary Society was founded in 1797 and was almost an auxiliary of the London Missionary Society, using Dutch personnel. Evangelicals in Germany organized a training school for missionaries in Berlin in 1804, and most of the graduates went out under the LMS, the NMS, or the CMS. A similar school opened in Basle in 1815, but in the second quarter of the century a number of German societies were organized, and the trained missionaries were sent through them. France saw its Paris Bible Society in 1818, and in 1828 a Paris-based Evangelical Missionary Society. The Danish Missionary Society came in 1821, and in the 1840's and 1850's similar organizations appeared among the Lutherans of the other Scandinavian countries. Soon there were literally hundreds of societies, enlisting the aid of hundreds of thousands of laymen on both sides of the Atlantic for the missionary cause. By 1830 every major denominational group in America had at least one missionary society, and many of them had dozens scattered throughout the country. In the period after 1860 the cumulative effect of this organizing trend began to show up in the rapid increase in evangelization in India, China, and Africa.

The Roman Catholics were also increasingly active in the cause of missions, though, as mentioned, there was a slowing on the part of the Spanish and Portuese. The French soon shot into the lead. In the century prior to World War I, France alone accounted for over half of the total missionary outreach of Roman Catholicism. Somewhere between two-thirds and three-fourths of all Catholic missionary priests were French, and 80% of the nuns and teaching brothers were also. Of 119 priests killed in the nineteenth century on the mission field, 95 were French. One of the remarkable parts of this development was the increasing use of women. Scores of different monastic orders were involved. In the late 1870s missionary women made up about 35,000 of the 60,000 Catholic missionaries, and by 1900 this had become

53,000 out of the total of 70,000.

Other elements helped to account for this great upsurge in Catholic missions. (1) There was a popular interest that had never been there before. The Society for the Propagation of the Faith, founded in Lyons in 1822, was one of the first of such lay societies among Catholics to sponsor missions. This particular society was of immense benefit to American Catholicism for the next century and more. Other associations came in France, Germany and elsewhere. By 1914 nearly two hundred such organizations had been founded; over half of the monies subscribed through them came from France.

(2) Another helpful element was that most of the Catholic countries, with governments that had declared themselves neutral in the ecclesiastical realm, were unable to use missions as instruments of policy as had been the case in earlier periods. In the Counter Reformation the Spanish, Portuguese, and French had all subsidized and controlled their missions. That was no longer possible, and the elimination of governmental interference probably encouraged more lay involvement and activity.

(3) Missions followed much of the rest of Catholic thought as it became Ultramontane. Earlier, Catholic missionary activity had been the expression of a particular country and loyalty to its king, but ultramontanism centered more loyalty and authority in Rome. Missions came more firmly under papal control than had been true of the Counter Reformation. France was the last holdout here, but by the end of the century, with French disestablishment at the turn of the century, papal control over

French missions became complete. In the twentieth century the religious orders all over the world came under the centralized control of the papal court.

(4) There was also a new maturity in methods used on the mission field. There were none of the mass conversions at the point of the sword that had taken place in earlier generations. Converts were brought in individually or in families, and they were expected to know something of the faith before undergoing baptism. The Catholic missions were not as observant of this as the Protestant missions were, but there was still a significant improvement over earlier Catholic practice.

The major fields of missionary emphasis in the 19th century were the undeveloped fields of Africa, Asia, and the islands of the South Pacific. Roman Catholicism still maintained a strong activity in Latin America, though the Catholicism of most of the population there was superficial in the extreme. There was little new activity there. India was considered an *old* field since the English and Danes had been working it for some time, and Catholics even longer, but there was renewed activity there. China opened up in the 19th century, though there were great struggles with the maintenance of Chinese identity, as was already suggested in the controversy surrounding the use of certain Chinese words for "God." Not until the Boxer Rebellion of 1899-1900 (brought on to a great extent by rejection of foreigners, including both commercial entrepreneurs and missionaries) was there general acceptance of missionary proselytizing. One of the great success stories in China was that of the China Inland Mission, established in 1865 by J. Hudson Taylor (1832-1905). For a time it was the largest mission in the world. By 1895 this single mission had 641 missionaries at work, drawn from many different countries.

Missions in the South Sea Islands had been going on ever since the great days of the whale boats and the China trade. American missionaries were active here, as well as Germans, particularly in Samoa. The work of Congregationalist missionaries in Hawaii was often heroic, though too often they tended to insist upon Yankee culture rather than relate the simple gospel to the simple Polynesian way of life.

The "disappearance" of David Livingstone (1813-1873) into Africa and his "discovery" by Henry Stanley (1841-1904) in 1871 focused attention on that continent and its possibilities as a missionary field. Increasingly in the 19th century Islam was retreating, and the Mediterranean was again becoming what it had been some 1200 years before — a Christian lake. This opened the way for colonial enterprise throughout the continent: first in North and South Africa, then along the coasts of the Atlantic and Indian Oceans, finally into the interior. In 1881 there was a wide-open grab for colonial stakes in Africa, and missionaries poured in along with troops and merchants. The French and British got the largest shares, but the Germans and Italians also got pieces, and the Portuguese held onto their toehold in Angola and Mozambique. In spite of all the problems of missionary identification with western culture — and the tendency to equate Christianity with modern plumbing, styles of dress, and democratic concepts — there were good aspects too. Protestantism as the Religion of the Book fostered literacy and schools. Many of the missionaries were genuinely sympathetic to the plight of the exploited

people and attempted to stop the worst of the depredations of colonialism and mercantile exploitation. One of
the heroic groups in Africa was the White Fathers,
founded by Archbishop Charles Lavigerie (1825-1892)
at Algiers in 1868. Beginning in Algeria and Tunisia,
they expanded into central and eastern Africa as well.
Named for their white cloak and scapular, their real
name was the Society of Missionaries of Africa. This
society, in addition to its actual missionary work, accomplished a great deal in working to abolish the African
slave trade.

The wave of missionary enthusiasm that climaxed in
the nineteenth century cannot be fully appreciated unless
one understands the wave of optimism that accompanied
it. In America there developed in 1886 the Student Volunteer Movement, originating out of a college-age conference hosted by the internationally known evangelist,
Dwight L. Moody. The SVM adopted as its motto, "The
evangelization of the world in this generation," and they
really meant it. Over five thousand missionaries were
recruited from among college students in the three
decades after its founding, leading to the apex of missionary activity in the years just prior to World War I. That
war, however, changed the entire scene, a story that must
await Chapter Twenty-Six. But there can be no arguing
with the label missions historians have adopted: the nineteenth century was indeed "the great century" of missions.

Bibliography for Chapter Twenty-Four

Latourette, Kenneth S. *A History of the Expansion of*

Christianity. 7 vols. New York: Harper & Row, Publishers, 1937-1945.

This is the major treatment of missions history in our lifetime, done by the highly respected dean of missions historians. Volumes 4, 5, and 6 deal with "The Great Century."

Neill, Stephen. *A History of Christian Missions.* "The Pelican History of the Church," Vol. VI. Baltimore: Penguin Books, 1964.

This book was already introduced in Chapter Seven. It is an excellent one-volume treatment of the topic, giving much more detail on the missions expansion covered in this chapter.

Questions and Projects for Chapter Twenty-Four

1. How much of the world was unevangelized in 1800? How much is still unevangelized?
2. Why has missionary success in the Orient been so much more difficult than in Africa? Do either of these provide any parallels to unchurched Americans?
3. Why are the more industrialized nations more active in missions? Is this a benefit or a liability?
4. What are the major differences between missions in the first eight centuries and missions in the last two centuries? Any similarities?
5. In light of the resistance of the Third World to western imperialism, what do you think is the future for missions in Africa and Asia?

Chapter Twenty-Five
RELIGION IN
MODERN AMERICA

As mentioned in Chapter Twenty-Three, religion in America during the colonial and early national period showed definite transitions from the original concepts of the first transplanted immigrants. Numerous denominations had been transplanted from Europe, and several additional American ones had developed. By the 1830's, Christianity in America had developed three basic tendencies: pluralism, voluntarism and activism. There were so many denominations in America that no single one of them was dominant, and they all had to live together — pluralism. None of them were state churches or had a monopoly on political influence, so all had to depend upon the initiative of the people to become members — voluntarism. And there was so much work

517

to be done in the churches that large numbers of lay people had to take responsibility for its accomplishment — activism. Added to this triad was a fourth characteristic, revivalism, which continues to be a major influence on religious thought and activity down to the present. One of the most significant developments which showed the combination of pluralism and activism was the Benevolent Empire. This phrase is applied to a series of agencies which Protestants developed in the first half of the nineteenth century in America. All of these agencies were geared to the common end of furthering the cause of Christian conversion and activism. Generally there were three layers of these societies: missionary, service or supply, and reform. All of them were voluntary, and most were interdenominational. Many were directed by laymen, and the whole group soon came to have an "interlocking directorate" of men who shared the work of numerous societies. These lay board members were usually wealthy merchants from the evangelical denominations, normally living in one of the urban areas of the east; New York was a common center.

Most of the denominations had developed missionary societies by the early part of the nineteenth century, and there were various important interdenominational ones as well, including the American Board of Commissioners for Foreign Missions (1810) and the American Home Missionary Society (1826). The second layer of associations, the service and support societies, supplied the needs for the missionary groups. Included here were such groups as the American Bible Society (1816), the American Tract Society (1825), and the American Sunday School Union (1824).

Evangelical activity directed itself not only to missions, but at reform causes as well; revivalistic evangelicalism showed concern not only for eternal salvation, but also for peace on earth and improvement in human welfare. Evangelicals organized the American Peace Society in 1828, but it was never a very strong movement. Evangelicals were much more consistent in their concern for temperance, organizing the American Society for the Promotion of Temperance (1826) and the United States Temperance Union (1833) which merged in 1836 to form the American Temperance Union. When the U.S. Congress passed a law in 1825 which required post offices to remain open on Sundays, concerned sabbatarians organized the General Union for Promoting the Observance of the Christian Sabbath (1828), but it had no significant success in reversing the trend toward a more relaxed sabbath observance. Other reform activities included the work of Dorothea Dix (1802-1877) in care of the insane, the labor of Horace Mann (1796-1859) in free public education, plus exertion in prison reform and women's rights. Most of this activity was either generated by or largely supported by Protestant evangelicals.

The most attention in these years was given, however, to the growing concern with slavery. Of all religious groups, the Quakers were the most sensitive to the slavery issue during the colonial period. The influential Philadelphia Yearly Meeting condemned it in 1758. Within a few years both Baptists and Presbyterians also passed regulations against the institution, although these were not applied against their own members. Antislavery agitation continued to grow slowly in the first quarter of the nineteenth century, but William Lloyd Garrison (1805-1879) gave it a big boost when he began his paper the *Liberator* in 1830. A Baptist with a strong evangelical commitment, Garrison declared war on slavery and became the catalyst for the growing abolitionist movement. Many revivalists who had been influenced by the leadership of C.G. Finney added slavery to their list of sins to be denounced.

By the 1840's abolition had become a matter of grave concern in several American denominations. In 1844 both the Methodists and Baptists divided over resolutions which had significant implications for slaveholding. Methodists demanded that a southern bishop release his slaves or resign; Baptists refused to appoint a missionary to Oklahoma Indians because he was a slaveholder. As a result, Southern Methodists and Southern Baptists organized their own denominational structures. Presbyterians also suffered schisms over the slavery issue, but their situation was more complicated because of earlier organizational tensions. For much of the pre-Civil War period the American churches struggled hard with the implications of their faith with regard to reform causes.

It was already obvious by the end of the first third of the nineteenth century that the Protestant evangelical denominations in America had arrived at an evangelical consensus which functioned as a near equivalent to a state church. This Protestant consensus, influenced both by revivalism and Pietism, set the tone for national ethics and encouraged a Protestant viewpoint in the public schools and the news media. Protestants, of course, saw no problems with this, but the arrival of large numbers of

Irish and German Catholics in the next decade or two greatly disturbed the Protestant euphoria.

Roman Catholics had been present in colonial America since the earliest beginnings, but they had been such a small portion of the colonial population that they were virtually ignored. In the first national census of 1790 Roman Catholics numbered only 25,000 out of a population of four million — less than 2/3 of 1%. By 1840 hundreds of thousands of additional Roman Catholics were arriving in America each decade, and they did not quickly blend into the national consensus.

Most of the Irish Catholics settled in the urban areas of the Atlantic seaboard where they soon took over the lower-paying jobs, creating some economic problems for "nativist" Protestants. Their clannishness seemed to be a threat to political stability, as their rising numbers prophesied a growing political power bloc. Most of all, English-speaking Protestants found it hard to forget the Catholic threats posed in 16th and 17th century England, which included papal connivance at assassination and rebellion.

These growing frictions needed only an incident to break into full fury. Lyman Beecher provided it in Boston in 1834 when he delivered a series of violent anti-Catholic speeches. The mob, sufficiently worked up, moved out and burned to the ground an Ursuline convent. No one died, but the perpetrators of the conflagration were acquitted by a partial court. The 1836 publication of *The Awful Disclosures of Maria Monk* by an alleged ex-nun was a lurid account of the bawdy tales of a convent in Montreal, filled with lusting priests, a Mother Superior who acted as a madam, and the death of nuns who refused to be complaisant partners in sexual degeneracy. This book and others of its type gave sensational ammunition to the Catholic-haters, even though the book was a fraud, ghostwritten by paranoid Protestant ministers from New York City.

Catholics were not helped when Bishop John Hughes (1797-1864) of New York in 1840 condemned the Protestant character of public schools for their use of the King James Version of the Bible; he demanded an appropriation of public funds for Catholic schools. Even worse was the action of a bitter priest in 1842 who openly burned some Protestant Bibles and tracts. Bloody riots broke out in Philadelphia in 1844, resulting in numerous deaths, two churches burned, and several blocks of Catholic neighborhoods burned out. Tension continued, with the creation of the American Republican Party in 1845 and the later American Party, the "Know-Nothings," who had phenomenal but ephemeral success in the 1854 elections. After that, tensions cooled somewhat, but they remained right under the surface, often emerging in personal encounters, though never again reaching such national proportions.

The evangelical consensus was also challenged by the erection of several deviant groups in this same period. One such development was Spiritualism, which originated in 1848 by the "rappings" of the Fox sisters in upstate New York. These two teenagers claimed to have communication with the spirits, and an entire movement resulted, complete with mediums and seances. Even when the girls later announced the whole thing had been a fraud (they had produced the rapping noises by cracking their toe joints), spiritualism lived on.

Another alternative to the Protestant consensus came from Mormonism. Joseph Smith printed the *Book of Mormon* in 1830, and he convinced hundreds of people that he was a special prophet, reestablishing the true religion of God and Christ with latter day saints. Moving out of New York, Smith and his followers were hounded out of Ohio and Missouri, settling for a while in Nauvoo, Illinois. By the early 1840's Smith had attracted well over twenty thousand followers, and he threatened to use his Mormon votes to gain concessions from Illinois politicians. When rumors of polygamy circulated around the Mormon community, it was too much, and civil disturbances resulted in Smith's assassination by an angry mob at the county jail. The Mormons relocated in Utah where they continued to grow, but in more obscurity.

Perhaps not as deviant, but certainly just as disturbing to the Protestant consensus was the chronological formulation worked out by William Miller (1782-1849). In 1818 Miller computed that the Second Coming of Christ would occur in 1843. Thousands of people were caught up in this eschatological expectation, and the Millerites, or the Adventists, received a great deal of attention until 1843 came and went with no appreciable sign that Christ had returned. Most of Miller's followers disappeared in embarrassment, although others formed themselves into new organizations, rationalized what had or had not happened in 1843-1844, and continued their existence as a new religious group in America.

Such were some of the problems that plagued the Protestant consensus in the early 19th century. Another problem was to try to meet the unique demands of religious life in urban America. Cities had never been neglected in pre-Civil War America, but the nation was predominantly a country of farms and small towns. Finney was the first major revivalist to see the importance of the cities, and thousands of farm boys saw it as soon as he did, abandoning the family farm for the glitter and novelty of the cities. Unless something could be done to evangelize the cities, these centers of influence and commercial strength would develop without proper Christian moorings and doom the remainder of the country.

As early as 1816 missionary societies for the cities were being formed in the major cities along the Atlantic coast. Rescue missions, seaman's institutes, and other slum-oriented missions continue this type of activity. Modern embodiments of this concern include the Salvation Army and its kindred Volunteers of America. A second form of Christian concern that was developed to deal with the cities was the Young Men's Christian Association. The first "Y" was formed in London in 1844 to improve the spiritual condition of young men learning the various commercial trades. The Y tried to provide a "home away from home" for these boys, most of them farm boys who had come to the city to better their position in life. The YMCA came to America in 1851 in Boston, and the idea spread rapidly through the country. The New York Y became the model, with its fourfold emphasis on developing the spiritual, social, mental, and physical capacities of its members. The young men of the Y were often evangelistic, and it was their involvement that spurred the "Businessmen's Revival" of 1857-1858.

A third form of Christian concern that directed attention primarily to the cities was the development of non-denominational professional revivalism. The greatest name here was that of Dwight L. Moody (1837-1899), and his career typified the situation of churches in mid-nineteenth century America. Born in rural Massachusetts, he went to Boston to seek his fortune, later transferring to Chicago where more money could be made. Already converted by his Sunday School teacher in Boston, Moody in Chicago threw himself into church work in his off-work hours. He took charge of an out-of-the-way mission station and developed it into a church of 1500 members. He left his business activities in 1861, worked for the YMCA, and by the early 1870's was holding revival meetings. When Moody and his singer Ira Sankey went to England in 1873 to hold a meeting, they stayed two years, winning an international reputation.

Moody's style was pure American homespun, and he appealed to the new masses in the cities, many of whom were recently transplanted villagers, just like himself. His messages were always plain and simple, portraying Bible incidents in language common to the day: the prodigal son became a farm boy coming to the city; Paul in Corinth was a traveling evangelist in a new city. Moody's message was a simple combination of American optimism and evangelical Arminianism. His theology was thoroughly orthodox, centered in God's redemptive love. For a century after Moody's initial success, mass-meeting revivals continued to be a major tool for evangelizing the cities.

As if the American Protestant consensus had not experienced enough difficulty by the arrival of Catholics and the development of home-grown alternatives, in the years after the Civil War the consensus was shattered by the theological implications of liberalism. In Chapter Twenty-One, we looked at the development of liberalism in nineteenth century Europe. These European intellectual currents did not seriously affect the American scene until the 1860's and later. But once the Civil War was over, American attention responded to influences from across the Atlantic.

The theological thrust of liberalism was often difficult to distinguish from humanism. Liberalism presented a Jesus who provided an example of selfless life, deeds of mercy, words of wisdom, and a magnetic personality. Jesus was Savior only in the sense of showing men how to apprehend the love of God and live a life of reconciliation with the Heavenly Father. Christ did not come to rescue man from hell, but to inspire him to live the abundant life in God. In their concept of man, the liberals were very optimistic. Man is potentially a Son of God; Jesus had only more fully realized the potentialities of man than any other. This combination of the place of Jesus with the precepts of liberalism was sometimes referred to as "evangelical liberalism."

The entire country did not immediately take to these new teachings, and some denominations had difficult heresy trials. David Swing (1830-1894), a Presbyterian preacher in Chicago, was brought before his presbytery in 1874 on charges of being out of harmony with the Confession of Faith. Crawford H. Toy (1836-1919) resigned from his teaching position at Southern Baptist Theological Seminary in 1879 because his views on inspiration were under attack. Probably the most famous case was that of Charles A. Briggs (1841-1913) at Union

Theological Seminary in New York in 1891. Denying verbal inspiration, he was acquitted by his presbytery, but convicted by the Presbyterian General Assembly. To escape a similar trial, A.C. McGiffert (1861-1933) of Union left the Presbyterians and became a Congregationalist. By the year 1900 liberalism dominated most of the leading seminaries in the country and gained the leadership of most major American denominations. This set the stage for further theological disturbances in the 1920's.

In the same years that American Protestantism was troubled by liberalism, American Catholicism went through a parallel series of difficulties that was called "liberal Catholicism," but it had nothing to do with the same theological problems. Catholic "liberals" and "conservatives" instead were fighting over the image Catholicism ought to be projecting in America in the attempt to make Catholicism attractive to American Protestants. The liberals were interested in evangelizing the native American Protestants, and thus they were willing to accept the rightness of certain Protestant positions, while still emphasizing that Catholicism had something definite to offer them. The conservatives felt this was undermining the solidity and integrity of the true church, and by definition Protestants were doomed to hell since they were outside its borders.

Conservative Catholics were much more interested in maintaining the Catholic identity of the newly arrived Catholic immigrants than they were in trying to reach the native Protestants. The liberals, however, felt this turned the church into an inward-looking group, rooted in European traditions. A further disagreement turned upon the place of Catholics with regard to American politics. Liberals argued that unless Catholics took up the burdens of democracy and acted like intelligent citizens, Protestants would never be impressed by their religion. Conservative Catholics were reluctant to become involved in a government that was (by their definition) non-Christian. Encouraging political participation in American democracy seemed like courting trouble. In addition there were perennial school problems. Catholics were committed to parochial education because of the Protestant consensus in the public schools, but the liberals were in favor of working with the public schools where necessary, to win the trust of American educators.

This entire question of adjusting to Protestant America climaxed when Pope Leo XIII condemned "Americanism" in a papal letter in 1899. Liberals ceased their aggressive programs, and the Catholic conservatives carefully controlled American Roman Catholicism until after World War II. As a result, all through the first half of the twentieth century, American Catholicism grew up in a "ghetto mentality," to a great extent shut off from the intellectual currents of the rest of the country, with a certain amount of an inferiority complex, isolated from their Protestant neighbors. American Protestants, reflecting the same isolation, continued to distrust the clannish Catholics. The implications of this separation continued down to the presidential election of 1960 which finally saw a Catholic win a national election.

The nineteenth century was an extremely formative period in American Protestantism. The early part of the century had seen the flourishing of a Protestant consensus. Buffeted by deviations, alternatives, and Catholic opposition, it survived in the years after the Civil War to prosper again. Challenged again by theological liberalism, it continued to hang on through the century, though it was becoming an empty shell. But in the decades after the Civil War, it looked very much alive and well. It was almost a cultural religion, a national religion, God and country welded together. American manifest destiny was religious in origin, though nationalistic and secular in execution. Additional agencies came forward to sustain the evangelical dominance: notably the Evangelical Alliance formed in 1867 and the Christian Endeavor society, formed in 1881. The American Sunday School Union adopted the Uniform Lesson Plan in 1872, whereby each denomination printed its own materials, but all studied the same texts. Thus all Protestant Sunday Schools studied the same texts on the same day, and in many cities the Sunday School teachers gathered on Saturday for an interdenominational seminar to gain material for preparing the next day's lesson.

Much of the flavor of Protestantism at the time was borrowed from American democracy and free enterprise capitalism. This was the era of the great Princes of the Protestant Pulpit — Henry Ward Beecher (1813-1887) in Brooklyn, Phillips Brooks (1835-1893) in Boston, and Russell Conwell (1843-1925) in Philadelphia. Conwell's most famous sermon was "Acres of Diamonds," which he delivered 6,000 times over a twenty-year period. In it he claimed, "Get rich, God wants you to become rich"; he insisted it was a Christian duty to become rich.

Many devout Protestants took Conwell at his word, including John D. Rockefeller (1839-1937) and the Scottish immigrant lad Andrew Carnegie (1835-1919). In

1889 Carnegie published his essay "The Gospel of Wealth," in which he said that wealth was a gift of God and ought to be treated with proper stewardship. For Carnegie this meant that the person who built up a fortune ought to give it away in his lifetime. He insisted that the man who died rich died disgraced. He himself gave away $300 million before his death in 1919.

Significantly, the churches that were accumulating all the wealth were the churches most influenced by religious liberalism. The social elite were attending elegant downtown churches, with eloquent pulpit orators getting their sermons published regularly in the newspapers. The majority of such preachers identified with the new liberalism. By contrast, the revivalists who were the most evangelical still identified with the conservative theological positions. Gradually there were significant segments of some denominations that were increasingly uncomfortable with the direction of things in their denominations. The triumphant evangelicalism was disappearing in the wake of a dissolving evangelical consensus. Prof. Ahlstrom calls this period a time of "dissent and reaction in Protestantism."[1]

Most of the denominational losses were felt by the Methodists. They were still emphasizing holiness and perfectionism but they were compromised by affluence. When the Holiness Revival hit the country around 1900, Methodists suffered the most numerical loss. The Nazarenes and other pentecostal groups arose, including the Assemblies of God. Thus theological liberalism and middle class affluence brought on another revival of the disinherited which fostered these new denominations; in another two generations they in turn became "mainline" middle class Protestant denominations.

But to say that most of the major denominations were moving into liberalism does not mean that they were inactive. Instead, their evangelical enthusiasm was being channeled into other activities, notably the Social Gospel. As we have seen, Ritschl had contributed the idea that Christianity was a message to the society at large, not just to individuals. Christianity must be corporate and thus deal with the problems of society, particularly the problems of labor-management friction, unrestricted competition, economic exploitation, and urban life. The Social Gospel was a move on the part of middle class Protestant churches to ameliorate the plight of lower-class city residents, most of whom were not attending urban Protestant churches.

The unexpected riots which followed the labor strikes of 1877, 1886, and 1892 indicated that the churches were not attuned to blue-collar needs. As a result, divinity schools began to provide courses in economics and sociology, while the Institutional Church League (1894) represented a whole alliance of churches that were trying to provide parish needs through their church facilities: a gymnasium, libraries, lecture rooms, youth centers, sewing classes, and English classes for the immigrants. By the 1890's there was emphasis on the Kingdom of God being established as a socialized Christianity. The major focus of preaching was on the social teachings of Jesus and how to apply His insights to the current economic and social problems. The Social Gospellers firmly believed in a Christian solution to the social crisis, although they often differed on the means. Such men as Washington Gladden (1836-1918) and Walter Rauschenbusch (1861-

1918) were the major theologians for the movement, a movement that had great influence on churches which stood on both sides of the theological issues. Conservative churches developed social concerns as well as liberal churches, although they combined them with a message of individual regeneration, which the liberal churches often ignored.

In addition, the turn of the century evangelical thrust included a renewed appeal for reform measures. This was the Progressive Era in national politics, and most leaders believed that the perfect society was in the last stages of genesis. The temperance movement was gaining great strength, although it was really a movement for abstinence and prohibition rather than for temperance. The Women's Christian Temperance Union (1874) was assisted by the Anti-Saloon League (1893). By 1903 24% of the country's population lived in areas made dry by local option, and by 1906 this swelled to 40%. The U.S. Congress passed the Prohibition Amendment in 1917, ratified by the necessary number of states early in 1919. It was a victory for many ardent church workers.

A similar popular crusade was for immigration restriction. Social conservatives supported it to keep out unwanted "foreigners," while social liberals supported it to limit the available pool of laborers, thus raising both industrial wages and working conditions. Through this combination of motives, immigration was greatly restricted by legislation in 1924.

Unfortunately, the theological and social tensions of the turn of the century resulted in a theological split in Protestantism. Resistance to liberalism occurred first in isolated groups, then in organized moves within some of the denominations, although these latter were uniform in their lack of success. The phenomenon known as fundamentalism grew out of disparate origins. The dispensational thinking of John Nelson Darby (1800-1882) arrived in America in the 1880's and soon merged with the Niagara Bible Conferences which emphasized biblical prophecy. At the same time conservative scholars at Princeton were emphasizing biblical inspiration and inerrancy, and these two influences teamed up to produce the classic fundamental points of Christianity listed at the 1895 Niagara Bible conference: verbal inerrancy, Christ's deity and virgin birth, substitutionary atonement, Christ's physical resurrection, and His bodily return.

Much of the fundamentalist controversy needs to be seen against the background of the famous evangelist Billy Sunday (1862-1935). Where Moody was polished and polite, Sunday was crude and rude. Sunday grew up in poverty in Iowa and became a flashy professional baseball player, but in 1886 he was converted while on a drinking spree in Chicago. He began working at the YMCA in 1891, two years later became assistant to a traveling evangelist, and in 1895 became an evangelist on his own. While Moody's preaching style was homey and sedate, Sunday's was wild, demonstrative, and often quite a performance. He did pantomimes to portray his point; he took off coat and tie when he got hot; he ran, jumped, slid, and gyrated all over the platform. He spoke in slang and called himself a "rube of the rubes." He declared war on the liquor traffic and defended America's entry into war against the Germans in 1917. He personally bought $25,000 out of the first issue of

Liberty Bonds and declared that "if Hell could be turned upside down, you would find stamped on its bottom, 'Made in Germany.' "

Sunday had big revivals in the largest cities in America, but he had never been accepted by the skeptical urban public. When World War I was over and people were disillusioned of fighting to make the world safe for democracy and all the other reform causes of the past generation, Billy Sunday became an anachronism. He was entirely out of step with the 1920s. Rural America might have still believed in the fundamentals, but Sunday was an embarrassment to suburban church people. By the 1920s fundamentalism was fighting a defensive, negative battle against secularism, hedonism, and evolution. Sophisticated America treated the 1925 Scopes Monkey Trial as a joke. Fundamentalism was identified with the attempt to freeze American culture in the comfortable mold of the late 19th century: ignore the modern issues and continue to condemn dancing, smoking, card-playing, drinking, biblical criticism, and the liberals. "Fundamentalism" came to be a synonym for anti-intellectualism and anti-progress. The evangelical consensus of the 19th century had disappeared, and fundamentalism was a crude embarrassment.

Unfortunately, however, the liberalism of the day proved to be no support for life and leadership when the frenzy of the twenties turned into the depression of the thirties. The hedonism of the Jazz Age replaced the optimism of the Progressive Era, only in turn to be replaced by the pessimism of the economic catastrophe. After 1929 the optimism and rationalism of the liberals became useless. It was then that America could listen to the new voice emanating from Europe, the appeal of Neo-Orthodoxy. Karl Barth (1886-1968), Emil Brunner (1889-1966), and others had discovered the emptiness of liberalism, and they had returned to emphasizing the cardinal doctrines of the Protestant Reformation — hence, a *neo*-orthodoxy. There was a renewed acceptance of the reality of sin (liberals had all but forgotten that word), and the majesty of God Who was still there, sovereign and transcendent. Neo-Orthodoxy had a renewed interest in Christology and biblical theology, although it did not totally abandon the conclusions reached by the recent biblical critics. Neo-Orthodoxy returned to much of the original Christian message, although it failed to accept the Scriptures as fully authoritative. Still, it was an improvement, and America went into World War II with more realism and courageous commitment than the previous generation had in entering World War I.

In the aftermath of World War Two, religion in America experienced a significant rise. The country reverted to a conservative mood, and American church membership continued to grow. Church membership rose from 15% in 1800 to 36% in 1900, 43% by 1920, 49% by 1940, 55% by 1950, 62% in 1960. Some figures show it as high as 70% in 1972 when about 40% of the American population were in church (or synagogue) on a given Sunday (Saturday). Church attendance even became popular in the intellectual communities of the universities.

A new era of revivalism also began in the post-war period, heralded by Billy Graham's Los Angeles crusade in 1949. From there, Graham (1918-   ) became an international evangelist, with crusades in most major

American cities, and countries around the world, both English speaking and non-English speaking. Throughout the 1950s there seemed to be a genuine religious revival in the country. Newspapers carried stories of Congressmen sponsoring Bible-study breakfasts, and in 1952 detective novelist Mickey Spillane converted to the Jehovah's Witnesses.

But at the same time the religious statistics went up, there was an uneasiness that religion in America was becoming more secular. Church membership had become increasingly easy to attain, and most Americans were putting religion into a private corner of their lives. A whole school of religious self-helps emerged. Norman Vincent Peale (1898-1993) and Bishop Fulton J. Sheen (1895-1979) both wrote books about "faith in faith"; peace of mind and confident living could be attained in the current age of anxiety through proper mental discipline. Dale Carnegie (1888-1955) created a successful organization in developing self-help techniques and proper mental attitudes through his seminars.

For many religion became merely a self-help tool. Peale's 1952 book, *The Power of Positive Thinking*, typified the trend. Bookstores offered such titles as *The Power of Prayer on Your Plants*, and *Pray Your Weight Away*. Juke boxes provided "He," and "Have You Talked to the Man Upstairs," both of which offended serious theologians. *Movie Screen* magazine ran a series on "How the Stars Found Faith," in which Jane Russell announced, "I love God. And when you get to know Him, you find he's a livin' doll!"

Then in 1952 Dwight David Eisenhower (1890-1969) won the campaign for the American presidency against the intellectual governor of Illinois, Adlai E. Stevenson (1900-1965). The button stated "I like Ike," and the people of the country cheered for the war hero rather than the witty, sophisticated Stevenson. Eisenhower was perhaps the last of the military heroes. The country went Republican by a wide margin — obviously voting for the man, not the candidate.

But Eisenhower's election was significant because he also represented the growth of Americanized religion. In 1948 Eisenhower, not a member of any church (though he soon joined the Presbyterians), claimed to be a religious man and insisted, "A democracy can not exist without a religious base. I believe in democracy." Shortly after his election in 1952 he stated, "Our government makes no sense unless it is founded on a deeply felt religious faith, and I do not care what it is."[2]

Eisenhower did care, of course; he was not talking about the Shintoist faith, or a Buddhist faith. He was talking about Protestantism, Catholicism, and Judaism — all of which said much the same thing from his perspective, for they upheld the moral and spiritual values of democracy. It was a classic case of "religion-in-general," but different from that of the Evangelical consensus of the 19th century. This was a Judaeo-Christian corpus devoid of any specific content.

The Eisenhower era brought in a new brand of civil religion. In 1954 Congress added the phrase "under God" to the Pledge of Allegiance. In 1956 "In God We Trust" was officially made the nation's motto. The American Legion began its Back to God movement, and Christianity-in-general became the civil religion of the country — a "quasi-establishment" of religion. Then

537

came the rude awakening in 1963 when Supreme Court justices announced that school boards did not have the constitutional authority to draft prayers for students. Although the Supreme Court did not "remove prayer from the schools," their decision came as quite a shock to many Americans who could find no distinction between Christian beliefs and American culture.

Other critics, however, noticed how it was that the God of the 1950s had become identified with middle class virtues. Consequently the turbulent 1960s saw a new generation turn their backs on the moral values of their parents, steeped in hypocrisy and shallow religious platitudes. They fought this religious establishment as well as the Great Society which decided to accelerate the war in Southeast Asia. These young people who were interested in a more meaningful, content-filled experience with the Divine turned not to the standard churches, but to underground churches, interest in the Occult, Oriental mysticism, or became the Jesus Freaks of the late 60s and early 70s.

The new generation did not necessarily come up with the right answers, but they did accurately detect the emptiness of their parents' inherited religious values: a value system that had more to do with the American Way of Life than it did with the Way of the New Testament. Some decades earlier the American theologian H. Richard Niebuhr referred to this kind of religion as "A God without wrath who brings men without sin into a kingdom without judgment through the ministrations of a Christ without a cross."

Meanwhile, of course, evangelical Christians in America have continued to live, witness, preach, and convert their neighbors to meaningful Christianity. The cutting edge of intellectual criticism often has little effect at the grass roots level. But the intellectual rationalizations both for and against Christianity in America in the last couple of decades have encapsulated the problem of modern American Christianity — the necessity to distinguish between American middle class idealism, and the reality of struggling to mature in Christian understanding and practice. Liberal churches continue to lose members, while conservative groups continue to grow because they offer a more meaningful religious option to Americans who are searching for answers in a frighteningly secular world. In a culture that is experiencing continual political, social and theological liberalism, no one can predict what the outcome will be in the next couple of generations.

Bibliography for Chapter Twenty-Five

Billington, Ray Allen. *The Protestant Crusade, 1800-1860: A Study of the Origins of American Nativism.* Chicago: Quadrangle Books, 1964.

This treatment gives excellent detail of the nativist resentment and response to the growing Catholic presence in America prior to the Civil War.

Carroll, Jackson W., Douglas W. Johnson, and Martin E. Marty. *Religion in America: 1950 to the Present.* Afterword by George Gallup, Jr.; New York: Harper & Row, Publishers, 1979.

An analysis of the strength of religion in America, broken down by denominations, with graphs, charts, and color-coded maps. An extremely useful guide.

Cauthen, Kenneth. *The Impact of American Religious Liberalism.* New York: Harper & Row, Publishers, 1962.

A good treatment of the development of liberalism, its ideas, and what it has meant to American Christianity.

Cross, Robert D. *The Emergence of Liberal Catholicism in America.* Chicago: Quadrangle Books, 1968.

A helpful insight into the struggles of Catholicism in its "liberal" period in the late nineteenth century.

Cross, Whitney R. *The Burned-Over District: The Social and Intellectual History of Enthusiastic Religion in Western New York, 1800-1850.* New York: Harper & Row, Publishers, 1965.

Cross gives an interesting insight into the development of deviant religious patterns in this period: this portion of New York gave birth to Mormonism, Adventism, and Spiritualism.

Ellis, William T. *Billy Sunday: The Man and His Message.* Chicago: The John C. Winston Company, 1936.

The "official" biography of Sunday by a staunch admirer.

May, Henry F. *Protestant Churches and Industrial America.* New York: Harper & Brothers, Publishers, 1949.

An incisive analysis of the social gospel and the churches' involvement in it.

Pollock, John. *Billy Graham: The Authorized Biography.* New York: McGraw-Hill Book Company, 1966.

The best biography of Graham, covering both his life and a major treatment of his evangelistic ministry.

Richey, Russell E. and Donald G. Jones (eds.). *American Civil Religion.* New York: Harper & Row, Publishers, 1974.

A collection of articles on the problem of civil religion — stimulating in its analysis, and disturbing in its assessment.

Tyler, Alice Felt. *Freedom's Ferment: Phases of American Social History from the Colonial Period to the Outbreak of the Civil War.* New York: Harper & Row, Publishers, 1962.

A thoughtful and classic study of American social reform, showing also the variety of reform issues the churches shared through the Benevolent Empire.

Questions and Projects for Chapter Twenty-Five

1. In light of the fact that a recent survey listed 1200 different denominations in America, is pluralism a blessing or a curse? Defend your answer in some detail.
2. Describe the history of the ups and downs of evangelical Protestantism in America since 1830. What do you think is its current status?
3. Prepare a paper giving a brief history of Catholicism in America from 1632 to the present. Describe the major transitions it has experienced.
4. Compare and/or contrast D.L. Moody, Billy Sunday, and Billy Graham. What were the strengths and weaknesses of each?
5. After doing some extra research, delineate the theological distinctions between fundamentalism, evangelicalism, neo-orthodoxy, and liberalism. How has each

influenced the modern religious situation in America?
6. How serious a threat is "civil religion" to modern
American Christianity? What can be done about it?

Notes for Chapter Twenty-Five

1. Chapter title in Sydney E. Ahlstrom, *A Religious History of the American People* (New Haven: Yale University Press, 1972), p. 805.

2. *The New York Times*, December 23, 1952, as quoted by Will Herberg in *Protestant-Catholic-Jew: An Essay in American Religious Sociology* (New York: Doubleday & Company, Inc., 1955), p. 84. See further comment on p. 258.

Chapter Twenty-Six
THE AGE OF ECUMENICITY

Christianity in twentieth century Europe has been marked by two factors that have also colored religious life in recent America: ecumenicity and secularity. The nineteenth century saw the great struggles between rising national powers and conservative Catholicism which led to clashes in Italy, *Kulturkampf* in Germany, and disestablishment in France. Protestantism, meanwhile, was being realigned by the theological reorientation of liberalism and the continuing critical studies of the Bible which tended to erode the traditional understandings of the Christian Scriptures. In this context, many religious leaders found themselves somewhat "at sea," looking for direction in a new world where the old concepts did not seem to apply any more.

It was at this point that the Ecumenical Movement was born. The word "ecumenical" comes from the Greek *oikoumene*, which means "the whole inhabited world." In its modern application, "ecumenical" refers to efforts at cooperation and unity among Christians throughout the world. Ecumenical concerns and ecumenical organizations are not necessarily the same thing, although there is a definite overlapping. Many Christians share an ecumenical concern — a concern for unity in the name of Christ — who cannot share in the activities of the World Council of Churches. In this chapter we shall look at the organizations, as well as the concerns that originated them.

The origins of ecumenical concern go back some centuries, but the traditional birth date for the movement is the World Missionary Conference held in Edinburgh in 1910. The nineteenth century was the great century of world missions, and under its influence many missionary agencies worked together to accomplish their goal on the field. Missionary societies on the home front pooled their resources, while at the same time missionary agencies on the fields themselves were also merging their efforts. Out of this continuing development came the concern for world organization with respect to missions.

English-language missionaries met in London in 1878 and 1888, and a more successful meeting occurred in New York in 1900. In addition, the Student Volunteer Movement under the chairmanship of John R. Mott (1865-1955) also shared in unity concerns. Mott was involved in YMCA work, and in 1891 he gathered delegates together to discuss an international student Christian fellowship, organized in 1895 as the World Student

Christian Federation. An English counterpart to some of these groups was the Student Christian Movement. All of these were preliminary to Edinburgh.

The World Missionary Conference was a delegated body, so it was able to act with authority on behalf of the various missionary societies represented. The conference was a deliberative body, formulating policy for the years ahead. Although it had no authority to legislate, its policy suggestions carried great weight. The Conference enjoyed wide representation and involvement, from Anglicans and Continental Protestants as well as Anglo-American Evangelicals. A Continuation Committee chaired by John R. Mott followed up many of the policy suggestions, and they also inaugurated a comprehensive scholarly journal, the *International Review of Missions*, to facilitate scholarly discussion of issues and implications. Over 1,200 delegates from 160 missionary boards or societies participated in the Edinburgh Conference.

The Continuation Committee formed an International Missionary Council in 1921 to promote missionary investigation, help coordinate missionary activity, promote unified action, publish the *Review*, and call additional world missionary conferences as desired. Under the leadership of the Council several missionary fields saw a unification of missions: China in 1922, India and Japan in 1923, the Congo in 1924, and a Near East Council in 1929. Mott was again chairman of the Council, and it met several times over the next several decades.

In between the Edinburgh Conference and the formation of the Council in 1921 occurred what its survivors called "The Great War." The impact of World War I must not be minimized. Seeing the nations of Christian Europe engaged in such a vicious, four-year war, the nations of the Third World developed serious reservations as to the validity of the Christian gospel. The period of great missionary expansion was over, for the nations of Europe no longer had the stamina, commitment, or enthusiasm to carry on missionary outreach.

In addition, the theological climate changed abruptly because of the realization that the heady liberalism of the pre-War years provided no answers for the moral and spiritual bankruptcy indicated by the war itself. Liberalism was discredited as Barth and Brunner introduced Neo-Orthodoxy among the shattered remains of a war-devastated Europe. Neo-Orthodoxy represented a return to a more traditional theological base, but it failed to capture the spirits and morals of the people of Europe. Instead, the 1920's and 30's saw a renewal of militarism in Europe as the Fascists in Italy, the Nazis in Germany and the Communists in Russia seemed to threaten European stability.

The Bolshevik victory in Russia was a signal for socialists in other countries to strive for victory, with the result that the 1920's was a decade of constant political agitation. In most countries of Europe the moderate classes in the middle turned away from the left toward the right, sensing the need for some bulwark against communism. In Italy Benito Mussolini (1883-1945) and his fascist Blackshirts took advantage of this very condition, and in 1922 they legally formed a new government with Mussolini as premier. The new Pope Pius XI (1922-1939) had just returned from Poland where he had seen the Red Army's depredations against the church and civil rights, so he firmly supported the new militarist government of Mussolini. A series of agreements between Mussolini and the Vatican led to the Lateran Pact of 1929 whereby the papacy came to an agreement over its lost estates, which had been absorbed into the new Italy in 1870.[1] Papal-Italian relations were not always peaceful, however. Mussolini clamped down on the activities of Catholic Action, organizations of Catholic laymen involved in church outreach. Mussolini saw Catholic Action interfering with the state's control over education and youth, and Pius' official protests against Fascist restrictions brought no relaxation on the part of the Italian government. However, Pius felt he could approve the 1935 war against Ethiopia, calling the Italian victory "a contribution to world peace," even though the League of Nations had branded it an illegal act.

Similar developments were happening in Portugal and Spain. In 1926 Portugal experienced a military coup against its republic. The Republic had disestablished the church in 1911, but the militarist government restored church property in 1940. Portugal also became the haven for the Spanish militarists planning the coup of 1936. General Francisco Franco (1892-1975), a devout Catholic, led the fight against the anticlerical Republic. In 1937 all but two Spanish bishops called the military coup a "crusade." In a famous encyclical of 1931, Pius XI stressed the evil results of free competition, and the incompatibility of socialism to Catholicism. He put such an emphasis on the "corporate state" that Fascists felt the letter supported their efforts.

Christianity under the Nazi regime in Germany did

not fare even as well as under the heavy-handed dictators of Italy, Portugal, and Spain. Hitler (1889-1945) came to power in 1933 and that same year signed a concordat with the Pope, similar to that signed with Mussolini.[2] The Catholic Center Party disbanded the same year, but by the next year the Nazis began to move against Catholic labor organizations and newspapers. In 1935 the government tried to force Nazi indoctrination into the Catholic schools. They accused the monasteries of being centers of currency smuggling and homosexuality. In 1937 in the encyclical *Mit brennender Sorge* Pius condemned the new teachings of blood and race, protested Nazi interference with Church and families, denounced Nazi breaches of the Concordat, and called Nazism fundamentally unchristian.[3] By 1939 Pius XI had become disillusioned with the political shift to the right and died a disappointed man. His successor, Pius XII (1939-1959) tried to reorient things more directly toward the liberal democracies.

Protestants in Germany were not any better off. By 1932 Hitler saw the German Protestant Churches as a threat, and he organized the counter "German Christians," who were more concerned about being loyal Nazis than Christians.[4] Taking advantage of the new Nazi force in the government, by 1934 the German Christians got their candidate appointed as head of the German Evangelical Church Federation, Ludwig Müller (1883-1946). Müller used his position to demand that all persons of Jewish ancestry and those opposed to National Socialism be barred from pastoral ranks. Phrases like "Amen," and "Hallelujah," being Jewish in origin, were to be excluded from Scripture, and the New

Testament was to be rewritten sufficiently to clarify the German ancestry of Jesus.

A resistance movement was soon under way, led by some influential city pastors, including Martin Niemöller (1892-   ) of Berlin. In 1934 these formed the "Confessing Church,"[5] and from 1937 to the end of the war Niemöller spent his time in a concentration camp. At one time 7,000 of the 15,000 pastors of Germany identified with the Confessing Church, including Karl Barth and Dietrich Bonhoeffer (1906-1945). Once the war was under way, restrictions became even heavier. It is estimated that 85% of the Confessing Church pastors were drafted into the army.

The general pattern that emerged from 1918 to 1945 was that originally the Catholic Church supported the fascist regimes because of their appeal to law and order against the communist world. Most Protestants supported the same regimes for the same reason. But in the pressures of the 1930's, Catholics changed their mind, and certainly by the time the war was over there was a radical shift of opinion. Generally Christians emerged from the war with a renewed commitment, although their forces had been pared down during the time of testing. Because the churches seemed to have so little to say during the times of crisis, and seemed to be in favor of the regimes in the beginning, many people lost confidence in them, and thus throughout Europe the process of secularity received another boost.

Meanwhile the ecumenical concerns had remained active. Nathan Soderblom (1866-1931), primate of Sweden as Archbishop of Upsala, was concerned with stimulating thought and action on the application of Christian faith and principles to social and international problems, so he organized a meeting on this topic, held in Stockholm in 1925. To see to it that there would be some continuity on this concern, the conference organized the Universal Christian Council for Life and Work. A second large meeting convened at Oxford in 1937.

Parallel to this development was another significant agency. An Episcopalian bishop, Charles Henry Brent (1862-1929) was convinced that the decision to avoid doctrine and polity at Edinburgh was an unrealistic and unfortunate choice. He felt church unity was a real possibility, but this meant that doctrinal discussions had to be conducted. He led in the planning for a World Conference on Faith and Order which assembled in Lausanne in 1927. Its second meeting was also at Oxford in 1937.

In 1938 these two bodies — Faith and Order and Life and Work — got together in Utrecht to draft a constitution for a World Council of Churches. World War II interrupted their plans but the meeting finally convened in Amsterdam in 1948 — 351 delegates from 147 church organizations in 44 countries. Although numerous large denominations refused to attend — Southern Baptists, Missouri Synod Lutherans, Roman Catholics and the Russian Orthodox — it was the largest, best represented assembly of its kind. The constitution of the body described it as a "fellowship of churches which accept our Lord Jesus Christ as God and Saviour."[6] The new World Council absorbed the work of the Life and Work and Faith and Order agencies, and it continued to study missionary issues as well as foster the growth of ecumenical consciousness.

Additional meetings of the World Council have occurred at irregular intervals since its origin, including a 1961 meeting in New Delhi which saw the Russian Orthodox join the movement. At that same meeting the International Missionary Council joined the World Council, and official observers were present from the Roman Catholic Church.

One of the main fears directed at the World Council in the minds of many evangelicals is that it represents an attempt to create a world church that will control all subsidiary bodies. Apparently a few people in the organization desire this, but they are decidedly in the minority. When the World Council was created, it was emphatically a "fellowship of churches," and definitely not a "church." The goal of the World Council is to provide a forum for discussion, including theological discussion. Most members of the WCC see it as providing a framework for joint action in the world rather than as a vehicle for ecumenical mergers. Although all Christians would admit that the stated goals of the World Council are good ones, most Protestant evangelicals hold little hope for the Council. In more recent years the Council has fallen under the control of those who are agitating for radical social change, using the church federation as a tool for forcing political changes in Third World countries, and all too often condemning the Western democracies out of proportion to their silence with regard to the Communist world. This has led numerous evangelicals to conclude that the WCC itself is a communist agent to aid in the weakening of the Christian faith in the West and ultimately to aid in the international communist takeover. Although these fears are probably exaggerated, there is enough correlation between the theory and the track record of the Council to give evangelicals pause concerning the future of the World Council.

At the same time that ecumenical organizations were developing at the international level, similar organizations were originating in America. We have already mentioned several of the groups that came out of the Protestant consensus of the late nineteenth century: the American Sunday School Union, the Evangelical Alliance, The American Congress of Churches formed at New Haven, Connecticut in 1885; its purpose was "to promote Christian union and advance the Kingdom of God by the free discussion of the great religious, moral, and social questions of the time." This organization soon died out but it represented the shape of things to come. In 1895 a number of clergymen organized the Federation of Churches and Christian Workers of New York City.

This city-wide organization saw the possibility of something on a national scale. By 1902 the general secretary of the organization, Elias B. Sanford (1843-1932), called for a national federation of churches, officially endorsed by the denominations. A planning session held in 1905 led to the creation in 1908 of the Federal Council of the Churches of Christ in America. Thirty denominations were charter members, including the Disciples of Christ.

Once the Federal Council got under way, additional interdenominational agencies followed. There were agencies for foreign missions, home missions, religious education, stewardship, and women's work. This proliferation caused such a duplication of effort that in 1950 they all combined into a new National Council of

Churches. Twenty-nine denominations went into this cooperative endeavor; it became the outstanding expression of united American Protestantism in the country.

However, most of these agencies were also tainted with theological liberalism. Fundamentalist and conservative-evangelical churches resented the monopoly the Federal Council seemed to have in speaking for the American churches. When the American government suggested that the Federal Council be allowed to allocate time for all religious radio broadcasting, the conservative churches foresaw disaster. Asserting that the Federal Council did not speak for all American churches, fundamentalist churches organized under Carl McIntire (1906-   ) to form the American Council of Churches in 1941. They demanded that their members practice strict separation from the liberalism of the Federal Council and the denominations it included. Other conservatives, not willing to be so separatist, formed the National Association of Evangelicals in 1942. For some time James DeForest Murch (1893-1973) was the editor of their major paper, *United Evangelical Action*.[7] Another agency assisting the evangelical grouping was the significant magazine, *Christianity Today*, founded in 1956 by Carl F.H. Henry (1913-   ).

American conservatives continue to distrust the National Council of Churches, just as they distrust the World Council, and for similar reasons. The National Council of Churches is a member of the World Council, and it reflects the same support for liberal political, social, and economic issues. The National Council has endorsed civil rights marches, reparation payments for injustices done to Blacks, and political activism against the government. Rightly or wrongly, many evangelicals see the National Council as communist-infiltrated, a threat to the American system, and a stain upon the integrity of American Protestantism.

A further aspect of ecumenical concern in America has to do with denominational mergers. The twentieth century has been the occasion for a number of "family reunions" within American Protestantism. Lutheran bodies have gone from twenty-four separate denominations to three large ones and a few small ones. Methodists have experienced a three-way reunion. Several Presbyterian bodies have united.

A more comprehensive view of ecumenical merger surfaced with the Blake-Pike proposal in 1960. This suggested a six-way merger of Presbyterians, Methodists, Evangelical United Brethren, Episcopalians, United Church of Christ, and the Disciples of Christ. This "Council on Christian Unity" (or "Church of Christ Uniting," both of which abbreviated into COCU) came to nothing, although the EUB did merge with the Methodists, and the UCC and the Disciples have continued union discussions.

Most conservative American Protestants have been leery of such developments. Denominational mergers too often smack of political compromise and an adjustment of established theological viewpoints. National levels of cooperation have further polarized liberal-conservative tensions between the National Council on the one hand, and the ACC and NAE on the other. Ecumenicity has its price, and most conservatives have been unwilling to forfeit their commitment to biblical norms.

As we mentioned, Roman Catholic observers attended

the 1961 meeting of the World Council in New Delhi. Indeed, since World War II, Catholicism has undergone a significant transition. Pius XII began to appreciate the western democracies, although he brought few changes into the Church. His death brought John XXIII to the papal throne (1958-1963), and John ushered in numerous significant changes. He desired to modernize the Catholic Church, and within three months after his election he indicated his plans to convene a new ecumenical council. Since Vatican I's pronouncement of papal infallibility, many people felt no additional council would ever be called, and many conservative Catholic councilors in the Vatican feared the calling of a council would only raise troubles for the Pope. But John was adamant, and the Second Vatican Council dutifully got under way in the fall of 1962.

Having sent observers to New Delhi, Pope John invited Protestant observers to come to Rome. Although they had neither voice nor vote, their presence was significant. At one point in the debates, a cardinal looked up to the Protestant galleries and referred to "our separated brethren" — a far cry from the terminology used at Trent. The observers were often asked to comment frankly on some of the documents the Council was working on, particularly when the subject matter dealt with ecumenical concerns. Often changes in wording and tone in the documents reflected this non-Catholic input.

In April of 1963 John issued his encyclical *Pacem in Terris*, pleading for peace on earth and urging the right of individuals to believe according to the dictates of their conscience. In the 1964 document *De Oecumenismo* the

Council mentioned there had been rifts in Christian society, with many people now separated from the successor
of Peter, but such people were embraced by the Catholic
Church as brothers anyway, acknowledged as Christians.
They were in communion with the Catholic Church,
though that communion was still imperfect, and they
lacked the unity Christ intended for his followers — a
unity that could be achieved when they returned to full
communion with the Supreme Pontiff.[8]

When John died in 1963, many people were concerned about what implications this would have for the
Council, still in session. But the new Pope Paul VI
(1963-1978) continued the Council without any interrup-
tion whatsoever. Soon after his election someone asked
him what the thrust of his pontificate would be. Paul
walked over to a window, threw it open and said, "To let
in some fresh air." Paul continued the new direction
begun by John, with the result that Catholic ferment has
created unrest in some circles. Some Catholics feel the
modernization has undermined some of the values of the
past, including the demand for Latin-only worship services. Other Catholics have wanted modernization to
increase: to include the marriage of clergy, and the
acceptance of artificial means of birth control. On these
issues, however, the Vatican is still holding to the old
line, underlined by Paul's 1968 encyclical *Humanae
Vitae*, which linked contraception to abortion and steril-
ization and condemned all three.

Yet Catholicism has definitely changed in the last half
century. In 1964 Paul journeyed to the Holy Land, meeting twice with the Patriarch of Constantinople, the first
pope in more than 500 years to hold conversations with

an Orthodox Patriarch. In 1965 he and the Patriarch issued joint nullifications of the excommunications decreed in 1054. In 1966 Paul received the Archbishop of Canterbury — the first such occurrence since the days of Henry VIII. In 1969 he abolished the Index of Forbidden Books, a carryover from the Counter Reformation. In 1974 Paul appointed commissions for relations with Islam and Judaism. Thus Paul continued the ecumenical concern of John, and indeed he modernized the church in various ways. He even worked to open renewed diplomatic relations with the communist countries of eastern Europe. The election of John Paul II in 1978, the first non-Italian pope since 1523, may be an indication of additional changes in the future.

Unfortunately, much of the world is not interested in Christianity. Because of population growth rates, Christians are an increasingly small percentage of the population of the world. And in both Europe and America, large numbers of people are disinterested in Christianity's claims on their lives. Both continents have witnessed a growth in cults and new varieties of oriental religions. In many of the free countries of Europe church attendance is less than 10% of the population on any given Sunday.

The Church which Christ established on Pentecost continues to the present, a church with an imposing history. Yet its place in the present is disputed. Some historians and intellectuals contend that we are now living in a "post-Christian" world. Yet the faith of millions of evangelical Christians continues the historic witness of the Church. We believe that the Church planted by God will continue on the earth until Christ comes back to reclaim His own. Faithful Christians will persevere, regardless of the pressures of the modern world with its hedonism, humanism, and secularity. In the meantime, true Christians continue to spread the gospel just as did those early Christians nineteen centuries ago. We are part of that great Body of Christ, and we are confident that God will accomplish His purposes through human history. Our task is to be faithful in our service to Him, realizing the necessity of His grace to cover our failures, but determined to be proper stewards of the opportunities He has provided our generation.

Bibliography for Chapter Twenty-Six

Detzler, Wayne A. *The Changing Church in Europe.* Grand Rapids: Zondervan Publishing House, 1979.

Detzler analyzes the situation of the church in modern Europe, giving an assessment of the major denominations and countries.

Hopkins, C. Howard. *John R. Mott, 1865-1955: A Biography.* Grand Rapids: William B. Eerdmans Publishing Company, 1979.

Mott was the most outstanding participant in the ecumenical activities of the first half of the twentieth century; this comprehensive biography portrays his role well.

Rouse, Ruth, S.C. Neill, and Harold E. Fey (eds.). *A History of the Ecumenical Movement.* 2 vols. Philadelphia: Westminster Press, 1954, 1970.

This is the standard and classical treatment of ecumenical developments. Vol. I treats 1517-1948 in historical essays; Vol. II treats 1948-1968 in thematic studies of ecumenical activities.

Questions and Projects for Chapter Twenty-Six

1. Prepare a brief paper on the major developments in international ecumenical activity since 1910. What broad patterns emerge? What do you think will happen in the next half century?
2. What impact have WWI and WWII had on the churches of Europe? What do you think it will take to revitalize European Christianity? Is the ecumenical movement a cause of this spiritual malaise, or is it an opportunity for revival?
3. Prepare a brief paper on the history of Catholicism in Europe since 1900. Have its church-state agreements given it strength, or caused it to lose strength?
4. Prepare an overview of how the churches have fared under totalitarian government in Europe in the last half century or so. What patterns emerge? What lessons for the future are suggested?
5. Based on recent developments, do you think Roman Catholicism will become active in the ecumenical movement? What results will this bring?

Notes for Chapter Twenty-Six

1. The Lateran Treaty is located in Barry, III, pp. 348-354.
2. The text of the Concordat with Germany is given in Barry, III, pp. 363-370.
3. The encyclical *Mit brennender Sorge* is located in Barry, III, pp. 370-380.

4. The Platform of the German Christians is given in Manschreck, pp. 529-530.

5. The Barmen Declaration establishing the Confessing Church is given in Manschreck, pp. 530-532.

6. The Constitution of the World Council of Churches as adopted in 1948 is given in Manschreck, pp. 495-498.

7. Murch also wrote the semi-official history of the NAE in *Cooperation Without Compromise* (Grand Rapids: Wm. B. Eerdmans Publishing Co., 1956).

8. This significant document is given in Barry, III, pp. 563-575.

Appendix A

ROMAN CATHOLIC POPES

This is the traditional list, and we use it without agreeing that Peter was the first pope. The dates of the first fifteen are conjectural. Anti-popes are listed indented.

42-67	Peter	311-314	Melchiades
67-76	Linus	314-335	Sylvester I
76-88	Cletus	336	Mark
88-97	Clement	337-352	Julius I
97-105	Evaristus	352-366	Liberius
105-115	Alexander I		355-365	Felix II
115-125	Sixtus I	366-384	Damasus I
125-136	Telesphorus		366-367	Ursinus
136-140	Hyginus	384-399	Siricius
140-155	Pius I	399-401	Anastasius I
155-166	Anicetus	401-417	Innocent I
166-175	Soter	417-418	Zozimus
175-189	Eleutherius	418-422	Boniface I
189-199	Victor I		418-419	Eulalius
199-217	Zephrinus	422-432	Celestine I
217-222	Callistus I	432-440	Sixtus III
	217-235	Hippolytus	440-461	Leo I
222-230	Urban I	461-468	Hilary
230-235	Pontius	468-483	Simplicius
235-236	Anteros	483-492	Felix III
236-250	Fabian	492-496	Gelasius I
251-253	Cornelius	496-498	Anastasius II
	251	Novatian	498-514	Symmachus
253-254	Lucius I		498-505	Lawrence
254-257	Stephen I	514-523	Hormisdas
257-258	Sixtus II	523-526	John I
259-268	Dionysius	526-530	Felix IV (III)
269-274	Felix I	530-532	Boniface II
275-283	Eutychian		530	Dioscurus
283-296	Caius	533-535	John II
296-304	Marcellinus	535-536	Agapetus I
308-309	Marcellus I	536-537	Silverius
309	Eusebius	537-555	Vigilius

556-561	Pelagius I
561-574	John III
575-579	Benedict I
579-590	Pelagius I
590-604	Gregory I
604-606	Sabinian
607	Boniface III
608-615	Boniface IV
615-618	Adeodatus I
619-625	Boniface V
625-638	Honorius I
640	Severinus
640-642	John IV
642-649	Theodore I
649-655	Martin I
654-657	Eugenius I
657-672	Vitalian
672-676	Adeodatus II
676-678	Donus
678-681	Agatho
681-683	Leo II
684-685	Benedict II
685-686	John V
686-687	Conon
687	Theodore
687	Paschal
687-701	Sergius I
701-705	John VI
705-715	John VII
715-731	Gregory II
731-741	Gregory III
741-752	Zachary
752	Stephen II
752-755	Stephen III
757-767	Paul I
767-769	Constantine
768	Philip
768-772	Stephen IV
772-795	Adrian I
795-816	Leo III
816-817	Stephen V
817-824	Paschal I
824-827	Eugenius II
827	Valentine

827-844	Gregory IV
844	John
844-847	Sergius II
847-855	Leo IV
855-858	Benedict III
855	Anastasius
858-867	Nicholas I
867-872	Adrian II
872-882	John VIII
882-884	Marinus I
884-885	Adrian III
885-891	Stephen VI
891-896	Formosus
896	Boniface VI
896-897	Stephen VII
897	Romanus
897	Theodore II
898-900	John IX
900-903	Benedict IV
903	Leo V
903-904	Christopher
904-911	Sergius III
911-913	Anastasius III
913-914	Lando
914-928	John X
928	Leo VI
928-931	Stephen VIII
931-935	John XI
936-939	Leo VII
939-942	Stephen IX
942-946	Marinus II
946-955	Agapetus II
955-964	John XII
963-965	Leo VIII
964-966	Benedict V
965-972	John XIII
973-974	Benedict VI
974	Boniface VII
974-983	Benedict VII
983-984	John XIV
984-985	Boniface VII, again
985-996	John XV
996-999	Gregory V

APPENDIX A

997-998	John XVI	1159-1164	Victor IV
999-1003	Sylvester II	1164-1168	Paschall III
1003	John XVII	1168-1178	Callistus III
1004-1009	John XVIII	1179-1180	Innocent III
1009-1012	Sergius IV	1181-1185	Lucius III
1012-1024	Benedict VIII	1185-1187	Urban III
1012	Gregory	1187	Gregory VIII
1024-1032	John XIX	1187-1191	Clement III
1032-1044	Benedict IX	1191-1198	Celestine III
1045	Sylvester III	1198-1216	Innocent III
1045	Benedict IX, again	1216-1227	Honorius III
1045-1046	Gregory VI	1227-1241	Gregory IX
1046-1047	Clement II	1241	Celestine IV
1047-1048	Benedict IX, again	1243-1254	Innocent IV
1048	Damasus II	1254-1261	Alexander IV
1049-1054	Leo IX	1261-1264	Urban IV
1055-1057	Victor II	1265-1268	Clement IV
1057-1058	Stephen X	1271-1276	Gregory X
1058-1059	Benedict X	1276	Innocent V
1059-1061	Nicholas II	1276	Adrian V
1061-1073	Alexander II	1276-1277	John XXI
1061-1072	Honorius II	1277-1280	Nicholas III
1073-1085	Gregory VII	1281-1285	Martin IV
1080-1100	Clement III	1285-1287	Honorius IV
1086-1087	Victor III	1288-1292	Nicholas IV
1088-1099	Urban II	1294	Celestine V
1099-1118	Paschal II	1294-1303	Boniface VIII
1100	Theodoric	1303-1304	Benedict XI
1102	Albert	1305-1314	Clement V
1105-1111	Sylvester IV	1316-1334	John XXII
1118-1119	Gelasius II	1328-1330	Nicholas V
1118-1121	Gregory VIII	1334-1342	Benedict XII
1119-1124	Callistus II	1342-1352	Clement VI
1124-1130	Honorius II	1352-1362	Innocent VI
1124	Celestine II	1362-1370	Urban V
1130-1143	Innocent II	1370-1378	Gregory XI
1130-1138	Anacletus II	1378-1394	Clement VII
1138	Victor IV	1378-1389	Urban VI
1143-1144	Celestine II	1389-1404	Boniface IX
1144-1145	Lucius II	1404-1406	Innocent VII
1145-1153	Eugenius II	1406-1415	Gregory XII
1153-1154	Anastasius IV	1394-1423	Benedict XIII
1154-1159	Adrian IV	1409-1410	Alexander V
1159-1181	Alexander III	1410-1415	John XXIII

1417-1431	Martin V		1769-1774	Clement XIV
1431-1447	Eugenius IV		1775-1799	Pius VI
1440-1449	Felix V		1800-1823	Pius VII
1447-1455	Nicholas V		1823-1829	Leo XII
1455-1458	Callistus III		1829-1830	Pius VIII
1458-1464	Pius II		1831-1846	Gregory XVI
1464-1471	Paul II		1846-1878	Pius IX
1471-1484	Sixtus IV		1878-1903	Leo XIII
1484-1492	Innocent VIII		1903-1914	Pius X
1492-1503	Alexander VI		1914-1922	Benedict XV
1503	Pius III		1922-1939	Pius XI
1503-1513	Julius II		1939-1958	Pius XII
1513-1521	Leo X		1958-1963	John XXIII
1522-1523	Adrian VI		1963-1978	Paul VI
1523-1534	Clement VII		1978	John Paul I
1534-1549	Paul III		1978-now	John Paul II
1550-1555	Julius III			
1555	Marcellus II			
1555-1559	Paul IV			
1559-1565	Pius IV			
1566-1572	Pius V			
1572-1585	Gregory XIII			
1585-1590	Sixtus V			
1590	Urban VII			
1590-1591	Gregory XIV			
1591	Innocent IX			
1592-1605	Clement VIII			
1605	Leo XI			
1605-1621	Paul V			
1621-1623	Gregory XV			
1623-1644	Urban VIII			
1644-1655	Innocent X			
1655-1667	Alexander VII			
1667-1669	Clement IX			
1670-1676	Clement X			
1676-1689	Innocent XI			
1689-1691	Alexander VIII			
1691-1700	Innocent XII			
1700-1721	Clement XI			
1721-1724	Innocent XIII			
1724-1730	Benedict XIII			
1730-1740	Clement XII			
1740-1758	Benedict IV			
1758-1769	Clement XIII			

Appendix B

ROMAN EMPERORS

27 BC-AD 14	Augustus	211-217	Caracalla
14-37	Tiberius	217-218	Macrinus
37-41	Caius Caligula	218-222	Elagabal
41-54	Claudius	222-235	Alexander Severus
54-68	Nero	235-238	Maximin
68-69	Galba, Otho, Vitellius	238-244	Gordian
69-79	Vespasian	244-249	Philip
79-81	Titus	249-251	Decius
81-96	Domitian	251-253	Gallus
96-98	Nerva	253-260	Valerian
98-117	Trajan	260-268	Gallien
117-138	Hadrian	268-270	Claudius II
138-161	Antoninus Pius	270-275	Aurelian
161-180	Marcus Aurelius	275-276	Tacitus
180-192	Commodus	276-282	Probus
193	Pertinax	282-284	Carus
193-211	Septimius Severus	284-285	Diocletian

Western		Eastern	
285-305	Maximian	285-305	Diocletian
305-306	Constantius	305-311	Galerius
306-324	Constantine	311-313	Maximin
		313-324	Licinius

324-337   Constantine

337-350	Constans	337-350	Constantius

350-361   Constantius
361-363   Julian
363-364   Jovian

364-375	Valentinian I	364-378	Valens
375-383	Gratian	379-392	Theodosius
383-392	Valentinian II		

392-395   Theodosius

A HISTORY OF THE CHURCH

395-423	Honorius
423-425	John
425-455	Valentinian III
455-456	Avitus
457-461	Majorian
461-465	Severus
465-467	Ricimer
467-472	Anthemius
472	Olybrius
473	Glycerius
473-475	Julius Nepos
476	Romulus Augustulus

Appendix C

EASTERN ROMAN (BYZANTINE) EMPERORS

337-361	Constantius	813-820	Leo V
361-363	Julian	820-829	Michael II
363-364	Jovian	829-842	Theophilus
364-378	Valens	842-867	Michael III
379-395	Theodosius I	867-886	Basil I
395-408	Arcadius	886-912	Leo VI
408-450	Theodosius II	912-913	Alexander
450-457	Marcian	913-959	Constantine VII
457-474	Leo I	919-944	Romanus I
474	Leo II		(Co-emperor)
474-491	Zeno	959-963	Romanus II
491-518	Anastasius I	963-969	Nicephorus II
518-527	Justin I	969-976	John I
527-565	Justinian I	976-1025	Basil II
565-578	Justin II	1025-1028	Constantine VIII
578-582	Tiberius II	1028-1034	Romanus III
582-602	Maurice	1034-1041	Michael IV
602-610	Phocus	1041-1042	Michael V
610-641	Heraclius	1042-1055	Constantine IX
641	Constantine III	1055-1056	Theodora
641	Heraclonas	1056-1057	(Michael VI
641-668	Constans II	1057-1059	Isaac I
668-685	Constantine IV	1059-1067	Constantine X
685-695	Justinian II	1068-1071	Romanus IV
695-698	Leontius	1071-1078	Michael VII
698-705	Tiberius III	1078-1081	Nicephorus III
705-711	Justinian II	1081-1118	Alexius I
711-713	Philippicus Bardanes	1118-1143	John II
713-715	Anastasius II	1143-1180	Manuel I
715-717	Theodosius III	1180-1183	Alexius II
717-741	Leo III	1183-1185	Andronicus I
741-775	Constantine V	1185-1195	Isaac II
775-780	Leo IV	1195-1203	Alexius III
780-797	Constantine VI	1203-1204	Alexius IV
797-802	Irene	1204	Alexius V
802-811	Nicephorus I	1206-1222	Theodore I
811	Stauracius	1222-1254	John III Ducas
811-813	Michael I	1254-1258	Theodore II

1258-1261	John IV
1261-1282	Michael VIII
1282-1328	Andronicus II
1328-1341	Andronicus III
1341-1347	John V
1347-1354	John VI
1355-1376	John V (Restored)
1376-1379	Andronicus IV
1379-1391	John V (Restored)
1390	John VII
1391-1425	Manuel II
1425-1448	John VIII
1448-1453	Constantine XI

Appendix D

HOLY ROMAN EMPERORS

800-814	Charlemagne	1273-1291	Rudolf I
814-840	Louis I	1291-1298	Adolf
840-855	Lothair I	1298-1308	Albert I
855-875	Louis II	1308-1313	Henry VII
875-877	Charles II the Bald	1314-1347	Louis IV
877-887	Charles III the Bald	1347-1378	Charles IV
887-899	Arnulf of Carinthia	1378-1400	Wenceslaus
899-911	Louis III the Child	1400-1410	Rupert
911-918	Conrad I	1411-1437	Sigismund
919-936	Henry I the Fowler	1438-1439	Albert II
936-973	Otto I the Great	1440-1493	Frederick III
973-983	Otto II	1493-1519	Maximilian I
983-1002	Otto III	1519-1556	Charles V
1002-1024	Henry II the Saint	1556-1564	Ferdinand I
1024-1039	Conrad II	1564-1576	Maximillian II
1039-1056	Henry III the Black	1576-1612	Rudolf II
1056-1106	Henry IV	1612-1619	Matthias
1106-1125	Henry V	1619-1637	Ferdinand II
1125-1137	Lothair II	1637-1657	Ferdinand III
1137-1152	Conrad III	1658-1705	Leopold I
1152-1190	Frederick I Barbarossa	1705-1711	Joseph I
		1711-1740	Charles VI
1190-1197	Henry VI	1742-1745	Charles VII
1198-1215	Otto IV	1745-1765	Francis I
1215-1250	Frederick II	1765-1790	Joseph II
1250-1254	Conrad IV	1790-1792	Leopold II
1254-1273	Interregnum	1792-1806	Francis II

Index

Arminius, Jacobus; Arminianism, 353, 525.
Arnulf of Carinthia, 201.
Arthur, 360, 362.
Articles of Confederation, 485.
Asbury, Francis, 494.
Assemblies of God, 530.
Athanasius, 98, 118, 126.
Athaulf, 133.
Athenagoras, 41-42.
Attila, 139, 151.
Augsburg Confession, 339.
Augustine of Canterbury, 151-152, 155, 258, 498.
Augustine of Hippo Regius, 58, 102, 103, 119, 134, 135, 190, 266.
Augustinian Canons, 266, 269.
Augustinian Hermits, 335.
Augustinus, The, 409.
Aurelian, 80.
Austin Friars, 270.
Avignon, 277-285, 290-292, 296-299, 306, 374, 430.

B

Babylonian Captivity of the Church, The, 336, 361.
Back to God, 537.
Baghdad, 169, 243.
Baldwin, 243.
Baltimore, Lord, 479.
Baptism, 12, 13, 26, 41, 55, 64, 81, 103, 139, 350, 479.
Baptist Missionary Society, 509.
Baptists, 351, 380, 470, 482, 508, 519-520, 526, 550.
Barmen Declaration, 560n
Barnabas, 24, 25.
Barth, Karl, 434, 535, 546, 549.
Basil, 116-117, 119.
Basil I, 227.
Basil II, 229.
Basle, Council of, 289, 303-311, 404.

Baur, F.C., 435-436, 438.
Beaton, David, 375.
Beecher, Henry Ward, 529.
Beecher, Lyman, 488, 492, 521.
Benedict of Aniane, 189, 258, 261.
Benedict of Nursia; Benedictines, 119-120, 204, 258-264, 270, 274, 394.
Benedict VIII, 207.
Benedict IX, 207, 208, 219.
Benedict XI, 277.
Benedict XIII, 296-300.
Benedict XIV, 503.
Benevento, 146, 179.
Benevolent Empire, 518, 541.
Bernard of Clairvaux, 243, 264-265, 267, 271, 273.
Berno, 203.
Bill to Establish Religious Freedom, 484.
Bill of Rights, 486.
Bishops, 19, 25, 26, 50-53, 59-66, 84, 86, 122, 198, 199, 392.
Bismarck, Otto von, 447-448, 452.
Black Stone, 163, 164.
Blake-Pike Proposal, 554.
Blandina, 44.
Boethius, 140, 141, 155.
Boleyn, Anne, 363-365.
Bolsheviks; Bolshevik Revolution, 466, 468-469, 546.
Bonhoeffer, Dietrich, 549.
Boniface, 178-181, 258, 498.
Boniface VIII, 276, 277, 295.
Book of Common Prayer, 367, 368, 371-372, 379.
Book of Kells, 125.
Book of Mormon, 491, 523.
Borgia, Alfonso, see Calixtus III.
Borgia, Cesare, 321, 322.
Borgia, Giovanni, 321, 322.
Borgia, Lucretia, 321.
Borgia, Rodrigo, 316, 319, 320; see also Alexander VI.

Charles Martel, 170, 178-180, 182.
Childeric I, 138.
Childeric III, 181.
Children's Crusade, 247-248, 254.
China, 499, 501, 503, 507-508,
510, 512, 545.
China Inland Mission, 512.
Chi-rho, 78.
Chlotilde, 138.
Christian IV, 396, 397.
Christian Endeavor Society, 529.
Christianity Today, 553.
Christopher, 202.
Church Missionary Society, 509.
Circuit Riders, 490.
Cistercians, 264-265, 267, 270.
City of God, 134.
Civil Constitution of the Clergy,
429.
Civil Religion, 528, 529, 535-538,
541.
Clare, 269.
Clement II, 208.
Clement V, 277-279.
Clement VII, 363, 364, 388-390.
Clement VII (antipope), 282-284,
296.
Clement XIV, 420.
Clement of Alexandria, 96.
Cleris laicos, 276.
Clermont, Council of, 238, 251.
Clovis, 138-139, 141.
Cluny; Cluniac Reform Movement,
204, 206, 209, 213, 237, 259-262,
267.
Colet, John, 325, 359.
Columban, 125.
Columbanus, 125.
Columbia University, 482.
Columbus, Christopher, 473-474.
Combes, Emile, 449-450.
Commodus, 45-46.
Communists, 468-470, 546, 551.
Compactate of Prague, 304.

Conciliarism, 290, 294-311.
Concord, Book of, 352.
Concord, Formula of, 352.
Concordat of Bologna, 324, 408.
Concordat of 1801, 431.
Concordat of London, 213, 262.
Concordat of Worms, 213, 262.
Confederation of the Rhine, 432.
Confessing Church, 549.
Confucianism, 501, 503.
Congregation of the Holy Office,
390.
Congregationalists, 475, 478-486,
489, 509, 513.
see also United Church of Christ.
Congress of Vienna, 441.
Conrad III, 243.
Consistory, 346-347.
Constance, Council of, 287-289,
298-302, 309, 310-311, 331, 404.
Constans II, 161, 162.
Constantia, 81.
Constantine, 76-87, 97-99, 101,
112, 113, 121, 129, 131, 182, 236.
Constantine IV, 162.
Constantine V, 181-182, 183, 224,
225.
Constantine VI, 224.
Constantinople, Patriarch of, 87,
99-101, 103, 104, 105, 146, 149,
161, 223, 224, 226-228, 230-233,
456-458, 464, 465, 556-557.
Constantinople, First Council of,
99-102, 142.
Constantinople, Second Council of,
145.
Constantinople, Third Council of,
162.
Constantinople, Fourth Council of,
227.
Constantius (father of Constantine),
73, 75, 76.
Constantius (son of Constantine),
98.

Hegira, 164.
Helena, 75, 236.
Henoticon, 142.
Henry I (Holy Roman Emperor), 204.
Henry I (King of England), 212.
Henry II (Holy Roman Emperor), 207.
Henry II (King of France), 399.
Henry III, 208.
Henry IV (Holy Roman Emperor), 210-212, 219, 238, 240, 452.
Henry IV (King of France), 400.
Henry VI, 214.
Henry VII, 360, 368, 374.
Henry VIII, 360-366, 369, 371, 374, 375, 389, 390, 557.
Henry of Langenstein, 296.
Henry of Navarre, 400; *see also* Henry IV (King of France).
Henry, Carl F.H., 553.
Henry, Patrick, 484.
Heraclius, 159-161, 168.
Herberg, Will, 455.
Herbert, Edward; Lord Herbert of Cherbury, 410-411.
Hermogen, 460, 461.
Hieria, Synod of, 224.
Hildebrand, 210; *see also* Gregory VII.
Hincmar, 199.
History of Dogma, 437.
Hitler, Adolf, 469, 548.
Hohenstaufens, 214, 245, 252, 275, 276.
Holiness Revival, 530.
Holy Alliance, 466.
Holy Roman Empire, 188, 432, 446.
Holy Synod, 463, 464.
Honorius (Byzantine Emperor), 123, 133.
Honorius I, 161, 162, 445.
Horns of Hattin, 244.

Hospitallers, 251.
Hugh of St. Victor, 267.
Hughes, John, 522.
Hugo, Victor, 441.
Hugoccio, 294.
Huguenots, 400-403, 408.
Humanae Vitae, 556.
Humbert, 232.
Hunchback of Notre Dame, 441.
Hundred Years' War, 280.
Huns, 131, 137-139, 151.
Hus, John; Hussites, 287-291, 301, 304, 331, 336, 337, 395.

I

Ibas of Edessa, 145.
Iconoclasm, 222-225, 234.
Ignatius (Bishop of Antioch), 50-52, 59, 60, 64, 66.
Ignatius (Patriarch of Constantinople), 226-228.
Immaculate Conception of the Blessed Virgin Mary, 444.
Index of Prohibited Books, 327, 392, 421, 440, 557.
India, 16, 499, 500, 503-505, 508, 509, 512, 545.
Indulgences, 251-252, 286, 288, 308, 335, 389, 392.
Infant Baptism, 103, 350.
Innocent III, 213-217, 219, 245, 251, 275-277, 294.
Innocent VIII, 319-320.
Inquisition, 270, 379, 386, 390.
Institutes of the Christian Religion, 345, 354.
Institutional Church League, 531.
Interdict, 215, 305.
Interlocking Directorate, 518.
International Missionary Council, 545, 551.
International Review of Missions, 545.

Kruschev, Nikita, 469-470.
Kulturkampf, 447-448, 452, 543.

L
Lambert, 200, 201.
Langton, Stephen, 215.
Lapsi, 62, 63, 65.
Lateran Council, Fourth, 216-217, 248.
Lateran Council, Fifth, 324.
Lateran Pact, 547.
Lateran Palace, 80, 182.
Latimer, Hugh, 371.
Latitudinarians, 412.
Laud, William, 379, 380.
Lavigerie, Charles, 514.
League of Nations, 547.
Leben Jesu, 435, 438.
Leo I, 105-107, 151.
Leo II, 162.
Leo III (Byzantine Emperor), 221-225.
Leo III (Pope), 186-188, 200.
Leo IV, 224.
Leo V, 202.
Leo IX, 209, 210, 230, 232.
Leo X, 320, 324, 335, 336, 388.
Leo XIII, 272, 442, 528.
Leo of Ochrida, 230.
Leopold II, 421-422.
Leslie, Charles, 412.
Liberalism, 433-441, 525-528, 530-532, 534, 538, 539, 541, 546, 553.
Licinius, 81-83, 97.
Life and Work, Universal Christian Council for, 550.
Lindisfarne Gospels, 125.
Liutprant, 179, 180, 182.
Livingstone, David, 513.
Locke, John, 411.
Loisy, Alfred, 440.
Lollards, 286, 360.
Lombards, 146-150, 179-184, 225, 229.

London Missionary Society, 509.
Lord's Supper, 26-27, 41, 51, 59, 60.
Lothair I, 192, 193.
Lothair II, 193, 199.
Louis I, 188, 190-192, 258.
Louis II, 193, 199, 200.
Louis VII, 243.
Louis IX, 249.
Louis XIII, 401.
Louis XIV, 380, 382, 401, 402, 408.
Louis XV, 417, 420.
Louis XVI, 428, 430.
Louis Napoleon, 448.
Loyalists, 483.
Loyola, Ignatius, 387, 403, 500.
Ludwig (Louis the German), 192, 193, 199-201.
Luther, Martin, 252, 324, 327, 333-341, 345, 352, 354, 385, 390, 414, 424.
Lutherans, 338, 339, 341, 347, 351, 352, 361, 366, 390-392, 394-396, 405-407, 423-424, 475, 481, 483, 504, 550, 554.
Lyons, 44, 52, 136, 171.

M
Macedonius; Macedonianism, 100.
Macrianus, 71-72.
Magna Carta, 216.
Major, Georg, 352.
Majorinus, 84.
Manicheanism, 102, 231.
Mann, Horace, 519.
Manzikert, Battle of, 237.
Mar Thomas Christians, 500.
Marburg Colloquy, 344.
Marcia, 45, 46.
Marcian, 105-106.
Marcion, 56-57.
Marcomanni Wars, 129.
Marcus Aurelius, 42-45, 61, 129.